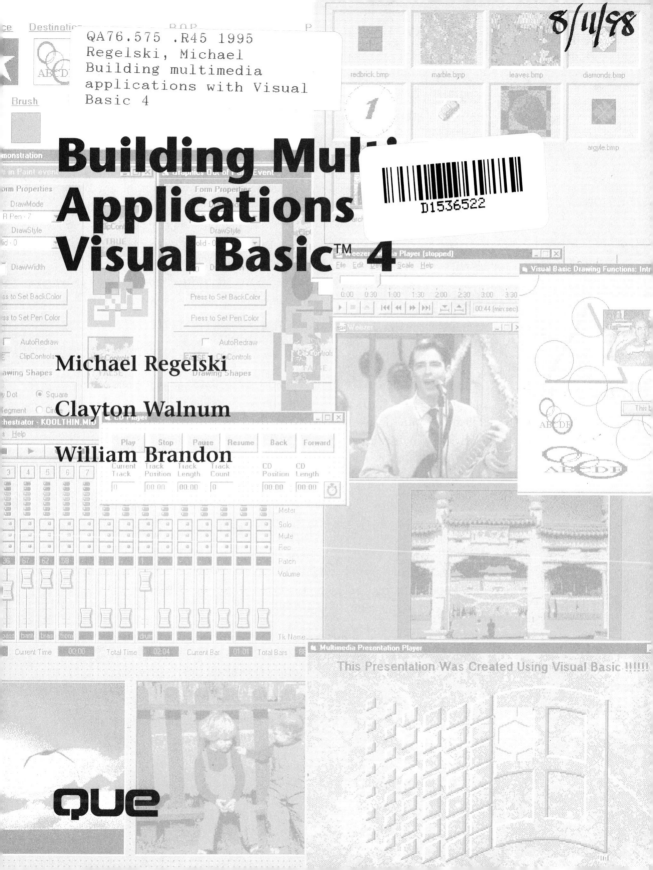

8/11/98

Building Multi
Applications
Visual Basic™ 4

D1536522

Michael Regelski

Clayton Walnum

William Brandon

que

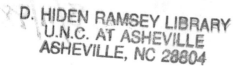
Building Multimedia Applications with Visual Basic 4

Copyright© 1995 by Que® Corporation

Library of Congress Catalog No.: 95-078874

ISBN: 0-7897-0139-1

97 96 95   6 5 4 3 2 1

Interpretation of the printing code: the rightmost double-digit number is the year of the book's printing; the rightmost single-digit number, the number of the book's printing. For example, a printing code of 95-1 shows that the first printing of the book occurred in 1995.

Screen reproductions in this book were created using Collage Plus from Inner Media, Inc., Hollis, NH.

Credits

President and Publisher
Roland Elgey

Associate Publisher
Joseph B. Wikert

Editorial Services Director
Elizabeth Keaffaber

Managing Editor
Sandy Doell

Director of Marketing
Lynn E. Zingraf

Senior Series Editor
Chris Nelson

Acquisitions Editor
Fred Slone

Product Directors
C. Kazim Haidri
Nancy D. Price

Production Editor
Caroline D. Roop

Editors
Judy Brunetti
Tom Cirtin
Susan Shaw Dunn
Patrick Kanouse

Assistant Product Marketing Manager
Kim Margolius

Technical Editors
Burt Harris
Russell L. Jacobs

Acquisitions Coordinator
Angela C. Kozlowski

Operations Coordinator
Patty Brooks

Editorial Assistant
Michelle R. Newcomb

Book Designer
Kim Scott

Cover Designer
Dan Armstrong

Production Team
Steve Adams
Angela D. Bannan
Chad Dressler
DiMonique Ford
Amy Gornik
Mike Henry
Michelle Lee
Bobbi Satterfield
Andy Stone
Jody York

Indexer
Kathy Venable

Composed in *Stone* and *MCPdigital* by Que Corporation

About the Authors

Michael Regelski is the Director of Software Development at Lenel Systems International. Lenel is one of the leading developers of Multimedia Development Tools and Multimedia Systems for the Windows, Windows NT, and Windows 95 platforms. Michael has a M.S. in Software Development and Management and a B.S. in Computer Engineering, both from Rochester Institute of Technology. Before joining Lenel, Michael was the lead design engineer for Access Control development at Eastman Kodak. When Michael is not developing software or writing, his interests include golf and basketball.

Clayton Walnum has been writing about computers for a decade and has published more than 300 articles in major computer publications. He is the author of books covering such diverse topics as programming, computer gaming, and application programs. His most recent book is *3D Graphics Programming with OpenGL*, also published by Que. His earlier titles include *Borland C++ Object-Oriented Programming, Borland C++ Power Programming, Creating Turbo C++ Games,* and *QBasic for Rookies* (Que); *PC Picasso: A Child's Computer Drawing Kit* and *The First Book of Microsoft Works for Windows* (Sams); *PowerMonger: The Official Strategy Guide* (Prima); and *C-manship Complete* (Taylor Ridge Books). Mr. Walnum is a full-time freelance writer and lives in Connecticut with his wife and their three children.

William Brandon is a human performance technologist who designs human systems to support mission-critical business outcomes. William has been a manager of business units, a classroom instructor and facilitator, and an author of computer-based training. William owns Accomplishment Technology Unlimited, and is carrying out projects in multimedia, training, and performance support for clients in a number of industries. He received his B.A. in History from the University of Texas at Austin, where he first learned to program. William did postgraduate work in Human Behavior at US International University in San Diego, and has completed extensive training in neurolinguistic programming. He lives near Dallas with his wife of twenty-five years. They have two daughters.

Acknowledgments

There have been a number of people who have contributed to this project and I would like to thank everyone for their time, effort and help in making this book a success. On the top of the list is Fred Slone who was the cornerstone of this project and put up with numerous delays, complaints and requests. Without Fred's patience and perseverance, this project would not have succeeded.

All of the staff at Que has been outstanding to work with and I would like to thank each and every one of them. Caroline Roop and Nancy Price have been tremendous editors and have been instrumental in delivering this book to the market. Also many thanks to the technical editors who have ensured the technical merit of all the applications in this book.

I would also like to thank Clay Walnum and Bill Brandon for their contributions to this project. Without their help and expertise in multimedia programming this book would not be possible. Also a special thanks to the Microsoft Developers Network, which provides more information than is humanly consumable.

Another important contributor has been Rudy and Elena Prokupets, the founders of Lenel Systems. Lenel Systems has provided the market with some of the most advanced multimedia tools on the market. The vision of Rudy and Elena have allowed Lenel to prosper and grow into a very successful company.

I would also like to thank all of the companies who have contributed products for inclusion on the enclosed CD-ROM.

Finally, I would like to give a special thanks to my wife Laura and son Andrew who have given me the more of their support than I thought possible. Their patience and understanding have been a blessing.

Trademark Acknowledgments

We'd Like to Hear from You!

As part of our continuing effort to produce books of the highest possible quality, Que would like to hear your comments. To stay competitive, we really want you, as a computer book reader and user, to let us know what you like or dislike most about this book or other Que products.

You can mail comments, ideas, or suggestions for improving future editions to the address below, or send us a fax at (317) 581-4663. For the on-line inclined, Macmillan Computer Publishing has a forum on CompuServe (type **GO QUEBOOKS** at any prompt) through which our staff and authors are available for questions and comments. The address of our Internet site is **http:// www.mcp.com** (World Wide Web).

In addition to exploring our forum, please feel free to contact me personally to discuss your opinions of this book: on CompuServe, I'm at 75767,2543, and on the Internet, I'm **nprice@que.mcp.com**.

Thanks in advance—your comments will help us to continue publishing the best books available on computer topics in today's market.

Nancy D. Price
Product Development Specialist
Que Corporation
201 W. 103rd Street
Indianapolis, Indiana 46290
USA

Contents at a Glance

Using Multimedia

The Graphics Interface

Video Capabilities

Special Techniques

Contents

II The Graphics Interface   119

5 Graphics and Palettes   121

7 Hypertext and Hot Spots   227

III Video Capabilities 267

A The MCI Command Reference   **505**

Introduction

For anyone wishing to develop a Windows multimedia application, title, or game, Visual Basic deserves serious consideration as the premier development environment for that project. Visual Basic is an easy-to-use but extremely powerful development environment that can access the latest features of Windows 95 and Windows NT.

Visual Basic has evolved from an easy method to prototype Windows application to a serious development tool for multimedia titles, corporate database applications, and games. The latest version of Visual Basic introduces features like support for OLE custom controls (OCXs), Windows 95 common controls, the JET 3.0 Database Engine, and support for the creation of OLE automation server .EXEs and .DLLs. The most important feature, though, is the capability to create both 16- and 32-bit applications from a single code base.

The ability to both create 32-bit applications and port 16-bit code to 32-bit code with a simple recompile will allow the market to become flooded with Windows 95 and Windows NT 32-bit applications. Because of Visual Basic's tight integration with Windows 95, developers can easily exploit the Windows 95 operating system and user interface to their advantage.

Visual Basic provides the power and flexibility of a true development language with the simplicity of a high-level authoring system. Visual Basic is the most extensive language on the market. There are more VBXs and OCXs on the market for Visual Basic than any other language.

Who Is this Book For?

This book is intended for anyone who wants to add multimedia capabilities to new or existing applications. The focus of this book is on developing multimedia applications. Techniques will be discussed that can be used in the development of all Windows applications.

This book contains topics that will appeal to all levels of developers. For developers new to Windows and Visual Basic, Chapters 1 and 2 focus on the development of multimedia applications using Visual Basic and Windows 95, while providing excellent insight into the multimedia capabilities of Visual Basic and Windows 95.

For the developers who are familiar with both Visual Basic and Windows 95, but would not classify themselves as gurus of either, there are chapters that will cover all of the multimedia types (graphics, animation, digital video, audio, and analog video) and how to use them. For the Visual Basic and Windows gurus, there are topics on the latest Windows multimedia technologies including digital video capture, MPEG video, and creating transition effects. There is even a chapter on how to develop your own OLE custom controls using the Microsoft Visual C++ compiler!

There are a number of third-party controls that are used in the sample applications and are included on the CD-ROM accompanying this book. All of the sample code and libraries used in the book are also included on the CD-ROM.

How to Effectively Use This Book

You will need the Professional Edition of Visual Basic 4 to create all of the applications in this book. The Standard Edition can be used but will not contain all of the OLE controls (for example, the MCI OLE control) used in the projects. The Enterprise Edition of Visual Basic can also be used to create all of the applications in this book.

Chapter 12, "Creating and Using OLE Custom Controls," extensively uses the Microsoft Visual C++ compiler 2.x or higher. This is only necessary for developers who desire to build their own OLE controls. The controls developed in this chapter are supplied on the CD-ROM so you will not need to re-create the OCXs.

All of the applications included with this book are both 16- and 32-bit enabled. This means that your computer can run either Windows 3.x, Windows 95, or Windows NT to develop the applications in this book. The primary focus of the book is on the Win32 API set and focused on Windows 95 particularly, due to the vast amount of multimedia capabilities built into the operating system.

If your computer can run Windows 95 and Visual Basic, then your computer meets the minimum requirements for developing the multimedia applications in this book. Your computer should also have an audio card, overlay video, and video capture board to build and run all of the applications in this book.

How This Book Is Organized

Building Multimedia Applications with Visual Basic 4 is divided into four parts. Each part deals with related multimedia programming topics. The content of each part is described in the following sections.

Part I: Using Multimedia

Part I provides you with an introduction to the multimedia features of both Windows 95 and Visual Basic. Chapter 1, "Multimedia Development Using Visual Basic," delves into the multimedia features included with Visual Basic 4. Chapter 2, "Multimedia Development with Windows," provides insight into the multimedia highlights and evolution of the multimedia features included in the Windows operating system. Chapter 3, "The Media Control Interface (MCI)," offers an in-depth look at exactly how the Windows MCI interface works with various multimedia files and devices. And finally, Chapter 4, "Visual Basic Audio Capabilities," demonstrates the audio capabilities available to the Windows developer.

Part II: The Graphics Interface

Part II explores the Windows graphics subsystem and is intended for developers of all experience levels. Chapter 5, "Graphics and Palettes," provides readers with a thorough understanding of the Windows Graphics Interface and how graphics and palettes are used under Windows. Chapter 6, "Creating Transition Effects," examines the techniques used to create special transition effects such as wipes and fades. Chapter 7, "Hypertext and Hot Spots," shows developers how to create applications that utilize hot-spots and hypertext links.

Part III: Video Capabilities

Part III delves into the Windows video capabilities. The primary focus is on time-based video, including digital video, overlay video, and animation. Chapter 8, "Digital Video Capture and Editing," starts off Part III with an in-depth look at capturing digital video (Video for Windows) on the Windows platform. Chapter 9, "Using Peripheral Devices for Overlay Video," looks at bringing overlay video into a Windows application through the use of video overlay boards, laser discs, and VCRs. Chapter 10, "Animation," demonstrates how to play MCI-based animation files and how to create palette and sprite animation. Finally, Chapter 11, "Using Digital Video Playback," focuses on how to play back digital video including Video for Windows and MPEG video.

Part IV: Special Techniques

Part IV looks at special techniques that can be applied to multimedia applications. Chapter 12, "Creating and Using OLE Custom Controls," takes a very low-level, in-depth look at how to build OLE custom controls (OCXs) and use them in Visual Basic applications. Chapter 13, "Creating Synchronized Presentations," looks at the details involved in synchronizing the playback of several multimedia elements at one time. A multimedia presentation package is developed in this chapter. And finally, Chapter 14, "Multimedia Databases Using the JET Engine," looks at how to store and retrieve multimedia from the JET Engine using Visual Basic.

Let's Get Started...

Writing this book has been a tremendous challenge. It also has been a lot of fun. Multimedia, Windows 95, and Visual Basic are technologies that cannot be ignored. The proliferation of multimedia into mainstream applications, such as the World Wide Web browsers, the Microsoft Network, and presentation packages, to name a few, will force Windows developers to adapt and learn the new skills required for multimedia development. With the techniques and information used in this book to construct multimedia applications, you will be armed with the latest multimedia knowledge available. Combining this knowledge with Windows 95 and Visual Basic will truly enable you to create stunning multimedia applications. We hope that you will enjoy and benefit from this book as much as we enjoyed writing it. Let the multimedia adventure begin!

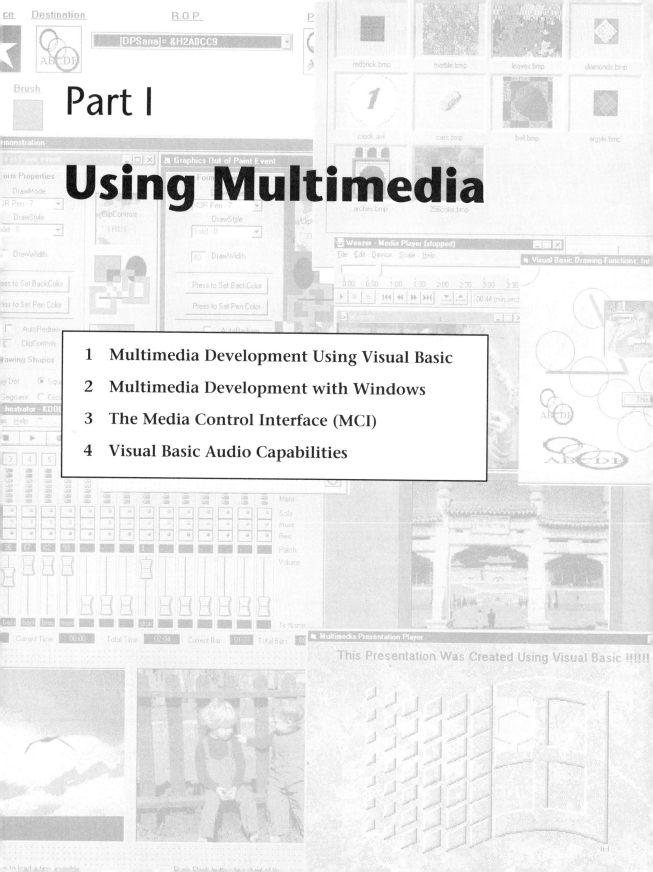

Part I

Using Multimedia

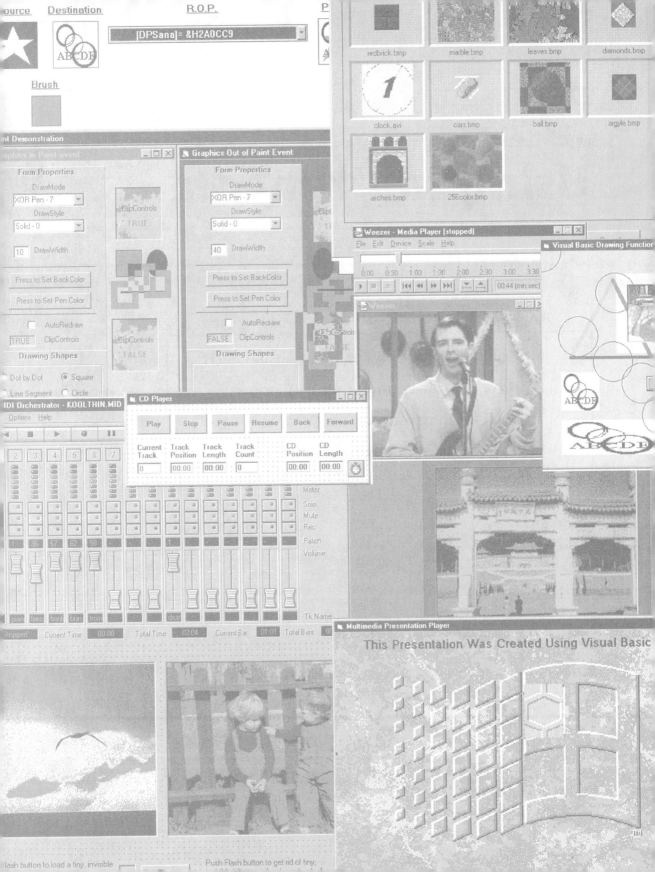

Chapter 1

Multimedia Development Using Visual Basic

Visual Basic, Microsoft's powerful visual programming and development environment, is quickly becoming one of the computer industry's leading environments for developing multimedia applications. This is due to its easy, non-threatening nature and its capability to take advantage of Microsoft's latest operating systems, especially Windows 95.

With Visual Basic 4.0, both 16- and 32-bit applications can be developed from the same code base. This helps to quickly flood the market with powerful 32-bit applications for Windows NT and Windows 95, as well as providing applications for the existing Windows 3.x and Windows for Workgroups platforms.

Multimedia development requires a total integration of many skills. Depending on your application, this can include audio, digital video, video capture, overlay video, animation, images, peripheral devices, CD-ROMs, and many other software and hardware technologies. This requires that your target platform (operating system) provides you with services to access or integrate these technologies. It also requires that your development environment has the capability to use these features. Visual Basic 4.0 is equipped with the power to run on the latest, most powerful versions of the Windows operating systems while providing user-friendly access to all of the capabilities of the operating system such as multimedia, common controls, and networking.

This chapter looks at the multimedia services provided by the Microsoft operating systems and Visual Basic 4.0. It provides an overview of built-in and add-on multimedia features that you can harness and integrate into your applications. In this chapter, you learn about the following items:

- What different types of multimedia elements are available

- Video for Windows capabilities

- High-level Windows multimedia services

- The audio services that Visual Basic can use

- How to add extensibility with OLE and VBX controls

- Multimedia database capabilities

Multimedia Elements

There are a variety of multimedia elements on the Windows platforms that are available to the developer. The multimedia elements consist of audio, digital video, analog video, animation, images, and text. These elements represent the six basic multimedia types available for use by the Visual Basic programmer.

Audio

When audio is mentioned with a multimedia program, the most typical type is *waveform audio*. There are other types of audio available for use and these include *CD Audio* and *MIDI (Musical Instrument Digital Interface)*.

Waveform Audio

Waveform audio represents electronically digitized sound that has been stored in a file on your computer's hard disk. Typically, waveform audio is captured through a soundboard connected to your PC. The sound source is connected to the audio input port on the soundboard and when recording commands are sent to the soundboard, the incoming audio is digitized and stored on the computer's hard drive. Figure 1.1 shows these connections.

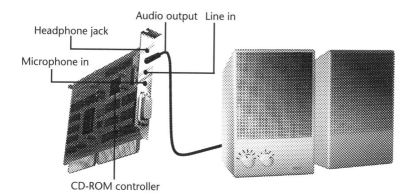

Headphone jack
Microphone in
Audio output   Line in
CD-ROM controller

Fig. 1.1
Typical connec-
tions made to a PC
audio soundboard.

I

Using Multimedia

Waveform audio can be digitized in a variety of formats depending on the capabilities of the soundboard and the requirements of your application. When soundboards first arrived on the market, they were 8-bit sound cards. The number of bits represents the number of sample points that can be saved during audio capture. Today, all of the audio board manufacturers produce 16-bit audio boards with 16-bit boards being the most popular and available.

> 8-bit audio boards can only capture 8-bit audio, while 16-bit audio boards can be programmed to capture either 8-bit or 16-bit audio.

The *sample rate* that audio is digitized at is the largest variable for the user. The sample rate refers to the number of samples of audio taken per second. There are many trade-offs with respect to quality versus space requirements. A higher sample rate requires more storage capacity for the digitized audio. The trade-off is that a high sample rate produces a higher quality audio recording because more audio samples are taken per second. Sample rates are measured in kilohertz. Table 1.1 lists the most common sample rates used in today's applications.

Table 1.1 Most Commonly Used Audio Sample Rates	
Sample Rate	**Description**
11.025 Khz	Used most often for voice grade audio.
22.05 Khz	Provides a good quality mix for music and voice.
44.1 Khz	CD Audio quality sampling. Provides the best quality for music.

Waveform audio can be digitized in mono or stereo mode. *Mono mode* is equivalent to AM radio, where one input source is simulated. *Stereo mode* is equivalent to FM radio, where two input sources are used. Stereo mode requires more space requirements than mono mode.

MIDI

MIDI (Musical Instrument Digital Interface) is a method of saving instrumental keynotes in a computer file. When these files are played back, the instruments that the notes represent are simulated. The MIDI file can also be played through a MIDI port located on a soundboard to control instruments, such as electronic keyboards and synthesizers, that accept the notes as inputs. MIDI files are played back through internal or external *sequencers*. A sequencer interprets the control events, which are stored in the MIDI file with the instrumental keynotes and communicates these events to the internal or external synthesizer.

MIDI audio requires much less storage capacity and lower data transfer rates than waveform audio because there are no actual audio samples stored in a MIDI file, only musical instrument events. This makes them ideal for providing background music for your applications. MIDI files can only contain musical instrument events or sequences; they cannot contain narrations or voice.

When using MIDI services on the Windows platform, messages are directed from the MIDI file to a *MIDI mapper*. The MIDI mapper is part of the Windows multimedia extensions and is responsible for redirecting MIDI output messages to a MIDI output device according to values stored in the MIDI map setup. The MIDI mapper can change the destination channel and output device for a message. It can also modify program-change messages, volume values, and key values.

The MIDI map setup is user-defined and controlled from the MIDI mapper applet in the Windows Control Panel. The MIDI map setup cannot be altered programmatically from an application.

CD Audio

CD Audio, often called *red book audio*, allows for CD musical titles to be played and controlled on a PC's CD-ROM drive. The PC's CD-ROM drive allows users to view non-audio CDs much like a hard disk directory. The CD-ROM device driver also recognizes red book audio format CDs (audio CDs) and allows PC software to control the CD much like a home stereo CD player. The audio outputs from the CD drive can be connected to the line-in input from the audio card; this allows for the audio to be heard from the same speakers as waveform audio, or it can be connected directly to a set of speakers. Often in multimedia PCs or in multimedia upgrade kits, the CD-ROM drive is connected internally to the sound card so no external connection is necessary.

CD Audio represents the highest quality digital reproduction of audio information but has the highest storage requirements. The typical storage rate for CD Audio is 176 kilobytes (K) per second, which yields about 73 minutes of CD Audio per CD-ROM.

Digital Video

Digital video creates a new dimension for the multimedia developer and for the end user. Digital video is video that has been digitized through a video capture board and stored in a file on the computer hard disk. Typical playback rates vary from about 15 fps (frames per second) to full-motion video at 30 fps. The playback rate is directly related to the computer hardware, the compression technology, and the size of the video being used.

Video for Windows and QuickTime

For the Windows operating systems, Microsoft's *Video for Windows (VFW)* is the standard file format. Video for Windows was introduced with Windows 3.1 and for the first time provided synchronized motion video and audio on the Windows platforms. Other competing standards are Apple Computer's *QuickTime* technology, *MPEG (Motion Photography Experts Group)* video, and *DVI (Digital Video Interactive)*. Both Video for Windows and QuickTime file formats use their own *codec* (compression and decompression driver) for the compression and decompression of the digital video.

Codecs provide tremendous flexibility for both capturing and playing back digital video. When you purchase a video capture board, it may have built-in video compression technology. An example of this type of video capture board is Intel's Smart Video Recorder. The Smart Video Recorder has the Intel Indeo's compression technology built directly into the board's firmware. This allows the video to be captured and compressed directly into a file. The compression is handled by the capture board's hardware.

If your video capture board does not contain video compression built into the hardware, a capture format is selected before capturing video. The capture format specifies the pixel depth and capture format to use. After the video is captured, a compressor is chosen and the file is saved using the chosen video compression technology.

When digital video is played back, the compressor used must be present on the playback system. Both the Video for Windows and QuickTime playback engines detect the codec that the video was captured in and then invoke that codec to decompress the video during playback.

Some video capture boards support *hardware assist* on the playback of captured video. Very often, these boards support their own capture format. When video is captured into these formats, the playback driver "detects" whether the native capture board is present during playback. If the board is present, the video is played back on the capture board's hardware frame buffer. This results in faster playback rates, clearer resolutions, and hardware-assisted scaling. If the video capture board is not present on the playback system or the video frame buffer is in use, the video plays back through software decompression on the VGA surface as with any other digital video file. Capture boards built with the MCT (Media Control Technology) and Auravision chip sets support this feature.

Because Video for Windows and QuickTime's codecs are largely software-based, the playback and capture rates of digital video are very hardware-dependent. The faster your CPU, video board, and capture board, and the more memory you have, the faster your playback and capture rates are. Faster systems also allow the video frame size to be larger without suffering performance degradation.

MPEG and DVI

MPEG and DVI are also file-based digital video formats, but unlike Video for Windows and QuickTime, they are hardware-based formats. This means that playback of both MPEG and DVI requires special video playback boards. The results of both MPEG and DVI are substantially better than the software-based solutions. MPEG and DVI can be played back at full-screen resolutions, with audio at 30 fps. The performance is much better, however, the cost is also substantially greater.

MPEG video is very expensive to produce because special capture hardware is required. In addition, off-line compression is required to produce the MPEG files. Currently, MPEG video cannot be captured on the PC platform. High-quality DVI video is also very expensive to produce but unlike MPEG, DVI video can be captured on the PC platform. A DVI capture board is available from IBM (ActionMedia II). The ActionMedia II board can capture video into DVI format, which can then be played back. Capturing DVI files on the PC produces a quality picture, but for the highest quality DVI files, off-line processing is required as it is with MPEG.

Because the costs for both DVI and MPEG are much greater, these solutions are reserved for the high-end applications. The gap between hardware- and software-based compression formats is rapidly decreasing. With a Pentium processor, a full quarter-screen Video for Windows file can be played at 30 fps. This was not true just a few short months ago. Carefully evaluate your application's needs before choosing between hardware- and software-based compression techniques.

Digital Video Capture

When Microsoft introduced Video for Windows, it not only became the standard digital video file format for the Windows platforms, but also the most popular. Currently, the only other competing standard is IBM's ActionMedia II video capture board, which captures DVI video. Apple's QuickTime and MPEG video currently cannot be captured in the Windows environment. QuickTime video is captured in the Macintosh platform and MPEG video is captured off-line with special video capture hardware.

Video for Windows consists of two parts, the Video for Windows runtime and the Video for Windows SDK. The Video for Windows runtime is a set of freely distributable DLLs and MCI driver, which provides the capability to play captured Video for Windows files. The Video for Windows SDK contains an array of programming APIs and tools to assist developers in the creation of video capture applications and to capture video content.

The Video for Windows SDK has allowed for third-party software developers to create tools that assist in the capture of digital video. One such tool is the MediaRecorder Toolkit from Lenel Systems International. The MediaRecorder Toolkit is a very powerful capture control that can be incorporated into your applications. This capture control allows for the capture of palettes, digital video, still images, and cropped images.

For the most flexibility and control, the Visual Basic programmer can write directly to the Video for Windows capture API. This API provides the most control and flexibility, but is also the lowest level API available. There is some C DLL code that must be written in order for Visual Basic to use this API.

For the Windows NT platform, there is a Video for Windows SDK, currently in its second beta. It is a very low-level API that can be accessed from the 32-bit version of Visual Basic. It also requires some C DLL programming in order to work. The Video for Windows SDK and other digital video capture tools will be covered in-depth in Chapter 11, "Using Digital Video Playback."

There are also several vendors who have complete video capture applications that can be used to capture and edit your digital video off-line, then incorporate the video into your application.

Analog Video

Analog video provides applications with the capability to play full-motion video at 30 fps, in a scaleable window, with no picture breakup. Unlike digital video, the source of information is not a file; instead it is an external device such as a laser disc, camera, or VCR. Analog video combines two different technologies to bring video solutions to the desktop. It is dependent upon an overlay video board for displaying video and upon external devices.

An overlay video board provides video pass-through for external video sources. Unless the overlay video board has built-in VGA capabilities, it connects to the VGA board through a feature connector on the top of the VGA card. The user selects a unique color from the VGA display known as the *key color*. Most overlay boards have a default of magenta as the key color. When an overlay video window is displayed, the background is filled with the key color. The result is that the external video source is shown on-screen wherever the key color is present (in this case, the overlay video window). This results in what is called *two-plane technology*—the VGA plane provided by the VGA adapter and the overlay plane provided by the overlay video board.

Peripheral devices such as cameras, VCRs, and laser discs provide a video source for the overlay video board. Some overlay boards have a built-in TV tuner so that there is no dependence on an external source. Most of the peripherals that are used in applications have a programmable interface. This is usually through a serial port. An application, such as emergency medical training, may have different video sequences of medical emergencies stored throughout a laser disc. During the training session, the application plays back a video clip that must be watched by the student. A test is then given on the proper response to the situation. In Chapter 9, "Using Peripheral Devices for Overlay Video," you learn how to create applications that utilize analog video without having to dissect the bowels of every peripheral device on the market.

Animation

Animation is the display of a series of graphics images that simulate motion and may also contain synchronized audio. There are two different types of animation: *cast-based* and *frame-based*.

Cast-based animation, also known as *object animation*, is a form of animation where each object in the presentation is an individual element with its own pattern, size, shape, color, and speed. A presentation script controls the placement and movement of the objects in each frame of the animation.

Frame-based animation is a series of screens or frames displayed in quick succession. The changing of the screen from frame to frame produces the animation. Frame-based animation is very similar to some digital video technologies. Each frame can be edited as a unique entity because it represents an actual picture that is shown for a specified time period. Animated cartoons are examples of frame-based animation.

Cast-based animation, by contrast, is strictly time-based. There are no individual frames that can be edited separately. Each frame is a time-slice that defines the usage and position of each element in the animation. As a result, there is no picture, only a collection of information defining the position and behavior of objects at an instance in time. Cast-based animation is created and edited through authoring packages that show all cast members relative to each other. The elements are then individually edited. An example of an application that creates cast-based animation is MacroMedia Director.

The technique used in cast-based animation, sometimes called *sprite animation*, can be applied to your application to give the illusion of motion. For example, this can be applied to a piece of text to give the impression that the text is moving across the screen.

images

Images or *graphics* represent a large part of multimedia programming. Images can be represented in two basic format types: *bitmap* or *vector*. Table 1.2 lists the most common bitmap and vector file formats.

Table 1.2 Common Windows Bitmap and Vector File Formats		
File Format	**File Type**	**Extension**
Windows Bitmap	Bitmap	.BMP, .DIB
Tagged Interchanged File Format	Bitmap	.TIF
Graphics Interchange Format	Bitmap	.GIF
Kodak Photo CD	Bitmap	.PCD

(continues)

Table 1.2 Continued		
File Format	**File Type**	**Extension**
Targa	Bitmap	.TGA
Icon	Bitmap	.ICO
Cursor	Bitmap	.CUR
PaintBrush	Bitmap	.PCX
Microsoft Run Length Endoded (RLE)	Bitmap	.RLE
GEM	Bitmap	.IMG
Joint Photography Experts Group (JPEG)	Bitmap	.JPG
Windows Metafile	Vector	.WMF
AutoCAD	Vector	.DXF

A bit-mapped image file contains the RGB (Red, Green, and Blue) components for each pixel that the image contains. These pixels can represent various depths such as 8-bits per pixel, 16-bits per pixel, or 24-bits per pixel. If the pixel depth is 8-bits per pixel, the RGB components map to a palette table that is contained within the file. The combination of RGB components and palette map represent the image.

A vector file doesn't contain pixel information about the image but instead contains a series of drawing instructions. This is called a *metafile*. Each of the drawing instructions is interpreted and sent to the Windows GDI for execution when the file is read. Vector files generally require less storage space than bitmap files and are very often used in architectural or engineering application programs such as AutoCAD.

Images are essential to multimedia programming. There are a number of techniques that can be used to provide transition effects from moving from one image to another. These techniques are only applicable to bitmapped images and are shown in Chapter 6, "Creating Transition Effects." Bitmaps are often used as backgrounds for presentations and applications.

Text

All the glamour and attraction in multimedia is thought to belong to elements such as digital video and sound. *Text*, however, is very crucial to the multimedia programmer, and an often-forgotten element. Even though a picture may represent a thousand words, a picture with a few descriptive quotes can provide much easier association and recognition than just the image alone.

Consider toolbars in Windows applications, for example. Toolbars became popular because they moved from a language metaphor to a graphic or iconic metaphor. The original thinking was that buttons with bitmapped images residing on toolbars would be intuitive for the end user. But these days, many toolbars are augmented by tool-tips, which are text pop-ups that appear each time the mouse passes over a button. Text is by no means a dead element.

There are a number of transitions and effects that can be applied to text elements. Text elements can be animated to move across the screen and paint themselves transparently over a bitmapped image. We examine this and other techniques as text is applied to applications in Chapter 10, "Animation."

High-Level Multimedia Services

Windows provides several high-level multimedia services to development environments. These services are in the form of the Media Control Interface (MCI) and audio APIs. Visual Basic supplements these services with controls, which provide an easy method to access them.

The Media Control Interface

The Media Control Interface (MCI), provides applications with a standard, device-independent method for communicating with different multimedia devices, peripherals, and drivers. MCI was established during the development of the Windows 3.0 Multimedia Extensions. It was added as a permanent part of all the Windows operating systems with the introduction of Windows 3.1.

The MCI was designed to communicate with various device types including waveform audio, MIDI Audio, CD Audio, digital video, overlay video boards, VCRs, laser discs, MPEG video, and various device types. The MCI is the most encompassing set of APIs for the Visual Basic programmer because of its power and flexibility in nature.

The MCI communicates with special MCI drivers. These MCI drivers interpret the MCI commands sent from the application and translate the user's commands into the device-specific commands necessary to implement the instruction.

The MCI has two methods for communicating with devices—the *string inter-face* and the *command interface*. The string interface sends text-based com-mands to the MCI driver. These commands are interpreted and translated into message-based commands, and sent to the MCI driver. The string inter-face is ideal for scripting languages or for quickly manipulating a device with a series of MCI commands.

The command, or message, interface is more cumbersome to implement but offers slightly improved execution speed because the string lookup and pars-ing are not needed. The command interface relies on structures for each com-mand type. These structures are filled with the appropriate commands, flags, and information and are sent to the device driver. Returned information is also contained in the structure.

High-Level Audio Services

The Windows API provides a few very high-level APIs for playing audio files. These APIs are extremely easy to use and require little knowledge of the Win-dows architecture or multimedia programming. There is a trade-off, though; for their ease of use, there is little to no flexibility in programmer control over the playback of audio. Depending on your needs, these APIs will prob-ably fill most of your programming requirements for audio playback.

The APIs that Windows provides for audio playback are two functions called MessageBeep and SndPlaySound. These are both one-line functions, which are associated with WIN.INI or registration database entries, that play wave-form sound files. These entries map a sound file to system events such as ApplicationClose or to application-defined entries.

Low-Level Audio Services

Windows provides several low-level audio services that are accessible to the Visual Basic programmer. These services control the playback of waveform sound files, MIDI files and control the auxiliary outputs for soundboards. While all of the APIs can be called from the Visual Basic environment, there are limitations inherent to Visual Basic that prohibit the use of certain audio playback strategies.

Low-level waveform audio APIs can be used to customize and control the buffering and playback of both MIDI files and waveform sound files. The buffering that is performed by the high-level audio APIs and the MCI inter-face might not be sufficient for the performance necessary for your application. This can play an important role in creating distributed or networked applications where customized buffering schemes can be deployed to prevent audio breakup. The low-level APIs also provide the best interface for creating audio editing, special effects and audio manipulation applications.

Low-Level Waveform Audio

The low-level waveform audio commands allow for the control of playback, volume, playback speed, and pitch. If your application needs to control these elements, then low-level audio services are your only choice. Fortunately, these APIs are fairly easy and straightforward to use.

Playing back audio with the low-level commands is going to be fairly difficult without the help of writing sections of code in a DLL with an external language such as C. This is necessary because the audio playback engine in the Windows operating system requires callback functions to a DLL when using the low-level APIs.

The low-level commands can be deployed, without requiring a callback function for playing back short waveform files, but there is no reason to do this when the MCI and high-level services already provide playback for you.

Low-Level MIDI Audio

Low-level MIDI audio playback falls into the same category as waveform audio. There is more control provided to the developer, but this control is only for situations for controlling volume, playback speed, pitch, and so on. The only time that the low-level MIDI audio functions would be used is if the MCI driver for the MIDI board was lacking functionality that was needed in your application, such as controlling volume.

The Auxiliary Audio Devices

The Windows operating systems define auxiliary audio devices that can be programmatically controlled. Auxiliary devices are often overlooked as part of the multimedia system. The auxiliary devices that can be controlled are actually part of the soundboard in your PC. These are the line-input and CD-ROM audio input line, if your audio board provides this channel and the CD-ROM is attached to it.

The auxiliary APIs can be used to control the volume settings for each input. This is important because if your application inputs CD Audio or external audio into the soundboard, this is your only means of controlling the volume settings.

Visual Basic Extensions: Adding Multimedia Power to Visual Basic

Visual Basic is a very powerful environment for developing multimedia applications. The environment is very user-friendly, easy to learn, and very tightly integrated with the Windows operating systems. One of Visual Basic's greatest assets, though, is its extensibility. The Visual Basic development environment has the largest available tool-chest of add-on software components of any environment on any platform.

The Visual Basic development environment can be extended through add-on tools and libraries such as Visual Basic custom controls (VBXs), OLE custom controls (OCXs), OLE automation servers, Dynamic Link Libraries (DLLs), and by creating your own Visual Basic automation components. There are also a variety of OLE controls distributed with the Visual Basic environment that simply need to be turned on to access them.

These add-on components can provide virtually any capability that can be developed or accessed from a low-level development environment like C.

DLL Support

A DLL (Dynamic Link Library) is a library of routines that can be called from many applications without the DLL code needing to be linked to the calling application. Unlike static libraries in languages like C or Pascal, where all code from a static library is linked into the client application, a DLL's code is linked to the application at run time.

Windows and most Windows applications are built on reusable DLLs. Using DLLs results in smaller executable (.EXE) files and usage of less physical memory when running programs that share common DLLs. Visual Basic, like most Windows development environments, provides support for external DLLs. Using DLLs is the mechanism that Visual Basic invokes when making calls to the Windows SDK. Windows is built on the concept of these shared code libraries.

DLLs can be shared among all Windows applications regardless of the language that they were developed in. This is because Windows provides a language definition for functions in a DLL library that ensures parameters are passed into the routine in a consistent manner and that stack cleanup on function exit is done in the same way regardless of whether the DLL was built in Pascal, C, or some other language.

The only exception is with C++ class methods. Exported C++ class interfaces cannot be easily accessed from applications other than other C++ applications; this is due to compiler mangling of the actual names of the methods when exporting the methods.

There are many multimedia tool vendors that sell add-on DLLs for capabilities like transitions, sprite animations, image processing, video capture, and many others. The Windows SDK is the most widely used source of DLLs for a Visual Basic programmer. All of the functions that will be used for the MCI, high and low-level audio examples are from the MMSYSTEM.DLL, which is part of the Windows 3.1 system. For Windows 95 and Windows NT, this DLL is called WINMM.DLL.

Visual Basic Controls (VBXs)

When Visual Basic was first released, it created a whole new industry for software-development vendors—the software component industry. This was not due to cognitive forethought by Microsoft, but because Visual Basic was the first commercially available program that allowed for easy-to-use add-on controls—the Visual Basic controls (VBXs).

Companies have been built on Visual Basic controls. The VBX provided a simple method for quickly and easily adding tremendous programming power to the Visual Basic environment. For multimedia programmers, this was a godsend. There is a proliferation of VBXs on the market today ranging from database controls to communications controls, networking and, of course, multimedia controls.

Today, there are VBXs for image display, image manipulation, transition effects, titling, overlay video control, and a host of other multimedia controls. VBXs are the fastest and most affordable method of extending the power of the Visual Basic development environment.

Unfortunately, VBXs are a dead-end investment. VBXs were designed only with the 16-bit Windows environment in mind. The architecture is not expandable to the 32-bit environment. VBXs are being replaced with a new technology—the OLE custom control (OCX). Visual Basic 4.0 continues to support VBX controls, but only in the 16-bit environments.

Microsoft provides a VBX to OLE control migration kit that makes porting from one architecture to the other fairly painless. This kit expedites the movement of your favorite VBX controls to OLE controls by your software vendor.

OLE Automation Servers

OLE automation is one of the greatest technological advances that Microsoft has ever provided to the Windows operating systems. Automation is part of OLE 2.0 that was introduced to the marketplace in 1993. OLE automation defines an interface with which applications can be made programmable regardless of the programming environment. Microsoft Word is an example of a programmable application. Developers can access the power of Word— for example, spell checking—within their own applications through Word's OLE automation interfaces.

When looking at the software-development industry, the puzzle that all developers are looking to solve is how to create application-independent software . This means code that can be used over and over again without modification: a software object with predefined functions that returns a predictable result when the functions are called. The software object is created so that the internal implementation doesn't matter, but the interface and the expected results do.

The VBX and DLL were solid first attempts at introducing reusable software. OLE automation is the first step to producing truly reusable software components. Automation objects are object-oriented components that are development-environment independent.

OLE automation provides *objects* to the programmer. These objects contain *properties* and *methods*. A property represents data variables that the container, which is the application using the object, manipulates to shape the appearance and behavior of the server object. A method is an action that the object performs.

The automation object is contained in a server. There are two types of OLE automation servers—an *in-process server* and a *local server*. An in-process server is a DLL while a local server is an .EXE. In the near future, there will be a third type of server called the *distributed server*, which will be an .EXE that runs on another computer. Currently, all automation servers run on a single computer.

Visual Basic is an OLE container. A *container* is a program that can embed or control OLE servers and can also control automation servers. The Visual Basic language provides constructs for supporting OLE automation with the `Object` variable type. The Visual Basic function `CreateObject` creates an instance of the automation server's object.

There are already several multimedia OLE automation servers on the marketplace. One of the most powerful automation servers is Lenel Systems

MediaDeveloper. MediaDeveloper is an automation server that provides a uniform interface to graphics, audio, digital video, analog video, and animation objects. There are several OLE automation server vendors that provide other types of multimedia services for developing applications. The latest list of OLE automation server vendors can be obtained from Microsoft's WINOBJ forum on CompuServe.

Creating OLE Automation Servers Using Visual Basic

Visual Basic 4.0 provides a very powerful feature that can now be incorporated into your multimedia applications—the capability to create your own OLE automation servers. In Chapter 12, "Creating and Using OLE Custom Controls," you build a multimedia OLE server application in Visual Basic.

By creating your own automation server, you can harness the power that your application contains, and provide all its features to other programs. For example, if your multimedia application reads in a specific file format such as a JPEG image file, you can provide a method that reads in a JPEG file and returns a handle to a Windows bitmap. Other programs can now use this method to read in an image file that they otherwise wouldn't support.

The capability to create OLE automation servers adds a new dimension to the types of applications that can be created. Developers now have the ability to multimedia-enable their applications and to multimedia-enable other applications.

The New Generation: OLE Custom Controls (OCXs)

Visual Basic 4.0 introduces support for the next generation of component software—the OLE custom control (OCX). An OCX provides similar capabilities as the VBX, but is built upon a new architecture that is designed to take advantage of today's operating systems and also tomorrow's.

The OLE control architecture is designed to be both 16- and 32-bit ready. This ensures that the controls you invest in today will protect your investment tomorrow. An OLE control is based on two key components of OLE: automation and in-place editing. An OLE control uses automation to provide access to the control's properties and methods.

Unlike a VBX, when the OLE control is activated during program run time, the programs menu can be altered and integrated with a controls menu, if the control provides one. If none is provided, the program functions as normal. This in-place editing feature allows for control-specific items to be invoked when using the control. For example, in a real estate application that uses digital video, there may be a capture control. When the control is activated, the program's menu becomes integrated with a video capture menu to control the capture of digital video.

Visual Basic's Multimedia Controls

Visual Basic provides several built-in multimedia controls—the MCI, picture and text controls—that assist in the development of multimedia applications. The controls included in Visual Basic are an easy method for starting multimedia development without making a significant cash or time investment.

In the previous versions of Visual Basic, the MCI control, picture control, and the text control were VBX controls. They have been upgraded to OLE controls for Visual Basic 4.0.

The MCI Control

The MCI control provides a basic interface to all MCI device types that you encounter for multimedia development. There are user-selectable buttons that provide an interface to various commands such as Play, Stop, and Pause. The interface can be made to be visible (by providing a control button to the end user when an application is run, for example) or can be made invisible. The developer can always write code to manipulate the control whether the control is visible or not.

The Image Control

The Image control is used for displaying some of the basic Windows image types. The Image control can read the image file formats listed in Table 1.3.

Table 1.3 Image File Formats Supported by the Visual Basic Image Control	
Image File Format	**File Extension**
Windows Bitmap	.BMP, .DIB
Windows Metafile	.WMF
Windows Icon	.ICO

The Image control can display the loaded files in either normal mode or stretched mode and can be used to establish a DDE link to other programs as well as support OLE 2.0 Drag and Drop. The Image control is not implemented as an OLE custom control.

The Label Control

The Label control, like the Image control, is not implemented as an OLE custom control. The Label control is used to display text. When the Label control is used with a transparent background, the text can be drawn over the top of another control, such as a Picture control, to provide effects such as titling of graphics or overlay video.

The Picture Clip Control

The Picture Clip control is an advanced control that can be used to store bitmap files for rapid display. This can be especially useful when creating animation or when you have a large number of bitmaps that need to be stored. One common use of the Picture Clip control is to store all of the different states of a button (normal, pressed, disabled) and use the `GraphicCell` property to select the appropriate bitmap and display it in either a Picture Box or an Image control.

The Picture Clip control is invisible at run time. You can specify rows and columns for the Picture Clip control, essentially creating an array of images out of one bitmap. These images are referenced by assigning the `GraphicCell` property to either a Picture Box control or an Image control. Visual Basic 4.0 comes with a sample program, which demonstrates the use of the Picture Clip control. It is located in the SAMPLES\PICCLIP subdirectory and the name of the project is REDTOP.VBP.

The Picture Box Control

The Picture Box control is similar to the Image control. The Picture Box control can read in the same file formats as the Image control (refer to Table 1.3).

The Picture Box control only displays the amount of the image that fits within the area of the picture box. If the image is smaller than the picture box, the image is displayed starting in the upper-left corner of the control. If the image is larger than the picture box, the image is drawn starting at the upper-left corner of the picture box and drawn. The portions of the image that fall outside of the picture box dimensions are not seen. This is a technique known as *image cropping*. The Picture Box control has an autosize property that automatically resizes the control to the size of the image.

Multimedia Database Development

Integrated with Visual Basic 4.0 is the powerful *JET Database Engine*. The JET Engine is a set of OLE automation objects that make creating multimedia database applications a snap. The Jet Engine is the same relational database that ships with Microsoft Access 2.0. The interfaces for using the JET Engine also allow connectivity to a variety of desktop database formats and can use ODBC (Open Database Connectivity) drivers to access client/server databases. The native format is MS Access; other desktop databases that can be used are Paradox, dBASE III and dBASE IV, FoxPro, and Btrieve. Flat files (text files) and spreadsheets can also be used. ODBC connectivity provides access to SQL client/server databases such as SQL Server, Oracle, Sybase and Informix database servers.

When developing multimedia applications as you will see in later chapters, there are two methods for accessing and storing multimedia data in a database system—a *file-based method* or a *BLOB (Binary Large Object) method*.

A file-based method can be used where your multimedia content resides somewhere on your hard disk or LAN. The name and path of the file are then stored in the database. When accessing the file, the file specification is retrieved and sent to your multimedia manipulation routines. This method is very straightforward and easy to implement. All database systems can be used—even text files or spreadsheets—and the files can be used by programs external to yours.

With a BLOB-based method, all of the multimedia data is stored in a field within database tables. This system treats your multimedia data the same as related alphanumeric data. All related record data is stored together. By using BLOB fields, all of your data is located in one place, within a set of database tables. There is no need to worry about files being deleted or moved.

Both methods—the file-based and BLOB-based—have advantages and disadvantages that need to be carefully examined before implementing your multimedia database application.

The following are the advantages and disadvantages of using a file-based multimedia database:

Advantages

> Easy to implement; multimedia field is a standard text field.

> Can be supported by any database type including text files and spreadsheets

> Multimedia files can be shared with external programs.

> Fast storage and retrieval of multimedia data

Disadvantages

> Difficult to move multimedia data to different locations without changing all database records

> Leads to data being located everywhere (local hard disks, LANs, remote PCs)

> Can lead to nonshareable or nonaccessible data. For example, different drive mappings among network users can lead to invalid file locations.

The following are the advantages and disadvantages of using BLOBs for multimedia applications:

Advantages

> All data is centrally located.

> Easy to move database files

> Data is accessible and shareable by all users.

Disadvantages

> Data cannot be shared by external applications without exporting it from the database application.

> Slow storage and retrieval

> Only database systems with BLOB support can be used.

The specific implementation strategies for each method will be covered in Chapter 14, "Multimedia Databases Using the JET Engine."

Hypertext and Hot Spots

Hypertext and hot spots are similar techniques where text or regions of an image are linked to other text or images. This creates an effect that allows the user to navigate through an application in a manner defined by the user. The most common example of this technique is the Windows Help Engine. When invoking a Windows Help file, the user can traverse from topic to topic looking at the subjects that interest him or her.

Visual Basic can access tools within the Windows operating environment such as the JET Engine, the Windows API and OLE structured storage, which provide methods of creating hypertext and hot spot regions within their applications. These techniques are essential for creating training and kiosk applications. Chapter 8, "Hypertext and Hotspots," covers these techniques in more detail.

From Here...

Visual Basic programmers have an assortment of multimedia capabilities built into the Windows platforms and included in the Visual Basic development environment. Understanding what these capabilities are and how to properly apply them in your application will allow you to easily construct multimedia applications. So have fun and enjoy as the multimedia programming excitement begins.

- For a look at the Windows MCI programming interface for all of the multimedia device types, see Chapter 3, "The Media Control Interface (MCI)." This chapter provides excellent insight into how Windows provides multimedia capabilities through the use of the MCI.

- To see how graphics and text can be manipulated to create transition effects, hot spots, and hypertext capabilities refer to Chapter 5, "Graphics and Palettes."

- To learn how to create and use OLE custom controls in multimedia development, see Chapter 9, "Using Peripheral Devices for Overlay Video." The OLE Custom Control Development kit is examined to demonstrate how to create your own controls. How to create OLE automation objects in Visual Basic 4.0 is also investigated.

- To see the techniques used for creating multimedia database applications, refer to Chapter 12, "Creating and Using OLE Custom Controls." This chapter contains an overview of the JET Engine and using BLOB fields.

Chapter 2

Multimedia Development with Windows

The term *multimedia* means different things to different people. The general meaning is the use of a medium other than text to deliver a message to an audience. This medium can be animation, images, audio, or video. For multimedia to be delivered to an audience, it must be integrated into an application or production. Often, a programmer can develop multimedia capabilities and include them in applications. But this method is very time-consuming and nonproductive for any organization. It would be much easier if multimedia capabilities were built into the operating system.

Including multimedia as a standard or even central component of an operating system is a concept that has been prevalent for many years in Apple platforms. It wasn't until late 1991 that Microsoft included multimedia as a core component of Windows. With the introduction of multimedia capabilities, the computing world had access to many previously unimaginable applications.

Understanding the capabilities and limitations of an operating system is crucial to the development and delivery of timely and robust applications. Nowhere is this more important than in the world of multimedia.

This chapter provides a detailed discussion of the design of Windows multimedia capabilities. It traces multimedia from the Windows 3.0 extensions through Windows 95. A clear understanding of what services are offered on each platform allows for a more comprehensive and complete development cycle.

In this chapter, you learn

- The design philosophies and methodologies used in designing the Windows multimedia interfaces

- What types of multimedia are available for Windows 95 and how they compare to Windows 3.1 and Windows NT

- What the Windows Media Control Interface (MCI) is and how it works

Integrating Multimedia Capabilities into Windows

When Windows 3.0 was released, it was the beginning of a major revolution for PC operating systems. Windows 3.0 was the first popular PC operating system with an intuitive graphical interface. Windows 3.0's graphical interface and multitasking capabilities allowed for a new class of applications to be developed. These applications provided users with advanced graphics, presentation, and drawing capabilities.

When Windows 3.0 exploded onto the computer scene, the Windows 3.0 SDK had no built-in multimedia capabilities. The *Windows SDK* provides developers with a programming interface to the capabilities of the Windows operating system. In late 1991, Microsoft released Windows multimedia extensions and the Windows *Multimedia Development Kit*. The APIs, or multimedia extensions, in the Multimedia Development Kit were a superset of the Windows 3.0 programming environment. The multimedia extensions provided application developers with a set of high- and low-level services for developing multimedia applications. The multimedia extensions provided an avenue of access to the extended capabilities of the multimedia PC.

The multimedia extensions that were previously sold as a separate product became a central component of Windows 3.1. The Windows 3.1 SDK included all the APIs and high- and low-level services that were part of the Windows Multimedia Development Kit. This was a significant event because for the first time on the PC platform, multimedia became a central component of the operating system rather than an add-on. Making multimedia a central component of the operating system moved multimedia applications into the mainstream. Special operating system requirements are no longer needed for multimedia applications.

The multimedia extensions have been integrated into all releases of Windows starting with Windows 3.1. Windows 3.1 and Windows for Workgroups are 16-bit operating systems with cooperative multitasking capabilities. The new generation of Windows—Windows NT and Windows 95—consists of 32-bit operating systems with preemptive multitasking capabilities.

The capability to create true 32-bit applications running in a 32-bit preemptive multitasking environment allows a new class of multimedia applications to be created. These applications include video conferencing, video on demand, continuous-media servers, multimedia training, and kiosks. All of these applications require the transmission of video or audio through LAN (Local Area Network), WAN (Wide Area Network), or telephone lines. A multitasking environment ensures that these applications will be given time to run, thus allowing for non-interruption of multimedia delivery.

For multimedia services to become integrated into the operating system, the multimedia services need to achieve the following goals:

- *Extensibility*. Future enhancements and features need to be added to the operating system easily and with backward compatibility. Advances in multimedia technology need to be added easily to the operating system without changing the operating system architecture.

- *Device independence*. All PC multimedia hardware and peripherals need to "simulate" using the same command set. Multimedia hardware should just be a Plug-and-Play commodity for application developers and end users.

The following sections examine the steps that the Windows architects took to achieve these design goals in 16-bit operating systems, from Windows 3.0 to Windows 3.1. You then look at the advances made in multimedia technologies for Windows NT and Windows 95.

The 16-bit Windows Multimedia Architecture

When the design engineers at Microsoft set out to add multimedia extensions to Windows, they had to meet the required design goals for the multimedia subsystem and ensure compatibility with the existing Windows architecture. The architects of the Windows multimedia system achieved the specified design goals by adding a new .DLL to Windows—MMSYSTEM.DLL. With the release of Windows 3.1, this .DLL became a standard Windows component.

MMSYSTEM.DLL provides a translation layer that isolates application code from system device drivers. All the multimedia application program interfaces (APIs) that the Windows multimedia system provides are contained within MMSYSTEM.DLL.

MMSYSTEM also provides run-time linking to the drivers that are needed. MMSYSTEM's APIs dynamically load the device drivers that are needed. This run-time linking is essential to the success of any operating system's multimedia capabilities. An application doesn't want to link to a specific hardware device driver. This limits the application to working only with the device driver that it's linked to.

The run-time linking is achieved through a well-defined, consistent device driver interface. Microsoft has defined an installable device driver interface. This interface provides a consistent interface that's followed by most of the existing multimedia hardware manufacturers. By following the defined interface, hardware vendors can guarantee that multimedia applications can take advantage of their hardware and, conversely, software vendors can guarantee that their applications are device-independent. The installable driver interface is defined in the Windows Multimedia Development Kit (MDK).

Figure 2.1 illustrates the relationship between Windows and the multimedia subsystem.

Fig. 2.1
The Windows multimedia system architecture.

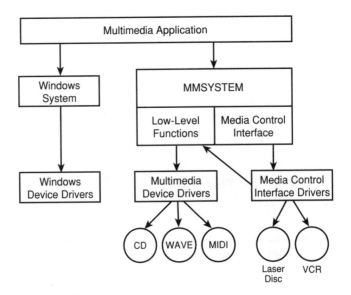

The MMSYSTEM.DLL is the component between the application code and the device driver code. The MMSYSTEM.DLL API contains the MCI APIs and the low-level multimedia support functions. These support functions include low-level support for the following devices:

- Waveform audio

- MIDI audio

- Auxiliary devices

- Low-level movie player support

- Multimedia timer services

- Joystick support

When an application accesses the Windows multimedia services, MMSYSTEM translates the function call into the correct device driver call. Figure 2.2 illustrates this point.

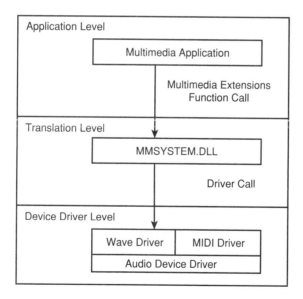

Fig. 2.2
How a multimedia API is sent to a device driver.

Extending Windows Multimedia to Include Digital Video

In 1992, Microsoft added another multimedia component to Windows. Known as Video for Windows 1.0, this component allowed for the capture and display of digital video on standard PCs.

Video for Windows provided *pseudo* full-motion video to be captured and displayed on the VGA monitor. I say pseudo because true full-motion video requires video playback at a rate of 30 frames per second (fps). This is the rate at which the human eye can't detect any pause or gap between video frames. With the introduction of Video for Windows 1.0, you could play back digitized video at a rate of 15 fps and at a size of 120×90 pixels with no audio breakup.

This important development for the PC platform meant that a technology was now available for full-motion video without the use of specialized hardware boards. This allowed title developers to extend the benefits of digital video to end users without the worry of system compatibility. Video for Windows also lets end users create digital video clips through the utilities VIDCAP.EXE and VIDEDIT.EXE, which allow for the capture and editing of digital video files.

Extending Multimedia Capabilities to 32 Bits

The core implementation of how the 16-bit Windows multimedia system was designed and developed has been extended into the 32-bit environments of Windows NT and Windows 95. The MMSYSTEM.DLL has been replaced with a new .DLL called WINMM. All the Video for Windows .DLLs are also now included as code operating system components. This is very significant because all the support for multimedia is now available to the developer and the end user just by using the operating system.

Even though the .DLL names have changed from 16-bit to 32-bit operating systems, the architecture hasn't. The architectural overview shown between the low-level multimedia services and the MCI-level services is still the same.

 All multimedia APIs except Video for Windows capture are contained in the WINMM.DLL. The Video for Windows capture APIs are contained in AVICAP32.DLL.

One interesting aspect of the 32-bit operating systems is how 16-bit applications can run and execute, even though the drivers for operating systems are 32 bit. Windows uses what's called the *thunk* layer, which allows address space mapping between 16- and 32-bit processes.

Windows NT: A 32-bit Multimedia Development Platform

When Windows NT 3.1 was first released in August 1993, little mention was made of it being a multimedia development environment. Windows NT was Microsoft's first operating system that included audio and digital video support as a standard component. Unlike Windows 3.1, where the digital video capture and playback components had to ship with each application using digital video, Windows NT and Video for Windows support is included.

Windows 95: Defining New Standards for Multimedia Development

Windows 95 represents a new level of opportunity for multimedia developers, content providers, and title developers. Windows 95 brings forward the best features of DOS, Windows 3.1, and Windows 95, as well as a new level of power for all multimedia enthusiasts.

DOS, although lacking the memory addressing, multitasking, and GUI that Windows provides, is the leading platform for games and game development. Games represent the only category where DOS-based applications outsell Windows applications.

DOS games are more popular than Windows games because DOS allows applications to have direct access to the VGA display hardware, allowing for super-fast graphics capabilities. DOS-based applications can take direct control of the video hardware because

- In DOS, only one application can run at a time, thus there's no worry about device conflicts over the display board or mapping of different palettes to the display at one time.

- DOS is an open, unprotected operating system, where a program can obtain direct access to any hardware device or I/O (input/output) port on the system.

With Windows applications, all graphics capabilities are mapped through the *GDI (Graphics Device Interface)*. The GDI provides a high-level abstraction to isolate and hide hardware interfaces from the developer. This virtually guarantees that any Windows-based application can run by using any video display adapter.

Windows 95 offers the following benefits for multimedia developers:

■ Plug-and-Play support for multimedia devices. This includes devices such as SCSI and IDE CD-ROMs, video overlay and capture cards, audio adapter cards, modems, and so forth.

■ Significant performance enhancements for CD-ROMs with the addition of a new 32-bit CD file system (CDFS).

■ *Spin and Grin,* or autoplay of CD-ROM support. This feature launches a CD-ROM viewer as soon as a new CD-ROM has been loaded.

■ Improved MIDI support through the Windows 95 polymessage MIDI feature, which allows transmission of complex MIDI messages with very little processor overhead.

■ New audio compression codecs. Windows 95 includes an ADPCM-based (Adaptive-Differential Pulse Coded Modulation) compression process for voice recording and playback called TrueSpeech. Windows 95 also has improved the audio codec (compression encoder/decoder algorithm) to allow for 4:1 compression ratios for music-quality audio with no noticeable fidelity loss.

■ A new CD-audio player that provides a programmable CD-audio interface. This feature allows for the selection and ordering of CD tracks.

■ Built-in digital video support. Video for Windows is now a standard part of Windows 95.

■ Display Control Interface (DCI), which allows for applications to take complete control of VLS (Video Local Bus) and PCI (Peripheral Control Interface) interface boards.

■ MCI device drivers for CD-audio devices, MIDI sequences, motion video devices, laser discs and VCRs, and wave audio devices.

Configuring Hardware with Plug and Play

The most frustrating experience for computer users of any level is adding a new hardware component to a computer system. This frustration is compounded for the multimedia enthusiast because there's always some type of hardware involved with multimedia.

Interrupt addresses (IRQs), memory addresses, and I/O ports all need to be configured, usually through DIP switches on the hardware board. These configurations need to match existing computer hardware to ensure that conflicts don't exist. Most computer users have no idea what this means, and hardware manufacturers haven't been much help in providing clear, concise instructions for hardware installation.

To solve this problem, Microsoft and Intel, in a joint initiative, introduced the concept of *Plug and Play*. Plug and Play is a standard that automates the process of adding new capabilities to your PC or changing PCMCIA (Personal Computer Memory Card International Association) adapters in notebook computers. Windows 95 is the first commercial operating system to fully support the Plug-and-Play interface.

Microsoft and Intel tackled this problem by introducing a specification for the Plug-and-Play BIOS. The Plug-and-Play BIOS is a ROM component in the computer motherboard that detects, manages, and configures computer hardware automatically, hiding all details from the user. When you boot the computer, the Plug-and-Play BIOS identifies the devices on the system during the Power-On Self-Test (POST). At a minimum, this includes a video display, keyboard, and disk drive.

The Plug-and-Play BIOS is only one component necessary for a fully operative Plug-and-Play system. For the BIOS to perform its duties, there must be hardware components that are Plug-and-Play compatible. Components such as PCMCIA boards, modems, video capture cards, audio cards, and disk controllers are examples of Plug-and-Play-compatible components. These components have a similar Plug-and-Play circuitry that can be auto-configured and detected.

The last component necessary for Plug-and-Play compatibility is the operating system. A fully Plug-and-Play-compatible operating system such as Windows 95 auto-detects existing and new hardware components and configures them on the fly for compatibility in your computer.

Multimedia enthusiasts benefit the most from Plug and Play because of the extra hardware necessary for multimedia applications and development. The Plug-and-Play architecture also reduces the amount of technical support calls received from application vendors and hardware manufacturers about configuring hardware. When you buy computer peripherals or systems, make sure that the components are Plug and Play-ready or Windows 95-ready so you can take advantage of this feature.

Duties of the Plug-and-Play BIOS

The Plug-and-Play BIOS is responsible for managing resources, run time, and events.

The management of basic system resources, such as DMA (direct memory access), I/O, IRQs, and memory addresses, is called *resource management*. These resources are shared by all hardware components on the system and are used by all applications. The resource manager is responsible for configuring the system's boot devices and managing the requests for system resources. You can get a list of all system resources from the System Properties program in the Windows 95 Control Panel. Figure 2.3 illustrates a typical Device Manager hardware listing.

Fig. 2.3

Use the Device Manager tab to view installed system hardware.

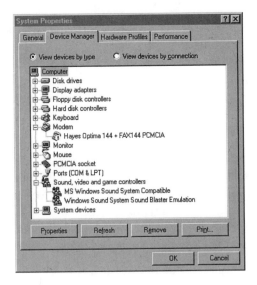

The event manager is responsible for detecting devices that are removed from or added to the computer while the system is running. Known as *hot-swapping*, this is reserved for PCMCIA devices in the initial release of the Plug-and-Play specification.

The run-time manager configures/reconfigures the devices that are added to or removed from the computer while the system is running. The run-time management of devices is especially useful for PCMCIA devices, where swapping of devices is commonplace.

Accessing CD-ROMs without MSCDEX

Windows 95—like its big brother, Windows NT—no longer needs the MSCDEX.EXE TSR (terminate-and-stay-resident) program to access CD-ROM drives. Instead, Windows 95 comes with a CDFS (CD-File System), which provides full 32-bit, protected-mode access to CD-ROM drives.

Because CDFS is a protected-mode driver, it's faster than MSCDEX, which must run in real mode. The CDFS driver doesn't use lower DOS memory for accessing the CD-ROM drive. Instead, it provides its own memory cache for buffering data transfers from the CD-ROM drive.

During installation, Windows 95 automatically detects the presence of a CD-ROM drive. This includes SCSI, Plug-and-Play SCSI, and IDE CD-ROM drives. If Windows 95 has a driver for your CD-ROM, the MSCDEX statement in AUTOEXEC.BAT is commented out, and the 32-bit Windows 95 driver is installed. If you have a CD-ROM drive that isn't recognized, such as a CD-ROM connected through a parallel port SCSI adapter, MSCDEX is not removed from AUTOEXEC.BAT and the CD-ROM is accessed through MSCDEX. The Windows 95 CDFS can always be circumvented by using your CD-ROM drivers and MSCDEX.

If you're not sure what mode Windows 95 is using for CD-ROM and fixed-disk access, you can check Control Panel's System applet to display your system settings. To determine how your system is configured, select the Performance tab of the System Properties sheet (see Fig. 2.4).

If your system uses the 32-bit CDFS and 32-bit fixed-disk drivers, the Performance property page will indicate that 32-bit drivers are used. You can enhance or modify the performance of CD-ROM drive access by clicking the File System button on the Performance tab. As Figure 2.5 shows, the optimization techniques used for the fixed-disk and CDFS VxDs can be modified to suit your system requirements. This includes changing the cache size and indicating the speed of the drive that your system is accessing.

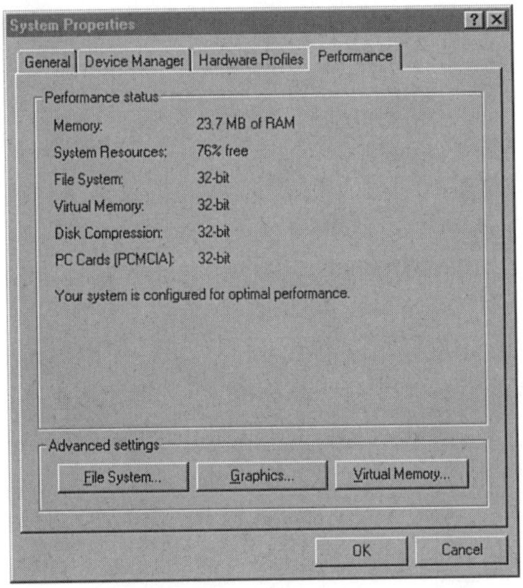

Fig. 2.4
This is where you determine whether your system is configured for optimal performance.

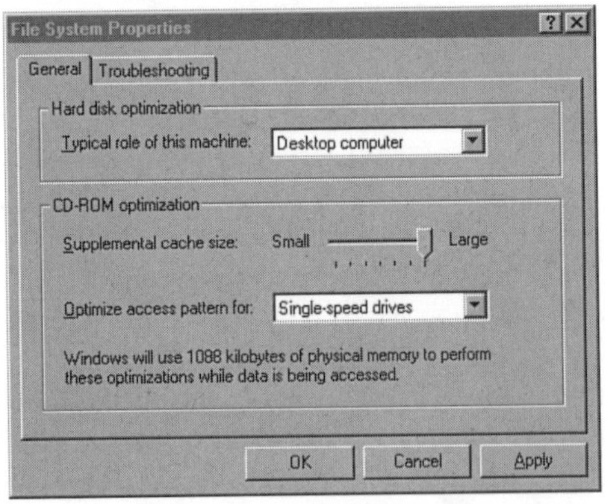

Fig. 2.5
How to use the Performance tab to configure Windows 95 VxDs for optimal CD-ROM and fixed-disk performance.

Additional Audio Compression Codecs

Windows 3.1 provided users with built-in audio support through APIs, MCI device driver support, and Control Panel audio applets. When Video for Windows was released as an add-on, the Audio Compression Manager (ACM) for Windows was also released. The Audio Compression Manager allowed for *audio codecs*, which allow for the capture and playback of compressed audio files. Compressed audio files allow for smaller audio file sizes and faster playback rates.

With the release of Windows 95, the playback of 44.1 kHz, 16-bit digital audio through software decompression makes Windows 95 a viable target platform for multimedia titles. Windows 95 includes two additional codecs that provide additional support for voice recording and playback, and for enhanced compression of audio music recordings without any appreciable audio fidelity loss.

Overall, Windows 95 includes six standard audio codecs. Each codec has its own particular merits and features. But before describing the audio codecs available with Windows 95, the following terms, which are used when discussing digital audio, need to be defined:

- *Digital audio.* Digital audio is captured through a process known as *sampling*. Sampling is a process of periodically measuring the loudness, or amplitude, of an incoming analog audio signal and representing this signal as a series of digital bits. The captured bits are stored in a waveform audio file (*.WAV) for playback.

- *Sample rate.* The periodic sampling of an incoming analog signal is called the *sample* or *capture rate*. For digital audio, the sample rate is expressed in kilohertz (kHz). Three typical sampling rates are used for digital audio: 11.025, 22.05, and 44.1 kHz. These values represent voice-grade audio, general-purpose audio, and CD-quality audio, respectively.

- *Sample resolution.* This is the number of bits that comprise a single audio sample. Typical audio cards offer 8- and 16-bit resolution. The number of bits in an audio sample determine the distinct values of the sample. An 8-bit sample can contain 256 different sample values. A 16-bit sample can contain 65,536 different sample values.

- *Codec.* The compression algorithm can be software only, as in the codecs provided with Windows 95, or the codecs can be contained in a DSP (digital signal processor) chip on the audio board. A codec compresses the audio stream on capture and decodes or decompresses the audio stream during playback. Codecs contained in hardware offer faster performance than software codecs but may also constrict the playback of the captured audio file to systems containing the audio board used for capture. If your audio board contains a hardware codec, make sure that a software-only codec exists for playback of the captured audio.

Choosing Audio Codecs for Capture and Playback

The Windows 95 Audio Compression Manager makes using audio codecs for capture and playback a painless experience. The Control Panel's Multimedia Properties lists all the multimedia devices on your system on the Advanced page. One entry is for Audio Compression Codecs (see Fig. 2.6). When the Audio Compression Manager determines which codec (if any) to use during audio capture, it looks at the priority given to each codec and uses the one with the highest priority. You can determine a codec's priority by selecting a codec from the list under Audio Compression Codecs and clicking the Properties button. A description of the codec is given, along with its usage priority (see Fig. 2.7). Altering the priority determines which codec is used first. If a codec allows for user-defined settings, the Settings button is enabled so that you can select the appropriate settings for that codec. Figure 2.8 shows a typical settings dialog box.

Fig. 2.6
Use the Advanced tab to see a tree view of the Windows 95 multimedia devices.

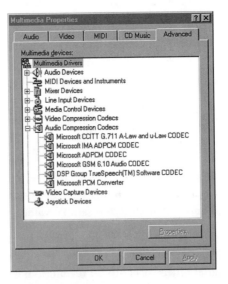

All the audio codecs supplied with Windows 95 are described as follows:

- *Microsoft ADPCM CODEC.* ADPCM stands for *Adaptive Differential Pulse Code Modulation.* Rather than save the actual values of each sample, this algorithm saves only the changes between samples. This general-purpose codec is included for backward compatibility with existing wave files that use this algorithm.

- *Microsoft IMA ADPCM CODEC.* This codec's primary purpose is for music recording. It offers up to 4:1 compression ratios of 16-bit audio without significant fidelity loss.

Fig. 2.7
Changing the
audio codec
priority is a snap
with Windows 95.

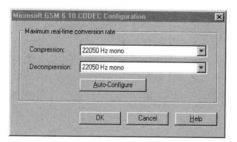

Fig. 2.8
How to create
user-definable
settings for the
Microsoft GSM
6.10 audio codec.

■ *Microsoft GSM 6.10 Audio CODEC.* GSM 6.10 is an algorithm that's used primarily for cellular telephone communications. This codec was developed according to the European Telecommunications Standards Institute's Group Special Mobile (ETSI-GSM).

■ *Microsoft CCITT G.711 A-Law and u-Law CODEC.* This codec follows the Consultative Committee for International Telephone and Telegraph's G.711 speech-compression algorithms. This is the algorithm primarily used for telecommunications in North America.

■ *Microsoft PCM Converter (Pulse Code Modulation).* This codec changes the sample rate and sample resolution of uncompressed wave files. It's automatically invoked by the Audio Compression Manager when a wave file is opened that has sample resolution and/or sample rates not supported by your audio board.

■ *DSP Group TrueSpeech(TM) Software CODEC.* The TrueSpeech codec was licensed by Microsoft from the DSP Group. The TrueSpeech codec is a specialized codec designed for voice-only recording and playback.

Using the Audio Compression Manager with Codecs

The Audio Compression Manager is a sophisticated software module that must determine not only what codec to use when playing or capturing a file, but also when to let the audio boards with built-in codecs handle the compression and decompression. To perform these tasks, the Audio Compression Manager uses the Windows 95 Wave Mapper.

When a wave file is opened, the Wave Mapper checks to see whether the file is compressed. This information is stored in the file header located at the beginning of the wave file.

If the wave file is compressed, the Wave Mapper tests the audio card to determine whether the file's compression method is supported by the audio card. If the compression method is supported, the data is sent directly to the audio card.

If the compression method isn't supported, the Audio Compression Manager searches through the list of available audio codecs for the first compatible codec. The priorities assigned to each codec determine the codec search order. If a compatible codec is found, the wave data is decompressed by the codec and piped to the audio card. If a compatible codec can't be found, the file can't be played.

Windows 95: The Digital Video Platform

Digital video is the technology that will make multimedia a mainstream technology. This statement has some merit because individual consumers, not corporations, bought the majority of multimedia computers last year. The typical multimedia computer purchased last year included a Pentium processor, a double-speed CD-ROM, a 16-bit audio soundboard, and a high-color display board. It should also be no surprise that the best-selling software consisted of multimedia titles and games.

When digital video technology first arrived on the Windows platform with the introduction of Video for Windows 1.0, many predicted that this would transcend immediately into the CD-ROM title and games markets. While this thinking had merit, the reality of the initial release of Video for Windows allowed only 160×120 size motion video at a rate of 15 frames per second. Not only was the playback size extremely small, but playback put a tremendous strain on the system CPU and the graphics subsystem. This was hardly the type of technology that would immediately benefit title or game developers.

Windows 95 ships with a 32-bit version of Video for Windows—the same version that now ships with Windows NT 3.5. The new 32-bit version allows for the playback of 320×240-sized video. While PC users are demanding full-screen motion video, the new Video for Windows is a step in the right direction. Digital video can now be used to enhance the appearance and messages delivered by multimedia titles and games.

Video for Windows uses the Audio-Video Interleaved (.AVI) file format for digital video files. When .AVI files are stored on CD-ROMs, adjacent tracks are used for the audio and video, which allows even slow CD-ROM drives to deliver synchronized sound with the video image. Within .AVI files, streams of video and audio data are interleaved, thus allowing for easy retrieval of audio and video data. To assist with the capture and playback performance of Video for Windows files, video codecs are used. For Video for Windows files that contain audio, the audio codecs are used to compress the audio data.

Like audio data, video data can be compressed and decompressed through codecs to improve storage requirements and increase playback speeds. Video data, however, is much more demanding than audio data. Whereas a sample of audio is represented in 1 (8 bits) or 2 (16 bits) bytes of information, video data is much more demanding.

For each video sample, a rectangle defining the capture area is saved. The capture area is composed of many pixels, with each pixel containing 1 (8 bits, 256 colors), 2 (16 bits, 64,000 colors), or 3 (24 bits, true color) bytes of video information. For a capture area of 320×240 pixels, this represents 76,800 pixels. True full-motion video can be captured and played back at a rate of 30 frames per second. Needless to say, video information is much more demanding than audio information.

Windows 95 ships with several video compression codecs, which can be found by running the Control Panel's Multimedia Properties and then clicking the Advanced tab (see Fig. 2.9).

Two types of video codecs can be found in Windows 95: *intraframe* and *interframe*. Interframe compression eliminates frame-to-frame duplication by using the key frame and delta technique. A key frame is used as a reference frame and a delta is the difference between the key frame and the subsequent frames. When setting up this type of codec, you indicate how often to create a key frame. The key frame is a reference point that's used for marking the changes or *deltas* that occur in subsequent frames until the next key frame is captured.

Fig. 2.9
Use the Advanced
tab to list the
Windows 95 video
compression
codecs.

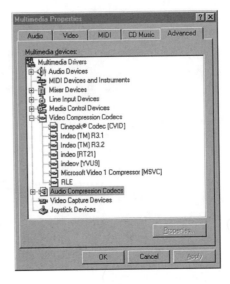

Intraframe compression is achieved on a frame-by-frame basis, where the codec compresses each individual frame independently of the others. Most of the codecs use both techniques, where the key frame is compressed individually and only the changes between the following frames are compressed.

The video codecs that are included in Windows 95 are

- *Cinepak Codec.* Cinepak is an intraframe codec that provides the best playback performance of all software codecs. Microsoft has licensed Cinepak from SuperMatch for inclusion in Video for Windows. Although the playback performance of Cinepak is outstanding, the time required to compress files using Cinepak is painstakingly slow. When using this codec, the video is captured either uncompressed or compressed using another codec. After capture, the video is then compressed into an .AVI file.

- *Indeo (RT21, YUV9, RT3.1, RT3.2).* Four separate Indeo codecs actually ship with Windows 95. The latest and greatest version of Indeo is RT3.2. The rest of the codecs are included for backward compatibility with .AVI files that are compressed using those formats. With the release of RT3.2, Intel has finally matched the Cinepak codec in performance features and is slightly faster in compression than Cinepak. Both Cinepak and Indeo are examples of interframe codecs.

- *Microsoft Video 1 Compressor.* The Video 1 compressor provides reasonable quality and sound for the capture and playback of digital video files. It doesn't match the performance of Cinepak or Indeo for compression of data, but it's a good general-purpose codec.

- *RLE (run-length encoding).* This is a sample codec primarily used for the compression of still-image bitmaps or animation. It doesn't perform well on digital video.

Controlling Your Multimedia Devices with MCI Drivers

Since the introduction of Windows 3.1, the Media Control Interface (MCI) has been the primary method of controlling board and peripheral devices. Windows 95 provides a suite of 32-bit MCI drivers for controlling many of the popular multimedia devices on the market today. The following list outlines the MCI drivers that ship with Windows 95:

- *CD Audio Device.* The CD Audio MCI driver provides an interface for controlling Red Book or audio CDs. This MCI driver has been included with Windows since Version 3.1. Windows NT was the first operating system to use a 32-bit version of the CD Audio MCI driver, and now Windows 95 includes the 32-bit MCI driver also.

- *MIDI Sequence Device.* The MIDI Sequence MCI driver is used for playing MIDI files. Like the CD Audio driver, this has been a standard part of Windows since Version 3.1. The MIDI sequence MCI driver was promoted to 32 bits with the release of Windows NT, and the 32-bit driver is now shipping with Windows 95.

- *Motion Video Device.* This is the 32-bit Video for Windows MCI driver, which uses the video compression codecs available on the system. This Video for Windows MCI driver is now included as a standard part of Windows 95 and Windows NT.

- *Pioneer LaserDisk Device.* This is the MCI driver used for controlling playback of the Pioneer LaserDisk. The LaserDisk device outputs an analog video signal that's displayed on the PC through an analog video card.

- *VISCA VCR Device.* This driver controls VCRs, laser discs, camcorders, and other devices that use the Sony VISCA protocol for PC control.

- *Wave Audio Device.* This is a 32-bit MCI driver for playing and recording digitized audio in wave files. The driver automatically uses codecs available through the Audio Compression Manager.

Windows 95 support for MCI device drivers isn't limited to the drivers included with Windows 95. Various third-party MCI drivers (16- and 32-bit) can be installed and used by MCI-compatible applications.

 Although 32-bit and 16-bit MCI drivers can be installed on the both Windows 95 and Windows NT platforms, the device drivers can't be used by all applications.

Native 32-bit applications can call the 32-bit MCI drivers but can't call the 16-bit MCI drivers. Native 16-bit applications can use the present 16- and 32-bit MCI drivers through something known as the *thunking* layer. The thunking layer is a software interface that maps 16-bit calls, variables, and so forth to 32-bit drivers or DLLs. All this is done with no program intervention.

From Here...

Understanding the multimedia architectures of your target operating system—and its capabilities and limitations—will yield better application performance and allow you to take full advantage of your operating system's features. This chapter examined the MCI multimedia architecture and how applications use MCI drivers. You also examined the features of Windows 95.

Refer to these chapters for more information on the subjects discussed in this chapter:

- For an in-depth look at the MCI implementation for all Windows systems and the various devices that can be controlled by the MCI interface, see Chapter 3, "The Media Control Interface (MCI)."

- For a glimpse at developing applications by using the audio capabilities of Windows and Visual Basic, see Chapter 4, "Visual Basic Audio Capabilities." Audio special effects, audio recording, and playback are among the topics covered in this chapter.

- For a discussion on how to effectively use digital video playback and MPEG video in your applications, see Chapter 11, "Using Digital Video Playback."

Chapter 3

The Media Control Interface (MCI)

Anyone who has tried to write a multimedia DOS application knows that dealing with the almost infinite number of device configurations possible on a PC is a nightmare of monstrous proportions. In fact, I'd go so far as to say that there's not even one DOS multimedia application that can run perfectly on every PC. There are just too many variables to consider, too many different components that can be installed on today's PCs, each with its own idea of how the job should be done. Take audio boards, for example. A PC owner can choose from hundreds of models of sound cards, which makes creating an application that uses sound a meticulous task, requiring months of testing to support even the most common sound requirements.

To a great extent, Windows 95 programmers are relieved of having to struggle with the details of implementing a particular multimedia device. This is because Windows 95 is a *device-independent environment*, which means that Windows 95 handles an application's interaction with the many devices that may be installed on a system. For example, to play a digital sound effect in a Windows 95 application, the programmer needs to do little more than send a play command to Windows. Windows then implements the command on the specific sound card installed in the user's system.

This device-independent system works surprisingly well, making multimedia applications easier to write and easier to install. The chances that a multimedia application won't run on a specific system are reduced significantly. The system works so well because the responsibility for making sure a device works properly under Windows is moved from the programmer to the manufacturer of the device. If the manufacturer wants his device to be Windows compatible, he must supply a Windows-compatible device driver. Because

Windows is the most-used operating system on desktop computers these days, few device manufacturers will overlook the chance to make their device Windows compatible.

From the multimedia programmer's point of view, Windows' device independence is largely housed in the Media Control Interface (MCI), which is a library of functions that enables programmers to easily control all types of multimedia devices, including everything from sound cards to laser disc players. Windows also supplies a number of high-level and low-level functions for manipulating specific multimedia devices. In this chapter, then, you get a general look at the MCI and what it can do for your multimedia applications. You also explore Windows' other multimedia services. The following topics are discussed in detail:

- Using MCI devices

- Working with high-level and low-level multimedia functions

- Using MCI command-string and command-message interfaces

- Programming multimedia audio services

- Programming videotape and laser disc services

- Working with multimedia video services

Multimedia Services and Visual Basic

Before you get too far in this chapter, you should know that Windows' multimedia services (of which the MCI is a large part) were designed to be accessed from C and C++ programs. With the exception of the multimedia control (see Fig. 3.1), which provides buttons that automatically control the MCI, Visual Basic has no built-in support for multimedia services. You can see that you can access the multimedia functions through Visual Basic, however, by declaring in your Visual Basic program the functions you want to use. You see how to do this throughout this book, starting with Chapter 4, "Visual Basic Audio Capabilities."

Fig. 3.1
Microsoft multimedia control.

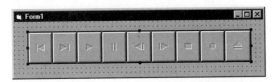

Because of the way the MCI sometimes works, you can't use it to its full advantage from within Visual Basic. For example, some MCI commands require something called a callback function. A *callback function* is a function that the MCI calls under certain conditions. When programming the MCI with C or C++, you can, for example, create a function called `SoundEnd()` (or anything you want to name it) and then have the MCI automatically call `SoundEnd()` when a sound effect is finished playing. Unfortunately, Visual Basic does not allow callback functions. Still, most MCI functions work under Visual Basic, certainly enough to program a killer multimedia application. (Note that the multimedia control, which is covered in more detail in Chapter 2, "Multimedia Development with Windows," does supply event procedures that respond to callbacks from the MCI.)

As you read the sections that follow, keep in mind that the multimedia services are a huge and complicated system. This chapter is meant only to give you an introduction to the capabilities provided by the multimedia services. If you don't understand some of the material in this chapter, don't panic. Much of the material presented here will be expanded upon in later chapters. The descriptions and function tables provided in this chapter are only meant to give you a general overview of Windows' multimedia services.

An Overview of Windows' Multimedia Services

As I said previously, multimedia services comprise libraries of functions that enable you to take control of various multimedia devices. This library is constructed so that you can access these devices at a number of levels. For example, it's possible to play a digital sound effect with a single function call. On the other hand, you can take full control of the sound effect, by using lower-level MCI commands. Similarly, you can play the tracks on a music CD with a few simple function calls, or you can dig in deep and control every aspect of playing the CD.

In addition to these various levels of control, you can access the MCI, which is a large part of Windows' multimedia services, through two different command interfaces. The *MCI command-string interface* enables you to control devices by sending command strings to the MCI functions. For example, to play an explosion sound effect that you have stored in a .WAV file, you might use the string command `Play EXPLODE.WAV`. The string interface is much easier to use than the command interface. It also enables you to accept text commands directly from the user or read in a script file containing plain text commands.

The *command-message interface* is much more Windows-like, requiring that your program send messages to the MCI in order to control multimedia functions. Because the command-message interface requires that you initialize complex data structures before calling MCI functions, it's much more difficult to use than the command-string interface, but provides greater control over the MCI and the devices it commands.

MCI Device Types

The MCI enables you to control two general types of devices: simple devices and compound devices. A *simple device* can function without an associated data file. A laser disc player, for example, is a simple device because all the data the device needs is contained on the media itself. Similarly, a CD player or a digital tape deck are also simple devices.

A *compound device* requires a data file that contains information the device needs in order to operate. A sound card is a compound device when it's used to play back a waveform (.WAV) file. A MIDI sequencer is also a compound device for playback, because it relies upon a file containing MIDI data.

The MCI currently lists ten classes of device types. These device types are listed in Table 3.1. As you can see from the table, the MCI provides a powerful library that can handle virtually any type of device you might want to use in a multimedia application. Moreover, because the MCI is an extensible library, as new devices become available, they can be easily incorporated into the library. Note that not all device types defined in Table 3.1 are currently supported by the MCI.

Table 3.1   MCI Device Types

Device Type	Description
animation	Animation device
cdaudio	CD audio player
dat	Digital audio tape player
digitalvideo	Digital video
other	Undefined device
overlay	Overlay video device
scanner	Image scanner

Device Type	Description
sequencer	MIDI sequencer
videodisc	Laser disc player
vcr	Videocassette recorder
waveaudio	Waveform audio device

Most multimedia devices share a basic set of capabilities. For example, most devices can be opened, played, paused, resumed, and closed. Because of these overlapping capabilities, the MCI provides two sets of commands for devices: *generic commands* and *extended commands*. Generic commands apply to all devices. For example, a CD player, MIDI sequencer, and a laser disc player all must be opened before they can be used. Table 3.2 lists the most commonly used generic commands that apply to MCI devices.

Extended commands give you access to capabilities that are unique to a specific device. An animation player, for example, may enable the user to view the animation sequence frame by frame. However, the concept of frames does not apply to a device like a CD player or a waveaudio device.

Table 3.2 Generic Device Commands

Command	Description
capability	Gets the capabilities of a device.
close	Closes a device.
info	Gets information about a device.
open	Opens a device.
pause	Pauses a device.
play	Plays a device.
record	Records on a device.
resume	Resumes a paused device.
seek	Moves to a new position in the media.
set	Sets control settings.
status	Gets the status of a device.
stop	Stops a device.

The Multimedia Audio Services

One of the most-used multimedia features is the playback of various types of audio information. Whether you want to have an alien ship explode on the screen, a musical soundtrack introduce your application, or even a digitized voice inform the user of his options, you provide audio by accessing Windows' audio services.

The multimedia services include both *high-level* and *low-level audio services.* The high-level audio services are the easiest to use, but are still powerful enough to be useful in most cases where you need to reproduce audio information. When you use the high-level audio services, Windows acts as an interface between your application and the audio device drivers.

The low-level audio services, on the other hand, provide the most control over the various audio devices, but also require a lot more programming effort to use. When you use the low-level audio services, you are communicating directly with a specific device driver.

Besides the different levels of service, the multimedia services provide interfaces for three types of audio devices: waveform audio, MIDI, and CD devices.

Waveform Audio

You're probably very familiar with Windows 95's famous "The Microsoft Sound" sound effect, which you hear when you start up the application. There are a lot of other sound effects—beeps, chimes, and chords—that you also hear throughout a Windows session (assuming, of course, that you have a soundboard installed and have the Windows' sound effects set to their default values). All of these sound effects are stored in what's called a *wave sound file,* which is digital sound information that's been recorded and saved on disk.

Wave sound files, which have a .WAV file extension, are perfect for all types of non-musical sound data, including voices and sound effects. Actually, you can also use waveform files to store digitized music. However, because digital sound data consumes so much hard-disk space (CD-quality sound can consume as much as 172K per second), it's often more practical to use the MIDI audio format (see the next section, "MIDI Audio") for music, unless the musical selection is only a few seconds long.

You record and play back wave sound files with a waveaudio device, which is usually just the soundcard installed in your computer. You control the waveaudio device with commercial or custom waveform applications.

For example, Windows 95 comes with an accessory called Media Player (see Fig. 3.2), which can play not only .WAV files, but other types of multimedia files as well.

Fig. 3.2
The Media Player application.

If you have an Ensoniq Soundscape soundcard, as I do, you can record and play .WAV files with the impressive Audiostation application (see Fig. 3.3).

Fig. 3.3
The Audiostation application.

On the other hand, Soundblaster users get Wave Studio (see Fig. 3.4), a special application that records, plays back, and edits waveform files.

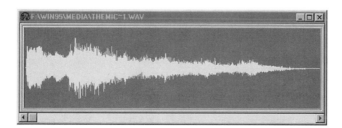

Fig. 3.4
The Wave Studio application.

All these multimedia applications have at least one thing in common. They call the multimedia services to get their work done. Table 3.3 shows the MCI command strings you can use to control waveform devices. These commands are usually all you need for most applications that must play .WAV files. You'll learn more about how to use these commands in Chapter 4, "Visual Basic Audio Capabilities." (In the table, the *<arg>* symbol indicates that an argument can be used with the command.)

Table 3.3 Waveform-Device Command Strings

Command String	Description
`capability waveaudio` *<arg>*	Gets information about the waveform device's capabilities. Arguments that can be used are `can eject`, `can play`, `can record`, `can save`, `compound device`, `device type`, `has audio`, `has video`, `inputs`, `outputs`, and `uses files`.
`close waveaudio`	Closes the waveform device.
`cue waveaudio` *<arg>*	Sets up a waveform device so that it can begin playing or recording with as little delay as possible. Arguments that can be used are `input` and `output`.
`delete waveaudio` *<arg>*	Deletes part of a waveform file. The argument can be `from` *position* or `to` *position* (where *position* is the position in the file).
`info waveaudio` *<arg>*	Gets information about the waveform device. The argument can be `input`, `file`, `output`, or `product`.
`open waveaudio` *<arg>*	Opens and initializes a waveform device. The argument can be `alias` *name* (where *name* is the alias name), `buffer` *size* (where *size* is the buffer size in seconds), `shareable`, and `type` *type* (where *type* is the device type).
`pause waveaudio`	Pauses the waveform device.
`play waveaudio` *<arg>*	Begins playing on a waveform device. The argument can be `from` *position* or `to` *position* (where *position* is a position in the file). In addition, several command flags can be appended to the command. These flags vary from device to device and include such commands as `fast`, `repeat`, `reverse`, and `slow`.

Command String	Description
`record waveaudio <arg>`	Starts recording on a waveform device. The argument can be `insert`, `from position`, `to position` (where `position` is a position in the file), or `overwrite`.
`resume waveaudio`	Resumes playing a paused waveform device.
`save waveaudio <arg>`	Saves a waveform file. The argument is the filename of the file in which to save the audio data.
`seek waveaudio <arg>`	Moves to a new position in the waveform file. The argument can be `to position` (where `position` is a position in the file), `to start`, or `to end`.
`set waveaudio <arg>`	Sets a waveform device attribute. The argument can be `alignment value` (where `value` is the alignment value), `any input`, `any output`, `audio all off`, `audio all on`, `audio left off`, `audio left on`, `audio right off`, `audio right on`, `bitspersample bits` (where `bits` is the number of bits per sample), `bytespersec bytes` (where `bytes` is the number of bytes), `channels number` (where `number` is the channel count), `format tag type` (where `type` is the format type), `format tag pcm`, `input number` (where `number` is the input channel number), `output number` (where `number` is the output channel number), `samplespersec rate` (where `rate` is the sample rate), `time format bytes`, `time format milliseconds`, and `time format samples`.
`status waveaudio <arg>`	Gets status information about the waveform device. The argument can be `alignment`, `bitspersample`, `bytespersec`, `channels`, `current track`, `format tag`, `input`, `length`, `length track number` (where `number` is a track number), `level`, `media present`, `mode`, `number of tracks`, `output`, `position`, `position track number` (where `number` is a track number), `ready`, `samplespersec`, `start position`, and `time format`.
`stop waveaudio`	Stops the waveform device.

If the command-string interface doesn't provide enough control for your application, you can resort to calling the high-level or low-level waveform-device functions offered by the multimedia services. These functions are summarized in Table 3.4.

Table 3.4 Waveform-Device Functions

Function	Description
MessageBeep()	Plays a sound defined by a system alert level.
PlaySound()	Plays a wave sound file (32-bit MCI).
sndPlaySound()	Plays a wave sound file (16-bit MCI).
waveInAddBuffer()	Gives a buffer to the waveaudio device.
waveInClose()	Closes the waveaudio device.
waveInGetDevCaps()	Gets the attributes of the waveaudio device.
waveInGetErrorText()	Gets an error string describing an input error.
waveInGetID()	Gets the input waveaudio device's ID.
waveInGetNumDevs()	Gets the number of waveform input devices.
waveInGetPosition()	Gets the current position of the input waveform.
waveInOpen()	Initializes the waveaudio device for recording.
waveInMessage()	Sends a message to an input waveaudio device.
waveInPrepareHeader()	Prepares a buffer for waveform input.
waveInReset()	Stops input and marks all buffers as done.
waveInStart()	Begins input (recording) on the waveaudio device.
waveInStop()	Stops input on the waveaudio device.
waveInUnprepareHeader()	Cleans up waveform input buffers.
waveOutBreakLoop()	Stops a playback loop on a waveaudio device.
waveOutClose()	Stops output on a waveaudio device.
waveOutGetDevCaps()	Gets the attributes for the output waveaudio device.
waveOutGetErrorText()	Gets an error string describing an output error.
waveOutGetID()	Gets the output waveaudio device's ID.
waveOutGetNumDevs()	Gets the number of output waveaudio device.
waveOutGetPitch()	Gets the current pitch setting for a waveaudio device.
waveOutGetPlaybackRate()	Gets the current playback rate for a waveaudio device.

Function	Description
waveOutGetPosition()	Gets the waveaudio device's current playback position.
waveOutGetVolume()	Gets the volume setting for a waveaudio device.
waveOutMessage()	Sends a message to an output waveaudio device.
waveOutOpen()	Initializes a waveaudio device for playback.
waveOutPause()	Pauses a waveform output device.
waveOutPrepareHeader()	Prepares a buffer for waveform output.
waveOutReset()	Stops output (playback) on a waveaudio device.
waveOutRestart()	Resumes the playback of a paused waveaudio device.
waveOutSetPitch()	Sets the pitch setting for a waveaudio device.
waveOutSetPlaybackRate()	Sets the waveaudio device's playback rate.
waveOutSetVolume()	Sets the waveaudio device's volume.
waveOutUnprepareHeader()	Cleans up waveform output buffers.
waveOutWrite()	Sends data to a waveform output device.

MIDI Audio

If you play any form of electronic keyboard, there's no way you could have avoided learning about *MIDI* (Musical Instrument Digital Interface). For those of you who don't know a synthesizer from a bagpipe, MIDI enables musicians (and multimedia programmers, of course!) to store musical information in much smaller files than those required for digital sound. How does MIDI manage this trick? By storing codes for musical events, rather than actually recording the sound produced by the instrument. That is, MIDI records what you need to do to reproduce the sound, rather than digitizing the actual sound.

For example, when you perform a musical selection on a MIDI-capable keyboard, you generate a number of MIDI messages. These include at least note-on and note-off messages, which indicate when a key is pressed and released. Other messages indicate other information, such as how hard the key was pressed or a change in volume. There are enough types of MIDI messages that any passage played and recorded on a MIDI keyboard can be played back almost perfectly just by feeding the MIDI commands back into the keyboard. In a way, you can think of a MIDI file as the electronic equivalent of the paper scroll used in a player piano.

Because MIDI commands control a MIDI device directly, reproducing the sound by actually replaying the passage on the MIDI device, the sound reproduction is stunning. Moreover, because MIDI messages can be sent to any one of sixteen different channels, you retain much more control over the musical passage.

Suppose, for example, you've composed a MIDI piece in which channel 1 controls the drums, channel 2 controls an organ, and channel 3 controls a synthesizer bass line. Now, suppose you decide that you want to use an electric piano instead of an organ. All you need to do is redirect channel-2 MIDI commands to the electric piano. On the other hand, if you had recorded the musical passage as a .WAV file, you would have no way to change the instruments—except by rerecording the entire passage from scratch.

Figure 3.5 shows MIDI Orchestrator, which comes with the Ensoniq Soundscape sound card. As you can see, this application enables you to control all 16 MIDI channels. In the figure, the current MIDI file has set up channel 1 for flute, channel 2 for piano, channel 3 for bass, channel 4 for baritone sax, and so on, up to channel 10, which holds the drum track. Using the slider controls, the user can change the volume of each instrument independently of any other instrument in the mix. The buttons enable the user to "solo" any particular channel or to shut off any channel.

Fig. 3.5
The MIDI
Orchestrator
application.

The user can even change the instrument used in a channel. Figure 3.6 shows the user changing the piano to a harpsichord.

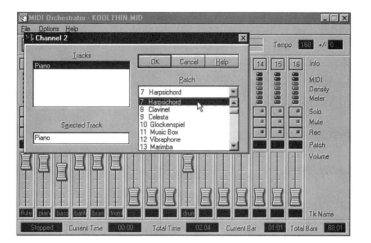

Fig. 3.6
Changing the piano to a harpsichord.

As you can see, MIDI provides a powerful way to record quality musical compositions. But keep in mind that the quality of the final music is based on the quality of the end user's sound card. Just as you wouldn't expect Windows to print as sharp a picture on a dot-matrix printer as it can on a laser printer, you can't expect an $80 sound card to sound as good as a $300 sound card.

MIDI files often have a .MID file extension, but MIDI data can also be stored as part of a *RIFF (Resource Interchange File Format)* file, which is a special file format for multimedia files.

As with waveform devices, you can control a MIDI device using the MCI command-string interface or by using the low-level multimedia functions. You learn more about MIDI in Chapter 4, "Visual Basic Audio Capabilities." Table 3.5 lists the MCI command strings you can use with a MIDI device.

Table 3.5 MIDI-Device Command Strings

Command String	Description
capability sequencer <arg>	Gets information about the MIDI device's capabilities. Arguments that can be used are can eject, can play, can record, can save, compound device, device type, has audio, has video, and uses files.

(continues)

Table 3.5 Continued

Command String	Description
close sequencer	Closes the MIDI device.
info sequencer *<arg>*	Gets information about the MIDI device. The argument can be file or product.
open sequencer *<arg>*	Opens and initializes a MIDI device. The argument can be alias (followed by the alias name), shareable, or type *type* (where *type* is the device type).
pause sequencer	Pauses the MIDI device.
play sequencer *<arg>*	Begins playing on a MIDI device. The argument can be from *position* or to *position* (where *position* is a position in the file).
record sequencer *<arg>*	Starts recording on a MIDI device. The argument can be from *position* or to *position* (where *position* is a position in the MIDI data), insert, or overwrite.
resume sequencer	Resumes playing a paused MIDI device.
save sequencer *<arg>*	Saves recorded MIDI data into a file. The argument is the name of the file in which to save the data.
seek sequencer *<arg>*	Moves to a new position in the MIDI file. The argument is to *position* (where *position* is a position in the MIDI data), to start, or to end.
set sequencer *<arg>*	Sets a MIDI device attribute. The argument can be audio all off, audio all on, audio left off, audio left on, audio right off, audio right on, master MIDI, master none, master SMPTE, offset, port *number* (where *number* is the port number), port mapper, port none, slave file, slave MIDI, slave none, slave SMPTE, tempo, time format milliseconds, time format song pointer, time format SMPTE 24, time format SMPTE 25, time format SMPTE 30, or time format SMPTE 30 drop.

Command String	Description
`status sequencer <arg>`	Gets status information about the MIDI device. The argument can be `current track`, `division type`, `length`, `length track number` (where *number* is a track number), `master`, `media present`, `mode`, `number of tracks`, `offset`, `port`, `position`, `position track number` (where *number* is a track number), `ready`, `slave`, `start position`, `tempo`, or `time format`.
`stop sequencer`	Stops a MIDI device.

If the command-string interface doesn't provide enough control for your application, you can resort to calling the low-level MIDI-device functions offered by the multimedia services. These functions are summarized in Table 3.6.

Table 3.6 MIDI-Device Functions

Function	Description
`midiInAddBuffer()`	Gives a buffer to the MIDI device.
`midiInClose()`	Closes the MIDI device.
`midiInGetDevCaps()`	Gets the attributes of the MIDI device.
`midiInGetErrorText()`	Gets an error string describing an input error.
`midiInGetID()`	Gets the MIDI device's ID.
`midiInGetNumDevs()`	Gets the number of MIDI input devices.
`midiInMessage()`	Sends driver-specific messages to an input MIDI device.
`midiInOpen()`	Initializes the MIDI device for recording.
`midiInPrepareHeader()`	Prepares a buffer for MIDI input.
`midiInReset()`	Stops input and marks all buffers as done.
`midiInStart()`	Begins input (recording) on the MIDI device.
`midiInStop()`	Stops input on the MIDI device.

(continues)

Table 3.6 Continued

Function	Description
midiInUnprepareHeader()	Cleans up MIDI input buffers.
midiOutCacheDrumPatches()	Preloads drum patches into the MIDI device.
midiOutCachePatches()	Preloads selected patches into the MIDI device.
midiOutClose()	Stops output on a MIDI device.
midiOutGetDevCaps()	Gets the attributes for the output MIDI device.
midiOutGetErrorText()	Gets an error string describing an output error.
midiOutGetID()	Gets the output MIDI device's ID.
midiOutGetNumDevs()	Gets the number of output MIDI devices.
midiOutGetVolume()	Gets the volume setting for a MIDI device.
midiOutLongMsg()	Sends a message to an output MIDI device.
midiOutMessage()	Sends a driver-specific message to an output MIDI device.
midiOutOpen()	Initializes a MIDI device for playback.
midiOutPrepareHeader()	Prepares a buffer for MIDI output.
midiOutReset()	Stops output (playback) on a MIDI device.
midiOutSetVolume()	Sets the volume for a MIDI device.
midiOutShortMsg()	Sends a non-system-exclusive message to a MIDI device.
midiOutUnprepareHeader()	Cleans up MIDI output buffers.

CD Audio

I don't know about you, but it's been one heck of a long time since I saw an old-fashioned vinyl record in a music store. These days, we buy almost all recordings on compact discs (CDs) with some people using cassette tapes instead. Because CDs are so popular, and because they provide unparalleled sound quality, no multimedia system would be complete without the ability to manage CDs. So, of course, Windows' multimedia services provide all the functions you need to play and manage CDs. In fact, using Visual Basic to control the MCI, you can even write a CD-player application that's almost as sophisticated as the one you have in your living room or den.

Figure 3.7 shows the CD Player accessory that comes with Windows 95. This handy program can not only play a CD, but also enables the user to move from track to track, to move quickly forward or backward through any specific track, and even pause, stop, or eject the CD currently in the computer's CD-ROM player. Information displayed by the application includes the current track number, the position within the current track, the length of the entire CD, and the length of the current track.

Fig. 3.7
The CD Player accessory.

As you may have guessed, you can control a CD player using the MCI's command-string interface. (There are no low-level functions specifically for controlling a CD player.) You learn more about controlling a CD player in Chapter 4, "Visual Basic Audio Capabilities." Table 3.7 shows the command strings you can use with a CD audio device.

Table 3.7   CD Audio-Device Command Strings

Command String	Description
capability cdaudio <arg>	Gets information about the CD device's capabilities. Arguments that can be used are can eject, can play, can record, can save, compound device, device type, has audio, has video, and uses files.
close cdaudio	Closes the CD device.
info cdaudio <arg>	Gets information about the CD device. The argument must be product.
open cdaudio <arg>	Opens and initializes a CD device. The argument can be alias name (where name is the alias name) or shareable.
pause cdaudio	Pauses the CD device.

(continues)

Table 3.7 Continued	
Command String	**Description**
`play cdaudio <arg>`	Begins playing on a CD device. The argument can be from *position* or to *position* (where *position* is a position on the CD).
`resume cdaudio`	Resumes play on a paused CD device.
`seek cdaudio <arg>`	Moves to a new position on the disc. The argument is to *position* (where *position* is the new position), to `start`, or to `end`.
`set cdaudio <arg>`	Sets a CD device attribute. The argument can be `audio all off`, `audio all on`, `audio left off`, `audio left on`, `audio right off`, `audio right on`, `door closed`, `door open`, `time format milliseconds`, `time format msf`, and `time format tmsf`.
`status cdaudio <arg>`	Gets status information about the CD device. The argument can be `current track`, `length`, `length track` *number* (where *number* is a track number), `media present`, `mode`, `number of tracks`, `position`, `position track` *number* (where *number* is a track number), `ready`, `start position`, and `time format`.
`stop cdaudio`	Stops the CD device.

Laser Disc Players

A popular source of video programs is the laser disc player. Laser disc (or videodisc) players work much like the CD-ROM player you have in your computer, except that laser discs used in a laser disc player are much larger and are double-sided. Laser discs provide much higher quality video and audio than videotapes. Moreover, information on a laser disc is quicker and easier to find than information on a videotape. What might take several minutes to locate on a videotape may take only a second or two to locate on a laser disc. In fact, comparing a videotape to a laser disc is a lot like comparing a cassette tape to a CD. The big disadvantage of a laser disc is that, like a CD, it is a read-only source. You cannot record information on a laser disc.

The MCI supports two types of laser discs: *CAV* and *CLV*. A CAV plays back one video frame for each revolution of the disk. This layout makes for perfect freeze frames, but allows only 30 minutes of video per side. The CLV laser disc contains one to three video frames per track (depending on how close to the center the track is). This layout allows for 60 minutes of video per side, but you can't perform frame-by-frame pausing and stepping.

Laser discs can hold two types of audio information: *analog* and *digital.* The digital sound tracks are most often used for the program's soundtrack, whereas the analog audio is often used for voice commentary. As with most MCI devices, you can use MCI commands to play, pause, seek, and step through a laser disc. In fact, computer-controlled laser discs are often used for training and education. However, only the Pioneer laser disc players with RS-232 ports can be used with your computer. (By the time you read this, there may be other machines that also function with the MCI.) These machines tend to be expensive and are not usually found in a typical video store.

As with other devices, you can control a laser disc player using the command-string interface. (There are no low-level functions specifically for controlling a laser disc player.) You learn more about controlling a laser disc in Chapter 9, "Using Peripheral Devices for Overlay Video." Table 3.8 shows the command strings you can use with a laser disc device.

Table 3.8   Videodisc-Device Command Strings

Command String	Description
capability videodisc `<arg>`	Gets information about the laser disc device's capabilities. Arguments that can be used are can eject, can play, can record, can reverse, can save, CAV, CLV, compound device, device type, fast play rate, has audio, has video, normal play rate, slow play rate, and uses files.
close videodisc	Closes the laser disc device.
escape videodisc	Sends a device-specific command string to a laser disc device. The argument is the command string to send.
info videodisc `<arg>`	Gets information about the laser disc device. The argument must be product.
open videodisc `[<arg>]`	Opens and initializes a laser disc device. The argument can be alias *name* (where *name* is the alias name) or shareable.
pause videodisc	Pauses the laser disc device.

(continues)

Table 3.8 Continued	
Command String	**Description**
play videodisc [<*arg*>]	Begins playing on a laser disc device. The argument is fast, slow, from *position*, to *position* (where *position* is a position on the disc), reverse, scan, speed *frames* (where *frames* is the speed in frames per second).
resume videodisc	Resumes play on a paused laser disc device.
seek videodisc <*arg*>	Moves to a new position on the laser disc. The argument is reverse, to *position* (where *position* is the new position), to start, or to end.
set videodisc <*arg*>	Sets a laser disc device attribute. The argument can be audio all off, audio all on, audio left off, audio left on, audio right off, audio right on, door closed, door open, time format frames, time format hms, time format milliseconds, time format track, video off, and video on.
spin videodisc <*arg*>	Starts or stops a laser disc spinning. The argument is down or up.
status videodisc <*arg*>	Gets status information about the laser disc device. The argument can be current track, disc size, forward, length, length track *number* (where *number* is a track number), media present, media type, mode, number of tracks, position, position track *number* (where *number* is a track number), ready, side, speed, start position, and time format.
step videodisc	Steps the laser disc playback frame-by-frame. The argument is by *number* (where *number* is the number of frames) or reverse.
stop videodisc	Stops the laser disc device.

Video Cassette Recorders

One of the most popular sources of video information is the video cassette recorder (VCR). Just about everyone owns one of these machines, which can record and play back video from a television or a video camera. The MCI provides extensive support for the control of Sony VISCA-compatible VCRs. (VISCA stands for Video System Control Architecture.) Using the MCI with a compatible VCR, you can perform the following functions:

- *Control tape movement.* These commands enable you to play, record, pause, step through, and seek through a videotape. You can monitor and control tape movement based on time codes or using the VCR's counter.

- *Set VCR controls.* These commands enable you to perform such tasks as setting the audio channel, setting the video channel, changing the channel to which the tuner is set, as well as adjusting other VCR functions such as time, counter setting, tracking, and speed.

- *Get status information.* Using the status group of commands, you can get specific information about a VCR, including the current channel, the speed, the audio and video sources, the time, the counter setting, and much more.

- *Frame capturing.* MCI commands can freeze and unfreeze a video image so that you can capture specific frames.

- *Input selection.* This set of commands enables you to set the input sources for the VCR, including line, auxiliary, tuner, and super video.

- *Record-track selection.* A VCR can usually record a video track, a timecode track, and one or more audio tracks. The MCI supplies commands for recording all tracks simultaneously (assemble mode) or for selecting a specific track to record (insert mode).

As you can see by this list, controlling a VCR can be a complex process. Moreover, because a VCR can take many minutes to locate and display information, it's useful mostly for video information that's played in serial fashion from beginning to end. A VCR is not capable of random access in the way a laser disc is.

The MCI command strings for controlling a VCR are listed in Table 3.9. (There are no low-level commands for controlling a VCR.) You learn more about using a VCR with a multimedia application in Chapter 9, "Using Peripheral Devices for Overlay Video."

Table 3.9   VCR-Device Command Strings

Command String	Description
capability vcr *<arg>*	Gets information about the VCR device's capabilities. Arguments that can be used are can detect length, can eject, can freeze, can monitor sources, can play, can preroll, can preview, can record, can reverse, can save, can test, clock increment rate, compound device, device type, has audio, has clock, has timecode, has video, number of marks, seek accuracy, and uses files.
close vcr	Closes the VCR device.
cue vcr *<arg>*	Prepares the VCR device to play or record. The argument can be input, output, from *position* (where *position* is a position on the tape), to *position*, preroll, and reverse.
freeze vcr *<arg>*	Freezes the VCR device's input or output. The argument can be output, input, field, and frame.
index vcr *<arg>*	Switches the VCR device's on-screen display on or off. The argument can be on or off.
info vcr *<arg>*	Gets information about the VCR device. The argument can be product or version.
list vcr *<arg>*	Gets the number and types of audio and video inputs on the VCR device. The argument can be audio source count, audio source number *index* (where *index* is an audio input index), video source count, and video source number *index*.
mark vcr *<arg>*	Records and erases marks on the VCR tape. The argument can be erase or write.
open vcr *<arg>*	Opens and initializes a VCR device. The argument can be alias *name* (where *name* is the alias name), shareable, or type.
pause vcr	Pauses the VCR device.
play vcr *<arg>*	Begins playing on a VCR device. The argument can be at *time* (where *time* is the time), from *position* (where *position* is the position on the tape), to *position*, reverse, and scan.
record vcr *<arg>*	Starts recording on a VCR device. The argument can be at *time* (where *time* is the time), initialize, from *position* (where *position* is the position on the tape), or to *position*.

Command String	**Description**
resume vcr	Resumes play on a paused VCR device.
seek vcr *<arg>*	Moves to a new position on the tape. The argument can be at *time* (where *time* is the time), mark, reverse, to *position* (where *position* is the new position), to start, or to end.
set vcr *<arg>*	Sets a VCR device attribute. The argument can be assemble record off, assemble record on, clock, counter *value* (where *value* is the counter value), counter format, door open, door closed, index counter, index date, index time code, length *length* (where *length* is the tape length), pause, power on, power off, preroll duration *length* (where *length* is the length), postroll duration *length* (where *length* is the length), record format EP, record format LP, record format SP, speed *factor* (where *factor* is the speed factor), time mode detect, time mode counter, time format hms, time format milliseconds, time format ms, time format frames, time format SMPTE 24, time format SMPTE 25, time format SMPTE 30, time format SMPTE 30 drop, time format msf, time format tmsf, video off, and video on.
setaudio vcr *<arg>*	Sets input, monitor, and record settings for the VCR device. The argument can be monitor to *type* number *number* (where *type* is aux, generic, mute, line, output, svideo, or tuner), off, on, record off, record on, record track *number* off (where *number* is the track number), record track *number* on, source to *type* number *number* (where *type* is aux, generic, mute, line, svideo, or tuner), track *number* off (where *number* is the track number), track *number* on.
settimecode vcr *<arg>*	Enables or disables timecode recording for the VCR device. The argument can be record off or record on.
settuner vcr *<arg>*	Switches the current tuner or changes the channel of the current tuner. The argument can be channel *channel* (where *channel* is the channel number), channel down, channel seek down, channel seek up, channel up, and number *number* (where *number* is the tuner number).

(continues)

Table 3.9 Continued	
Command String	**Description**
setvideo vcr <arg>	Sets the input, monitor, and record settings for the VCR device's video track input. The argument can be monitor to type number number (where type is aux, generic, mute, line, svideo, or tuner), off, on, record off, record on, record track number off (where number is the track number), record track number on, source to type number number (where type is aux, generic, mute, rgb, line, svideo, or tuner), track number off, track number on.
status vcr <arg>	Gets status information about the VCR device. The argument can be assemble record, audio, audio monitor, audio monitor number, audio record, audio record track number (where number is the track number), audio source, audio source number, audio track number (where number is the track number), channel, channel tuner number number (where number is the channel number), clock, clock id, counter, counter format, counter resolution, current track, frame rate, index, index on, length, length track number (where number is the track number), media present, media type, mode, number of audio tracks, number of tracks, number of video tracks, pause timeout, play format, position, position start, position track number (where number is the track number), power on, preroll duration, postroll duration, ready, record format, speed, timecode present, timecode record, timecode type, time format, time mode, time type, video, video monitor, video monitor number, video record, video record track number (where number is the track number), video source, video source number, and write protected.
step vcr <arg>	Steps the VCR playback frame-by-frame. The argument can be by number (where number is the number of frames) or reverse.
stop vcr	Stops the VCR device.
unfreeze vcr <arg>	Turns off the freeze command on the VCR device. The argument can be input or output.

Digital Video

Digital video is a big part of today's multimedia applications. That's not surprising when one considers the amount of time the average person spends in front of the TV set. Nothing brings you closer to "being there" than watching a well-produced video or movie. After all, watching TV is a lot like looking through a window and seeing another world beyond. Perhaps the power of video was best demonstrated when the entire country sat at home and watched the human race take its first tentative steps on the moon, live as it happened.

Obviously, video is an important way to present information. Using the MCI's digital video interface, you can display actual video sequences, sort of like using an on-screen window as a mini television. These video sequences can include not only the video images themselves, but also digitized sound and still pictures. To store all the types of data that must be included in a digital video file, Microsoft came up with the Audio-Video Interleaved (.AVI) file format, which stores video sequences as a series of bitmaps. Also included in the file is the digitized sound (in wave sound format) that accompanies the video sequence.

As you learned previously, a single second of CD-quality sound can eat up as much as 176K of hard disk space. This is nothing compared to the amount of space necessary to store video sequences. If it were possible to display TV-quality video on today's computers, a single second of full-screen video would require almost 28MB of hard disk space! Besides the storage space, you can probably see another significant problem. Even if you had enough space to store even a short 30-second video clip, your hard drive sure couldn't transfer 28MB of data a second.

To solve this problem, a video standard of 15 frames per second, with a 160×120 resolution and 256-color palette has been adopted for use with video under Windows. Using this standard, a video sequence including digitized sound eats up about 300K per second. This standard makes software-only video possible on today's machines. As more and more machines incorporate specialized video hardware, even greater quality video will be possible.

Figure 3.8 shows the Media Player accessory that comes with Windows 95 playing a video clip from the Video for Windows Developer's Kit. As you can see, the Media Player enables you to control the playing of the video sequence in much the same way you can control the playing of an audio sequence. You can jump to any location within the sequence, as well as fast forward, fast reverse, pause, and stop the video sequence.

Fig. 3.8

Playing an .AVI file with Media Player.

The MCI command strings for controlling digital video are listed in Table 3.10. You learn more about using digital video with a multimedia application in Chapter 8, "Digital Video Capture and Editing."

Table 3.10 Digital Video Command Strings	
Command String	**Description**
`capability digitalvideo` *`<arg>`*	Gets information about the digital video device's capabilities. Arguments that can be used are `can eject`, `can freeze`, `can lock`, `can play`, `can record`, `can reverse`, `can save`, `can stretch`, `can stretch input`, `can test`, `compound device`, `device type`, `has audio`, `has still`, `has video`, `uses files`, `uses palettes`, and `windows`.
`close digitalvideo`	Closes the digital video device.
`configure digitalvideo`	Brings up a dialog box for configuring digital video.
`cue digitalvideo` *`<arg>`*	Prepares the digital video device to play or record. The argument can be `output` or `to` *`position`* (where *`position`* is a workspace position).
`info digitalvideo` *`<arg>`*	Gets information about the digital video device. The argument can be `file`, `product`, `version`, `window text`.

Command String	Description
open digitalvideo *<arg>*	Opens and initializes a digital video device. The argument can be alias *name* (where *name* is the alias name), parent *hwnd* (where *hwnd* is a handle to a window), style *style* (where *style* is overlapped, popup, or child), or type AVIVideo.
pause digitalvideo	Pauses the digital video device.
play digitalvideo *<arg>*	Begins playing on a digital video device. The argument can be from *position* (where *position* is the position on the tape), to *position*, fullscreen, or window.
put digitalvideo *<arg>*	Specifies a rectangle for cropping or scaling. The argument can be destination, destination at *rect* (where *rect* is four values specifying a rectangle), source, source at *rect*, window, window at *rect*, window client, or window client at *rect*.
realize digitalvideo *<arg>*	Requests the digital video device to select and realize its palette. The argument can be background or normal.
resume digitalvideo	Resumes play on a paused digital video device.
seek digitalvideo *<arg>*	Moves to a new position in the video data. The argument can be to *position* (where *position* is the new position), to start, or to end.
set digitalvideo *<arg>*	Sets a digital video device attribute. The argument can be audio all off, audio all on, seek exactly off, seek exactly on, speed *factor* (where *factor* is the speed factor), time format *format* (where *format* is frames or ms), video off, or video on.
setaudio digitalvideo *<arg>*	Changes audio settings for the digital video device. The argument can be off, on, and volume to *value* (where *value* is the new average volume).
setvideo digitalvideo *<arg>*	Changes video settings for the digital video device. The argument can be off, on, or palette handle to *palette* (where *palette* is the palette handle).

(continues)

Table 3.10   Continued

Command String	Description
`signal digitalvideo <arg>`	Specifies when to send a signal. The argument can be at `position` (where `position` is the frame position), `cancel`, `every interval` (where `interval` specifies the time between signals), `return position`, or `uservalue id` (where `id` is a user-defined signal value).
`status digitalvideo <arg>`	Gets status information about the digital video device. The argument can be `audio`, `forward`, `length`, `media present`, `media type`, `mode`, `monitor`, `nominal frame rate`, `number of tracks`, `palette handle`, `position`, `ready`, `reference frame` (where `frame` is a frame number), `seek exactly`, `speed`, `start position`, `time format`, `unsaved`, `video`, `volume`, `window maximized`, `window minimized`, or `window visible`.
`step digitalvideo <arg>`	Steps the digital video playback frame-by-frame. The argument can be `by number` (where `number` is the number of frames) or `reverse`.
`stop digitalvideo`	Stops the digital video device.
`update digitalvideo <arg>`	Redraws the current video frame. The argument can be `hdc hdc at rect` (where `hdc` is a handle to a device context and `rect` is the clipping rectangle), `hdc hdc` (where `hdc` is the device context handle), or `paint hdc hdc` (where `hdc` is a handle to a device context).
`where digitalvideo <arg>`	Gets the rectangle defined by the last put command. The argument can be `destination`, `destination max`, `source`, `source max`, `window`, or `window max`.
`window digitalvideo <arg>`	Sets the window used to display video by the digital video device. The argument can be `handle hwnd` (where `hwnd` in the window's handle), `handle default`, `state value` (where `value` is `hide`, `minimize`, `restore`, `show`, `show maximized`, `show minimized`, `show min noactive`, `show na`, `show noactive`, or `show normal`), or `text text` (where `text` is the text for the window caption).

Overlay Video

Another type of video you can use through the MCI is overlay video. *Overlay video*, which is sometimes called "analog video-in-a-window," is different from digital video in that the video sequences are not read in from a file of digitized bitmaps and sounds. Instead, special hardware merges a live, analog video signal with your computer's VGA display. This video system allows for such cool pastimes as watching a mini TV on your screen.

The command strings for controlling overlay video are listed in Table 3.11. For more information on overlay video, see Chapter 9, "Using Peripheral Devices for Overlay Video."

Table 3.11   Overlay Video Command Strings

Command String	Description
`capability overlay <arg>`	Gets information about the overlay video device's capabilities. Arguments that can be used are `can eject`, `can freeze`, `can play`, `can record`, `can save`, `can stretch`, `compound device`, `device type`, `has audio`, `has video`, `uses files`, and `windows`.
`close overlay`	Closes the overlay video device.
`freeze overlay <arg>`	Freezes the overlay video device. The argument can be at `rect` (where `rect` is four values specifying a rectangle).
`info overlay <arg>`	Gets information about the overlay video device. The argument can be `file`, `product`, or `window text`.
`load overlay <arg>`	Loads data into the video buffer. The argument is the path and filename of the file to load. This can be followed by at `rect` (where `rect` is four values specifying a rectangle).
`open overlay <arg>`	Opens and initializes an overlay video device. The argument can be `alias` *name* (where *name* is the alias name), `parent` *hwnd* (where *hwnd* is a handle to a window), `shareable`, `style` *style* (where *style* is overlapped, popup, or child), `style child`, `style overlapped`, `style popup`, or `type` *device* (where *device* is the device type).

(continues)

Table 3.11 Continued	
Command String	**Description**
`put overlay <arg>`	Defines a capture rectangle, receiving rectangle, a source rectangle, or a destination rectangle. The argument can be `destination`, `destination at` *rect* (where *rect* is four values specifying a rectangle), `frame`, `frame at` *rect*, `source`, `source at` *rect*, `video`, or `video at` *rect*.
`save overlay <arg>`	Saves the video buffer to a file. The argument is the path and filename of the file to which to save. The filename can be followed by `at` *rect* (where *rect* is four numbers specifying a rectangle).
`set overlay <arg>`	Sets an overlay video device attribute. The argument can be `audio all off`, `audio all on`, `audio left off`, `audio left on`, `audio right off`, `audio right on`, `time format milliseconds`, `video off`, or `video on`.
`status overlay <arg>`	Gets status information about the overlay video device. The argument can be `media present`, `mode`, `ready`, `stretch`, or `window handle`.
`unfreeze overlay <arg>`	Unfreezes an overlay video device. The argument can be `at` *rect* (where *rect* is four values specifying a rectangle).
`where overlay <arg>`	Gets the video, destination, frame, and source rectangles. The argument can be `destination`, `frame`, `source`, or `video`.
`window overlay <arg>`	Sets the window used to display video by the overlay video device. The argument can be `fixed`, `handle` *hwnd* (where *hwnd* in the window's handle), `handle default`, `state` *state* (where *state* is hide, iconic, maximized, minimize, minimized, no action, no activate, normal, or show), `stretch`, or `text` *text* (where *text* is the text for the window caption).

Animation

The problem with digital video is that you need special hardware to capture and record the video signal. An easier way to add action sequences to your application is to use animation. Usually, an animation sequence is comprised of many drawn images that, when displayed one after the other, give the illusion of movement. This is exactly the same way a cartoon works. The advantage of animation is that you can draw the frames that make up the sequence rather than have to invest in a lot of expensive video hardware to capture the images.

The MCI provides a set of functions specifically for controlling animation. The MCI command strings for controlling animation are listed in Table 3.12. For more information on animation in Visual Basic, refer to Chapter 10, "Animation."

Table 3.12 Animation Command Strings

Command String	Description
capability animation `<arg>`	Gets information about the animation device's capabilities. Arguments that can be used are can eject, can play, can record, can reverse, can save, can stretch, compound device, device type, fast play rate, has audio, has video, normal play rate, slow play rate, uses files, uses palettes, and windows.
close animation	Closes the animation device.
info animation `<arg>`	Gets information about the animation device. The argument can be file, product, or window text.
open animation `<arg>`	Opens and initializes an animation device. The argument can be alias *name* (where *name* is the alias name), nostatic, parent *hwnd* (where *hwnd* is a handle to a window), shareable, style *style* (where *style* is a window style), style child, style overlapped, style popup, or type *device* (where *device* is the device type).
pause animation	Pauses the animation device.
play animation `<arg>`	Starts playback on an animation device. The argument can be fast, from *position* (where *position* is a position in the animation data), to *position*, reverse, scan, slow, or speed *frames* (where *frames* is the speed in frames per second).
put animation `<arg>`	Defines source and destination rectangles. The argument can be destination, destination at *rect* (where *rect* is four values specifying a rectangle), source, or source at *rect*.
realize animation `<arg>`	Selects and realizes the animation device's palette. The argument can be background or normal.

(continues)

Table 3.12 Continued

Command String	Description
resume animation	Resumes playback on a paused animation device.
seek animation <arg>	Moves to a new position in the animation data. The argument can be to *position* (where *position* is the new position), to start, or to end.
set animation <arg>	Sets an animation device attribute. The argument can be audio all off, audio all on, audio left off, audio left on, audio right off, audio right on, time format frames, time format milliseconds, video off, or video on.
status animation <arg>	Gets status information about the animation device. The argument can be current track, forward, length, length track *number* (where *number* is the track number), media present, mode, number of tracks, palette handle, position, position track *number* (where *number* is the track number), ready, speed, start position, stretch, time format, or window handle.
step animation <arg>	Steps the animation playback frame-by-frame. The argument can be by *number* (where *number* is the number of frames) or reverse.
stop animation	Stops playback on the animation device.
update animation <arg>	Redraws the current animation frame. The argument must be hdc *hdc* (where *hdc* is the device context handle). You can follow the argument with at *rect* (where *rect* is four values specifying a rectangle).
where animation <arg>	Gets destination and source rectangles. The argument can be destination or source.
window animation <arg>	Sets the window used to display video by the animation device. The argument can be fixed, handle *hwnd* (where *hwnd* in the window's handle), handle default, state *state* (where *state* is hide, iconic, maximized, minimize, minimized, no action, no activate, normal, or show), stretch, or text *text* (where *text* is the text for the window caption).

From Here...

This chapter gave you a quick look at Windows' multimedia services, including the MCI, a large and complex library of functions designed to make multimedia applications under Windows easier to write. If you'd like to learn more about using multimedia services from within Visual Basic, you can find more information on related topics in the following chapters:

■ For an introduction to multimedia applications and programming techniques, see Chapter 1, "Multimedia Development Using Visual Basic."

■ Windows' device independence means that handling sound cards is a snap! For more on this topic, read Chapter 4, "Visual Basic Audio Capabilities."

■ Learn to create your own AVI files in Chapter 8, "Digital Video Capture and Editing."

■ All the news that's fit to print about laser discs, videotapes, and overlay video boards can be found in Chapter 9, "Using Peripheral Devices for Overlay Video."

Chapter 4

Visual Basic Audio Capabilities

In these days of multimedia, audio has become an important element of even the most serious applications. In short, sound is no longer the domain of computer games! Voice annotations and digital sound effects can often be used even in applications like spreadsheets and word processors—and especially in multimedia help systems. In fact, audio is the multimedia feature most commonly used in programs. This chapter, then, teaches you to add audio to your own programs.

In this chapter, you learn to

- Declare and call both 16-bit and 32-bit Windows functions from within a Visual Basic program

- Play waveform files with high-level Windows functions

- Use the MCI command-message interface to control waveform devices

- Use the MCI command-string interface to control and play compact discs

- Use the MCI command-string interface to play MIDI files

High-Level Waveform Functions

Windows multimedia functions come in both high-level and low-level forms. The easiest way to play a sound from within your application is to call one of the high-level functions. These functions enable you to do everything from play a waveform file to record and create MIDI files. Unfortunately, it would take an entire book to cover all of the MCI's high-level functions. In this section, you get a look at how to use the multimedia high-level functions to control waveform audio.

Waveform audio, the most common type of audio, is digitized sound data stored in a file with a .WAV extension. Windows supplies three high-level functions for playing waveform files: `MessageBeep()`, `sndPlaySound()`, and `PlaySound()`.

Using the *MessageBeep()* Function

You can use the `MessageBeep()` function whenever you want to play a sound that's associated with one of Windows' alert levels. These sounds include the ubiquitous "ding" and other system sounds that inform you of various events. For example, if you click outside of a dialog box that's waiting for input, you hear a beep that reminds you to deal with the dialog box before you can continue with your application.

If you've ever fiddled with Windows, you may have discovered that you can assign whatever sounds you like to Windows' alert levels and various Windows events by opening the Control Panel and clicking on the Sounds icon (see Fig. 4.1).

Fig. 4.1
Associating sounds with system events.

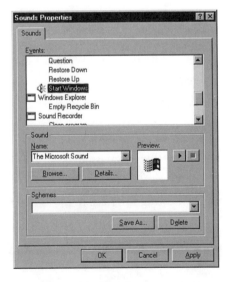

In a program, the various sounds associated with the Windows' alert levels are defined by the constants MB_ICONASTERISK, MB_ICONEXCLAMATION, MB_ICONHAND, MB_ICONQUESTION, MB_ICONINFORMATION, and MB_ICONSTOP.

When you use one of these constants in a call to MessageBeep(), the system plays the associated sound effect. Of course, to use MessageBeep() in a Visual Basic program, you must first declare the function as well as define the constants for the various alert levels, as shown in Listing 4.1.

Listing 4.1 LIST4_1.BAS. *MessageBeep()'s declaration.*

```
Declare Function MessageBeep Lib "User" _
    (ByVal AlertLevel As Integer) As Integer

Const MB_ICONHAND = &H10
Const MB_ICONQUESTION = &H20
Const MB_ICONEXCLAMATION = &H30
Const MB_ICONASTERISK = &H40
Const MB_ICONINFORMATION = MB_ICONASTERISK
Const MB_ICONSTOP = MB_ICONHAND
```

A typical call to MessageBeep() in a Visual Basic program then looks something like this:

```
Dim ErrorCode As Integer
ErrorCode = MessageBeep(MB_ICONASTERISK)
```

The function returns a zero if it fails and a nonzero value if it succeeds.

Using the *sndPlaySound()* Function

Whereas the MessageBeep() function limits you to only those sounds associated with system alert levels, the sndPlaySound() function can play any waveform sound you like, including alert sounds. In a Visual Basic program, sndPlaySound() is declared, as shown in Listing 4.2.

Listing 4.2 LIST4_2.BAS. *sndPlaySound()'s declaration.*

```
#If Win32 Then
    Private Declare Function sndPlaySoundA Lib "WinMM" _
        (ByVal SoundName As String, ByVal Flags As Integer) _
        As Integer
#Else
    Private Declare Function sndPlaySound Lib "MMSystem" _
        (ByVal SoundName As String, ByVal Flags As Integer) _
        As Integer
#End If

Const SND_ASYNC = &H1
Const SND_LOOP = &H8
Const SND_MEMORY = &H4
```

(continues)

Listing 4.2 Continued

```
Const SND_NODEFAULT = &H2
Const SND_NOSTOP = &H10
Const SND_SYNC = &H0
```

As you can see, `sndPlaySound()` also requires that you define a number of constants. You see how to use these constants with the function shortly.

Notice that the 32-bit version of `sndPlaySound()` is actually called `sndPlaySoundA()` and is found in WINMM.DLL rather than in MMSYSTEM.DLL. The name change is due to the fact that Win32 supports *UNICODE*, which is a kind of fancy new ASCII code that supports character sets requiring more than one byte per character. Because Windows must now support both regular character strings and UNICODE strings, every function that uses strings must have two definitions.

If you were programming in C++, you would just include the MMSYSTEM.H header file into your program, and then the `sndPlaySoundA()` (the regular version) or `sndPlaySoundW()` (the UNICODE version) function would be mapped to `sndPlaySound()`. In other words, you can call `sndPlaySound()` in a C++ program whether you're using regular or UNICODE strings. Visual Basic, however, knows nothing about the MMSYSTEM.H file and so has no way of mapping `sndPlaySoundA()` or `sndPlaySoundW()` to `sndPlaySound()`. You'll run into this problem again and again as you try to use the 32-bit multimedia functions.

The `sndPlaySound()` function requires two parameters. The first is the name of the sound or .WAV file that you want to play. The function first searches the `[sounds]` section of the system registry for the sound. The sound names found there are not the names of waveform files, but rather names assigned to specific Windows events. A typical `[sounds]` section looks like this:

```
[sounds]
SystemAsterisk=chord.wav,Asterisk
SystemHand=chord.wav,Critical Stop
SystemDefault=C:\WINDOWS\DING.WAV,Default Beep
SystemExclamation=chord.wav,Exclamation
SystemQuestion=chord.wav,Question
SystemExit=chimes.wav,Windows Exit
SystemStart=tada.wav,Windows Start
```

To play the `SystemAsterisk` sound, you provide `sndPlaySound()` with the string `SystemAsterisk` as its first parameter. If `sndPlaySound()` can't find the sound represented by the string, the function assumes that the sound string is the name of a waveform file. Then `sndPlaySound()` searches for the file in the current directory, the main Windows directory, the Windows system directory, or directories included in the user's PATH environment variable. If the function can't find the file, it tries to play the SystemDefault sound. Finally, if it can't find this sound, it returns an error.

The second parameter for sndPlaySound() is the sound-play option, which can be one or more of the following:

Parameter	Description
SND_ASYNC	The sound is played asynchronously (the function returns immediately after the sound begins). You must call sndPlaySound() with a first parameter of 0 to end the sound.
SND_LOOP	The sound plays repeatedly. To stop the loop, you must call sndPlaySound() with a first parameter of 0. (You must also include the SND_ASYNC flag along with SND_LOOP.)
SND_MEMORY	Indicates that the first parameter in the sndPlaySound() call points to a waveform sound in memory.
SND_NODEFAULT	If the sound specified in the first parameter can't be found, the function returns without playing the default sound.
SND_NOSTOP	The function does not play the requested sound if a sound is already playing. In this case, sndPlaySound() returns 0.
SND_SYNC	The sound is played synchronously (the function returns only when the sound ends).

A typical call to sndPlaySound()—or sndPlaySoundA()—in a Visual Basic program looks something like this:

```
Dim ErrorCode As Integer
ErrorCode = sndPlaySound("c:\windows\chimes.wav", _
   SND_SYNC Or SND_NODEFAULT)
```

The function returns 0 if it fails and a nonzero number if it succeeds.

Using the *PlaySound()* Function

The last high-level waveform function is PlaySound(). As you can see by its declaration in a Visual Basic program that is shown in Listing 4.3, it is a little more flexible than its cousin sndPlaySound().

Listing 4.3   LIST4_3.BAS. *PlaySound()'s declaration.*

```
#If Win32 Then
    Declare Function PlaySound Lib "WinMM" _
        (ByVal SoundName As String, ByVal handle As Integer, _
        ByVal Flags As Long) As Integer
#Else
    Declare Function PlaySound Lib "MMSystem" _
        (ByVal SoundName As String, ByVal handle As Integer, _
        ByVal Flags As Long) As Integer
#End If

Const SND_ALIAS = &H10000
Const SND_FILENAME = &H20000
Const SND_RESOURCE = &H40004
Const SND_NOWAIT = &H2000
```

Like sndPlaySound(), there are a number of flags you can use with
PlaySound(). Besides SND_ASYNC, SND_NODEFAULT, and SND_SYNC, which you
already defined for sndPlaySound(), the PlaySound() function can use the
SND_ALIAS, SND_FILENAME, SND_NOWAIT, and SND_RESOURCE flags. These flags have
the following meanings:

Flag	Description
SND_ALIAS	Indicates that the first parameter in the PlaySound() call is a sound name in the system registry.
SND_FILENAME	Indicates that the first parameter in the PlaySound() call is the filename of a .WAV file.
SND_NOWAIT	Indicates that the call to PlaySound() should fail if the waveform device is busy.
SND_RESOURCE	Indicates that the first parameter in the PlaySound() call is a resource name.

A typical call to PlaySound() in a Visual Basic program looks something like
this:

```
Dim ErrorCode As Integer
ErrorCode = PlaySound("c:\windows\chimes.wav", 0, _
    SND_SYNC Or SND_NODEFAULT Or SND_FILENAME)
```

The arguments for the function are the sound name (system name, resource
name, or filename), the handle of the module that owns the resource (if the
SND_RESOURCE flag is used), and the appropriate flags. The function returns 0 if
it fails and a nonzero number if it succeeds.

Using the MCI to Play Waveform Files

As you learned in the previous chapter, the MCI provides two high-level interfaces for controlling waveform devices: the command-string interface and the command-message interface. Later in the section, "Constructing the CDPLAYER Application," you will see how to use the command-string interface to control CD and MIDI devices. Using the command-string interface with waveform devices is very similar. In this section, you get an introduction to the command-message interface as you learn how to gain more control over the playing of waveform devices.

Using the *mciSendCommand()* Function

The function sndPlaySound() is one of the highest-level functions available for playing waveform files in Windows. As such, it allows only a few options and always plays a sound from beginning to end. What if you want more control over the sounds in your programs? You could step down one level and use the mciSendCommand() function to send specific commands to your sound device.

Although using mciSendCommand() requires learning a few Windows messages that are specially designed for multimedia applications, it is still a straightforward process. In this process, devices are treated much like tape recorders with features such as play, stop, pause, and resume. By using these different functions, you can stop a waveform file from playing at any point, or pause the waveform file and resume playing exactly where it paused. You can even give the user control of the sounds, as you'll soon see.

The first step in using the MCI command-message interface from within Visual Basic is to declare the mciSendCommand() function, which is the function that sends commands to the system. Listing 4.4 shows that Visual Basic declaration, along with declarations for related constants.

Listing 4.4   LIST4_4.BAS. *mciSendCommand()'s declaration.*

```
#If Win32 Then
    Private Declare Function mciSendCommandA Lib "WinMM" _
        (ByVal DeviceID As Integer, ByVal Message As Integer, _
        ByVal Param1 As Long, Param2 As Any) As Long
#Else
    Private Declare Function mciSendCommand Lib "MMSystem" _
        (ByVal DeviceID As Integer, ByVal Message As Integer, _
        ByVal Param1 As Long, Param2 As Any) As Long
#End If
```

(continues)

Listing 4.4 Continued

```
Const MCI_OPEN = &H803
Const MCI_CLOSE = &H804
Const MCI_ESCAPE = &H805
Const MCI_PLAY = &H806
Const MCI_SEEK = &H807
Const MCI_STOP = &H808
Const MCI_PAUSE = &H809
Const MCI_INFO = &H80A
Const MCI_GETDEVCAPS = &H80B
Const MCI_SPIN = &H80C
Const MCI_SET = &H80D
Const MCI_STEP = &H80E
Const MCI_RECORD = &H80F
Const MCI_SYSINFO = &H810
Const MCI_BREAK = &H811
Const MCI_SOUND = &H812
Const MCI_SAVE = &H813
Const MCI_STATUS = &H814
Const MCI_CUE = &H830
Const MCI_REALIZE = &H840
Const MCI_WINDOW = &H841
Const MCI_PUT = &H842
Const MCI_WHERE = &H843
Const MCI_FREEZE = &H844
Const MCI_UNFREEZE = &H845
Const MCI_LOAD = &H850
Const MCI_CUT = &H851
Const MCI_COPY = &H852
Const MCI_PASTE = &H853
Const MCI_UPDATE = &H854
Const MCI_RESUME = &H855
Const MCI_DELETE = &H856
```

Notice that, besides the function declaration, you must also define the constants that represent the various commands you can send to the MCI. You must also declare several data structures that hold information the MCI needs in order to complete the MCI commands your application sends. In Visual Basic, these data structures look like those in Listing 4.5.

Listing 4.5 LIST4_5.BAS. MCI data structure declarations.

```
Type MCI_OPEN_PARMS
    dwCallback As Long
    wDeviceID As Integer
    wReserved0 As Integer
    lpstrDeviceType As Long
    lpstrElementName As Long
    lpstrAlias As Long
End Type
```

```
Type MCI_PLAY_PARMS
    dwCallback As Long
    dwFrom As Long
    dwTo As Long
End Type

Type MCI_GENERIC_PARMS
    dwCallback As Long
End Type
```

These structures hold the many parameters needed to open, play, and otherwise control a sound device. With the function, constant, and data-structure
declarations complete, you can now call the MCI command-message interface from within your Visual Basic program. However, you do need to consider the problem of dealing with strings in functions that were originally
intended to be called from C or C++. The following section covers this sticky
problem.

Generating String Addresses

Because some members of the MCI data structures require addresses to strings
(something that Visual Basic isn't set up to provide), you have to do a little
Visual Basic trickery. Specifically, you need a special type of fixed-length
string. You declare such a string type like this:

```
Type StringX
    Str As String * 256
End Type
```

In a moment, you see how to use this new string type with MCI multimedia
functions.

To play a sound file from the beginning by using the default sound device,
you first initialize the MCI_OPEN_PARMS structure. The first step toward completing this task is to declare the variables you need. Listing 4.6 shows these declarations.

**Listing 4.6 LIST4_6.BAS. Declarations of variables needed to play
waveform sounds.**

```
Dim mciOpen As MCI_OPEN_PARMS
Dim mciPlay As MCI_PLAY_PARMS
Dim mciGeneric As MCI_GENERIC_PARMS
Dim ElementName As StringX
Dim AliasName As StringX
```

Next, you initialize mciOpen's dwCallback, wDeviceID, wReserved, and lpstrDeviceType members to 0, as shown in Listing 4.7.

Listing 4.7   LIST4_7.BAS. Initialization of *mciOpen* members.

```
mciOpen.dwCallback = 0&
mciOpen.wDeviceID = 0
mciOpen.wReserved0 = 0
mciOpen.lpstrDeviceType = 0&
```

Now, you must use the fixed-length string data type you created earlier, in order to generate addresses to strings that contain the name of the .WAV file you want to play (ElementName) and the alias you want to give to the device (AliasName). (The alias name is optional.) You start by assigning the filename of the .WAV file to ElementName. Because C functions expect to receive strings that end with a 0, you add the 0 to the string using the Chr$(0) function, for example:

```
ElementName.Str = "c:\win95\media\chimes.wav" & Chr$(0)
```

Next, you do the same thing with the AliasName string, except you initialize it to the name you want to give to the device, for example:

```
AliasName.Str = "wave" & Chr$(0)
```

Now comes the tricky stuff. Because Visual Basic does not allow you to generate the addresses of strings, you have to resort to a C function call. The Windows API provides three functions that return string addresses: AnsiNext(), lstrcat(), and lstrcpy(). Of the three functions, lstrcat() seemed like the best candidate because it performs two functions: it returns a string address as well as concatenates two strings. Therefore lstrcat() is the one chosen for this discussion. (The others work fine, as well.)

Of course, because lstrcat() is a Windows API function, before you can call it in a Visual Basic program, you must first declare it like this:

```
Declare Function lstrcat Lib "Kernel" (Str1 As Any, _
    ByVal Str2 As Any) As Long
```

As with many other functions, the normal-string, 32-bit version of lstrcat() has an "A" appended to its name. Also, the 32-bit version lives in KERNEL32.DLL rather than in KERNEL.DLL. That declaration looks like this:

```
Declare Function lstrcatA Lib "Kernel32" (Str1 As Any, _
    ByVal Str2 As Any) As Long
```

Normally, a C programmer would use `lstrcat()` to *concatenate* (join together) two strings, which are called `Str1` and `Str2` in the argument list. What makes `lstrcat()` useful to a Visual Basic programmer is that it returns the address of the newly concatenated string. So, to get the address of the `ElementName` string, which now holds the filename of the .WAV file you want to play, you would use the following Visual Basic code:

```
NullString = Chr$(0)
mciOpen.lpstrElementName = lstrcat(ElementName, NullString)
```

By concatenating `NullString` onto `ElementName`, you're not changing the `ElementName` string at all. (Basically, you're saying "add nothing to `Str1`.") After the above lines execute, however, `mciOpen`'s `lpstrElementName` member contains the address of the zero-terminated string that holds the .WAV filename.

Finally, you do the same thing for the `AliasName` string:

```
mciOpen.lpstrAlias = lstrcat(AliasName, NullString)
```

At this point, your `MCI_OPEN_PARMS` data structure is fully initialized, which means it's time to send your first MCI command.

Opening the Device

Before you can play a waveform file (or any other type of audio), you must open the appropriate device. You do this by using `mciSendCommand()`—or `mciSendCommandA()`—to send an `MCI_OPEN` command to the system, like this:

```
ErrorCode = mciSendCommand(0, MCI_OPEN, _
    MCI_OPEN_ELEMENT Or MCI_OPEN_ALIAS, mciOpen)
```

The function's four arguments are a device ID (always 0 with the `MCI_OPEN` command), the command message, the flags for the command message, and the data structure containing the required information (in this case, an `MCI_OPEN_PARMS` data structure). The flags you can use with the `MCI_OPEN` command are declared in a Visual Basic program, as shown in Listing 4.8.

Listing 4.8   LIST4_8.BAS. Declaration of *MCI_OPEN* flags.

```
Const MCI_OPEN_SHAREABLE = &H100&
Const MCI_OPEN_ELEMENT = &H200&
Const MCI_OPEN_ALIAS = &H400&
Const MCI_OPEN_ELEMENT_ID = &H800&
Const MCI_OPEN_TYPE_ID = &H1000&
Const MCI_OPEN_TYPE = &H2000&
```

These flags have the following meanings:

Flag	Description
MCI_OPEN_ALIAS	Indicates that the lpstrAlias member of the MCI_OPEN_PARMS data structure contains a pointer to an alias name.
MCI_OPEN_ELEMENT	Indicates that the lpstrElementName member of the MCI_OPEN_PARMS data structure contains a pointer to the element name.
MCI_OPEN_SHAREABLE	Indicates that the device or element is shareable.
MCI_OPEN_TYPE	Indicates that the lpstrDeviceType member of the MCI_OPEN_PARMS data structure contains a pointer to a device-type string.
MCI_OPEN_TYPE_ID	Indicates that the lpstrDeviceType member of the MCI_OPEN_PARMS data structure contains an device-type identifier in the form of an integer.

Checking MCI Return Code Errors

The mciSendCommand() function returns a code that indicates whether the command was completed. This return code will be 0 if the command was executed successfully or an error code if the command failed. If you want information about an error code, you can call the mciGetErrorString() function, which is declared in a 16-bit Visual Basic program like this:

```
Declare Function mciGetErrorString Lib "MMSystem" _
    (ByVal dwError As Long, ByVal lpstrBuffer As String, _
    ByVal wLength As Integer) As Integer
```

The 32-bit version of mciGetErrorString() is called mciGetErrorStringA() and is found in WINMM.DLL. You would declare the 32-bit version like this:

```
Declare Function mciGetErrorStringA Lib "WinMM" _
    (ByVal dwError As Long, ByVal lpstrBuffer As String, _
    ByVal wLength As Integer) As Integer
```

A typical call to mciGetErrorString() in a Visual Basic program looks like that which is shown in Listing 4.9.

Listing 4.9 LIST4_9.BAS. A call to *mciGetErrorString( )*.

```
Dim ReturnCode As Integer
Dim ErrorString As String * 256
ReturnCode = mciGetErrorString(ErrorCode, ErrorString, 255)
MsgBox ErrorString
```

The mciGetErrorString() function's three arguments are the error code for which you want information, the string in which the function will return the information, and the maximum length of the string. After the call to mciGetErrorString(), you can display the returned error information by calling MsgBox() with the error string. When you do, you see something like the message box shown in Figure 4.2.

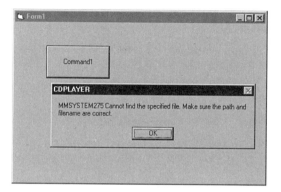

Fig. 4.2
Displaying an MCI error string in a message box.

Playing the Device

If the MCI_OPEN command has been completed successfully, your application is ready to play the sound. To do this, first save the device ID returned in the mciOpen data structure, and then initialize mciPlay (the MCI_PLAY_PARMS structure), as shown in Listing 4.10.

Listing 4.10 LIST4_10.BAS. Initialization of the *mciPlay* data structure.

```
DeviceID = mciOpen.wDeviceID
mciPlay.dwCallback = 0&
mciPlay.dwFrom = 0&
mciPlay.dwTo = 0&
```

Ordinarily, the dwCallback member of the mciPlay structure would hold the handle of the window that should receive MCI messages. Because Visual Basic cannot respond to these messages, dwCallback is set to 0. The dwFrom and dwTo members specify the starting and ending locations within the data to play. To play the entire sound, you just set these members to 0.

Next, another call to mciSendCommand() plays the sound. That call looks like this:

```
ErrorCode = mciSendCommand(DeviceID, MCI_PLAY, MCI_WAIT, mciPlay)
```

Here, the function's arguments are the device ID, the MCI command, the flags that augment the play command, and the MCI_PLAY_PARMS structure. The flags can be one or more of the following constants:

Constant	Description
MCI_FROM	Indicates that the MCI should start playing from the location stored in the dwFrom member of the MCI_PLAY_PARMS data structure.
MCI_NOTIFY	Indicates that, upon completing the command, the MCI should send a MM_MCINOTIFY message to the window whose handle is stored in the dwCallback member of the MCI_PLAY_PARMS data structure. (You'll never use this flag in a Visual Basic program.)
MCI_TO	Indicates that the MCI should stop playing the sound at the location stored in the dwTo member of the MCI_PLAY_PARMS data structure.
MCI_WAIT	Indicates that the play command be completed before the MCI returns control to the application.

You define these mciSendCommand() flag constants in a Visual Basic program, as shown in Listing 4.11.

Listing 4.11   LIST4_11.BAS. Declaration of the *mciSendCommand()* flags.

```
Const MCI_NOTIFY = &H1&
Const MCI_WAIT = &H2&
Const MCI_FROM = &H4&
Const MCI_TO = &H8&
```

Closing the Device

When the sound has finished playing, you must close the waveform device. You do this by calling mciSendCommand() yet again, only this time with the MCI_CLOSE command and an MCI_GENERIC_PARMS data structure:

```
mciGeneric.dwCallback = 0&
ErrorCode = mciSendCommand(DeviceID, _
  MCI_CLOSE, MCI_WAIT, mciGeneric)
```

Notice that mciGeneric's single member, dwCallback, gets set to 0. Again, Visual Basic cannot respond to MCI messages so it cannot specify a callback function.

The WAVEPLAY Program

Listings 4.12 and 4.13 are a complete program that plays a waveform file. Before running the program, be sure that the BEAMUP.WAV sound file included with the program on this book's CD-ROM is in your VB directory on drive C. When you run the program, you will see the windows shown in Figure 4.3. Just click the Play button to hear the sound effect.

Fig. 4.3
The .WAV Player program.

Listing 4.12 WAVEPLAY.FRM. The WAVEPLAY program's main form.

```
VERSION 4.00
Begin VB.Form Form1
   BackColor       =   &H00E0FFFF&
   Caption         =   "WAV Player"
   ClientHeight    =   1470
   ClientLeft      =   1875
   ClientTop       =   1815
   ClientWidth     =   2580
   BeginProperty Font
      name         =   "MS Sans Serif"
      charset      =   1
      weight       =   700
      size         =   8.25
      underline    =   0   'False
      italic       =   0   'False
      strikethrough =  0   'False
   EndProperty
   Height          =   1875
   Left            =   1815
   LinkTopic       =   "Form1"
   ScaleHeight     =   1470
   ScaleWidth      =   2580
   Top             =   1470
   Width           =   2700
   Begin VB.CommandButton btnPlay
      Caption      =   "Play"
      Height       =   975
      Left         =   720
      TabIndex     =   0
      Top          =   240
      Width        =   1095
   End
End
```

(continues)

Listing 4.12   Continued

```
Attribute VB_Name = "Form1"
Attribute VB_Creatable = False
Attribute VB_Exposed = False
Option Explicit

' Windows API Function Declarations
#If Win32 Then
    Private Declare Function mciSendCommandA Lib "WinMM" _
      (ByVal DeviceID As Integer, ByVal Message As Integer, _
      ByVal Param1 As Long, Param2 As Any) As Long
    Private Declare Function mciGetErrorStringA Lib "WinMM" _
      (ByVal dwError As Long, ByVal lpstrBuffer As String, _
      ByVal wLength As Integer) As Integer
    Private Declare Function lstrcatA Lib "Kernel32" _
      (Str1 As Any, ByVal Str2 As Any) As Long
#Else
    Private Declare Function mciSendCommand Lib "MMSystem" _
      (ByVal DeviceID As Integer, ByVal Message As Integer, _
      ByVal Param1 As Long, Param2 As Any) As Long
    Private Declare Function mciGetErrorString Lib "MMSystem" _
      (ByVal dwError As Long, ByVal lpstrBuffer As String, _
      ByVal wLength As Integer) As Integer
    Private Declare Function lstrcat Lib "Kernel" _
      (Str1 As Any, ByVal Str2 As Any) As Long
#End If

' MCI Command Constants
Const MCI_OPEN = &H803
Const MCI_CLOSE = &H804
Const MCI_PLAY = &H806

' Flags for the MCI_OPEN Command
Const MCI_OPEN_ELEMENT = &H200&
Const MCI_OPEN_ALIAS = &H400&

' Flag for the MCI_PLAY Command
Const MCI_WAIT = &H2&

' Wave Device ID
Dim DeviceID As Integer

Private Sub btnPlay_Click()
    Dim mciOpen As MCI_OPEN_PARMS
    Dim mciPlay As MCI_PLAY_PARMS
    Dim mciGeneric As MCI_GENERIC_PARMS
    Dim ElementName As StringX
    Dim AliasName As StringX
    Dim ReturnCode As Integer
    Dim ErrorCode As Long
    Dim NullString As String * 1

    mciOpen.dwCallback = 0&
    mciOpen.wDeviceID = 0
    mciOpen.wReserved0 = 0
```

```
    ElementName.Str = "c:\vb\beamup.wav" & Chr$(0)
    AliasName.Str = "wave" & Chr$(0)
    mciOpen.lpstrDeviceType = 0&
    NullString = Chr$(0)

    #If Win32 Then
        mciOpen.lpstrElementName = _
          lstrcatA(ElementName, NullString)
        mciOpen.lpstrAlias = lstrcatA(AliasName, NullString)
        ErrorCode = mciSendCommandA(0, MCI_OPEN, _
          MCI_OPEN_ELEMENT Or MCI_OPEN_ALIAS, mciOpen)
    #Else
        mciOpen.lpstrElementName = lstrcat(ElementName, NullString)
        mciOpen.lpstrAlias = lstrcat(AliasName, NullString)
        ErrorCode = mciSendCommand(0, MCI_OPEN, _
          MCI_OPEN_ELEMENT Or MCI_OPEN_ALIAS, mciOpen)
    #End If

    If ErrorCode = 0 Then
        DeviceID = mciOpen.wDeviceID
        mciPlay.dwCallback = 0&
        mciPlay.dwFrom = 0&
        mciPlay.dwTo = 0&
        mciGeneric.dwCallback = 0&

        #If Win32 Then
            ErrorCode = mciSendCommandA(DeviceID, _
              MCI_PLAY, MCI_WAIT, mciPlay)
            ErrorCode = mciSendCommandA(DeviceID, _
              MCI_CLOSE, MCI_WAIT, mciGeneric)
        #Else
            ErrorCode = mciSendCommand(DeviceID, _
              MCI_PLAY, MCI_WAIT, mciPlay)
            ErrorCode = mciSendCommand(DeviceID, _
              MCI_CLOSE, MCI_WAIT, mciGeneric)
        #End If
    End If
End Sub
```

Listing 4.13 WAVEPLAY.BAS. The WAVEPLAY program's data structure declarations.

```
Type MCI_OPEN_PARMS
    dwCallback As Long
    wDeviceID As Integer
    wReserved0 As Integer
    lpstrDeviceType As Long
    lpstrElementName As Long
    lpstrAlias As Long
End Type
```

(continues)

Listing 4.13 Continued

```
Type MCI_PLAY_PARMS
    dwCallback As Long
    dwFrom As Long
    dwTo As Long
End Type

Type MCI_GENERIC_PARMS
    dwCallback As Long
End Type

Type StringX
    Str As String * 256
End Type
```

As you can see, using the MCI's command-message interface can be a lot of work. In the previous section, you learned how to handle only the most basic open, play, and close commands. There are many other commands that you can use with the command-message interface, but because the command-string interface is so much easier to use, the rest of this chapter concentrates on how to handle multimedia devices using command strings.

Constructing the CDPLAYER Application

Although the MCI's command-message interface can be more flexible, the command-string interface is much easier to use yet still offers the programmer plenty of power—enough power, in fact, to write just about any type of multimedia application using the command-string interface. The best part is that you don't have to monkey with all those complicated data structures like MCI_OPEN_PARMS, MCI_PLAY_PARMS, and MCI_GENERIC_PARMS.

In Chapter 3, "The Media Control Interface (MCI)," you got a quick look at the commands that you can use with the command-string interface. At this point, you should have a pretty good idea of what you can do with these commands. In this section, then, you build the CDPLAYER program, which is a full-featured CD application that can play any music CD you place in your computer's CD-ROM drive.

The CDPLAYER application is fully 16-bit and 32-bit capable; just compile the application with the appropriate version of Visual Basic. Figure 4.4 shows the form as you should construct it with Visual Basic.

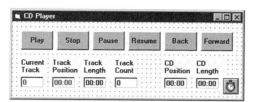

Fig. 4.4
The CDPLAYER
application's main
form.

A list of all the controls used for this application and their attributes are shown in Listing 4.14. In addition to the main form, you need several CommandButton and TextBox controls, as well as a Timer control.

Listing 4.14   LIST4_14.BAS. Controls used for the CDPLAYER application.

```
VERSION 2.00
Begin Form Form1
   BackColor       =   &H00E0FFFF&
   Caption         =   "CD Player"
   ClientHeight    =   1980
   ClientLeft      =   1875
   ClientTop       =   1815
   ClientWidth     =   6150
   Height          =   2385
   Left            =   1815
   LinkTopic       =   "Form1"
   ScaleHeight     =   1980
   ScaleWidth      =   6150
   Top             =   1470
   Width           =   6270
   Begin TextBox txtTrackCount
      Height       =   285
      Left         =   2760
      TabIndex     =   17
      Text         =   "0"
      Top          =   1440
      Width        =   615
   End
   Begin TextBox txtCDLength
      Height       =   285
      Left         =   4920
      TabIndex     =   15
      Text         =   "00:00"
      Top          =   1440
      Width        =   615
   End
   Begin TextBox txtCDPosition
      Height       =   285
      Left         =   4080
      TabIndex     =   5
```

(continues)

Listing 4.14   Continued

```
    Text            =     "00:00"
    Top             =     1440
    Width           =     615
End
Begin TextBox txtCurrentTrack
    ForeColor       =     &H000000FF&
    Height          =     285
    Left            =     240
    TabIndex        =     13
    Text            =     "0"
    Top             =     1440
    Width           =     615
End
Begin CommandButton btnForward
    Caption         =     "Forward"
    Height          =     495
    Left            =     5040
    TabIndex        =     11
    Top             =     240
    Width           =     855
End
Begin CommandButton btnBack
    Caption         =     "Back"
    Height          =     495
    Left            =     4080
    TabIndex        =     10
    Top             =     240
    Width           =     855
End
Begin TextBox txtTrackLength
    Height          =     285
    Left            =     1920
    TabIndex        =     4
    TabStop         =     0     'False
    Text            =     "00:00"
    Top             =     1440
    Width           =     615
End
Begin TextBox txtTrackPosition
    ForeColor       =     &H000000FF&
    Height          =     285
    Left            =     1080
    TabIndex        =     6
    TabStop         =     0     'False
    Text            =     "00:00"
    Top             =     1440
    Width           =     615
End
Begin Timer Timer1
    Interval        =     100
    Left            =     5640
    Top             =     1440
End
```

```
Begin CommandButton btnResume
    Caption         =    "Resume"
    Height          =    495
    Left            =    3120
    TabIndex        =    3
    Top             =    240
    Width           =    855
End
Begin CommandButton btnPause
    Caption         =    "Pause"
    Height          =    495
    Left            =    2160
    TabIndex        =    2
    Top             =    240
    Width           =    855
End
Begin CommandButton btnStop
    Caption         =    "Stop"
    Height          =    495
    Left            =    1200
    TabIndex        =    1
    Top             =    240
    Width           =    855
End
Begin CommandButton btnPlay
    Caption         =    "Play"
    Height          =    495
    Left            =    240
    TabIndex        =    0
    Top             =    240
    Width           =    855
End
Begin Label Label5
    BackColor       =    &H00E0FFFF&
    Caption         =    "Track Count"
    Height          =    375
    Left            =    2760
    TabIndex        =    16
    Top             =    960
    Width           =    495
End
Begin Label Label3
    BackColor       =    &H00E0FFFF&
    Caption         =    "CD Length"
    Height          =    495
    Left            =    4920
    TabIndex        =    14
    Top             =    960
    Width           =    735
End
Begin Label Label2
    BackColor       =    &H00E0FFFF&
    Caption         =    "CD Position"
    Height          =    375
```

(continues)

```
Listing 4.14   Continued
         Left          =   4080
         TabIndex      =   9
         Top           =   960
         Width         =   735
      End
      Begin Label Label1
         BackColor     =   &H00E0FFFF&
         Caption       =   "Current Track"
         Height        =   495
         Left          =   240
         TabIndex      =   12
         Top           =   960
         Width         =   615
      End
      Begin Label Label6
         BackColor     =   &H00E0FFFF&
         Caption       =   "Track Length"
         Height        =   495
         Left          =   1920
         TabIndex      =   8
         Top           =   960
         Width         =   735
      End
      Begin Label Label4
         BackColor     =   &H00E0FFFF&
         Caption       =   "Track Position"
         Height        =   375
         Left          =   1080
         TabIndex      =   7
         Top           =   960
         Width         =   735
      End
   End
End
```

Using the *mciSendString()* Function

To use the MCI's command-string interface, you must call the
mciSendString() function. In fact, the command-string interface is so easy to
use that the only function you need to declare in your Visual Basic program
is mciSendString(). That declaration looks like this:

```
Declare Function mciSendString Lib "MMSystem" _
   (ByVal lpstrCommand As String, ByVal lpstrRtnString As Any, _
   ByVal wRtnLength As Integer, _
   ByVal hCallback As Integer) As Long
```

For 32-bit programs, you should declare mciSendStringA(), like this:

```
Declare Function mciSendStringA Lib "WinMM" _
   (ByVal lpstrCommand As String, ByVal lpstrRtnString As Any, _
```

```
            ByVal wRtnLength As Integer, _
            ByVal hCallback As Integer) As Long
```

When you call the mciSendString() function, you must supply four arguments: the command string, the return string, the maximum length of the
return string, and the handle of a callback function. Because you can't use
callback functions with Visual Basic, the last argument will always be 0.

Initializing the Program

Like most programs, when the CDPLAYER application first starts up, it must
perform a few initialization tasks. Specifically, the program must disable all
the CommandButton controls except the Play button. The program must also
disable the Timer control so that timer messages don't start arriving before the
player has started playing the CD. These tasks are handled in the Form_Load()
procedure, which Visual Basic calls when the program starts. That procedure
is shown in Listing 4.15.

Listing 4.15   LIST4_15.BAS. CDPLAYER's *Form_Load()* procedure.

```
Sub Form_Load ()
    btnPlay.Enabled = True
    btnStop.Enabled = False
    btnPause.Enabled = False
    btnResume.Enabled = False
    btnBack.Enabled = False
    btnForward.Enabled = False
    Timer1.Enabled = False
End Sub
```

Playing the CD

The first thing the user will do when the CDPLAYER application appears on
the screen is click the Play button. This triggers the btnPlay_Click() command procedure, as shown in Listing 4.16.

Listing 4.16   LIST4_16.BAS. CDPLAYER's *btnPlay_Click()* procedure.

```
Sub btnPlay_Click ()
    Dim ErrorCode As Integer
    Dim ReturnStr As String * 256

    btnPlay.Enabled = False
    btnPause.Enabled = True
    btnStop.Enabled = True
    btnBack.Enabled = True
```

(continues)

Listing 4.16 Continued

```
      btnForward.Enabled = True

  #If Win32 Then
      ErrorCode = mciSendStringA("open cdaudio alias cd", _
        ReturnStr, 255, 0)
      ErrorCode = mciSendStringA("play cd", ReturnStr, 255, 0)
  #Else
      ErrorCode = mciSendString("open cdaudio alias cd", _
        ReturnStr, 255, 0)
      ErrorCode = mciSendString("play cd", ReturnStr, 255, 0)
  #End If

      Timer1.Enabled = True
  End Sub
```

This procedure first disables the Play button (the user doesn't need it while a CD is playing!) and then enables the Pause, Stop, Back, and Forward buttons, which are available now that the user has started playing a CD.

As with any MCI device, you must first open the device before you can use it. In the btnPlay_Click() procedure, this task is accomplished by the first call to mciSendString(), which sends the command string open cdaudio alias cd. This command not only opens the cdaudio device, but it also gives the device the name (or alias) cd. Throughout the program, functions can now refer to the newly opened cdaudio device as cd.

Once the cdaudio device is open, a second call to mciSendString() with the command string play cd starts playing the CD. When the mciSendString() function returns, the program enables the Timer control so that the application can start gathering timer messages. At this point, the user can go about his business, starting and using other applications, while the CD continues to play in the background.

Pausing the CD
While listening to a CD, the user may get a phone call or a visitor may enter his office. The user may want to pause the CD so that he can continue playing where he left off after he takes care of the business at hand. The user clicks the Pause button, which causes Visual Basic to call the btnPause_Click() command procedure, as shown in Listing 4.17.

Listing 4.17   LIST4_17.BAS. CDPLAYER's *btnPause_Click()* procedure.

```
Sub btnPause_Click ()
    Dim ErrorCode As Integer
    Dim ReturnStr As String * 256

    btnPause.Enabled = False
    btnResume.Enabled = True
    btnBack.Enabled = False
    btnForward.Enabled = False

    #If Win32 Then
        ErrorCode = mciSendStringA("pause cd", ReturnStr, 255, 0)
    #Else
        ErrorCode = mciSendString("pause cd", ReturnStr, 255, 0)
    #End If
End Sub
```

This procedure first disables the Pause, Back, and Forward buttons and then enables the Resume button, which leaves only the Resume and Stop buttons usable. The program then pauses the CD by calling mciSendString() with the command string pause cd.

Resuming the CD

When the user wants to continue listening to the CD, the user clicks the application's Resume button and Visual Basic calls the btnResume_Click() command procedure, as shown in Listing 4.18.

Listing 4.18   LIST4_18.BAS. CDPLAYER's *btnResume_Click()* procedure.

```
Sub btnResume_Click ()
    Dim ErrorCode As Integer
    Dim ReturnStr As String * 256

    btnResume.Enabled = False
    btnPause.Enabled = True
    btnBack.Enabled = True
    btnForward.Enabled = True

    #If Win32 Then
        ErrorCode = mciSendStringA("play cd", ReturnStr, 255, 0)
    #Else
        ErrorCode = mciSendString("play cd", ReturnStr, 255, 0)
    #End If
End Sub
```

This procedure first disables the Resume button (since the CD is no longer paused) and then enables the Pause, Back, and Forward buttons. Finally, another call to mciSendString(), this time with a command string of play cd, resumes playing the CD.

Skipping Tracks on the CD

Often the user may want to skip ahead or back to a favorite track, or just skip over a selection he doesn't like. For each, click on the Forward button, the CD advances one track. And (as if it weren't already obvious) the Back button does the same thing in reverse. These button clicks are handled by the btnForward_Click() and btnBack_Click() command procedures, which are shown in Listing 4.19.

Listing 4.19   LIST4_19.BAS. CDPLAYER's *btnForward_Click()* and *btnBack_Click()* procedures.

```
Private Sub btnForward_Click()
    Dim ErrorCode As Integer
    Dim ReturnStr As String * 512
    Dim TrackNumber As Integer
    Dim CommandStr As String

    #If Win32 Then
        ErrorCode = mciSendStringA("stop cd", ReturnStr, 255, 0)
        ErrorCode = mciSendStringA("status cd current track", _
            ReturnStr, 255, 0)
    #Else
        ErrorCode = mciSendString("stop cd", ReturnStr, 255, 0)
        ErrorCode = mciSendString("status cd current track", _
            ReturnStr, 255, 0)
    #End If

    TrackNumber = Val(ReturnStr) + 1
    CommandStr = "status cd position track " & Str$(TrackNumber)

    #If Win32 Then
        ErrorCode = mciSendStringA(CommandStr, ReturnStr, 255, 0)
    #Else
        ErrorCode = mciSendString(CommandStr, ReturnStr, 255, 0)
    #End If

    CommandStr = "seek cd to " & ReturnStr

    #If Win32 Then
        ErrorCode = mciSendStringA(CommandStr, ReturnStr, 255, 0)
        ErrorCode = mciSendStringA("play cd", ReturnStr, 255, 0)
    #Else
        ErrorCode = mciSendString(CommandStr, ReturnStr, 255, 0)
        ErrorCode = mciSendString("play cd", ReturnStr, 255, 0)
    #End If
End Sub
```

```
Private Sub btnBack_Click()
    Dim ErrorCode As Integer
    Dim ReturnStr As String * 512
    Dim TrackNumber As Integer
    Dim CommandStr As String

    #If Win32 Then
        ErrorCode = mciSendStringA("stop cd", ReturnStr, 255, 0)
        ErrorCode = mciSendStringA("status cd current track", _
            ReturnStr, 255, 0)
    #Else
        ErrorCode = mciSendString("stop cd", ReturnStr, 255, 0)
        ErrorCode = mciSendString("status cd current track", _
            ReturnStr, 255, 0)
    #End If

    TrackNumber = Val(ReturnStr) - 1
    CommandStr = "status cd position track " & Str$(TrackNumber)

    #If Win32 Then
        ErrorCode = mciSendStringA(CommandStr, ReturnStr, 255, 0)
    #Else
        ErrorCode = mciSendString(CommandStr, ReturnStr, 255, 0)
    #End If

    CommandStr = "seek cd to " & ReturnStr

    #If Win32 Then
        ErrorCode = mciSendStringA(CommandStr, ReturnStr, 255, 0)
        ErrorCode = mciSendStringA("play cd", ReturnStr, 255, 0)
    #Else
        ErrorCode = mciSendString(CommandStr, ReturnStr, 255, 0)
        ErrorCode = mciSendString("play cd", ReturnStr, 255, 0)
    #End If
End Sub
```

Both of these procedures work similarly, so you'll examine only the
btnForward_Click() procedure. In order to move forward one track, the program needs to gather some information about the current status of the CD.
To be sure that the program has complete control over the cdaudio device,
the first call to mciSendString() stops the CD with the stop cd command
string. A second call to mciSendString(), this time with a command string of
status cd current track, gets the current track number. This track number is
returned in ReturnStr.

Next, the program needs to know the position on the CD of the next track.
To get the number of the next track, the program increments the track number returned from the second call to mciSendString(), and then builds a command string by concatenating the command status cd position track with

the track number. If, for example, the current track is 4, the resulting command string would be `status cd position track 5`, which will get the starting position of track 5.

The third call to `mciSendString()` sends this newly constructed command string to the MCI, which then returns the next track's position in `ReturnStr`. Now, the program needs to construct a command string to move to the track's starting position. The program does this by concatenating the command string `seek cd to` with the position stored in `ReturnStr`. The next call to `mciSendString()` hands this command string off to the MCI, which positions the CD at the beginning of the track. The last call to `mciSendString()` starts the CD playing at the new position.

Stopping the CD

There may be times when the user wants to stop the CD before it has finished playing. He can do this by clicking the Stop button, which is handled by the `btnStop_Click()` command procedure. That procedure is shown in Listing 4.20.

Listing 4.20 LIST4_20.BAS. CDPLAYER's *btnStop_Click()* procedure.

```
Sub btnStop_Click ()
    Dim ErrorCode As Integer
    Dim ReturnStr As String * 256

    btnStop.Enabled = False
    btnPause.Enabled = False
    btnPlay.Enabled = True
    btnResume.Enabled = False
    btnBack.Enabled = False
    btnForward.Enabled = False

    #If Win32 Then
        ErrorCode = mciSendStringA("stop cd", ReturnStr, 255, 0)
        ErrorCode = mciSendStringA("close cd", ReturnStr, 255, 0)
    #Else
        ErrorCode = mciSendString("stop cd", ReturnStr, 255, 0)
        ErrorCode = mciSendString("close cd", ReturnStr, 255, 0)
    #End If

    Timer1.Enabled = False

    txtCurrentTrack.Text = "0"
    txtTrackPosition.Text = "00:00"
    txtTrackLength.Text = "00:00"
    txtTrackCount.Text = "0"
    txtCDPosition.Text = "00:00"
    txtCDLength.Text = "00:00"
End Sub
```

This function first disables all buttons except for Play. Next, the program stops the CD with the `stop cd` command string and closes the `cdaudio` device with the `close cd` command string. Because the application should no longer respond to timer messages, the program disables the `Timer` control. Finally, the program sets all the `TextBox` controls to their default values.

Displaying CD Status Information

Now you get to the most complicated part of the program. When the user starts playing a CD, the `Timer` control sends a timer message to the application every 100 milliseconds. These messages are handled by the `Timer1_Timer()` function, which is shown in Listing 4.21.

Listing 4.21   LIST4_21.BAS. CDPLAYER's *Timer1_Timer( )* procedure.

```
Private Sub Timer1_Timer()
    Dim ErrorCode As Integer
    Dim ReturnStr As String * 256
    Dim CommandStr As String
    Dim StartMinutes As Integer
    Dim StartSeconds As Integer
    Dim CurrentMinutes As Integer
    Dim CurrentSeconds As Integer
    Dim TrackMinutes As Integer
    Dim TrackSeconds As Integer
    Dim MinuteStr As String
    Dim SecondStr As String
    Dim CurrentTrackStr As String

    #If Win32 Then
        ErrorCode = mciSendStringA("status cd position", _
          ReturnStr, 255, 0)
    #Else
        ErrorCode = mciSendString("status cd position", _
          ReturnStr, 255, 0)
    #End If
    CurrentMinutes = Val(Left$(ReturnStr, 2))
    CurrentSeconds = Val(Mid$(ReturnStr, 4, 2))
    txtCDPosition.Text = Left$(ReturnStr, 5)

    #If Win32 Then
        ErrorCode = mciSendStringA("status cd current track", _
          ReturnStr, 255, 0)
    #Else
        ErrorCode = mciSendString("status cd current track", _
          ReturnStr, 255, 0)
    #End If
    txtCurrentTrack.Text = ReturnStr
    CurrentTrackStr = ReturnStr
```

(continues)

Listing 4.21 Continued

```
CommandStr = "status cd length track " & CurrentTrackStr
#If Win32 Then
    ErrorCode = mciSendStringA(CommandStr, ReturnStr, 255, 0)
#Else
    ErrorCode = mciSendString(CommandStr, ReturnStr, 255, 0)
#End If
txtTrackLength.Text = Left$(ReturnStr, 5)

CommandStr = "status cd position track " & CurrentTrackStr
#If Win32 Then
    ErrorCode = mciSendStringA(CommandStr, ReturnStr, 255, 0)
#Else
    ErrorCode = mciSendString(CommandStr, ReturnStr, 255, 0)
#End If
StartMinutes = Val(Left$(ReturnStr, 2))
StartSeconds = Val(Mid$(ReturnStr, 4, 2))

If StartSeconds > CurrentSeconds Then
    CurrentMinutes = CurrentMinutes - 1
    CurrentSeconds = CurrentSeconds + 60
End If

TrackMinutes = CurrentMinutes - StartMinutes
TrackSeconds = CurrentSeconds - StartSeconds

If TrackMinutes < 10 Then
    MinuteStr = "0" & TrackMinutes
Else
    MinuteStr = MinuteStr & TrackMinutes
End If

If TrackSeconds < 10 Then
    SecondStr = "0" & TrackSeconds
Else
    SecondStr = SecondStr & TrackSeconds
End If

txtTrackPosition.Text = MinuteStr & ":" & SecondStr

#If Win32 Then
    ErrorCode = mciSendStringA("status cd number of tracks", _
        ReturnStr, 255, 0)
#Else
    ErrorCode = mciSendString("status cd number of tracks", _
        ReturnStr, 255, 0)
#End If
txtTrackCount.Text = ReturnStr

#If Win32 Then
    ErrorCode = mciSendStringA("status cd length", _
        ReturnStr, 255, 0)
#Else
    ErrorCode = mciSendString("status cd length", _
        ReturnStr, 255, 0)
```

```
        #End If
        txtCDLength.Text = Left$(ReturnStr, 5)

        If txtCDPosition.Text = txtCDLength.Text Then
            btnStop_Click
        End If
End Sub
```

The `Timer1_Timer()` procedure is responsible for keeping the program's `TextBox` controls up-to-date, as well as for checking whether the CD has finished playing. The `TextBox` controls display the following information:

- *Current track.* The number of the currently playing track.

- *Track position.* The position at which the current track is playing. This position is measured from the beginning of the track to the currently playing CD position.

- *Track length.* The total length of the track. When track position is the same as track length, the track is finished playing.

- *Track count.* The total number of tracks on the currently playing CD.

- *CD position.* The position at which the CD is currently playing. This position is measured from the beginning of the CD (position 00:00:00) to the currently playing position.

- *CD length.* The total length of the CD. When CD position is the same as CD length, the entire CD has finished playing.

The `Timer1_Timer()` procedure first gets the current CD position by sending the command string `status cd position`. After this function call, `ReturnStr` will contain a time in the format `mm:ss:ms`, in which `mm` is minutes, `ss` is seconds, and `ms` is milliseconds. (This is the default position format for the `cdaudio` device.) The program uses the `Left$()` and `Val()` functions to extract the current minutes and seconds, which are stored in the integer variables `CurrentMinutes` and `CurrentSeconds` for later use. Because `ReturnStr` contains the current CD position, the `TextBox` control `txtCDPosition` is set to the first five characters in `ReturnStr`, which displays the current minutes and seconds in the form `mm:ss`.

Next, the program needs to know which track is currently playing. Sending the command string `status cd current track` to the MCI gets the track number into `ReturnStr`. The program sets the `TextBox` `txtCurrentTrack` to the contents of this string and then saves the string in the `CurrentTrackStr` variable for later use.

The program next gets the length of the current track. It does this by concatenating the command status cd length track with the track number stored in CurrentTrackStr and then passing the command string on to the MCI. The track length is returned to ReturnStr in the form mm:ss:ms. Because the program only needs to display the minutes and seconds, the txtTrackLength TextBox is set to the first five characters in ReturnStr.

Getting the current position within a track is a little tricky: the program must subtract the starting position of the track from the current CD position. First, the program constructs a command string by concatenating the command status cd position track with the track number stored in CurrentTrackStr. If, for example, the CD were currently playing track 6, this process would create the command string status cd position track 6. The program passes this command string on to the MCI, which returns the starting position of the current track in ReturnStr in the form mm:ss:ms. The program uses the Left$(), Mid$(), and Val() functions to extract the minutes and seconds into the integer variables StartMinutes and StartSeconds.

Because the program will be subtracting the starting seconds from the current CD seconds, it has to be sure that it doesn't end up with a negative number. For example, suppose the track's starting position is 12:45 and the CD's current position is 15:21. Although the position 15:21 is farther along the CD than position 12:45, you still have a situation in which subtracting the starting seconds from the CD position seconds will result in a negative number.

To avoid this problem, the program checks whether StartSeconds is greater than CurrentSeconds. If it is, the program subtracts 1 from CurrentMinutes and adds 60 to CurrentSeconds. Then, subtracting the starting time from the current time will produce a positive number.

After performing this check on the variables, the program does the subtraction. The results are stored in TrackMinutes and TrackSeconds, which represent the position within the currently playing track. The program uses these values to construct MinuteStr and SecondStr, which is just the current time in the string form mm and ss, respectively. The program uses these strings to set the contents of the txtTrackPosition TextBox.

Getting the total number of tracks on the CD is a simple matter of sending the status cd number of tracks command string to the MCI and setting the txtTrackCount TextBox to the contents of ReturnStr. Similarly, the command string status cd length fills ReturnStr with the CD's total length, which the program places in the txtCDLength TextBox.

The last task of `Timer1_Timer()` is to check whether the CD is finished playing. Normally, the MCI would send a message to a callback function, informing the program that the CD has reached the end. But Visual Basic programs can't have callback functions, so the CDPLAYER program must use a little trickery to close down the CD device when the CD is finished playing. Actually, this so-called trickery is not very tricky at all. The program merely checks whether the current CD position is equal to the CD length. If it is, then the CD is finished and `Timer1_Timer()` calls the `btnStop_Click()` command procedure to shut down the CD player.

Playing MIDI Files

MIDI (Musical Instrument Digital Interface) is a way of storing a musical-instrument performance in a file. Rather than holding the actual sounds that the MIDI instrument produces, however, a MIDI file holds digital commands that, when sent to the instrument's MIDI input port, cause the instrument to almost exactly duplicate the performance. A MIDI file, then, is like a piano roll for a player piano but constructed of digital data instead of paper.

Although a MIDI file is completely different from a waveform file or data stored on a CD, the MCI enables your program to play a MIDI file in almost exactly the same way you would play any other multimedia file. For example, all the usual commands—open, play, pause, and stop—are available for use on a MIDI device. Moreover, you use these commands just as you would with any other multimedia device; the only difference is that you're controlling the sequencer device rather than cdaudio, waveform, or other devices you've learned about.

The MIDIPLAY application (found on this book's CD-ROM) is a MIDI player program that can play back MIDI files. (MIDI files have the .MID extension.) When you run the program, you see the window shown in Figure 4.5.

Fig. 4.5
The MIDIPLAY application at startup, (*MIDIPLAY.FRM*).

Before you can play a MIDI file, you must select one using the File menu's Open command. When you select this command, you see the dialog box shown in Figure 4.6. Select any MIDI file you happen to have on your system. If you have no MIDI files, you can use the ITSSHOP.MID file (which is one of the MIDI files that comes with the Ensoniq Soundscape sound card) included on this book's CD-ROM.

Fig. 4.6
Selecting a MIDI file to play.

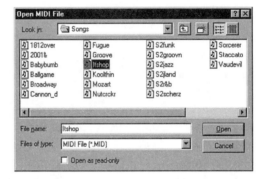

After selecting the file, play it by clicking the Play button. When you do, information about the MIDI file appears in the program's text boxes, as shown in Figure 4.7. The Track Position box shows the current position in the file. This value constantly changes as the file is played. The Track Length box shows the length of the MIDI file, which is also the last playable position in the file. The Tempo box contains the speed setting for the MIDI file. Finally, the File Name box contains the filename of the currently playing MIDI file.

Fig. 4.7
The MIDIPLAY application playing a MIDI file.

The program's Settings menu enables you to change the speed at which the file plays. Select the Increase Tempo command to increase the playback speed by 10, or select the Decrease Tempo command to reduce the playback speed by 10. The maximum speed allowed by the application is 500 and the minimum is 10.

You can also use the Ctrl+I and Ctrl+D key combinations to select the tempo commands without having to open the Settings menu.

Recording Multimedia Audio Files

It is, of course, possible to use the MCI to record your own waveform or MIDI files. However, unless you're planning to write a waveform editor or a MIDI sequencer application, there's really no need to get into the programming side of recording multimedia files. Such a discussion would take up much more space than this chapter has been allotted. The fact is that most sound cards come with all the programs you need to record waveform or MIDI files. Once you've recorded the files, you can then use them in your applications by employing the programming techniques described in this chapter.

If your sound card did not come with sound-recording utilities, or if you want more sophisticated tools than those that typically come with a sound card, there are many commercial products to choose from. Ask about them at your local software store. For MIDI products, you can also get software information from music stores that cater to professional musicians. Commercial MIDI programs range from very basic applications to full-fledged, multitrack "studios." Choose the program that best fits your needs.

From Here...

This chapter gave you a quick look at how to play multimedia audio files in your applications. If you would like to learn more about multimedia files and MCI commands, you can find more information on related topics in the following chapters:

- The MCI provides easier access to all kinds of multimedia devices, see Chapter 3, "The Media Control Interface (MCI)."

- Nothing adds more pizzazz to a multimedia application than digital video, see Chapter 8, "Digital Video Capture and Editing."

- Custom controls, whether "homegrown" or purchased, can take a lot of the frustration out of multimedia programming, see Chapter 12, "Creating and Using OLE Custom Controls."

Part II

The Graphics Interface

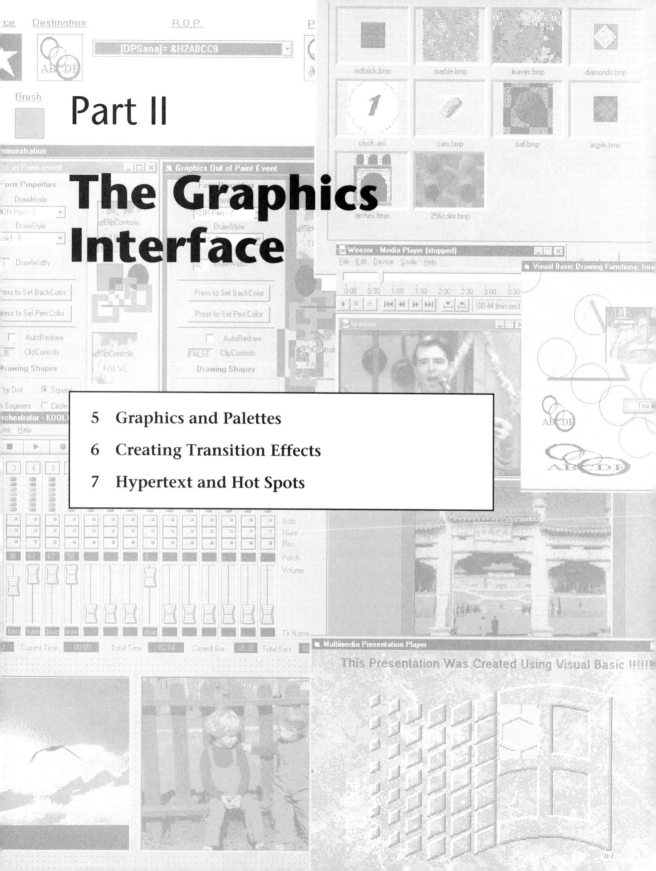

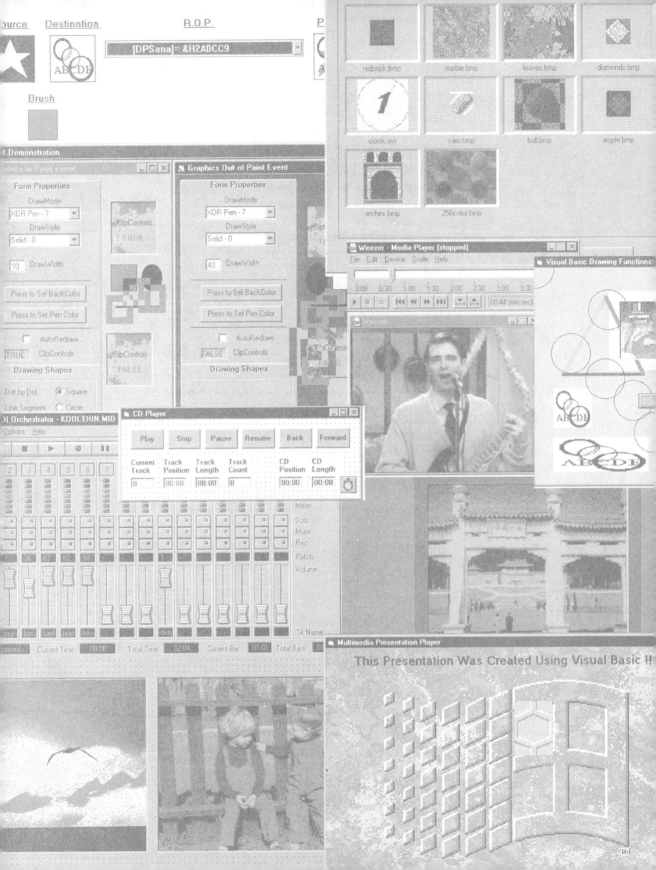

Chapter 5

Graphics and Palettes

Windows relies on graphics to communicate with the user, and Visual Basic shares and supports this characteristic. Besides the pictorial nature of the forms and controls, Visual Basic provides a fundamental set of graphics functions, statements and methods to directly create line, color and image on the screen. Other features of Visual Basic make it possible to manipulate the location and appearance of objects.

An essential purpose of Visual Basic is to make it easy to create Windows applications. The built-in functions and methods make it possible to write multimedia programs that will run in any environment supported by Visual Basic. However, these features may not meet all the demands of every multimedia project.

For this reason, Visual Basic supports calling directly on the Windows *API* (Applications Programmer's Interface), a set of several hundred functions in various categories. One of these categories, and a very large one, is known by the collective name of *GDI* (Graphics Device Interface). This GDI includes most of the drawing and display functions of Windows. It is one of two main sources of programming power for multimedia developers.

The other important source of programming power is the Media Control Interface, or MCI. There is a library of functions associated with the MCI that provides simple methods to add multimedia playback and recording capabilities to applications you program in Visual Basic. Visual Basic 4, as opposed to its predecessors, is much more able to use the MCI.

In this chapter and the next, you will learn to use both the native Visual Basic capabilities and the GDI functions to create and manipulate line, color, and image. This is a fascinating area and one where you will probably find yourself learning something new with every new application you develop.

In this chapter, you'll see examples that teach you how to:

- Use Visual Basic to create a simple "slide show" player

- Use Visual Basic functions and object properties to create graphic effects

- Deal directly with color palettes in both Visual Basic and the GDI

- Accommodate the limitations of Windows and Visual Basic when it comes to handling color

- Use the Windows API to create simple animation effects

Using Visual Basic's Built-in Capabilities

Many multimedia applications are developed for the general market. Whether written as a "shrink wrap" product to be sold at retail, or as a custom program for use within an organization, your code may have to run under up to three different operating systems—Windows 3.1, Windows NT, and Windows 95. Because you don't have any control over how your application will be used, you must write code that can run under any of these operating systems. This is not a trivial problem.

Visual Basic 4 is designed to help you cope with this diverse operating environment. While some tasks may necessitate calls to the API or use of custom controls, a surprising amount of multimedia can be done well with plain vanilla Visual Basic. To minimize problems for your users and to speed development, it would be smart to do as much as possible without resorting to methods that will lock your application to a given operating system. Sticking with native Visual Basic also makes it easier to distribute and maintain your applications.

Visual Basic offers a number of essential tools for multimedia programmers: *graphical properties*, *functions* and *methods*. The more familiar you are with these, the more you will be able to do within Visual Basic. This chapter is designed to facilitate your learning about the six most critical fundamental elements of Visual Basic for multimedia programming:

- `AutoRedraw` and `ClipControls` properties of forms and picture controls

- The "layering" approach used by Windows to determine what the user sees on-screen

- `DrawMode` property of forms and shape controls, and related properties, such as `BackColor` and `ForeColor`, which interact with `DrawMode`

- Picture and image display technology

- Factors affecting speed and memory use

- The `Paint` event

AutoRedraw **and** *ClipControls*

These two properties control more aspects of your multimedia than you would suspect from their names. When forms don't paint right, images flicker, or controls disappear, check your settings for these properties.

The key to understanding both of these properties and their operation is to realize that everything you see on your display screen under Windows is a *bitmap*. To the user, a bitmap is a pattern of colored dots. To the computer, a bitmap is also an array of data in memory. Much of the GDI, in fact, is concerned with manipulation of these bitmaps.

Windows relies on certain illusions to create a direct, clear, consistent user interface. So the user may see what appears to be a pushbutton on a gray panel underneath an inset picture. If a dialog box pops up while the user is looking at this display, the box will appear to be resting on top of the pushbutton, panel and inset picture. But this sequence of objects and appearances is really only a sequence of changes to a bitmap.

When the dialog box appeared on top of the panel, the array of data in memory (the actual bitmap) was changed. The data bits that represented whatever the box appeared to cover were replaced by the data bits for the box itself. This leaves you with a problem. What happens when the dialog box is closed? If you haven't saved the "covered up" data bits somewhere, your nice pushbutton-panel-picture bitmap will have a neat, square hole in it where the dialog box was.

One purpose of `AutoRedraw` is to allow bitmaps to be moved around the screen without appearing to tear "holes" in each other. When `AutoRedraw` for a form or control is set to `True`, an image of the form or control is kept in memory. If the object needs to be repainted, the appropriate part is copied to the screen from the virtual copy.

It's important to remember that the default setting for `AutoRedraw` is `False`. This is done to save memory resources. If you set `AutoRedraw` for a form or picture box to `False`, any graphics you create with graphics methods (`Point`,

Pset, Line, Circle or PaintPicture) will be lost if another window covers them for a time. Graphics that extend beyond the edge of the form or picture box will also be lost if the form is enlarged by the user.

You can change the AutoRedraw setting as desired during run time. In multi-media work, you may often want AutoRedraw to be set to True. This forces normal layering (discussed in the next section), so that graphical controls and labels, nongraphical controls and graphics methods can all work together without interfering with each other.

Achieving this level of cooperation does not come without a price, however. When AutoRedraw is True, the memory demands can cause reduced performance. Consider conserving memory and enhancing performance through the following methods:

- Keeping forms small.

- Creating a picture box for all drawing effects, and setting AutoRedraw to False for the form but True for the picture box (only the contents of the picture box will be saved in memory).

- Leaving AutoRedraw set to False for the form and picture boxes, and having your program redraw graphics as needed.

ClipControls works something like the masking tape you use when you paint your house. When ClipControls is True (the default setting), only the background gets changed or updated during a Paint event. However, protecting what you have drawn by setting ClipControls to True also means it takes longer for forms to repaint. ClipControls sometimes creates an undesirable "flicker" effect during repainting. You may, therefore, want to turn off ClipControls.

When you paint your house, you can dispense with the masking tape and try to cut in straight lines by hand with your brush. Of course, you know that you may get some paint in areas you hadn't intended. If you turn off ClipControls to speed things up and to eliminate the flicker, you may get some similar undesired effects.

To completely understand how AutoRedraw and ClipControls work, and how to manage them, it is necessary to understand how Windows layers graphical controls and graphical methods. The main thing to remember, though, is that you want to do any graphical work on your forms in the Paint event. Failure to maintain normal layering can lead to unpredictable results.

DrawMode and Related Properties

DrawMode, BackColor, and ForeColor are three properties shared in common by forms and picture boxes. Shape controls also use DrawMode and BackColor. You use DrawMode together with BackColor and ForeColor to produce visual effects in various ways.

BackColor determines the color of the visual surface on which your program draws images. This color can be selected at design time and changed while your program is running. ForeColor identifies the color of the "ink" used for drawing on the visual surface. Like BackColor, it is selected by the designer, but unlike BackColor, the color you see when actually drawing is not necessarily the one selected. This depends on the value of the third property, DrawMode.

DrawMode is the chameleon of Visual Basic. It determines the actual color of the lines drawn by the graphics methods or by Shape or Line controls. Depending on the choices made by the programmer, DrawMode can lay those lines down using pure black or white, or it can combine the color of the pixels beneath the line with the current ForeColor in any of 14 ways to determine the final line color.

DrawMode is useful to the multimedia programmer for animation effects and in a number of other ways. You'll see it used in this chapter to draw and erase frames around images, for example.

Picture and Image Controls

You have two choices for controls to display images in Visual Basic. Image controls are "light" controls. That is, they don't make much demand on system resources, and they don't offer much in the way of properties. However, they repaint faster than the alternative.

The alternative is the PictureBox control. This is a much more versatile control, but it may be overkill for simple requirements. When in doubt, try to make do with an Image control. If that doesn't work, then use the PictureBox. For simple applications, of course, the difference is trivial, but complex multimedia programming requires careful choices.

In either case, you can display graphics from any of three kinds of bitmap (BMP, RLE4 and RLE8), and from icons and metafiles. You can also use most of the graphics methods (Circle, Cls, Line, Point, Print, and Pset) in either a PictureBox or an Image control. In addition, you can use PaintPicture (a new and powerful method added in Visual Basic 4) in a PictureBox or on a form.

A *bitmap* is an image represented by pixels and stored as a set of bits in which one or more bits map to a single pixel. The .BMP is the familiar Windows bitmap file format. RLE4 and RLE8 are compressed bitmap formats that save storage space and are worth considering for many projects. An *icon* is a picture that consists of a bitmapped image (typically 32×32 pixels) and a mask to create transparent parts of the picture. *Metafiles* are stored drawing instructions that are played back into your control to re-create the original drawing.

Speed and Memory Use

Two of the factors affecting speed and memory use in Visual Basic multimedia applications have been mentioned already: `AutoRedraw` and `ClipControls`. The way your program handles images is another major factor.

In general, Image controls are faster and less demanding of memory than are PictureBoxes. In both Image controls and PictureBoxes, you have the choice of loading an image at design time, or loading at run time. A single image will display most quickly if it is embedded in the form (loaded at design time).

However, most multimedia is going to involve multiple image displays. You could place a large number of Image controls on your form, change their `Visible` properties to `False` and then turn them on and off one at a time to display them. While this would make your program run quickly, it would also use up available memory. Bitmaps tend to be large, and just because you can't see them doesn't mean they aren't there.

In most cases, you will be loading images one at a time, as needed, using the `LoadPicture` command. Here, you must make another trade-off. Images stored in the .BMP format take up the most space on the hard drive, but they load faster than any other format. RLE-format bitmaps, because they must be decompressed take slightly longer to load and display, but take up less hard disk space. Metafiles (whether stored as .WMF or .EMF) take up very little disk space, but they are not photorealistic and they take much longer to display because they must be reconstructed via mathematical means.

As you can see, there are a number of trade-offs to make in designing your multimedia image displays. The time spent optimizing the display is well worth it.

Studies show that nothing affects user acceptance as much as display speed. If it takes over a half-second for a visual response to a user action, the program will be perceived as slow.

The *Paint* Event

As far as the user is concerned, nothing happens in Visual Basic multimedia until the form gets painted. The `Paint` event is where your choices for Image controls, drawing methods, and control properties all come together to determine what the user sees on the display.

The safest way to proceed in the design of any multimedia application is to be sure that all use of graphics methods (`Circle`, `Cls`, `Line`, `Point`, `Print`, `PaintPicture` and `Pset`) takes place within the `Paint` event for the form or container. Failure to do this can result in a number of undesirable effects. For example, graphical controls (`Image`, `Label`, `Line` and `Shape`) and certain of the 3-D controls (3-D panels especially) can be overpainted, disappear, or be laid down in the wrong order.

Creating a Slide Show Engine

The most basic kind of multimedia application is probably a simple slide show. As it happens, this application is also a good way to demonstrate many of the points made in the preceding sections.

In any multimedia project, it is best to start by thinking about the finished product. What do the users require? What facilities must be built into the application?

In the case of slide shows, these are fairly simple questions to answer. You want to be able to display any number of images in a predetermined sequence. It is important for the display to meet common aesthetic standards for presentation (layout, color, and so on). For the person who will be putting together the slide show, the engine should be easy to use and customize for a variety of situations.

For this project, assume that the slide show engine must show one image at a time. The user can resize the form during the show. Each image is to appear as if matted and mounted in a picture frame. This means providing a background of a neutral color and a wide border around the picture. All images are not necessarily the same size, but each is to appear optically centered on the form. Images are to change when the user clicks on a button. You would like to have the first image display as soon as the program begins to run, and to have a notice to the user appear after the final image has been shown. The final image is not to be visible behind this notice.

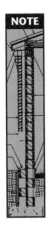

NOTE The files for this Slide Show project are on the CD-ROM as a 16-bit application (EZPICS16.VBP, EZPICS16.FRM) and as a 32-bit application (EZPICS32.VBP, EZPICS32.FRM). The actual code in both versions of the files is identical. Several .BMP images are also used. You may load either the 16-bit or the 32-bit version. In the discussion that follows, EZPICS refers to both versions. The executable versions on the CD-ROM are EZPICS16.EXE and EZPICS32.EXE.

If you prefer to build the program as you read the description, refer to Figure 5.1 to see how to set the form up. An MCI control is shown on the form and is used by the code on the CD-ROM, but will not be discussed here. You should refer to Chapter 3, "The Media Control Interface (MCI)" for details. Most of the code is in the form declarations, and in the Form_Load, Form_Paint, Form_Resize, and Form_Unload events.

Fig. 5.1
For EZPICS, place
the controls
approximately as
shown here.

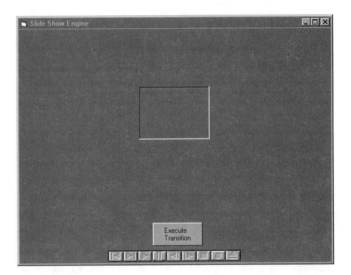

Coding the *Form_Load* and *Form_Paint* Events

All of the components on the form visible when the program starts running are positioned by code in the Form_Load event. Basic arithmetic is also used to visually center the form on-screen. Refer to the actual code in EZPICS.FRM to see how this is done. This is not anything peculiar to multimedia work, so it will not be discussed.

The heart of the image player is in the Form_Paint event, the first part of which is shown in Listing 5.1. For this project, the images are hard coded by name. A variable, intCounter, is used to keep track of where you are in the list.

> **Caution**
>
> The bitmap path names shown in Listing 5.1 will not be correct for your system. Please edit them as needed to point to the path you used when you installed the examples. As a matter of fact, it is usually a bad idea to hard-code anything. Use resource files for images and text.

Listing 5.1   EZPICS.FRM. The form declarations and the hard-coded image files in the *Form_Paint* event.

```
Public strNextPicture As String
Public intCounter As Integer
Select Case intCounter
      Case 1
          strNextPicture = "C:\VB\CHINA2.BMP"
      Case 2
          strNextPicture = "C:\VB\CHINA1.BMP"
      Case 3
          strNextPicture = "C:\VB\BITMAPS\ASSORTED\BIRD1A.BMP"
      Case 4
          strNextPicture = "C:\VB\BITMAPS\ASSORTED\KIDS1A.BMP"
      Case 5
          strNextPicture = "C:\VB\BITMAPS\ASSORTED\DOG1A.BMP"
      Case 6
          Msg = "No more pictures!"
          MsgBox Msg, 16
          End
   End Select
```

As a general matter, there are several other ways to handle the task of storing and retrieving the images.

- You could list the images in order in a separate text file (one image filename per line), have the player program read each line and store the filename in strNextPicture, and display on command.

- You could place all the image files in the same subdirectory as the player with the files named sequentially (IMAGE01.BMP, IMAGE02.BMP, etc.), and the program would use intCounter to increment the digits in the names, read each in turn into strNextPicture, and go on about the business of display.

- You could place all the images into one large bitmap and use the Picture Clip control to pull out the image you want.

Using *DrawMode* and *Visible* Properties

In the Form_Load event, the central area of the form was already covered (including the Image control) with a Shape control named shpCoverIt. In the Form_Paint event, the Shape control's DrawMode is changed to 13 (Copy Pen). The Shape is set by default to the BackColor for the form. The Copy Pen setting simply covers whatever is beneath the Shape.

```
shpCoverIt.DrawMode = 13
```

EZPICS is your introduction to the power of DrawMode. You will find many uses for it in your multimedia work. The DrawMode property is available to Form objects, Shape controls, Line controls, and PictureBox controls.

DrawMode actually causes Visual Basic to perform what is known as a *binary raster operation* to determine the way the color of a line, shape, or image drawn at run time combines with colors already on the screen. The color you see applied to any given pixel is the result of a bitwise operation involving two color values (which is why it's called binary), that of a pixel in the draw pattern and that of the corresponding pixel on the display.

NOTE Visual Basic and the GDI make use of two kinds of raster operation to control the way lines, shapes, and other graphic elements are drawn. Binary raster operations (abbreviated ROP2) determine the appearance of output from graphics methods or the appearance of a Shape or Line control. Ternary raster operations (abbreviated ROP) are bitwise operations that are used in manipulating or moving bitmaps. Ternary raster operations will be discussed in Chapter 6, "Creating Transition Effects."

There are sixteen values for DrawMode, corresponding to sixteen different binary raster operations. You can see these listed in the Help selection for the DrawMode property.

The way the bitwise operation works is easiest to understand in the case of a monochrome pattern being laid down over a monochrome background. For these monochrome situations, a black pixel is represented by a single bit set to 0, and a white pixel is represented by a single bit set to 1. Table 5.1 illustrates how some of the DrawMode settings work in black and white.

Table 5.1   The Effect of *DrawMode* Settings in Monochrome

DrawMode	ForeColor	BackColor	Result
1—Blackness (all pixels become 0)	0 1	1 0	0 0
16—Whiteness (all pixels become 1)	0 1	1 0	1 1
13—Copy Pen (all pixels set to value of ForeColor property)	0 1	1 0	1 0
7—Xor Pen (combines colors in ForeColor and BackColor, but not both)	0 1 1 0	1 1 0 0	1 0 1 0
11—Nop (drawing turned off)	0 1	1 1	1 1
15—Merge Pen (combines ForeColor and BackColor)	0 1	1 0	0 1
2—Not Merge Pen (inverse of Merge Pen)	0 1	1 0	1 0

To give you some idea of how complex this can get, Table 5.2 shows what happens when you draw on a blue background with ForeColor set to white, using various DrawMode settings.

Table 5.2   The Results of Drawing a White Line on a Blue Background with Different *DrawModes*

DrawMode	Result
1—Blackness	Black line
16—Whiteness	White line
9—Mask Pen	Blue line same color as background
5—Mask Pen Not	Red/green line
3—Mask Not Pen	Black line
7—Xor	Red/green line

II

The Graphics Interface

You'll have more chances to see how this works and to experiment with it in the next two projects (FRMDRAW.VBP in the section titled "Layering in Visual Basic," and PAINT.VBP in "Experimenting with DrawMode and Other Drawing Tricks"). For now, notice when you run EZPICS that in drawing the frame, a color was specified (&HC0& or dark red) for the line in the code. When you see the line on-screen after the program is run, it will not appear as the same shade of red that was specified. In fact, it may not appear to be red at all. This is because the Xor function combines the BackColor from the form with the ForeColor of the line. This same Xor function will be used to erase the frame as well.

Another way to see what happens when different DrawMode settings combine ForeColor and BackColor, where a color image is involved, is to change the setting for shpCoverIt to any number between 1 and 16. If you use 1 or 16, of course, you will always get solid black or solid white, respectively.

Once the picture is covered, you need to load the image designated by strNextPicture into the Image control imgCurrentPicture. Listing 5.2 illustrates this process and a bit more as well. You will find that if the Image control is visible, you can see the picture "flickering" as AutoRedraw does its work. To prevent this, set the Visible property of the Image control to False. When the image is loaded, the control is re-centered on the form, DrawMode for the form is changed to Xor, and the Line method is used to frame the image. After that, the image can be made visible again. The DrawMode of the covering Shape control is set to 11, or Nop (*No Operation*), meaning that whatever is underneath the Shape is simply copied onto the top of the Shape.

Listing 5.2 EZPICS.FRM. This code from the *Form_Paint* event eliminates flicker and manages the framing of the images.

```
imgCurrentPicture.Visible = False

imgCurrentPicture.Picture = LoadPicture(strNextPicture)

' Position loaded image control to visual center of form
imgCurrentPicture.Left = (frmEZPICS.Width -_
   imgCurrentPicture.Width) / 2
imgCurrentPicture.Top = (frmEZPICS.Height -_
   imgCurrentPicture.Height) / 3

' Place frame around image control by XORing a pen
' color with the form color
```

```
frmEZPICS.DrawMode = 7 ' Change DrawMode to XOR
Line ((imgCurrentPicture.Left - 250), _
  (imgCurrentPicture.Top - 250))-_
  Step((imgCurrentPicture.Width + 500), _
  (imgCurrentPicture.Height + 500)), &HC0&, _
  BF
frmEZPICS.DrawMode = 13 ' Change DrawMode_
  back to CopyPen so any new drawing will be_
  "normal" looking

' Make the Current Picture visible
imgCurrentPicture.Visible = True
shpCoverIt.DrawMode = 11
```

The DrawMode was changed to Xor because of an interesting property of this setting. If you draw a line or a figure on a form in Xor DrawMode, and then draw over that line again in Xor DrawMode, that line disappears. In effect, it is erased without a trace and without affecting anything else on-screen. As you will see in the next section, each frame will be erased before the next image is put up and framed. If you didn't do that, the old frames would just stay on-screen and create visual litter.

> Make the form ForeColor and BackColor the same dark gray. Delete &HC0& from the Line function. You still get a wide picture border—in black (any color Xord with itself yields black).

When you are done drawing the line, the DrawMode property is returned to the default of 13. This code may be reused in another program in which other drawings on the same form may take place. By keeping DrawMode at CopyPen, you help the programmer who recycles your code to get his or her drawing to appear the way he or she intended it to look.

Changing Pictures with the Command Button *Click* Event

Once the first image is loaded, framed and revealed, the program waits for the user to click on the command button, cmdExecuteXition. Here are the four lines of the cmdExecuteXition_Click event:

```
Private Sub cmdExecuteXition_Click()
    intCounter = intCounter + 1
    shpCoverIt.DrawMode = 13
    Form_Paint
End Sub
```

When this event fires, the intCounter variable is increased by one, the DrawMode for the covering Shape is changed back to 13, and you are returned to the Form_Paint event to display the next image.

In the Form_Paint event, the first thing you must do is to Xor the old frame. This "erases" the frame before moving the Image control to its new position and reframing it. Listing 5.3 shows you this process.

Listing 5.3 EZPICS.FRM. The *Form_Paint* event, showing the use of *Xor* to remove the frame as part of changing images.

```
' Cover the image and frame to hide the changes
    shpCoverIt.DrawMode = 13

    ' Eliminate the frame that was around the previous image,
    ' by XORing the pen color originally used with the background
    ' color
    frmEZPICS.DrawMode = 7 ' Change DrawMode to XOR
    Line ((imgCurrentPicture.Left - 250), (imgCurrentPicture_
      .Top - 250))-Step((imgCurrentPicture.Width + 500),_
      (imgCurrentPicture.Height + 500)), &HC0&, BF
    frmEZPICS.DrawMode = 13 ' Change DrawMode back to CopyPen
```

Setting Up the *Form_Resize* Event

The only actual problem left to contend with is the matter of resizing the form. In the condition the program is in now, if the user clicks on the Maximize button or drags the form to a larger dimension in one direction or the other, the image and the command button will be left uncentered. Nothing fatal, just unsightly.

You can fix this by placing some code in the Form_Resize event to relocate the command button and the Shape control (see Listing 5.4). Any actual drawing (relocating the image and the frame) must be left in the Paint event to ensure that normal layering is maintained. A flag is also set in the Form_Resize event to let the Paint event know which image to display.

Listing 5.4 EZPICS.FRM. Placing code in the *Form_Resize* event to relocate the image and command button.

```
    Public intResizeFlag As Integer
    Private Sub Form_Resize()
        intResizeFlag = 1

        ' Relocate command button well out of the way at bottom_
        ' center of form
        cmdExecuteXition.Left = (frmEZPICS.Width -_
          cmdExecuteXition.Width) / 2
        cmdExecuteXition.Top = (frmEZPICS.Height -_
          (cmdExecuteXition.Height + 550))
```

```
        ' Recover center area of form with shpCoverIt
        shpCoverIt.Left = frmEZPICS.Left + 100
        shpCoverIt.Top = frmEZPICS.Top + 100
        shpCoverIt.Width = frmEZPICS.Width - (2 * shpCoverIt.Left)
        shpCoverIt.Height = frmEZPICS.Height - (4 * shpCoverIt.Top)

        Form_Paint
    End Sub
```

At this point, you can run the slide show. You'll see the form shown in Figure 5.2 placed neatly and attractively on the screen. As you step through the images, each one will be positioned at the visual center of the form, even though all the images are of different sizes. Try resizing the form and using the Maximize and Restore buttons. The image and the command button relocate themselves. Finally, when the last slide has been shown, you will see the small dialog box announcing that the slide show is over.

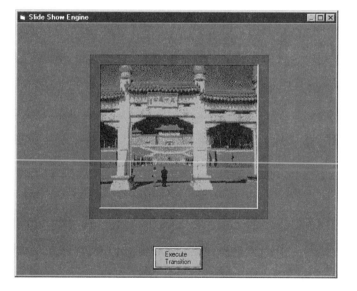

Fig. 5.2
When EZPICS first runs, this is what you will see.

The Graphics Interface

Layering in Visual Basic

Imagine looking through a triple-glazed window, one with three layers of glass. Suppose that on each layer of this window, someone has painted part of a picture. On the layer most distant from you, the artist painted a background scene. On the middle layer, she drew some items so that they appeared to be closer to you than the background. And on the layer closest to you, she placed the figure of a cartoon character.

As long as you are looking through the window, you probably aren't aware that there are three layers contributing to the final picture you see. Yet they are there, each one covering part of the one behind it. This is a metaphor for the way that layering works in Windows and Visual Basic.

In Visual Basic, the layer on the bottom of the stack, most distant from you, is where the graphics methods (`Line`, `Circle`, `Cls`, `Point`, `Print`, `Pset`) paint. If normal layering is maintained, nothing you do on this layer will affect the other two layers. Within the layer, the most recently painted line or shape will go on top of anything that was already there.

Whatever you create using the graphical controls (`Line`, `Shape`, `Image` and `Label`) at design time goes in the middle layer of this window. Finally, nongraphical controls (most of the rest of the controls) appear in the layer closest to you and are on top of everything else.

There are four methods for achieving and maintaining normal layering:

- Set `AutoRedraw` and `ClipControls` both to `True`.

- Set `AutoRedraw` to `True` and `ClipControls` to `False` (may result in faster painting if you have many controls that do not overlap).

- Set `AutoRedraw` to `False` and `ClipControls` to `True` (that is, leave both properties in their default conditions) and only use graphics methods in the `Paint` event.

- Set `AutoRedraw` and `ClipControls` both to `False` and only use graphics methods in the `Paint` event.

In putting the slide show project together, some important details were glossed over in the way the drawing functions, the graphic methods, and the various properties work together to produce the final effect. Because there are a huge number of combinations of these elements, it is easier to show how things work than to explain them. This section provides a laboratory in which you can experiment with basic layering in Windows. The files for the Layering Laboratory application are on the CD-ROM as FRMDRAW16.VBP and FRMDRAW16.FRM for the 16-bit version, and as FRMDRW32.VBP and FRMDRW32.FRM as 32-bit. Both versions of each file are identical. The executable files are on the CD-ROM as FRMDRW16.EXE and FRMDRW32.EXE, respectively. In the discussion that follows, FRMDRW refers to both versions.

Figure 5.3 shows the layout for the laboratory. Some Shape and Line controls have been placed on the form in arbitrary locations. A PictureBox and two Image controls were added, all with images loaded. The Image controls contain the same image, but the `Stretch` property of one is set to `True` and the other to `False` to show the effect of stretching the bitmap. Most of the code is contained in the `Form_MouseDown` and `Form_Paint` events. The `Form_Load` event simply sizes and positions the form on the screen.

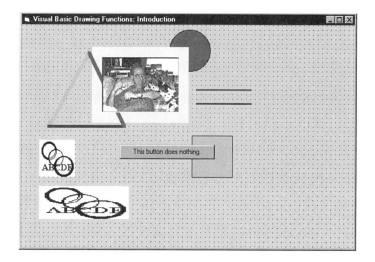

Fig. 5.3
Here's the start of the drawing demo: top and middle layers in place.

Drawing on a Form Containing Graphical and Nongraphical Controls

Load and run FRMDRW.VBP. This program is set up with `AutoRedraw` set to `False` and `ClipControls` set to `True`, one of the four recommended combinations for creating normal layering mentioned in the beginning of the "Layering in Visual Basic" section. These settings also happen to be the defaults for `AutoRedraw` and `ClipControls`.

The way in which the different controls overlay each other was determined at design time. That is, as controls were added, the last controls went "on top" of the ones that were already there. The exceptions to this pecking order are the nongraphical controls: the `PictureBox` and the command button. The nongraphical controls are in the top layer of the window. The other controls are in the middle layer. The bottom layer is occupied by the colored background of the form itself.

At this point, this is interesting but not very useful. We need to make something happen to see how drawing takes place in this layered world.

One way to make something happen is to arrange the form so that when the mouse button is clicked, the program draws a circle around the cursor location. Listing 5.5 shows how to capture the mouse position in the `Form_MouseDown` event and pass it to the `Form_Paint` event. In the `Form_Paint` event, you execute the `Circle` (graphics) method.

II

The Graphics Interface

Listing 5.5   FRMDRW.FRM. The *Form_MouseDown* and *Form_Paint* events cause a circle to be drawn where the mouse is clicked.

```
Private Sub Form_MouseDown()
Dim intX As Single
Dim intY As Single
Dim intPaintNow As Integer
Private Sub Form_MouseDown(Button As Integer, Shift As _
  Integer, X As Single, Y As Single)
    intX = X
    intY = Y
    Form_Paint
End Sub
Private Sub Form_Paint()
    Static intHoldIt As Integer
    intHoldIt = intHoldIt + 1
    intPaintNow = True
    If intPaintNow + intHoldIt Then
        Circle (intX, intY), 500
     End If
    intPaintNow = False
End Sub
```

When you have added these lines, run the program. After you have spent some time clicking away and making circles, your screen may look something like Figure 5.4.

Fig. 5.4
Here's what the demo looks like after a few mouse clicks.

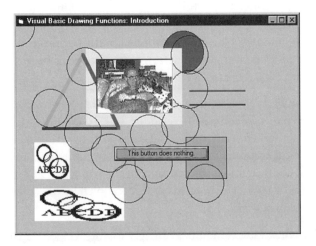

It's clear that the Circle method will not draw on top of the command button or the PictureBox. These are both nongraphical controls, and are in the top layer. When normal layering is in force, nongraphical controls cannot be overdrawn by graphical methods like Circle.

Manipulating the Way Visual Basic Paints the Screen

You will recall from the earlier discussion on layering that Image, Line, Label and Shape controls paint in the middle layer and the graphics methods, including `Circle`, are supposed to paint in the bottom layer. But in this demo, the `Circle` method also draws on top of the Image, Line and Shape controls! This is the result of the way the `Paint` event and `ClipControls` operate.

First, setting `ClipControls` to `True` will keep lines from being drawn on top of nongraphical controls such as the `PictureBox` and the command button. However, it has no such "masking" effect on Line, Shape, Label, and Image controls. Therefore the circles float on top of these controls, waiting for the form to be repainted.

The form is only repainted in response to certain triggers. One of these is provided by `AutoRedraw`; this property is set to `False` for this demo. Another trigger takes place when the form is enlarged. The third trigger is provided if a window that was covering the form is removed. Finally, if a `Refresh` method is called in the `Form_Resize` event, the form will be repainted.

You can test this easily by grabbing the right side of the form and dragging it to make the form larger. All those circles suddenly sink to their correct layer. The same thing happens if you click on the Maximize button. But notice that if you create some circles while the form is maximized and then click on the Restore button, the new circles stay on top of the graphical controls.

Add the following three lines to the `Paint` event. These lines only run the first time the `Paint` event is called, immediately after the form is loaded.

```
If intHoldIt < 1 Then
        Line (2000, 300)-(5000, 3500), RGB(125, 255, 125), BF
    End If
```

The rectangle created by the `Line` command is painted along with the rest of the form, in the appropriate layer, when the program runs. But if you minimize the form and then restore it, the rectangle disappears. It is not redrawn by the `Paint` event because of the conditions set up in the `If` statement.

Run the program again with these three lines included. Pop up the Debug window or the Project window to the front of the form. Then click on any visible part of the demonstration to bring it back to the front. The parts of the box that were covered by the other window are not refreshed because `AutoRedraw` is turned off.

Next, leaving the three new lines in the `Paint` event, change `AutoRedraw` to `True` and run the program. You now have "persistent" graphics enabled. You can no longer keep the circles on top of anything except the new rectangle. The rectangle stays visible when you pop up another window or minimize and then maximize the form. This is because the rectangle is part of the image that AutoRedraw is keeping in memory.

You may now see a brief "flicker" each time you make a new circle, as AutoRedraw brings its stored image in from memory. Notice that you can see all of the circles, very briefly, on top of the graphical controls. Then normal layering is enforced by the Paint event and the circles sink to their proper layer.

What would happen if you used a graphics method outside the Paint event? Take out the three lines just entered, change AutoRedraw back to False, and place the single line below in the Form_MouseDown event.

```
Line (2000, 300)-(5000, 3500), RGB(125, 255, 125), BF
```

Now the rectangle covers up all the graphical controls. Not only that, but if you click so as to create circles on top of the rectangle, only the most recent circle will stay on top. This is because the rectangle is being redrawn each time you click the mouse and the Paint event is unable to affect the layer in which the rectangle appears. However, because AutoRedraw is off, you can cause part of the rectangle to disappear by popping up a window on top of it. (Bringing the Debug window to the front should do the trick.)

Change AutoRedraw to True and run the program again. Now when the mouse button is clicked, the rectangle is redrawn as before, but AutoRedraw brings the previous image back in from memory and appears to force normal layering. You can tell that the layering isn't normal, however, because circles drawn on top of the rectangle disappear with the very next mouse click anywhere on the form.

Cut the line you just typed into the Form_MouseDown event and paste it into the Form_Load event. Now when you run the program with AutoRedraw set to True, everything appears to run normally. But you are still doing your drawing outside of the Paint event, and things are not always as they seem.

Change AutoRedraw to False and the new rectangle never appears, despite the fact that it is actually being drawn when the form loads. In the Form_MouseDown event, the code calls the Form_Paint event. When Form_Paint runs, the controls that were placed on the form at design time are repainted, but Form_Load isn't run again. As a result, the rectangle is never visible to the user.

As you have seen, there are several ways to affect what the user sees on the screen when your application runs. The usual path to predictable results is to maintain normal layering and keep all drawing inside the Paint event. You can change the layering and draw outside the Paint event and get useable results but you must exercise some caution.

Experimenting with *DrawMode* and Other Drawing Tricks

The PAINTDEM.VBP application presented in this section makes it easier to experiment with combined effects of controls and properties, used within and outside the Paint event. Experimentation is the best way to understand some of the properties, especially DrawMode.

> The PAINTDEM.VBP project is on the CD-ROM as PAINT16.VBP, PAINT16.FRM, PAINT32.VBP, PAINT32.FRM, FRMVBDIN.FRM and FRMVBDOU.FRM. The source code in both versions of the files is identical. The executable files are PAINT16.EXE and PAINT32.EXE. As before, "16" and "32" indicate a 16-bit or a 32-bit application respectively, and "PAINT" in the discussion that follows refers to both versions. You should simply load PAINT.EXE and run it to follow along with this discussion. Figure 5.5 shows how it looks in operation.

The Graphics Interface

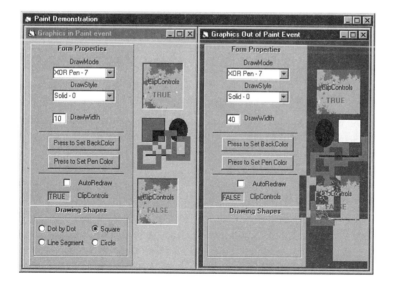

Fig. 5.5
This demo makes it easy to try out drawing and painting effects.

The purpose of the application is to provide two nearly identical forms, loaded up with controls that will make it easy to set a number of critical properties. On one of the forms, though, the graphics methods will be applied outside the Paint event. You will see what happens to certain 3-D controls when you enable AutoRedraw under these circumstances.

Another difference between the two forms is that one of them has ClipControls set to True, and the other has it set to False. ClipControls cannot be changed while a program is running, so a side-by-side comparison seemed the best way to go.

You can learn a lot from this apparently simple application. For example, when you change the BackColor on a form, all of the graphics drawn on the bottom layer are erased, but the controls in the middle and top layers are not affected. Another thing you might notice is that the ClipControls status for the form has precedence over the ClipControls settings for the Image controls.

The main use of this little application is experimentation with the DrawMode. You had your first look at DrawMode in the EZPICS project and in Table 5.2. But the DrawMode property makes it possible to do a number of seemingly impossible things with drawn objects on your screen very easily. Let's look at a few of them.

Seeing *DrawMode* in a Systematic Way

A systematic approach is best for experimentation. As you will recall, DrawMode calls on sixteen binary raster operations. These operations can involve combining up to two colors at a time and applying the results to the pixels in the path of the electronic "pen."

The system that is best for experimenting is based on the observation that the two colors you are combining will fall into one of three relationships:

- They may be identical.

- They may be opposites, or "color complements" (in binary terms, if a color is represented by 01010101, its complement will be 10101010).

- They may be related in some other way, including no logical relationship at all.

In the project called COLOR.VBP, in the section titled "Exploring How Visual Basic Handles Color," you will be given a tool, identifying the digital formula for any color that can be displayed on your screen under Visual Basic. Until then, you may want to stay with the first two relationships in your experimentation.

The colors that can be involved are the color of the pixel to be changed (not necessarily the same thing as the BackColor property of the form) and the color of the pen (the ForeColor property of the form). Either color can be combined "as is" with the other, or it may be changed in some way before the combination. And the color that results from the combination of the pen and destination pixel colors can itself be changed. All of these combinations and changes involve performing bitwise mathematical operations on the data held in memory that represents the color of the pixel to be affected.

The DrawMode functions fall into five categories, according to complexity. As these categories are outlined in this section, you may want to be running PAINT and trying out various combinations of ForeColor (pen color), BackColor, and DrawMode. Select either circle or square for the shape, and set your DrawWidth to 40 or more. Whether you are using the "In Paint Event" or "Out of Paint Event" side of the demonstration in Figure 5.5, click its Maximize button so that you have plenty of room to work. (It doesn't matter which side you use.) Leave AutoRedraw unchecked.

Using the Simplest *DrawMode* Functions

The simplest category contains four functions that do one of the following operations:

- Change all the color data for the pixel to 0, therefore making the pixel black (DrawMode = 1, or Blackness).

- Change all the color data for the pixel to 1, therefore making the pixel white (DrawMode = 16, or Whiteness).

- Leave the color data for the pixel exactly as it is, therefore performing no operation at all (DrawMode = 11, or NOP).

- Change all the color data for the pixel to its complement (i.e., changes 0 to 1 and vice versa), therefore changing the pixel to its complementary color (DrawMode = 6, or Invert).

Notice that the DrawMode in this first category doesn't care what the ForeColor is. The functions in the category operate only on the present actual color of the pixel.

Learning *DrawMode* Functions Involving the Pen Color

The next category in order of complexity contains two functions, each of which involves only the pen color (ForeColor):

II

The Graphics Interface

- Change all the color data for the pixel to equal the ForeColor specified (DrawMode = 13, or Copy Pen).

- Change all the color data for the pixel to the complement of the ForeColor (DrawMode = 4, or Not Copy Pen).

Neither DrawMode cares what the current pixel color may be; they only operate using the ForeColor.

Using the *Xor*-Related Functions

The third category still only contains two functions, but they involve both the ForeColor and the color of the target pixel:

- Perform a bitwise Xor operation to combine the color data for the current pixel and the ForeColor (DrawMode = 7, or Xor Pen).

- Perform a bitwise Xor operation to combine the color data for the current pixel and the ForeColor, then perform a bitwise Not operation on the result (DrawMode = 10, or Not Xor Pen).

These are the first two operations that offer some unique capabilities for multimedia. (That is, if you don't count the ability of Invert to switch between colors and their complements.)

If you set DrawMode to Xor Pen and leave the BackColor and pen color (or ForeColor) at their defaults, nothing seems to happen when you click on the drawing area. Xor requires two colors in order to do anything, and when you first run PAINT, only the BackColor is set.

If you set the pen color to any value and then click, you will notice that the line drawn does not match the color you chose. This is because what you are seeing is the color of the background pixels combined with the pen color by the Xor operator. If you click to create a line, then click again without moving the mouse, the line disappears. Xor is very useful to animators because of this property.

You can also use Not Xor Pen to make drawing disappear. It accomplishes this by first combining the pen and destination colors, using the Xor operator, and then performing an Invert operation on the result. For this reason, Not Xor Pen will produce a result even if the ForeColor has not been set (it is just doing an Invert operation on the background pixels).

As noted earlier, any color combined with itself via the Xor operator yields black. Logically, any color combined with itself using the Not Xor operator yields white. If you use Xor to combine a color with its complement (yellow with blue, for example), you get white. If you combine a color with its complement by using Not Xor, you get black.

Using the Paint Demonstration project, set DrawMode to Xor. Draw a square (set a DrawWidth of 40), using dark blue for the BackColor and yellow for the pen color. Then draw another square with the same settings so that it just slightly overlaps the first square. Where the two white squares overlap, you will get a swatch of dark blue.

Just below these two squares and slightly overlapping them, use Not Xor to create a third square. Then repeat the operation to make a fourth Not Xor square, which just overlaps the third.

> Did you notice that changing `DrawMode` doesn't affect anything that has already been done?

You will see that where the black Not Xor squares overlap only each other, another dark blue swatch has appeared. Where either black Not Xor square overlaps only one of the white Xor squares, you have yellow pixels. And finally, in the very center, you may have a small area in which one of the black Not Xor squares overlaps the blue swatch created by the overlapping white Xor figures. This small area will be black, but can you tell why? These results depend on your selection of the correct shades of blue and yellow from the color dialog box. I used row 5, column 5 for the blue, and row 2, column 2 for the yellow.

Finding Uses for the Merge Group of Operations

The fourth category of binary raster operations is the Merge group. All four of the operations in this group use both the destination and pen colors, and apply the logical `Or` operation to them, with or without a logical `Not`:

- Combine the color data for the destination pixel with the pen color, using a logical `Or` (DrawMode = 15 or Merge Pen).

- Combine the color data for the destination pixel with the pen color, using logical `Or`, and then `Not` the result (DrawMode = 2, or Not Merge Pen).

- Perform a logical `Not` on the pen color, then combine the result with the color data for the pixel by using a logical `Or` (DrawMode = 12, or Merge Not Pen).

■ Perform a logical Not on the color data for the destination pixel, then combine the result with the pen color, using logical Or (DrawMode = 14, or Merge Pen Not).

This group can have some complex interactions. Here is an interesting observation that may prove useful to you in your work, and may get you started on your experimentation:

Set the ForeColor (pen color) and BackColor so that they are color complements (blue and yellow or red and green, to name a couple of possible pairs). Select a square drawing shape, set DrawWidth to 40, and select Copy Pen as your DrawMode. Using this combination, "stamp" a square somewhere on the working area of PAINTDEM.

Now change your DrawMode to Merge Pen, place the cursor in the middle of one of the squares and click the mouse. You will get a white square that appears to be under the first square, like a shadow.

If you haven't already tried this, switch to the Graphics Out of Paint Event form in the Paint Demonstration. The ClipControls are set to False. Change your DrawMode to Xor Pen. Then cover one of the small pastel fractal bitmaps on the form with a square or round shape. Change DrawMode again to Merge Pen or Mask Pen. As you can see, DrawMode works on pixels in bitmaps and controls as well as on pixels on the back layer of a form.

Applying Members of the Mask Group

The fifth and final group of DrawMode properties is the Mask group. In these four properties, the destination and pen colors are combined using the And operator, with or without the Not operator:

■ Perform a logical And between the color data for the destination pixel and the pen color (DrawMode = 9, or Mask Pen).

■ Perform a logical And between the destination pixel and the pen color, and then invert the result with logical Not (DrawMode = 8, or Not Mask Pen).

■ Invert the pen color with a logical Not, then logical And the result with the color data for the destination pixel (DrawMode = 3, or Mask Not Pen).

■ Invert the destination pixel color with logical Not, then logical And the result with the pen color (DrawMode = 5, or Mask Pen Not).

As for the `Merge` group, you can use `Mask Pen` to create a shadow for a figure created with `Copy Pen`. As long as the destination pixels and the pen color are color complements, the shadow will be black.

Exploring How Visual Basic Handles Color

Because color is so important in a graphical user interface, Visual Basic is loaded with ways to handle this property. At the same time, all versions of Windows have specific ways of controlling color. These methods came about to support the variety of hardware where Windows 3.1, Windows 95, and Windows NT run, and to ensure backward compatibility. These issues will affect your work in multimedia.

You have already seen color handled in three ways in the earlier projects. In EZPICS, perhaps you noticed that a hexadecimal value (`&HC0&`) was entered when specifying a dark red color for the frame around the images in the slide show. Hexadecimal color values are expressions consisting of the red, green, and blue (RGB) components used by your hardware and software to determine the color ultimately seen on-screen.

Later, in the FRMDRW.VBP, an RGB triplet was used to establish the color of a filled box drawn on the form at run time: RGB(125,255,125). The numbers represent the amount of red, green and blue, respectively, in the color of that box. In this system, each component is identified by a number between 0 and 255. Table 5.3 shows the RGB components for the sixteen standard VGA colors.

Table 5.3 The RGB Components for the Standard Windows Colors

Color	Red	RGB Components Green	Blue
Black	0	0	0
White	255	255	255
Red	255	0	0
Dark Red	128	0	0
Green	0	255	0

(continues)

II

The Graphics Interface

Table 5.3   Continued

Color	Red	RGB Components Green	Blue
Dark Green	0	128	0
Blue	0	0	255
Dark Blue	0	0	128
Yellow	255	255	0
Dark Yellow	128	128	0
Magenta	255	0	255
Dark Magenta	128	0	128
Cyan	0	255	255
Dark Cyan	0	128	128
Gray	192	192	192
Dark Gray	128	128	128

NOTE   In addition to the RGB function, Visual Basic offers a QBColor function; this converts color values used by other versions of Basic to the RGB system.

PAINT.VBP used a color dialog box to specify the form's BackColor. This is a convenient way to help users pick or customize colors within a multimedia application.

Visual Basic offers one more method for identifying a color, and that is the use of *intrinsic constants*. An intrinsic constant is provided by an application. You can use the Object Browser to find the Visual Basic constants stored in the VB Object library. All that is required to use one of these constants is to enter the constant name in the code. It is not necessary to declare the constant. Table 5.4 lists the eight intrinsic constants for colors.

Table 5.4   Visual Basic Offers Eight Intrinsic Constants to Define Colors

Color	Intrinsic Constant
Black	`vbBlack`
Blue	`vbBlue`
Cyan	`vbCyan`
Green	`vbGreen`
Magenta	`vbMagenta`
Red	`vbRed`
White	`vbWhite`
Yellow	`vbYellow`

In addition, there are 25 more intrinsic constants that allow you to tie the colors of your application to the system colors chosen by the user. Table 5.5 shows your choices. If you specify one of these constants for the color of a form or control, the color of that form or control will match the color of the corresponding part as determined by the user's Control Panel settings. The great value of this is that no matter what the user has selected for a "color scheme" (for example, Pumpkin, Rose 256, or Celery), your application will look like it was designed to fit into it.

> It is generally a bad idea to hard code the colors of the forms and controls in your applications. Instead, let Windows and Visual Basic work for you. The default value for the BackColor of most controls and of all forms is set to a constant that will cause the BackColor to change appropriately to match the system colors chosen by the user. By using the default or the intrinsic constants in Table 5.5, you can be sure that your application will "look right."

NOTE

Table 5.5   These intrinsic constants match the colors in your application to the System Colors selected in the Windows Control Panel.

System Color	Constant	Value Matches Color Of
vbScrollBars	0x80000000	Scroll bars
vbDesktop	0x80000001	Desktop

(continues)

II

The Graphics Interface

Table 5.5 Continued		
System Color	**Constant**	**Value Matches Color Of**
vbActiveTitleBar	0x80000002	Active window title bar
vbInactiveTitleBar	0x80000003	Inactive window title bar
vbMenuBar	0x80000004	Menu background
vbWindowBackground	0x80000005	Window background
vbWindowFrame	0x80000006	Window frame
vbMenuText	0x80000007	Text on menus
vbWindowText	0x80000008	Text in windows
vbTitleBarText	0x80000009	Text in title bar
vbActiveBorder	0x8000000A	Active window border
vbInactiveBorder	0x8000000B	Inactive window border
vbApplicationWorkspace	0x8000000C	MDI app background
vbHighlight	0x8000000D	Control items selected
vbHighlightText	0x8000000E	Control text selected
vbButtonFace	0x8000000F	Command btn face shading
vbButtonShadow	0x80000010	Command btn edge shading
vbGrayText	0x80000011	Grayed text
vbButtonText	0x80000012	Text on pushbuttons
vbInactiveCaptionText	0x80000013	Text in inactive caption
vb3DHighlight	0x80000014	3D element highlights
vb3DDKShadow	0x80000015	3D element dark shadows
vb3DLight	0x80000016	3D element light parts
vbInfoText	0x80000017	Text in ToolTips
vbInfoBack	0x80000018	ToolTips background

Why did Microsoft find it necessary to provide all these different methods for specifying colors? The main answer is in one word: diversity. As mentioned earlier, your multimedia applications may be required to run under a variety of operating systems, on many different kinds of hardware and in the company of a bewildering array of display drivers. Some systems will support only sixteen colors, and others will support millions of colors. Your objective, of course, is to have an application that looks the same on all of them. Each method of specifying color supports your efforts in this regard.

Demonstrating Visual Basic Color Functions

It is easier to demonstrate how to use these color functions than to go into very long explanations. The COLOR.VBP application shows how to use numerical methods and the intrinsic constants to specify a color. It also provides a way to determine the RGB components of any color your system can display.

This demonstration, which enables you to set and read color in Visual Basic is on the CD-ROM as a 16-bit application (COLOR16.VBP and COLOR16.FRM) and as a 32-bit application (COLOR32.VBP and COLOR32.FRM). No other files are used. The code in both sets of listings is identical. The executable versions are on the CD-ROM as COLOR16.EXE and COLOR32.EXE, respectively. Throughout the discussion that follows, "COLOR" refers to both versions of all files.

As you see in Figure 5.6, COLOR.FRM uses quite a few controls. However, the exact layout is not critical. The PictureBox control in the center of the form is where the results of your choices will be shown. The radio buttons at the upper left are used to select the method for specifying colors. After this, depending on the radio button chosen, you can pick colors from the respective list box, from the color dialog box (it appears when the Color Dialog radio button is selected), or by entering values for red, green and blue. The hexadecimal values for the color selected will be displayed in the labels at the upper right.

NOTE

Print out the program listing for COLOR.FRM and refer to it as you read the description in the text.

The Graphics Interface

II

Fig. 5.6

This application displays specified colors and translates color to numerical values.

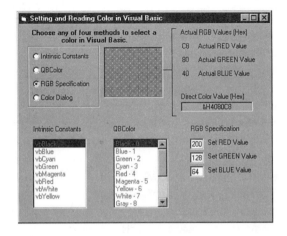

Using ListBox Controls for Color Selection

With the intrinsic constants and the QBColor function, you are dealing with small sets of pre-specified colors and associated constants. To make it easy to select a specific color and constant, you will use a pair of ListBox controls to hold all of them.

The intrinsic constants could give us a bit of a problem. Each of these constants is identified by a string expression (for example, vbRed) but this name represents a number. The name can be displayed in the ListBox, but it will be treated as a string when read.

Caution

If you try to set the BackColor value of the PictureBox control with this string, you'll get a type mismatch error.

The solution is to read the intrinsic constants into an array during the Form_Load event (refer to the actual code on the CD-ROM, in COLOR.FRM). Then order the array to match the ListIndex property of the ListBox and use the constant name stored in the array to specify the color. The lboColorConstants_Click() event handles the actual selection. Just to show that you can use the intrinsic constants directly, one is called in the Form_Load event to initially paint the PictureBox control red.

```
picColorBox.BackColor = vbRed
```

At the end of the `Form_Load` event, there are a number of lines that are re-marked out with `'`. These begin with the following lines:

```
'frmColor.BackColor = vbDesktop
'frmOptions.BackColor = vbDesktop
'Options(1).BackColor = vbHighlight
'Options(1).ForeColor = vbHighlightText
```

Go through and remove the single quotes. Then go back to the Control Panel, select Display and turn to the Appearance tab. Change the color scheme (try "Pumpkin"), then go back to Visual Basic and run COLOR.VBP. This illustrates the effect of the intrinsic constants that match application colors to system colors. If you have a strong stomach, put the single quotes back on these lines and run COLOR.VBP again under the new color scheme to see how bad hard-coded gray panels look with color schemes other than the Windows standard.

The code for `QBColor` can be handled a bit more directly because `QBColor`'s argument is an integer, just like `ListIndex`. If you will refer to the program code in the `Form_Load` event, under the remark line `'Load List Box for QBColors`, you can see that you only need to place the items in the list box. The code for the `lboQBColors_Click()` event can pull out the number right from the listing, rather than having to fool around with an index.

Capturing, Translating, and Displaying Color Values

From either ListBox control, program execution is sent to the `picColorBox_Paint` event (see Listing 5.6). The purpose of this move is to capture the color that has just been placed in the control, translate it to hex values and display these values.

Listing 5.6 COLOR.FRM. For undithered colors, this code in *picColorBox_Paint* pulls out the color values from a single point and prints them.

```
Private Sub picColorBox_Paint()
    Dim strColorValue, strPadding As String
    Dim intAddPad, intCounter As Integer

    'Use the Point function to capture the color
    lblDirectColorValue.Caption = "&&H" & Hex(pic _
      ColorBox.Point(10, 10))
    strColorValue = Hex(picColorBox.Point(10, 10))

    'Pad strColorValue with zeroes to the left.
    intAddPad = 6 - Len(strColorValue)
    For intCounter = 0 To intAddPad
        strPadding = strPadding & "0"
    Next intCounter
    strColorValue = strPadding & strColorValue
```

(continues)

The Graphics Interface

II

Listing 5.6 Continued

```
'Print RGB values for solid colors
lblRedValue.Caption = Mid$(strColorValue, Len(str _
   ColorValue) - 1, 2)
lblGreenValue.Caption = Mid$(strColorValue, Len( _
   strColorValue) - 3, 2)
lblBlueValue.Caption = Mid$(strColorValue, Len( _
   strColorValue) - 5, 2)

End Sub
```

Getting the color value by looking at a single point works well with the intrinsic constants and the QBColor function. Both of these cause a standard display to be painted with pixels all of the same color.

 Because of the way display systems are designed and the way Windows uses them, many color values must be simulated. The process is called *dithering*.

Sometimes Windows can't create a pure color as specified on your system. When this happens, it fills the area in question with a combination of differently colored pixels that will give the impression of the pure color. In these cases, you won't be able to rely on a single point to give the color value.

This problem comes up in working with colors that are specified using the RGB function. It is fairly simple to cause the color of the PictureBox to change as the red, green and blue values are entered individually. To get the complete color value from the painted box, you have to get the hexadecimal number that Visual Basic uses to describe the BackColor. Listing 5.7 shows how this is done for the blue component. The code for the red and green components is contained in the txtSetRed_Change and txtSetGreen_Change events. Only the last line in each of these events is different from the other two.

Listing 5.7 COLOR.FRM. This *Change* event procedure builds an RGBexpression from text the user enters, reads back the actual hex value and prints it.

```
Private Sub txtSetBlue_Change()
    Dim strColorValue, strPadding As String
    Dim intAddPad, intCounter As Integer

    'Build the RGB expression from the TextBox values.
    picColorBox.BackColor = RGB(Val(txtSetRed.Text), _
        Val(txtSetGreen.Text), Val(txtSetBlue.Text))
```

```
'Capture the Color Value from the BackColor
strColorValue = Hex(picColorBox.BackColor)
'Print the full value in the DirectColorValue
 lblDirectColorValue.Caption = "&&H" & str _
    ColorValue
'Make the value exactly 6 characters long
intAddPad = 6 - Len(strColorValue)
For intCounter = 0 To intAddPad
     strPadding = strPadding & "0"
Next intCounter
strColorValue = strPadding & strColorValue

'Pull out just the part that we need
lblBlueValue.Caption = Mid$(strColorValue, Len(str _
    ColorValue) - 5, 2)

End Sub
```

There is a similar problem for the colors specified by the color dialog box,
which is displayed by selecting the Color Dialog radio button: many of them
are dithered. In this case, though, you can capture the Color property and
hold it in strColorValue. Listing 5.8 shows the lines in the Option1_Click
event that do this.

**Listing 5.8   COLOR.FRM. These lines in the *Option1_Click* event
capture, dissect, and display the code for the color selected from
the Common Dialog.**

```
cdlColorDialog.ShowColor

picColorBox.BackColor = cdlColorDialog.Color
strColorValue = Hex(cdlColorDialog.Color)

lblDirectColorValue.Caption = "&&H" & strColorValue

'Pad strColorValue with zeroes to the left.
intAddPad = 6 - Len(strColorValue)
  For intCounter = 0 To intAddPad
    strPadding = strPadding & "0"
  Next intCounter
strColorValue = strPadding & strColorValue

'Print RGB values for colors
lblRedValue.Caption = Mid$(strColorValue, _
   Len(strColorValue) - 1, 2)
lblGreenValue.Caption = Mid$(strColorValue, _
   Len(strColorValue) - 3, 2)
lblBlueValue.Caption = Mid$(strColorValue, _
   Len(strColorValue) - 5, 2)
```

II

The Graphics Interface

The real lesson is that you can capture the value used to send color information to your display. It is not special in any way. Like any value, it can be changed to a string, or it can be added, multiplied and divided. This is very useful in creating multimedia effects.

Suppose you created a Shape control on your form at design time, and you wanted the FillColor in this Shape to vary smoothly as the program ran, indicating changes in the intensity of something. For example, to show changes in pressure on a steel beam, you could change the color from the lightest pink to the darkest red, simply by using math to manipulate the FillColor value. Visual Basic gives you a lot of control over color in your applications.

Using Code to Select Color Specification Methods

The selection of methods is made using the option buttons and a Case statement in the Option1_Click event, shown in Listing 5.9. As each control is enabled, the other controls are disabled. This is an ordinary procedure; a single case will give you the idea as to what goes in the code

Listing 5.9 COLOR.FRM. This is the start of the *Case* statement, which handles option button selections.

```
Private Sub Option1_Click(Index As Integer)
Dim strColorValue As String
      ' Make selection of method
      Select Case Index
          Case 0
              lboColorConstants.Enabled = True
              lboQBColors.Enabled = False
              txtSetBlue.Enabled = False
              txtSetGreen.Enabled = False
              txtSetRed.Enabled = False
              ...
      End Select
End Sub
```

At this point, you have seen most of the functions in Visual Basic that are especially suited for multimedia work. These (plus one function, PaintPicture, to be presented in Chapter 6, "Creating Transition Effects") will be all that is required for many projects. As said earlier, it is highly desirable to do as much of your work as possible using just Visual Basic functions. Such an approach takes advantage of the cross-operating system capabilities. It also helps to keep your application compact and easy to maintain.

There is one topic that still needs to be discussed before you proceed to look under the hood of the API. This topic is one that every Visual Basic multimedia programmer faces on a fairly regular basis.

Palette Flash When Using 256 Colors

Earlier it was mentioned that Windows has some problems in handling color. The most serious of these problems arises when there are more colors than Windows is prepared to deal with. The result of this overload is known as *palette flash*.

Palette flash is easy to describe in one word: ugly. All the colors in the bitmaps in the active window suddenly change to various psychedelic shades. Just as quickly, some colors return to approximately what they were, while others remain permanently altered. In severe cases, colors in other windows are also affected.

Actually, the "flash" happens because Windows must remap the way that colors are assigned to the palette. The *palette* is a data structure containing the codes for the colors Windows can display at any given time. The existence of palette flashing is a hint that interesting effects might be possible if you could manipulate the palette at will. The Windows API (specifically, the GDI) contains a number of functions that help Windows manage its use of color. Some of these are available to you as a Visual Basic programmer.

You will be going deeply into the methods Windows uses to deal with color in the last part of the chapter. But there is a certain amount of palette management that you can do without getting into the GDI functions. First, here is an example of palette flash.

Make sure your display system is in 256-color mode. You may have to go to the Control Panel in Windows to do this. Palette flashing only happens in 256-color mode, for reasons that will be explained later. However, a great many of your users will be running your application on systems set to this mode. It's important to be able to cause palette flashing on purpose because that's the first step to learning how to avoid palette flashing. Load the project FLASH16.VBP (16-bit version) or FLASH32.VBP (32-bit version) from the CD-ROM.

The form for FLASH (either the 16-bit or the 32-bit version) is very straightforward, as you can see in Figure 5.7. There are two bitmaps loaded on it now. The program loads three tiny bitmaps in turn into the small Image control at the bottom of the form, every other time the Flash button is clicked.

II

The Graphics Interface

Fig. 5.7
FLASH.VBP uses
this form setup to
demonstrate
palette flashing.

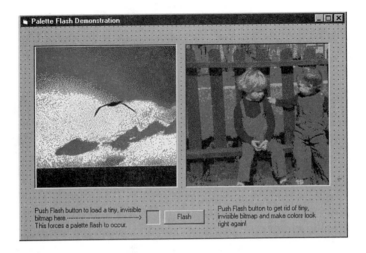

These three bitmaps (RAINBOW.DIB, PASTEL.DIB, and BRIGHT.DIB) were
supplied with your copy of Visual Basic. Each one consists of just a single
pixel, but each one also has attached to it a complete color palette. The code
in Listing 5.10 shows how these bitmaps are switched in and out of the small
Image control. This is the entire program for FLASH. All the color action you
see when you run the program is the result of palette flashing.

**Listing 5.10 FLASH.FRM. This code switches between three tiny
bitmaps that cause the palette flashing.**

```
Private Sub Command1_Click()
    Static Time As Integer
    Time = Time + 1
    If (Time Mod 2) Then
        If (Time Mod 3) = 1 Then
            Picture3.Picture = LoadPicture("RAINBOW.DIB")
        ElseIf (Time Mod 3) = 2 Then
            Picture3.Picture = LoadPicture("PASTEL.DIB")
        ElseIf (Time Mod 3) = 0 Then
            Picture3.Picture = LoadPicture("BRIGHT.DIB")
        End If
      Label1.Visible = False
      Label2.Visible = True
    Else Picture3.Picture = LoadPicture()
      Label1.Visible = True
      Label2.Visible = False
    End If
End Sub
```

Run FLASH and click on the command button to operate the demonstration.
(You can run FLASH16.EXE or FLASH32.EXE from the CD-ROM if you prefer.)
Notice how the labels at the bottom of the form change to let you know

where you are in the process. When the palette flash is over, the colors in the images are noticeably different.

As the tiny bitmaps are cycled in and out of the PictureBox control, the colors in the two larger bitmaps suddenly turn vividly wrong. In fact, if you have another application running in the background you may notice that some of its colors change as well.

Understanding Palette Flash

The problem is that while your system may be capable of displaying millions of colors, Windows can only handle so many of them at a time. The set of colors Windows happens to be using at any given time is called the *system palette*. So long as the number of individual colors in this palette is 256 or less, everything is fine. But when the number of colors required to draw all the objects on-screen goes over the limit, something has to give.

When you first start Windows on your computer, the system palette is probably very small. Only 20 system colors are required to draw everything that you see on a normal Windows desktop. Each time you run an application or display a bitmap, it notifies Windows of the colors it would like to have available to use. If there are enough unused palette entries available, Windows accommodates the request.

There are not always enough palette entries available to give the application running in the foreground all the colors it needs. In this case, Windows clears enough entries to fill the request. The "flash" that you see happens as Windows makes room in the system palette, adds the colors needed by the new arrival, and redraws the screen. This process is called *realizing the palette*.

That's fine for the foreground application or the latest bitmap, but what about all the others? Windows fills their requests with the closest available color. That's why some of the colors in the other applications and bitmaps stay changed after the flash is over.

This explains a lot about what you see happening in the demonstration. In FLASH, the flashes are not of equal intensity and the after-effects of each tiny bitmap's palette on the large bitmaps are not the same. PASTEL.DIB, the first of the additions, is mostly shades of blue, green and red. You can tell that it doesn't have a lot of yellow in it from the effect on the bird image. RAINBOW.DIB, the second small bitmap, seems to have more entries in common with the two visible bitmaps. Each of them looks almost normal. The worst match of the three is BRIGHT.DIB, which is made up of highly saturated colors. The effect might be satisfactory for a retrospective of psychedelic experiences in the 60s, but not for much else.

Avoiding Palette Flash

There are six general ways to avoid palette flashes. Each of them will work under some circumstances and none of them is a universal solution.

- *One method is to show one image at a time on-screen.* When bringing a new image on to replace the one you just removed, load it into a Picture control with the `Visible` property set to `False`. If there is a palette flash in the image as it is loaded, it won't be seen. Then change the `Visible` property to `True`. You saw this technique used in the EZPICS project at the start of the chapter. Of course, this won't prevent flashes in background windows that may be open and visible. The solution for that is to maximize your application's window if possible.

- *A second method is to use only the 16 standard VGA colors for everything in your application.* This will require dithering to simulate other colors. Flashing is completely eliminated by this approach. Unfortunately, viewers may not find the limited range of colors to be terribly exciting. Some dithered colors won't fool anybody. In addition, if you are trying to show areas of graduated color, such as fading a screen from dark at the top to light at the bottom, you can easily get a "banded" appearance instead of a smooth transition.

- *A third method is to plan your image sets so that no more than 236 colors plus the 20 system colors are ever required.* This is difficult to do if you have a lot of images to display, but it is sometimes possible.

- *A fourth method is to scan all your images at the same time.* That is, scan them all in a single pass. If you are scanning in a few photos and can get them all on the scanner at the same time, this is a great solution. It forces all the images to use the same palette.

- *A fifth method forces all images to use a common palette by loading a single-pixel bitmap onto the form and using code to force this bitmap to the top of the Z-order.* In other words, you can load RAINBOW.DIB or BRIGHT.DIB onto the form just as we did here. This has the effect of degrading the color in most images, but it does eliminate the flashing. You can also use a palette utility to create a single-pixel bitmap with a palette optimized for the images to be shown. Palette utilities are commonly provided with high-end graphics programs. Microsoft includes one with its Video for Windows development kit as well.

- *The final method involves the use of a palette utility to synchronize all the colors in all the images you are going to display.* That is, you find a set of

236 colors that comes close to satisfying all the needs of your images. Then you modify the colors used in the bitmaps as necessary, before loading the bitmaps into your application, so that none will require any color not included in that optimized palette. In this case, when you load the first image it brings with it a set of color requirements that will satisfy all the images that follow.

Introducing the Windows GDI, Palettes, and Animation

In spite of what was just said about palette flashing, there are times when you will want color to change while your application is running. Of course, you will want these to be controlled, intentional color changes, not random and unpredictable. As of yet, there is no way to do this directly from Visual Basic, but all versions of Windows certainly offer you the capability from the GDI.

Palette animation is a technique for causing selected colors in one part of the display to shift in a controlled fashion. With planning, this can create the illusion of motion without requiring the amount of work normally associated with animation. Sometimes you will see the term *color cycling* applied to this technique.

Demonstrating Palette Animation

Load PALAN16.EXE (or PALAN32.EXE for the 32-bit version) from the CD-ROM and run it now. Note that your system must be set up for 256-color mode in order for the palette animation to occur. You will see what appears to be a wide horizontal slot across the center of the form. The color of the slot appears to be evenly graduated from black on the left to bright red on the right. If you look very closely, you will see that the even graduation is made up of many narrow rectangles, each just the tiniest bit lighter in shade than its neighbor to the left.

When you click on the command button, the darkest area will begin moving to the left. To the viewer, the color will seem to be flowing through a pipe. This works much like the marquee lights at a theatre. Nothing is actually moving; each rectangular element is only cycling rapidly in color intensity, from very dark to very light. Each element is always exactly one shade ahead of the element on one side, and one shade behind the element on the other side.

II

The Graphics Interface

To explain how this is done, you need to take a look at the way Windows and your system handle color. Then in the section headed, "Building a Palette Animation Project" you will see how the code was constructed for the PALAN.EXE demonstration you just saw.

Calculating How Many Colors are Available on a System

Every picture is made up of pixels. Each pixel's color is the result of combined intensities of red, green, and blue. The earlier project COLOR.VBP showed you how the color of items on the screen is set using the QBColor function and individual color intensities from within Visual Basic.

It might seem that any pixel could be any shade of any color. Unfortunately, this isn't the case because all computer display systems are not created equal. Table 5.6 tells you how many colors a pixel can be in the most common multimedia display systems.

Table 5.6 How Many Colors Can a Pixel Be?		
Bits	**Colors**	**Common Name**
1	2	Monochrome
4	16	Standard VGA
8	256	Super VGA
24	16,777,216	True Color

The "bit" part of some names for these systems refers to the number of bits required to store the information for a single pixel. To translate this into the maximum number of colors available, raise two to the "bit" power. For example, a *four-bit color* system can display 2^4 colors. In other words, a four-bit color system has a 16-color VGA card in it.

The range of displays that your applications must contend with is the result of computer evolution, the marketing cycle, and economics. However, a surprising number of businesses are still using 16-color VGA. For now, plan on VGA and SuperVGA systems. Fortunately, all the applications that you write for these systems will run just fine on 24-bit systems. Visual Basic itself is a 256-color application, so the advance of display technology will not invalidate your work.

Determining Actual Pixel Colors

Given that each pixel in any display system can only be one color at a time, and that there is only a finite range for those colors, how does a pixel get to be the shade of mauve you need? Let's walk back from the front of the display clear to the program code to find out.

In COLOR.VBP, the intrinsic constants and QBColor simply sent each pixel a single signal made up of intensities for one or more primary colors: red, green, and blue. But you may also have noticed, in dealing with the RGB function and the color dialog box, that many colors can't be produced this directly. Instead adjoining pixels are set to different colors in order to trick the eye into "seeing" a shade that isn't there. As you learned earlier in the chapter, this is called dithering.

In general, it only takes pixels of two different colors selected from the basic 16 VGA colors to simulate much of what viewers would understand as the complete visible spectrum. For example, many of those shades of "green" that you see in the color dialog box are simulated by black pixels and green pixels. A light blue takes a few blue pixels thrown together with a lot of white pixels. A few colors require three differently colored pixels to be shown together in order to fool the eye. Those dark violet-purples in the color dialog box are made up of red, blue and black pixels.

Dithering is made necessary by the limits of video systems; in particular, the graphics adapter that actually creates the video signal, which paints the image on your screen. The explanation that follows really only applies to 16-color and 256-color systems. However, Windows will appear to work in the same way for you if you have a system with a higher color resolution.

In a 16-color VGA system, the 16 colors are hard-coded into the graphics adapter. What happens when the graphics adapter receives a signal from the system that doesn't match one of those standard colors? It dithers the output, according to instructions that are also hard-coded into the adapter. What you see is a simulation of what the system intended for you to see. This produces acceptable results if the programmer was thinking about and could adapt to the limitations of 16-color.

In a true Super VGA (SVGA) system, you can display up to 256 colors at the same time. Depending on the actual hardware design, these 256 colors are selected from a much larger number of possibilities—up to 16.7 million, to be exact.

There is a name for the 256 colors that can be shown at any given moment on an SVGA system. This collection of hues is called the *system palette* or sometimes the *hardware palette*. The "hardware" referred to is the graphics adapter, where the current system palette entries are stored in a table.

Managing the Palette

Every image you display will require the use of color. If the image is a bitmap, it comes with the collection of colors it would like to show as part of the data. This color data table is a palette. Your application may have certain sets of colors that it would like to use in displaying its output. This is also a palette. These are usually referred to as *logical palettes* and are stored in memory until they are needed to display the image or the output.

In order for Windows to work as advertised, a program running in one window should not have any affect on the programs running in other windows. As a practical matter, the window that is currently in the foreground gets first choice in many areas. This would include the right to set the colors in the system palette. Each version of Windows has a *palette manager function* to determine which window controls the palette and to manage changes to the palette as required.

When an application gets the foreground, it specifies the colors it wants to use. If, out of the 256 slots for color entries, there are enough empty entries to accommodate the logical palette requested, the palette manager function just adds them in. If there are not enough spaces, the palette manager clears enough entries and loads the new palette. The logical palette of the foreground application is now known as the *foreground palette*. Palettes of other applications are mapped to the closest equivalent to what was requested. Their palettes now become *background palettes*. As mentioned before, the process of putting a palette in the foreground or background is known as realizing the palette.

Understanding Palette Animation

To cause palette animation to occur, an application must do four things:

- Create a logical palette consisting of the colors to be animated (this palette can have just a few entries, or it can have up to 236).

- Draw or paint on the active window, using the logical palette entries.

- Get control of the current palette for the active window.

- Call a special GDI function, `AnimatePalette`, which immediately maps each entry in the logical palette to an entry in the system palette.

`AnimatePalette` is called over and over, with changes in the mapping as required to obtain the effect wanted. Usually, this means changing the palette entry to the next immediately following or preceding, although other arrangements are possible. The affected colors in the active window are changed immediately, without anything having to be redrawn. As you saw when you ran the demonstration, the effect is to create the illusion of motion.

Keeping a Handle on Palettes and Other Objects

What you see on your display and what your system sees are two completely different things. In looking at PALAN.EXE while it is running, *you* see a number of graphical shapes and rapidly changing colors. You identify each of those shapes as an object (form, control, and so on) and you know that each of the tiny pulsating rectangles is a box drawn and filled (as will be explained shortly) by the `Line` method.

What Windows sees is a collection of devices. The major window in which your applications are running is a device. The Picture control is a device. There are some devices seen by Windows but not by you. For example, drawing and painting on your screen is done by devices known as *pens* and *brushes*, respectively.

> For the sake of clarification, it should be pointed out that many of the things referred to here as *devices* may already be known to you as *objects*. In the discussions in this chapter, think of an object as describing programming code, while a device describes any place where input or output takes place.

NOTE

In order for Windows to deal with a device, it needs some information. It needs to know where the device is, how to read the input, and how to write the output. The way Windows gets this information is in the *device context* (sometimes called a DC). The device context links your application, a device driver, and a device.

Let's take the output device used for PALAN.EXE (the display on your monitor). As said earlier, the actual video image you see is not determined by the monitor itself, but by the graphics adapter card in your monitor and by the display driver (VGA.DRV, for example) that is loaded into your computer's memory. So when PALAN.EXE is running, one of the dozen or so device contexts that Windows is managing is a *display device context* (display DC).

Suppose it's time to place graphic output into PALAN.EXE's window, such as those colored rectangles. The Windows GDI (which assigned the window to PALAN to begin with) calls routines in the display driver, through the display device context, and uses those routines to operate the graphics adapter. At the time that the GDI assigned the display device context to the window, it passed Visual Basic a handle to that device context. This handle is referred to in code as *hDC*. The actual hDC is simply an integer.

> The key point about handles is that if your program has a handle, it can send or receive information to or from any device context. The hDC is like a Zip code. It makes sure that messages get delivered efficiently to their intended destinations.

Handles are usually indirect pointers to data, and every object has a handle. A program cannot directly access the internal structure of an object or the system resource that the object represents. Instead, an application must obtain the handle to the object and use that handle to examine or modify the system resource.

The PALAN program uses the handle every time it needs to identify the window it is using and to send output to that window. The program can also use the handle to obtain information about the display device, such as its size and display resolution. The handle is a unique identifier for PALAN's window only. In this way Windows keeps programs from interfering with each other.

To summarize things to this point, there may be several palettes in use at any given time. There is the hardware or system palette, stored on the graphics adapter and actually used to determine output. There is a copy of the system palette that is maintained by the Palette Manager. There is the foreground palette, which is the logical palette of the active window. There may be a number of background palettes, which are the logical palettes of applications that are in the inactive windows. The system palette is some combination of all of these, up to a total of 256 colors.

Each palette is a separate object. As such, it is assigned a *handle*, a simple integer the system uses to keep track of the palette. Every object, including the device contexts where input and output take place, has a handle. To pass data to and from a device, your program must have the handle to that device.

You should have enough information now to make sense of the actual code in the Palette Animation demonstration.

Building a Palette Animation Demonstration

The Palette Animation demonstration is on the CD-ROM as PALAN16.VBP and PALAN32.VBP (16-bit and 32-bit, respectively) and two associated files, PALANIM.BAS and FRMPAL.FRM. The latter two files contain source code for both 16- and 32-bit versions, with one set or the other REMarked out. The chief difference is that each version must call certain functions only from 16-bit or 32-bit libraries, as appropriate. The 16-bit version may not call functions from a 32-bit library, and vice versa.

No other files or graphics are required. In the discussion that follows, "PALAN" refers to both the 16-bit and the 32-bit versions. For clarity, only the 16-bit code is shown in the text.

The form for the project, FRMPAL.FRM, is shown in Figure 5.8. There's not much to it: the form, one picture box control, a timer and a command button. The exact location of these items when you set up the form is not important; each will be positioned by code in the Form_Load event.

The application is fairly complex. You should print out PALANIM.BAS and FRMPAL.FRM to refer to during the discussion of the code.

NOTE

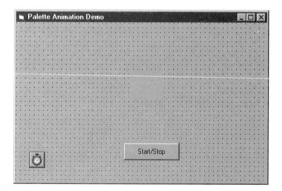

Fig. 5.8
This is the form for the palette animation demo, as it appears at design time.

You will also be using a code module in this project. To create a code module, open the Insert menu and click on Module. The finished product is PALANIM.BAS (on the CD-ROM), which starts with a collection of types, declarations and constants used in palette animation, plus some public declarations. The rest of the code module consists of special functions written just for this application. They should be clear enough to serve as models for your own efforts.

The actual amount of code required to build this application is quite small, but what the program is doing and how it was built won't be clear from the code listing. So that it will be easier to follow the development process and to understand the way PALAN actually operates, here are the three steps that result in palette animation:

■ Build the logical palette that will be animated and store it on the Windows Clipboard.

■ Draw the filled rectangles that appear in the Picture control on the form, and assign each rectangle a single entry from the logical palette.

■ Animate the palette.

Building a Logical Palette

You will need a logical palette, made up entirely of shades of red. The number of shades in the palette will determine how smoothly graduated the colors in the Picture control will appear. Windows will allow you to easily build a logical palette containing up to 236 entries, although for most purposes 16 to 32 shades of any given color should be plenty.

The logical palette is created by the code module. You will make your first use of information related to the GDI in the first 20 lines of PALANIM.BAS. Specifically, you will declare the following:

■ Two data types (PALETTEENTRY and LOGPALETTE) needed to create a palette.

■ A constant (PC_RESERVED) required for palettes that are to be animated.

■ A variable name for the handle of the logical palette you will create.

■ A name for the logical palette object itself.

■ The function (CreatePalette), which actually creates the logical palette that will be animated.

■ A constant of your own creation (PALENTRIES), specifying how many shades of red you want.

Any time you do palette animation, you will need to declare the first five of these six items. It is up to you in each project to decide whether you need the PALENTRIES constant. Listing 5.11 shows the actual entries used in the project.

Listing 5.11 PALANIM.BAS. These entries will appear in any project in which you are going to do palette animation.

```
Option Explicit
Const PC_RESERVED = &H1
Const PALENTRIES = 32
Type PALETTEENTRY
    peRed As String * 1
    peGreen As String * 1
    peBlue As String * 1
    peFlags As String * 1
End Type
Type LOGPALETTE
    palVersion As Integer
    palNumEntries As Integer
    palPalEntry(PALENTRIES) As PALETTEENTRY
End Type
Declare Function CreatePalette Lib "GDI" _
  (lpLogPalette As LOGPALETTE) As Integer
Public hDemoPalette As Integer
Public LogicalPalette As LOGPALETTE
```

PALETTEENTRY is a four-byte structure that is used to hold the color values for each palette entry. One byte each is used for the red, green and blue intensities, and the fourth byte is used for a flag. The flag tells Windows how to map this particular entry. There are a number of choices for this fourth value, but when using an entry for palette animation, the only acceptable value is described by the constant PC_RESERVED.

The other type declaration is LOGPALETTE. This structure defines a logical palette, and consists of three elements. The first, palVersion, identifies the version of the LOGPALETTE structure; it will always be &H300 for all versions of Windows through Windows 95 and Windows NT 3.51. The second element, palNumEntries, identifies the number of entries in the palette. In this case, it will be set equal to PALENTRIES. Finally, palPalEntry can be either a string buffer or an array that holds the actual PALETTEENTRY structures. An array is used because it is simpler to handle.

Creating the Actual Palette for Animation

The function CreatePalette does the work of creating a new logical palette. This function returns a handle to the newly created palette. Handles will be discussed, but for now consider the handle as a tag by which Visual Basic keeps track of objects.

To use this function, first build an array, using the LOGPALETTE and PALETTEENTRY structures, of the entries in your logical palette. Listing 5.12 shows what this looks like, and it is all contained in PALANIM.BAS.

Listing 5.12 PALANIM.BAS. This code creates the palette entries, turns them into a logical palette in memory, and returns a handle to the palette.

```
Sub CreateDemoPalette()
    Dim EntryNum As Integer

    LogicalPalette.palVersion = &H300
    LogicalPalette.palNumEntries = PALENTRIES

    For EntryNum = 0 To PALENTRIES - 1
        LogicalPalette.palPalEntry(EntryNum).peRed = _
            Chr$((255 * EntryNum) / PALENTRIES)
        LogicalPalette.palPalEntry(EntryNum).peGreen = _
            Chr$(0)
        LogicalPalette.palPalEntry(EntryNum).peBlue = _
            Chr$(0)
        LogicalPalette.palPalEntry(EntryNum).peFlags = _
            Chr$(PC_RESERVED)
    Next EntryNum

    hDemoPalette = CreatePalette(LogicalPalette)

End Sub
```

This Sub is called from the Form_Load event with a single line in FRMPAL.FRM:

```
CreateDemoPalette
```

Storing the Palette Safely for Later Use

At this point, you have your palette data stored somewhere in RAM. This data can be overwritten at any time by another application, by Windows, or by PALAN itself. It would be well to move it to a more secure location. While it is possible to create a file to hold the information, it is more convenient and faster to put the palette on the Windows Clipboard, where it will not be overwritten.

NOTE If you haven't worked with the Clipboard before from the applications development side, this may seem strange. You can have several items on the Clipboard at the same time so long as each is in a different format. The palette is just bits of data comprising an object, not color as the viewer will eventually perceive it.

You are going to store and recall the palette information from the Form_Load event. However, it is necessary to declare three more Windows API functions first in PALANIM.BAS.

```
Declare Function OpenClipboard Lib "User" _
  (ByVal hWnd As Integer) As Integer
Declare Function SetClipboardData Lib "User" _
  (ByVal wFormat As Integer, ByVal hMem As Integer) As Integer
Declare Function CloseClipboard Lib "User" () As Integer
```

You will notice a couple of new expressions in those declarations. The ones that start with lowercase h are the handles that Windows needs to find the object being referenced. hWnd, in particular, is a handle to a window, usually a form.

Incidentally, you may wonder why the API is being used. It's because the API functions are more flexible when dealing with the Clipboard. It is true that Visual Basic has three functions that can be used to clear the Clipboard, store information on the Clipboard, and retrieve information from it. Although these functions will allow you to store and retrieve a palette as well as text and graphics, there is a catch. The catch is that the palette must be stored as part of a bitmap file. In PALAN, unfortunately, it is not.

You will need a handle for the Clipboard since the Clipboard is another object. This is declared at the beginning of the Form_Load event as Dim inth As Integer.

You are going to see another of those intrinsic constants used here: vbCFPalette. This specifies that the Clipboard format being stored and retrieved is for a palette, and saves you from having to make another declaration. When the palette is safely on the Clipboard, simply copy it to the Picture property of the Picture control. This action actually realizes the logical palette into the foreground palette, by the way. The whole thing only takes four lines of code:

```
inth = OpenClipboard(frmPalAnim.hWnd)
inth = SetClipboardData(vbCFPalette, hDemoPalette)
inth = CloseClipboard
picPalAnim.picture = Clipboard.GetData(vbCFPalette)
```

Making and Coloring the Rectangles

The red palette is now safely stashed on the Clipboard. The next step is to set up and color in those little rectangles in the Picture control.

Because this procedure will use a graphics method, it will be done from within the picPalAnim_Paint event. The event (in FRMPAL.FRM) only has one line in it, calling a Sub created for the occasion:

```
Private Sub picPalAnim_Paint()
    MakeSpectrumSegments
End Sub
```

The `MakeSpectrumSegments` code, shown in Listing 5.13, comes from
PALANIM.BAS. You use the constant `PALENTRIES` to establish the number of
rectangles in the PictureBox. The only unusual thing in this listing is the use
of the `Set` function, which somewhat simplifies the code and makes it easier
to tell what is happening. Otherwise, this is just a straight use of the `Line`
method until the last statement in the `Sub`.

Listing 5.13 PALANIM.BAS. This *Sub* creates the small rectangles in the Picture control on the form and calls another function to color them using the palette created earlier.

```
Sub MakeSpectrumSegments()
    Dim TotalWidth, StartPoint, EndPoint As Integer
    Dim Pic As Control
    Dim Counter As Integer
    Set Pic = frmPalAnim.picPalAnim
    TotalWidth = Pic.ScaleWidth
    For Counter = 0 To PALENTRIES - 1
        StartPoint = (TotalWidth * Counter) / PALENTRIES
        EndPoint = (TotalWidth * (Counter + 1)) / PALENTRIES
        Pic.Line (StartPoint, 0)-(EndPoint, Pic.ScaleHeight), _
          SegmentColor(Counter), BF
    Next Counter
End Sub
```

The last line in the `Counter` loop draws each rectangle and colors it in with
the corresponding entry from the palette that was built in the "Building a
Logical Palette" section. The function called to do the coloring is
`SegmentColor()`, shown in Listing 5.14. `MakeSpectrumSegments` passes the value
of its counter to `SegmentColor()`, which uses it as the number of the palette
entry to be retrieved. In this step, you use the `RGB` function to build and return a long integer, which contains the color value for the rectangle. The
long integer is built up from the data in the logical palette itself.

II

The Graphics Interface

Listing 5.14   PALANIM.BAS. This short function returns the RGB value of the palette entry required for the rectangle being drawn by *MakeSpectrumSegments*.

```
Function SegmentColor(Entry As Integer)
    Dim lngStoredRed As Long
    Dim lngStoredGreen As Long
    Dim lngStoredBlue As Long
    Dim pe As PALETTEENTRY
    LSet pe = LogicalPalette.palPalEntry(Entry)
    lngStoredRed = Asc(pe.peRed)
    lngStoredGreen = Asc(pe.peGreen)
    lngStoredBlue = Asc(pe.peBlue)
    SegmentColor = RGB(lngStoredRed, lngStoredGreen, lngStoredBlue)
End Function
```

Animating the Palette

By now it is probably beginning to make sense to you why so few Windows programmers ever get into palette operations! There is a lot of detail to attend to when you go outside the safe haven of Visual Basic. But believe it or not, you are nearly finished. The only thing left to do is to actually animate the palette. The AnimatePalette function was called in the opening lines of PALANIM.BAS:

```
Declare Sub AnimatePalette Lib "GDI" (ByVal hPalette As _
    Integer, ByVal wStartIndex As Integer, ByVal wNumEntries _
    As Integer, lpPaletteColors As PALETTEENTRY)
```

By now, you may be able to figure out what most of that means, but let's go over it anyway. First, hPalette is a handle to a logical palette. wStartIndex is the number of the first entry in the palette to change and wNumEntries is the number of entries to be changed. There must be at least this many entries in the array that is referenced, lpPaletteColors. This last item is the first entry in an array of PALETTEENTRY structures that will replace the current entries in the system palette.

Next stop is the Timer event in FRMPAL.FRM, from which you call a Sub of your own that uses AnimatePalette. Incidentally, you adjust the Interval value of the Timer to change the speed of the animation:

```
Private Sub tmrTimer1_Timer()
    AnimateDemoPalette
End Sub
```

The AnimateDemoPalette called is shown in Listing 5.15. There are actually three parts to this Sub's code, not counting the declarations at the beginning.

Listing 5.15 PALANIM.BAS. After getting control of the palette and setting up a simple cycle of the palette entries, this code does the actual palette animation.

```
Sub AnimateDemoPalette()
    Dim EntryNum As Integer
    Dim HoldEntry As PALETTEENTRY
    Dim hCurrentPalette As Integer
    Dim hSystemPalette As Integer

    hSystemPalette = GetStockObject(DEFAULT_PALETTE)
    hCurrentPalette = SelectPalette(frmPalAnim.picPalAnim.hDC, _
      hSystemPalette, False)
    hSystemPalette = SelectPalette(frmPalAnim.picPalAnim.hDC, _
      hCurrentPalette, False)

    LSet HoldEntry = LogicalPalette.palPalEntry(0)
    For EntryNum = 0 To PALENTRIES - 2
        LSet LogicalPalette.palPalEntry(EntryNum) = _
          LogicalPalette.palPalEntry(EntryNum + 1)
    Next EntryNum
    LSet LogicalPalette.palPalEntry(PALENTRIES - 1) = HoldEntry

    AnimatePalette hCurrentPalette, 0, PALENTRIES, _
      LogicalPalette.palPalEntry(0)

End Sub
```

Getting the Handle to the System Palette

To use `AnimatePalette`, you need the handle to the actual current system palette. There is, however, no direct way to obtain this handle either in the GDI or in Visual Basic. Luckily, there is a GDI function, `SelectPalette`, that will return the handle to the *previous* logical palette for a device context.

There is also a GDI function called `GetStockObject` that will retrieve any of 17 standard Windows objects that can be used by any Windows application. Most of these standard objects are brushes, pens, or fonts, but one of them is the default Windows color palette.

To obtain the handle to the actual current system palette, do the following:

1. Declare two functions in the declarations section of PALANIM.BAS.

```
Declare Function SelectPalette Lib "User" (ByVal hDC As Integer, _
  ByVal hPalette As Integer, ByVal bForceBackground As Integer) _
  As Integer
Declare Function GetStockObject Lib "GDI" (ByVal nIndex As _
  Integer) As Integer
```

2. Use `GetStockObject` to select the default palette into the system palette.

```
hSystemPalette = GetStockObject(DEFAULT_PALETTE)
```

3. Use `SelectPalette` to get the handle to the system palette.

```
hCurrentPalette = SelectPalette(frmPalAnim.picPalAnim.hDC, _
    hSystemPalette, False)
```

4. Use `SelectPalette` again to set the system palette back the way it was.

```
hSystemPalette = SelectPalette(frmPalAnim.picPalAnim.hDC, _
    hCurrentPalette, False)
```

Making the Palette Entries Loop

The result of all this effort is the handle to the actual system palette, captured as `hCurrentPalette`.

The next task is to set up some code to loop the palette entries, so that every time the `Timer` event fires, each entry will be replaced by the next higher entry. To make the loop complete, you need to have a *holding entry* in the pattern as well. The `Lset` statement serves well for this purpose.

```
LSet HoldEntry = LogicalPalette.palPalEntry(0)
    For EntryNum = 0 To PALENTRIES - 2
        LSet LogicalPalette.palPalEntry(EntryNum) = _
            LogicalPalette.palPalEntry(EntryNum + 1)
    Next EntryNum
    LSet LogicalPalette.palPalEntry(PALENTRIES - 1) = HoldEntry
```

In the last line of the `Sub`, you call `AnimatePalette` and give it the handle to the system palette. In return, `AnimatePalette` immediately loads into the system palette the current values of the logical palette entries. On the display, each little rectangle immediately brightens by one "notch," except for the one that had contained the palette entry for the brightest shade of red. That last one turns black. To the viewer, it appears that each rectangle has moved one place to the left.

The last thing to do is to create the code for the command button. This is a simple toggle for the `Timer.Enabled` property, in the FRMPAL.FRM file:

```
Private Sub cmdAnimate_Click()
    tmrTimer1.Enabled = Not tmrTimer1.Enabled
End Sub
```

Palette Animation Tricks

In the PALANIM.BAS file on the CD-ROM, you will find two groups of lines in the `MakeSpectrumSegments` `Sub` that have been `REM`'d out. One of these is preceeded by a comment line: `Eastbound/Westbound effect`. Listing 5.16 shows you how to split the single Picture control in top and bottom halves and make the color cycle in opposite directions in each half. The trick here is to reverse the order of segment colors in the top half of the control.

Listing 5.16   PALANIM.BAS. This code will give you two lanes in one Picture control, with colors cycling in opposite directions.

```
' Eastbound/Westbound effect
   'For Counter = 0 To PALENTRIES - 1
   '    StartPoint = (TotalWidth * Counter) / PALENTRIES
   '    EndPoint = (TotalWidth * (Counter + 1)) / PALENTRIES
   '    Pic.Line (StartPoint, 0)-(EndPoint, Pic.ScaleHeight / 2), _
   '        SegmentColor((PALENTRIES - 1) - Counter), BF
   'Next Counter
   'For Counter = 0 To PALENTRIES - 1
   '    StartPoint = (TotalWidth * Counter) / PALENTRIES
   '    EndPoint = (TotalWidth * (Counter + 1)) / PALENTRIES
   '    Pic.Line (StartPoint, Pic.ScaleHeight -_
(Pic.ScaleHeight / 2))-(EndPoint, Pic.ScaleHeight), _
   SegmentColor(Counter), BF
   'Next Counter
```

There are better, more compact ways to code this, but I have left it this way to make it easier to follow. This one is kind of fun to watch. You can also make the colors cycle in a vertical Picture control.

The other trick involves splitting the Picture control into three horizontal segments and "staggering" the palette entries so that the moving color seems to form a simple arrow shape. The code is shown in Figure 5.17, and it can also be modified to make the arrows move the other way.

Listing 5.17   PALANIM.BAS. These lines, when substituted for *MakeSpectrumSegments*, create a moving arrow effect.

```
' Arrow effect
   For Counter = 0 To PALENTRIES - 1
       StartPoint = (TotalWidth * Counter) / PALENTRIES
       EndPoint = (TotalWidth * (Counter + 1)) / PALENTRIES
       Pic.Line (StartPoint, 0)-(EndPoint, Pic.ScaleHeight / 3), _
         SegmentColor(Counter), BF
   Next Counter
   For Counter = 0 To PALENTRIES - 1
       StartPoint = (TotalWidth * Counter) / PALENTRIES
       EndPoint = (TotalWidth * (Counter + 1)) / PALENTRIES
       Pic.Line (StartPoint, Pic.ScaleHeight - (Pic.ScaleHeight _
         / 3))-(EndPoint, Pic.ScaleHeight - (Pic.ScaleHeight / 3)* 2), _
           SegmentColor(Counter + 1), BF
   Next Counter
   For Counter = 0 To PALENTRIES - 1
       StartPoint = (TotalWidth * Counter) / PALENTRIES
       EndPoint = (TotalWidth * (Counter + 1)) / PALENTRIES
       Pic.Line (StartPoint, (Pic.ScaleHeight / 3) * 2)- _
         (EndPoint, Pic.ScaleHeight), SegmentColor(Counter), BF
   Next Counter
```

From Here...

This part of your exploration of Visual Basic's graphics capabilities is complete. You will probably want to return to and study the palette animation project (PALAN.VBP) thoroughly. It presents nearly everything that you will need to know about palettes for most multimedia work.

The following is a list of chapters for information pertaining to the topics discussed:

- To add sound to your slide show, refer to the discussion of the MCI control in Chapter 3, "The Media Control Interface (MCI)."

- To look at transition effects and make your efforts look professional, you will find more information in Chapter 6, "Creating Transition Effects."

- To make great use of what you've learned here about palettes, see Chapter 10, "Animation."

Chapter 6

Creating Transition Effects

In Chapter 3, "The Media Control Interface (MCI)," you saw how you can use Visual Basic to bring video into multimedia programs. There are many special video effects that enhance the viewer's experience. However, those effects are part of the video, and you can't change them. The good news is that Visual Basic makes tools available to create similar effects inside forms and objects. In Chapter 5, "Graphics and Palettes," you learned about the Graphics Device Interface (GDI) where Windows stores the most powerful of these tools.

Now you'll expand your ability to use the Graphics Device Interface from within Visual Basic to produce special animation effects called transitions. You probably know the names given to some of these effects, such as wipe, fade, dissolve, and fly-on. These are common in videos and in business presentations. You may have wondered how to get an image to slowly appear in a picture box or to roll smoothly onto the screen. By the end of this chapter, you'll be able to do the following:

- Use Visual Basic and the Windows GDI tools

- Build and manipulate special bitmaps for visual effects

- Create flip, wipe, and fade effects

- Design your own special effects using these tools

Using Transition Effects in Multimedia

Transitions are important in multimedia for three reasons. First, they help viewers follow a presentation. When you use multimedia to present ideas, your principal role is that of a communicator. Helping someone get the point isn't easy, even with the help of technology. In ordinary face-to-face communication, most of the meaning comes from context and from nonverbal elements. The same thing is true in multimedia.

The second reason transitions are important in multimedia is that they keep viewers alert and involved. The brain notices movement and pays closer attention when changes take place in things seen or heard. A good communicator appeals to this human love for variety. Transitions, by emulating movement and providing changes in sensory levels, keep the brains of the audience involved.

Third, transitions can build suspense, amuse the viewer, and create the eager interest needed to motivate action. Effective communication succeeds by fostering anticipation, enthusiasm, and enjoyment. Transitions are an important part of building positive responses to a message.

Nine Common Transitions

There are many possible transition effects. Table 6.1 shows the nine that are the most useful.

Table 6.1 Nine of the Most Common Multimedia Transition Effects	
Effect	**Description**
Cut	The next image instantaneously replaces the current image.
Fade Out/Fade In	The current image slowly and uniformly darkens to total black (Fade Out), or slowly and uniformly appears from a black screen (Fade In).
Dissolve	The current image is slowly and uniformly transformed into the next image.
Wipe	The next image appears sequentially across the current image.
Slide	The next image slides smoothly into position on the screen from an edge or a corner.

Effect	Description
Pop On/Pop Off	The next image appears immediately on the screen or disappears immediately.
Pull Down/Pull Up	The next image comes down from the top of the screen like a window shade, and returns the same way.
Flip	An image in a frame appears to "flip" over and reveal the next image on the other side.
Spin	An image appears in a spinning frame.

Multimedia applications use all of these, both in small areas of the screen and over the whole screen. You will see how to create three of these in this chapter, and you will be given a good start on the others.

All of these transition effects involve animation, which creates the illusion of change or motion. The actual images on the screen do not move, but they seem to do so. In the movies, this illusion is created by recording separate images on film and then playing them back fast enough so that the brain is tricked into thinking it sees movement. In multimedia transitions, the separate images are created by rapidly combining bitmaps or copying them from one place to another.

Visual Basic and the Windows API provide powerful tools for creating this illusion. In some cases, creating a transition effect is as simple as changing the run-time `Visible` property of a label or a picture box to `True`. However, in many cases you will need to call on the Windows GDI to create the transition you want.

Creating Simple Animation Effects with Visual Basic

Visual Basic comes with several tools that can be used directly to create animations. These include the `Move` and `PaintPicture` methods.

It is important to understand that you are not limited to doing only one thing at a time on the display screen. The first project for this chapter, "Flip Transition Effects," will put two transitions on the screen, running simultaneously. You can even position one of the transitions on top of the other.

The Flip Transition Effects demonstration is on the CD-ROM as FLIP16.VBP, FLIP32.VBP, FLIP16.FRM, and FLIP32.FRM. The executable files are

FLIP16.EXE and FLIP32.EXE. The source code for the 16-bit and the 32-bit versions is identical. "FLIP" in the discussion that follows refers to both versions of the .VBP, .FRM, and .EXE files. Other files used in this program are CHINA1.BMP, CHINA2.BMP, and RINGS2.BMP.

As you can see in Figure 6.1, FLIP.FRM uses two timers, three picture boxes and a command button. The `Form_Load` event will position two of the picture boxes where needed. The third one can be placed anywhere, so long as it is the last of the controls to be added to the form.

Print out the program listing and you will see that most of the action takes place in the `Paint` events for two of the PictureBoxes. This code uses the `PaintPicture` and `Move` methods to produce the animation that creates the "flip" effect on the display.

Fig. 6.1

Setup of form and controls for FLIP.

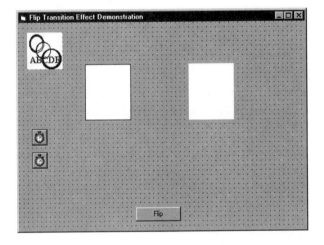

Load and run FLIP.VBP before you go through the code. The small geometric design at the upper left will "flip" continuously as long as the program is running. As it alternates showing its two sides, realize that this is being done by manipulating a single bitmap. The reversing of the image is done automatically by Visual Basic.

The large photo will flip over and show a second image on its virtual back side when you click the command button. This transition is produced in exactly the same way as the one in the upper-left corner of the form. However, since there is not much point in showing an actual photograph reversed, this transition smoothly takes the viewer from one image to the next.

Understanding the Small Transition

The small bitmap is made to busily spin away by the code in the `picSpinner_Paint` event, which is in turn called by the `tmrFlip_Timer` event. Most of the `Paint` event code is simply used to keep track of where the logo is in its virtual rotation. The work is done in the three lines in the middle of each `If` statement. These lines are all slight variations on the same theme.

```
PicSpinner.PaintPicture picSpinner.picture, 0, 0,picSpinner.Width
picSpinner.Width=picSpinner.Width - intSpinDelta
picSpinner.Move(picSpinner.Left+intSpinAdjust), picSpinner.Top, _
    picSpinner.Width
```

You may have used the `Move` method, seen here in the third line of code, in other projects. `Move` provides a simple, convenient way to produce smooth movement and resizing of forms and controls. It has four parameters: `left`, `top`, `width`, and `height`. The only parameter that must be present is the first one, which gives the x-coordinate of the left edge of the object being moved. However, if you want to use the `width` parameter, you must also give the parameter for the `top`, as done in the last line above. In the present demonstration, `height` is not needed, so it is omitted.

`Move` is used in FLIP.FRM to resize the `picSpinner` control, repositioning the left and right sides to give the illusion that the control is spinning around a central vertical axis. `Move` can be just as effective in creating the impression of rotation around a horizontal axis.

Introducing *PaintPicture*

The real star of this show is `PaintPicture`. This is a new method in Visual Basic. `PaintPicture` provides the programmer with an easy way to copy part or all of a bitmap from one place and quickly paste it down in another. In FLIP.FRM, the pasting is done almost "in place," but the Picture control is resized in the middle of the operation. `PaintPicture` obligingly stretches or squeezes the image to fit the new surroundings. This is how the foreshortening effect is created in FLIP.FRM, to trick the viewer's eye into thinking that something is rotating.

`PaintPicture` has another useful feature. In some of the sections of the `picSpinner_Paint` event, you will see lines that look like this:

```
picSpinner.PaintPicture picSpinner.picture, _
    picSpinner.Width,0,picSpinner.Width
```

This line, and the others like it, is where the "flip" takes place. To see how this is done, look at the syntax for the `PaintPicture` method.

```
object.PaintPicture picture, x1, y1, width1, height1…
```

II

The Graphics Interface

(Another five parameters are given for the method, but only the first five are important to this discussion.)

You could sort out from the context that *picture* must be where the image comes from that is to be drawn onto the *object*. What is not so obvious is that the source of the image can be the object itself.

It is the other four parts that make it possible to flip images. The keys are *x1* and *y1*, the Cartesian coordinates where the top left corner of *picture* will be placed on *object*. To flip an image around the vertical axis, give *x1* the value of the width of *picture*, and give *width1* the same value, but negative. In effect, this makes the upper-left corner into the upper-right corner of the image—as if you were looking at the image from the back.

To flip an image around the horizontal axis, give *y1* the value of the height of *picture*, and give *height1* the negative of this value.

In setting up your own flips and spinners, study the way that the AutoResize and AutoRedraw properties have been set in this short example. These make the difference between PaintPicture working or not working, as the author found out. Their functioning is not addressed in the Microsoft manuals that come with Visual Basic!

Understanding the Large Transition

The transition between the two large images on the FLIP form is also done with PaintPicture and Move. However, it had to be set up a little differently because it is a foundation for making a series of transitions between images.

It wasn't important to show each image reversed, and there had to be a place to change pictures. It was also necessary to take into account the possibility that the images might not be the same size. As a result, picProduct_Paint looks different from picSpinner_Paint. In addition, by tracking certain key events and using them to detect whether the image is getting larger or smaller, it was possible to make the code a little more compact.

There are two main sections in the Paint event. One section drives the program when the image is getting smaller, and the other drives when the image is getting larger. In fact, the key to understanding how this works is to forget about illusions and rotations.

Imagine a rectangle with a vertical line drawn through its center as in Figure 6.2. You start with the rectangle at maximum width. When the first half of the transition is finished, the rectangle will have been reduced to a very narrow strip on either side of the center line. The width will be reduced in a number of equal increments, or *deltas*. In the second half, the rectangle is incrementally expanded to accommodate the width of the new image.

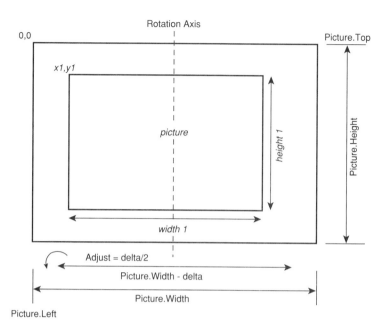

Fig. 6.2
The variables used in animating a flip effect.

It is the way in which this reduction and enlargement is done that determines how smooth the transition appears. In the code, the width of the rectangle is reduced by one increment (delta), the image is redrawn (shrunken or stretched to fit) into the new rectangle, and the Move method adjusts the rectangle by sliding it over one-half increment to the left or right. By adjusting the speed of the timer and the size of the increment, the programmer produces the effect sought. Figure 6.3 shows the completed program in operation.

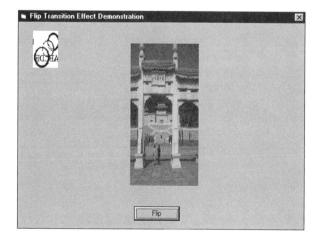

Fig. 6.3
Two transitions—flipping and spinning—on one screen!

Creating Simple Animation Effects with the GDI

As you have just seen, Visual Basic provides the basics for multimedia. However, the native functions are not powerful enough or fast enough to do everything that you might want to do.

Fortunately, the GDI contains two important sets of tools to fill this capability gap. These are the block transfer functions and the ternary raster operations. You can use these tools to copy and combine up to three bitmaps at the same time, manipulate images in various ways, and present the results on the display screen. If you perform your manipulation and presentation very quickly, the viewer "sees" motion.

Using the Block Transfer Functions

Within the GDI, Windows provides three functions for quickly transferring bitmap images between locations on the screen and between the screen and memory. Two of these functions can stretch an image if necessary to get it to fit in its new location. One of them fills areas with a repeating pattern, or brush.

All three block transfer functions use ternary raster operation codes (abbreviated ROP). These codes define how the GDI combines colors from a source bitmap, a possible brush bitmap, and the destination bitmap to produce the final colors in the destination bitmap.

NOTE   You saw *binary* raster operations (abbreviated ROP2) in Chapter 5 when you were working with the drawing functions. In this chapter, you will be using only the ternary raster operations, or ROPs.

Table 6.2 summarizes the functions and their capabilities.

Table 6.2 Block Transfer (blt) Functions that Make Transition Effects Possible	
Block Transfer Function	**What It Does**
BitBlt *(Bitmap Block Transfer)*	Transfers a bitmapped image, or a rectangle area of one, from one device context to an *equal-sized* area of another. Can convert color bitmaps to monochrome, and vice versa. If the destination area is a different size than the source area, BitBlt automatically calls StretchBlt to make the transfer.

Block Transfer Function	What It Does
StretchBlt *(Block Transfer and Stretch)*	Transfers a bitmapped image, or a rectangular area of one, from one device context to either a *different-sized* or a *same-size* area on another. Can convert color maps to monochrome, and vice versa. If necessary, use the GetDeviceCaps API function to determine whether the device context supports raster functions involved in such a transfer.
PatBlt *(Pattern Block Transfer)*	Fills a device context with a pattern. The pattern is determined by the currently selected brush and by the raster operation specified when the function is called. PatBlt works with "destination -only" ROPs. It will fail if the ROP refers to a source.

The actual movement is a simple process. The bitmap (or a rectangular selection from it) is copied into memory. BitBlt or StretchBlt then copies the image from memory back to the new display location.

To the computer, of course, the bitmap is just data, not an image as the viewer understands an image. Because this data is not in a file or some other convenient package, Windows must have a means to identify and track it during the transfer and any manipulation that takes place. Windows does this with the same techniques you saw in the previous chapter: device contexts and handles.

The details of the most useful of these blt functions, BitBlt, also describe the way that StretchBlt works. PatBlt will be demonstrated in the section of this chapter titled "Creating an ROP Brush Demonstration." PatBlt will also be put to work near the end of the chapter in "Creating the Fade Effect Demonstration."

This is what BitBlt's declaration looks like. It is similar in many ways to other API functions called when working with palettes, as discussed in the previous chapter.

```
Declare Function BitBlt Lib "GDI" (ByVal hDC As Integer, ByVal _
X As Integer, ByValY As Integer, ByVal nWidth As Integer, ByVal _
nHeight As Integer, ByVal hSrcDC As Integer, ByVal Xsrc As _
Integer, ByVal YSrc As Integer, ByVal dwROP As Long) As Integer
```

This isn't as bad as it may appear (fortunately). It's long, but most of the arguments merely define two rectangular areas:

- ■ hDC—The device context (DC) for the destination. You first learned the concept of a device context in Chapter 5, "Graphics and Palettes." In this case, you are retrieving the device context by using the hDC (handle) property.

- ■ X, Y—The coordinates of the upper-left corner of a rectangle within the destination device context. If the ScaleMode of the picture box holding the destination bitmap is pixels, then the coordinates will be measured in pixels.

- ■ nWidth, nHeight—The width and height of the destination rectangle (and also of the rectangle being transferred from the source).

- ■ hSrcDC—The device context for the source.

- ■ XSrc, YSrc—The coordinates of the upper-left corner of the source rectangle within the source device context. This rectangle will have the same dimensions as the one in the destination, but the coordinates of the corner may be different.

- ■ dwROP—This is the 32-bit value for the ternary raster operation (ROP) that will combine bitmaps during the transfer.

NOTE For the rest of this chapter, the initials "DC" or "hDC" will be used when referring to the actual integer that will be supplied by Windows as the device context handle, or to a reference in the Visual Basic code. The phrase "device context" refers to the concept or to the specific device context linking your application, a device driver, and a device. Refer to the discussion of device contexts and handles in Chapter 5, under "Keeping a Handle on Palettes and Other Objects."

To use BitBlt, specify the area on the destination bitmap to combine in some way with a portion of the source bitmap. It is as if you cut out a rectangular piece of the destination bitmap and combined this with an equal-sized piece of the source bitmap. You can take the pieces from different parts of their bitmaps. For example, you could combine the upper-left corner of the source and the lower-right corner of the destination. Figure 6.4 is a sketch of the way it works.

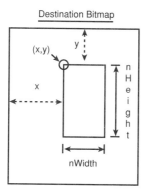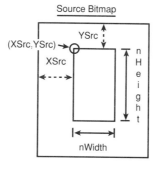

Fig. 6.4
This visualization
shows how the
arguments used by
BitBlt identify
the sections of two
bitmaps to
combine.

BitBlt uses the calling convention Call By Value instead of the default Call
By Reference. When used with numeric data, a copy of the parameter value
passes to the DLL function. The copy changes, not the actual parameter.
BitBlt does not alter the "original" bitmap in picSource in any way.

Understanding Ternary Raster Operations (ROPs)

As you saw in the previous section, you can move a bitmap around with
BitBlt. In the most basic case, the value of each bit in the destination device
context changes to the value of the corresponding bit in the source bitmap.
You might think of this as "rubber stamp mode."

Windows is much more capable than this, however. There are 255 ways in
the GDI for setting the bits on any given destination device context. These
255 methods are collectively known as ternary raster operations, usually abbreviated as ROP. Unlike the binary raster operations (ROP2) you learned about
in Chapter 5, these ROPs can combine up to three bitmaps at a time.

For the rest of this chapter, "raster operation" will refer only to the ternary variety
(unless otherwise stated). When you see the abbreviation "ROP," it refers to the actual
32-bit parameter value or intrinsic constant that is entered in a Visual Basic program.
The term "raster operation" will be used when discussing the concept or when referring to ROPs collectively.

Each ROP is a 32-bit value used to implement a Boolean equation. The equation specifies what the destination DC bit values will be. Values derived from
up to three different sources may be involved. The current value of the destination DC bit is one of these values. The value of the source DC bit is another.
Finally, some ROPs will also combine the value of the bits in the currently
selected brush with either or both the source and destination bits.

Fifteen of the 255 ROPs have names, shown at the top of Table 6.3. While these probably appear in programs more often than the other 240, they are by no means the only useful raster operations. Twenty-seven of the nameless variety are in the table, and you will see all of them used in this chapter.

Table 6.3 Fifteen Named *ROPs* and Some that Have No Common Names		
Raster Operations	**Boolean Equations**	**32-Bit Parameters**
The Named Operations		
BLACKNESS	0	&H42
WHITENESS	1	&HFF0062
DSTINVERT	Dn	&H550009
PATCOPY	P	&HF00021
PATINVERT	DPx	&H5A0049
PATPAINT	DPSnoo	&HFB0A09
SRCAND	DSa	&H8800C6
SRCCOPY	S	&HCC0020
SRCERASE	SDna	&H440328
SRCINVERT	DSx	&H660046
SRCPAINT	DSo	&HEE0086
MERGECOPY	PSa	&HC000CA
MERGEPAINT	DSno	&HBB0226
NOTSRCCOPY	Sn	&H330008
NOTSRCERASE	DSon	&H1100A6
Operations with D and S Only (This is the whole list of this type.)		
	DSan	&H7700E6
	DSna	&H220326
	DSxn	&H990066
	SDno	&HDD0228

Raster Operations	Boolean Equations	32-Bit Parameters
Operations with P and S Only (This is the whole list of this type.)		
	PSan	&H3F00EA
	PSna	&H30032A
	PSo	&HFC008A
	PSno	&HF3022A
	PSon	&H0300AA
	PSx	&H3C004A
	PSxn	&HC3006A
	SPna	&H0C0324
	SPno	&HCF0224
Operations with P, S, and D (This is only a small fraction of the over 200 *ROPs* of this type.)		
	DPa	&HA00C9
	DPan	&H5F00E9
	DPo	&HFA0089
	DPna	&H0A0329
	DPSaa	&H8003E9
	DPSaan	&H7F03C9
	DPSana	&H2A0CC9
	DPSanan	&HD50CE9
	DPSano	&HBF08C9
	DPSao	&HEA02E9
	PDna	&H500325
	PDno	&HF50225
	SSPxPDxaxn	&H2B1D58
	SPDSxax	&HAC0744

II

The Graphics Interface

Any ROP, named or not, can be identified by the Boolean equation that defines it. These equations appear in the second column of Table 6.3. From one to three operands can be specified in an ROP equation:

D is the value of the bit in the destination device context.

S is the value of the bit in the source corresponding to a bit in the destination device context.

P is the value of the bit in a pattern determined by the currently selected brush.

These operands can combine using any of our of the Boolean operations introduced in Chapter 5. These are designated in the table by lowercase letters:

a is the AND operation

n is the NOT operation

o is the OR operation

x is the XOR (exclusive OR) operation

Raster operations equations are written in *Reverse Polish Notation (RPN)*. This means the operations in the equation are read from left to right. Each operation affects the operand to its left. For example, the equation for SRCINVERT is DSx. The source bitmap combines with the destination bitmap, using the XOR operator. As another example, the equation for SRCCOPY is just S, meaning that the source bit overwrites the destination bit.

Finally, each ROP has a 32-bit parameter value for passing to the function that calls the ROP. The 32-bit values for the 15 named ROPs appear as constants in WIN31API.TXT. You can copy them into your programs at design time by using the API viewer. Table 6.3 shows the parameters for 42 ROPs.

Using Intrinsic Constants and the Object Browser

At the time this chapter was written, 13 of the ROPs were available as intrinsic constants in Visual Basic, meaning that they can simply be named for use with methods and properties. So, instead of declaring Const SRCCOPY = &HCC0020 and then calling SRCCOPY where needed, you just use vbSrcCopy where needed in your code without any declarations. In other words, for these 13 common ROPs, you never have to type or copy in the 32-bit parameters.

You can use the Object Browser to locate and include the specific intrinsic constant you require. With the Code window for a form open, and with your insertion point located where you want the constant to appear, click on View in the menu bar, and then Object Browser. (Instead of going to the menu bar, you can just press F2 to open the Object Browser directly.) At the top of the Object Browser dialog box, open the Libraries/Projects list and select VB-Visual Basic Objects and Procedures. Then click on the word Constants in the Classes/Modules list. Locate and highlight the intrinsic constant you want in the Methods/Properties list. Click on the Paste button at the upper right of the Object Browser dialog box and Object Browser will paste the constant name into your code at the specified location.

The ROP constants set up this way are identified and defined in VB Help; use the Search for Help On option and click on the Find tab, where you should type **ras**. This will bring up the word RasterOp in the middle list box. The phrases RasterOp Constants and Visual Basic Constants will appear in the bottom list box. Highlight RasterOp Constants and click Display.

Complete details on all 255 of the ternary raster operations, their Boolean equations, and 32-bit values can be found in the Windows 95 PDK, as part of the Win32 Programmer's Reference.

Demonstrating Block Transfers and Simple Raster Ops

It's time to see how all this works in practice and to begin understanding how to code transition effects.

Let's start with a demonstration that illustrates the use of BitBlt and ROPs. This first demonstration will also start building some basic structures for use in later projects in this chapter.

To keep things simple and easy to follow, the ROP Demonstration project will use only two monochrome bitmaps: black and white, no color, and no brushes. However, you will see the effect of the named ROPs and several of the unnamed ROPs as well.

The program listings for this ROP Demonstration are on the CD-ROM as ROPDEM16.VBP and ROPDEM16.FRM (16-bit version) and as ROPDEM32.VBP and ROPDEM32.FRM (32-bit version). The source code for both the 16-bit and the 32-bit versions is identical, and in the discussion that follows, "ROPDEM" refers to both versions. The bitmaps are STAR1.BMP and RINGS2.BMP.

Notice that, for all three picture boxes, AutoSize = True and ScaleMode = 3 - Pixel. Also notice the naming convention for the PictureBoxes. The form is set up as in Figure 6.5. From left to right, the PictureBoxes are picSource, picDestination, and picProduct.

The code is all in the form, with no other modules being used. Everything in this demonstration is done from the general declarations section and three events: Form_Load, picProduct_Paint, and cboROPList_Click.

Fig. 6.5
Setup of form and controls for ROPDemo.

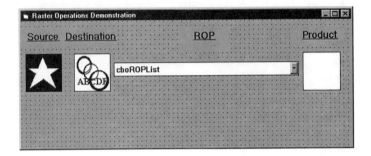

Combining Bitmaps in the *picProduct_Paint* Event

When the demonstration runs, initially the bitmap in the Destination box will simply be copied to the Result box by BitBlt. An ROP called SRCCOPY does the copying. Both BitBlt and SRCCOPY were declared in the general declarations section of ROPDEM.FRM.

SRCCOPY is one of the five simplest ROPs. The Boolean formula is just plain S. It only copies the source bitmap to another device context, replacing anything that was there before. Like the other raster operations, SRCCOPY passes its 32-bit parameter (&HCC0020) to functions that require it.

The following line of code in the picProduct_Paint event copies the image in the picDestination PictureBox exactly to the picProduct PictureBox as the demonstration begins.

```
intCombination = BitBlt(picProduct.hDC, 0, 0, 65, 65, _
picDestination.hDC, 0, 0, lngSRCCOPY)
```

However, you won't actually see this copying because in the same Paint event, the contents of the picProduct box clear out as soon as a new ROP is chosen in the combo box. By default, the first ROP on the list (BLACKNESS) is chosen at the start of the demonstration.

As shown in Listing 6.1, the program uses a string function (Mid$) and the Val function to pull the 32-bit parameter for the selected ROP code out of the menu of ROPs loaded at run time. Finally, BitBlt combines the images.

Listing 6.1   ROPDEM.FRM. The *picProduct_Paint* event.

```
Private Sub picProduct_Paint()
    Dim lngROP32BitParameter As Long
    Dim strROPChosen As String
    Dim intCombination As Integer

    picProduct.Cls
    strROPChosen = cboROPList.Text
    lngROP32BitParameter = Val(Mid$(strROPChosen,_
        InStr(strROPChosen, "=") + 1))

intCombination = BitBlt(picProduct.hDC, 0, 0, 65, 65,_
    picSource.hDC, 0, 0, lngROP32BitParameter)

End Sub
```

Running ROPDEM

Where did the ROP list come from? It was set up by the Form_Load event. In addition to the 15 named ROPs, the list includes four unnamed ROPs purely for demonstration purposes.

The action will be triggered by the cboROPList_Click event, which then sends execution to the picProduct_Paint event. This is the entire event:

```
Private Sub cboROPList_Click()
    picProduct_Paint
End Sub
```

Figure 6.6 shows how the program should look in operation. When you run ROPDEM, notice the effects of the various ROPs. Some of these can produce attractive transitions. For example, with two images and no brush selected, you could use the following series of ROPs with BitBlt to smoothly transform one image into another:

```
SRCCOPY
SRCAND
DSxn
SRCINVERT
PATINVERT
```

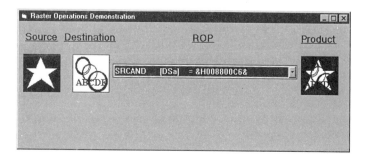

Fig. 6.6
This is the ROP demonstration in action.

Experimenting with ROPs is a good way to become familiar with the range of effects they can produce. Try using color bitmaps and notice what happens with certain combinations. Or use the ROPs you have now to create transitions that only affect a small part of the screen. For example, you can easily "transition" a label on a chart into another label. Or you can put a trail of dinosaur tracks across the screen. Many new possibilities are open now, and you are just starting.

You probably noticed that four of the ROP codes in the list don't seem to do much. PATCOPY, PATINVERT, PATPAINT, and MERGECOPY all require the presence of a brush. You'll have a chance to see them do their stuff in a few more pages.

Creating the Wipe Effect

In this section, you will create the Wipe Effect demonstration. The wipe makes use of the fact that BitBlt stakes out a rectangular area on one bitmap and moves it to cover a rectangular area on another bitmap.

In a wipe, the new image appears to be wiped or rolled across the old image. Imagine an image painted on a wall. The new image is on a roll of paper. You glue the loose edge to the wall along an edge of the old image. Then you unroll the new image little by little across the old one. The old image stays in place and the new one progressively covers it. Figure 6.7 is a picture of this effect in operation.

Fig. 6.7
This is a wipe in progress, showing the image of the gate rolling from left to right across the image of the ornate building facade.

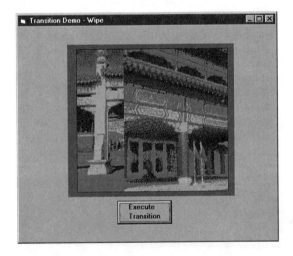

A wipe is a very simple animation. Although the leading edge of the new image appears to be moving across the old image, in fact no movement is taking place at all. Instead, the two images are being progressively combined and redisplayed in order to create the effect.

You need only two GDI functions and a little math for the wipe effect. One of the functions is BitBlt; the other is SRCCOPY. The math locates the right part and stakes out an identical-sized piece on the source.

The Wipe Effect demonstration is on the CD-ROM as WIPEFX16.VBP and WIPEFX16.FRM (for the 16-bit version) and as WIPEFX32.VBP and WIPEFX32.FRM (for the 32-bit version). The source code in both sets of files is identical. The executable version of the demonstration is on the CD-ROM as WIPEFX16.EXE and as WIPEFX32.EXE. In the discussion, "WIPEFX" refers to both 16- and 32-bit versions. The demonstration uses two bitmapped images, CHINA1.BMP and CHINA2.BMP. In a normal project, you would probably use standard modules for the variables and for the actual wipe. Placing it all in the form for now makes things a bit easier to follow.

Once again, AutoSize is set to True for both picture boxes and ScaleMode is set to Pixel. However, picCurrentPicture is on top of picNextPicture. The Visible property for picNextPicture is set to False. This demonstration uses the form general declarations and three events: Command_Click, Form_Load, and Timer_Timer. The form and controls are set up as shown in Figure 6.8.

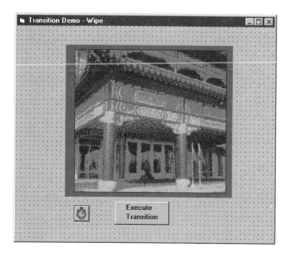

Fig. 6.8

Set up your form like this for the wipe demonstration.

II

The Graphics Interface

Stepping through the Wipe

The wipe effect in the demonstration is a series of steps:

1. The program sets up two picture boxes. One of these is for the image the viewer will see (the "current picture" box). The other holds the next picture for display (the "next picture" box), hidden behind the current picture.

2. The program loads a bitmap in the current picture box. This image is the Destination bitmap. It loads a second bitmap in the next picture box. This image is the Source bitmap. The bitmaps do not have to be the same size, although they probably will be in most cases.

3. The program locates the upper-left corner of the current image, where the wipe will begin. It uses a constant that identifies how many "steps" to use in the wipe. The more steps used, the smoother the effect. It also calculates how much of the image in the current picture box to cover with each step.

4. The BitBlt and SRCCOPY define and copy the first piece of the next picture onto the current picture, in the right place.

5. Some basic arithmetic increases the size of the piece being copied by one step-size increment. BitBlt and SRCCOPY paste this next piece of the Source image onto the current picture, again in the right place.

The program repeats this last step to cover the first image. What was the Source image is now in the current picture box.

If another wipe is to follow, the image in the current picture box is now the Destination image. Have your program load the new bitmap into the next PictureBox, making it the Source image. The program then repeats the wipe procedure, beginning with the third step.

There are a couple of subtle points to consider when you set up your own wipe effects:

■ First, you want to set the ScaleMode for both your picture boxes to pixels. This ensures that all the mathematical operations involved will work out right for any screen resolution.

■ Second, to provide the best quality effect, place the Source bitmap in memory. Fortunately, this is easy to do in Visual Basic. If you set the

AutoRedraw property of a PictureBox to True, and the Visible property to False, the PictureBox becomes a memory device context. In the demonstration, the picNextPicture PictureBox is such a context. SRCCOPY will do its work in memory and BitBlt will then immediately place the finished product into a visible PictureBox. The viewer does not see any of the actual pixel-by-pixel changes.

Setting Up the Declarations for a Wipe

In the form general declarations, the program calls BitBlt and sets up a constant to specify SRCCOPY as the operation of choice. Listing 6.2 shows the one function to be declared, plus two constants and four variables required in the operation.

Listing 6.2   WIPEFX.FRM. Form general declarations for the wipe effect.

```
' We'll be using the API Function BitBlt to perform the
' wipe effect.
Private Declare Function BitBlt Lib "GDI" (ByVal hDC As _
    Integer, ByVal X As Integer, ByVal Y As Integer, ByVal _
    nWidth As Integer, ByVal nHeight As Integer, ByVal _
    hSrcDC As Integer, ByVal XSrc As Integer, ByVal YSrc As _
    Integer, ByVal dwROP As Long) As Integer

' The Raster Operation (ROP) SRCCOPY combines the next image
' with the current image during the transition. The effect
' created makes it appear that the next image is being
' painted over the current one.
Const lngSRCCOPY = &HCC0020

' The wipe is actually a number of discrete "steps"; vary this
' constant and the timer interval to get the wipe speed
' and appearance desired.
Const intSTEPS = 64

' These variables set up the actual wipe operation.
Dim intCurrentPictureWidth As Integer, intWidthChange As _
    Integer, intPieceToAdd As Integer, intNextPiece As Integer
```

Understanding the Wipe Engine

Most of the work in the demonstration is done by just a few lines of code. A timer event controls execution, as shown in Listing 6.3.

II

The Graphics Interface

Listing 6.3   WIPEFX.FRM. The *tmrWipeTimer_Timer* event.

```
Private Sub tmrWipeTimer_Timer()
    Dim intI As Integer 'Counter to keep track of pieces
    ' Each time the timer event fires, add the next piece of
    ' the next picture.
    intNextPiece = BitBlt(picCurrentPicture.hDC, 0, 0, _
        intPieceToAdd, picCurrentPicture.ScaleHeight, _
        picNextPicture.hDC, 0, 0, lngSRCCOPY)
    intPieceToAdd = intPieceToAdd + intWidthChange
    intI = intI + 1
    ' When all the pieces are added, turn off the timer.
    If (intI - intSTEPS) > 0 Then tmrWipeTimer.Enabled = False
End Sub
```

As written, this will produce a wipe from left to right across the full height of the current PictureBox. By manipulating the elements within the statements, you can also produce right-to-left, top-to-bottom, bottom-to-top, and corner-to-corner wipes. Other wipes can be produced by using multiple narrow strips or small square patches; these will look like horizontal or vertical blinds, checkerboard and diamond patterns, and even spirals.

When the program runs, you first see a photo of a colorful building front. Click on the command button. The image of a ceremonial plaza and gateway is wiped across the first photo. You can vary the speed of this wipe by changing the timer Interval property. Adjust the smoothness of the effect by changing the constant intSTEPS.

A command button will kick off the wipe in the demonstration. Listing 6.4 shows the procedures to compute the amount by which the wipe will proceed with each tick of the timer. The last line transfers control to the timer.

Listing 6.4   WIPEFX.FRM. *The cmdExecuteXition_*Click event.

```
Private Sub cmdExecuteXition_Click()
    ' These procedures are used within the wipe
    ' operation, but they must be set up here.
    intCurrentPictureWidth = picCurrentPicture.ScaleWidth
    intWidthChange = intCurrentPictureWidth \ intSTEPS
    intPieceToAdd = intWidthChange

    ' Transfer control of the effect to the Timer
    tmrWipeTimer.Enabled = True
End Sub
```

In the Form_Load event, Listing 6.5, the only matter to attend to is loading the pictures. These pictures are the same size, by the way. In doing wipes to transition from one picture to the next, you may want to have bitmaps that are either the same size, or progressively larger. If the bitmap being wiped "onto" the display is smaller than its predecessor, you will leave the edges of the preceding image showing. If this is the effect you want (like a series of photos piled on top of a table), fine. If you want only one image showing at a time, you will have to wipe on a suitable plain or textured background bitmap in between the differently sized ones.

Listing 6.5   WIPEFX.FRM. The *frmXitionDemo_Load* event.

```
Private Sub frmXitionDemo_Load()
    'Load the pictures
    picCurrentPicture.Picture = LoadPicture("\vb\china1.bmp")
    picNextPicture.Picture = LoadPicture("\vb\china2.bmp")
End Sub
```

Dealing with Palette Incompatibilities

This demonstration should run well for you. However, as you substitute other bitmaps, you will surely find some problems created by palette incompatibilities. The second bitmap, or perhaps the entire Windows screen, suddenly looks like a painter's nightmare.

The problem appears because a Windows palette can contain only 256 colors, as you learned in Chapter 5. Windows will do the best it can to match the colors specified for succeeding bitmaps from the ones in the first palette. Sometimes the results are interesting, but most of the time they're garish.

To recap, here are some methods you can use to avoid palette flash when doing wipes:

■ Show one image at a time on-screen. Wipe on an image, then either make the PictureBox or Image control invisible and unload it, or wipe a plain colored or textured background over the first image. After that, wipe on the next image.

■ Use only the 16 standard VGA colors for everything in your application.

■ Plan your image sets so that no more than 236 colors are ever required at the same time.

■ Scan all of your images at the same time, in one pass. This will force all of them to use the same palette.

■ Use a palette utility to synchronize all the colors in all the images you are going to display.

Using Brushes with Raster Operations

To this point, you know how to use about a dozen ROPs and the `BitBlt` function to create interesting but simple transition effects. There is much more potential in the 243 ROPs that involve combining a pattern brush with the other bitmaps.

Now you want to show the kind of results you get when you combine a brush with a Source or Destination bitmap. This is an essential part of producing a fade transition and other special visual effects.

In addition to fades, brushes enable you to separate and emphasize different elements on your screens. They also make it possible to add visual texture to screens, and this helps to maintain viewer interest.

A brush is a very small bitmap, just eight pixels on a side. To be effective with this tool, you need to be able to make your own brushes. This means learning to make bitmaps from scratch.

The next project (on the CD-ROM as MAKBRUSH.VBP) will show you how to make your own brushes. After that, another small program (on the CD-ROM as BRDEM16.VBP for the 16-bit version or BRDEM32.VBP for the 32-bit version) will demonstrate 27 of the brush-wielding ROPs for your edification. BRDEM16.VBP and BRDEM32.VBP also add another block transfer tool to your kit— `PatBlt`.

As you go, you'll put the code into modules that can easily be reused. The form used in BRDEM16.VBP and BRDEM32.VBP, for example, is an improved version of the one in ROPDEM.VBP at the beginning of the chapter.

Studying Bitmap Structures

To make brushes for use in creating transition effects, you need to know a couple of things about bitmaps. You will also need to know about the functions provided by Windows and Visual Basic to create both brushes and bitmaps.

A bitmap, when loaded into a context, becomes *device-dependent*. This means that it only works with devices that have the same internal configuration. In Windows, all bitmaps (except one) are device-dependent. The monochrome bitmap is compatible with all devices, so it is the one exception. Even though these examples all use monochrome bitmaps, you might one day soon need to use something more complex.

This presents a problem for you as a developer, however. It is never safe to make any assumptions about the kind of internal format the viewer's video device is going to require of bitmaps. The solution provided by Windows is the *device-independent bitmap* or DIB.

The DIB can hold an image that is compatible with any raster device. A raster device defines images in terms of scan lines and allows access to individual pixels. All Windows display screens and many printers fall into this category.

Device-independent bitmaps use a standard format for the bitmap data. They include the definitions of the colors represented by that data. DIBs are also the only way to ensure accurate color conversions when transferring images between devices.

Any DIB is created by setting up two data structures and then following them with the pixel data. The BITMAPINFOHEADER is defined first. It establishes the size and type of the DIB, and tells the type of compression in effect (if any) and the number of colors. After this come the BITMAPINFO structure and a color table.

Reviewing Brush-Building Methods

I have gone into the details of bitmap structure so that the explanation that follows will make more sense. Windows offers you four functions and three methods for building a bitmap. Each of the methods has its advantages and its disadvantages.

It is possible to create a monochrome bitmap directly, using only the pixel data. In this method, you don't need the BITMAPINFOHEADER, the BITMAPINFO, or the color table. (Remember that the monochrome bitmap is compatible with all devices.) You can use CreateBitmap() or CreateBitmapIndirect() to do this.

Both of these functions use device-dependent pixel data and produce device-dependent bitmaps. Neither will convert a device-independent bitmap. This is a problem if you need to create a color bitmap, because the pixel data must specify the colors and their locations in the system palette. Getting this information takes extra programming steps and is one more place for bugs, errors, and gremlins to creep into your program.

Another function that Windows provides for creating bitmaps, and one that directly applies to the task of making pattern brushes, is the function CreateDIBPatternBrush(). This function creates a brush by referring to a structure called a *packed DIB*. The packed DIB is a block of memory containing a BITMAPINFO structure and a device-independent bitmap. If a monochrome brush is the objective, the DIB information isn't used. The function uses the text and background colors for the window instead. While this is certainly handy, creating the packed DIB requires the use of tools to manage global memory blocks. This is a more advanced topic, beyond the scope of the present book.

The third method, the one to be used in the rest of this chapter, is to create a device-dependent bitmap based on a DIB. `CreateDIBitmap()` is the function that does this. The advantages of the third method are that it will work with color brushes, that it does not require information about the system palette, and that it does not require the use of global memory. It isn't as direct as the other two methods, but it is certainly easy to use.

Making Your Own Brush

To make and use brush bitmaps, you will find it convenient to have two standard modules that you can use over and over again in your own multi-media projects. The Brush-Making Modules project shows you how to build these standard modules.

One of the modules, TRANSDEC.BAS, holds the type statements, declarations, and constants that appear over and over in transition effects. The other standard module, MAKBRUSH.BAS, makes an evenly patterned brush bitmap; you can change this module to produce any desired brush.

Neither of these modules will "run" on its own. Each provides functions needed by other functions or by event procedures. As a result, there are no associated forms or controls.

The finished code for the Brush-Making Modules project is on the CD-ROM as three files. MAKBRUSH.VBP is the project file. TRANSDEC.BAS is a standard module of declarations commonly used in transition effects. MAKBRUSH.BAS contains a program that creates a 50% gray brush and can be used to create other brushes.

Let's begin with TRANSDEC.BAS, creating the declaration module. To set up, follow these steps:

1. Select <u>N</u>ew Project from the Visual Basic <u>F</u>ile menu.

2. Highlight the Form module in the Project Dialog and then click on <u>R</u>emove File in the <u>F</u>ile menu.

3. Save the project as **MAKBRUSH.VBP.**

4. Then pull down the Insert menu and click on Module.

5. Save this File as **MAKBRUSH.BAS**.

6. Repeat Step 4 and save the resulting Module 2 as **TRANSDEC.BAS**.

If you haven't done one of these before, you just created a "formless" project.

Open TRANSDEC.BAS. There are a number of items that will go here eventually, but the most important ones are covered first.

Declaring *CreateDIBitmap*

The first item to place in TRANSDEC.BAS is the declaration for `CreateDIBitmap`, the function of choice for most of the brush-making process. The best way to bring this into your code is to use the API Text Viewer.

To use the API Text Viewer, minimize Visual Basic. Click Start button, open Programs and Visual Basic folder. Click API Text Viewer, load WIN31API.TXT, select API Type (`Declares` in this case), and scroll down to CreateDIBitmap and highlight it. Then click the Add and Copy buttons. Exit the API Text Viewer. Restore Visual Basic by clicking on it in the taskbar.

When you have copied the declaration into TRANSDEC.BAS, this is what it will look like:

```
Declare Function CreateDIBitmap Lib "GDI" (ByVal hDC As Integer, _
    lpInfoHeader As BITMAPINFOHEADER, ByVal dwUsage As Long, _
    ByVal lpInitBits As String, lpInitInfo As BITMAPINFO, _
    ByVal wUsage As Integer) As Integer
```

The reason for using this function is to transform device-*independent* bitmap data into a device-*dependent* bitmap that will work on the user's system. The following is a list of arguments that you will deal with:

■ `hDC`—An integer handle to the device context that will define the configuration of the device-dependent bitmap under construction. In this case, it will be the handle to the `picBrush` PictureBox.

■ `lpInfoHeader`—A long (32-bit) pointer to the data structure `BITMAPINFOHEADER`. This structure describes the format of the device-independent bitmap that is being converted. More on this in the next section.

- dwUsage—A long (32-bit unsigned, or double word) integer used to indicate to Windows whether to initialize the bitmap data. This is zero if the bitmap is not going to be initialized. If the bitmap will be initialized according to the next two parameters, the value of this argument is filled by the constant CBM_INIT. Because you want to base the bitmap on the BITMAPINFOHEADER, you'll be using the constant.

- lpInitBits—Either a string or a long integer, this is a pointer to the bitmap data in DIB format specified by the next argument, lpInitInfo. In this case, you'll be using the string version.

- lpInitInfo—A long pointer to the data structure BITMAPINFO, which describes the format and colors of the bitmap data pointed to by lpInitBits.

- wUsage—An integer indicating one of two possible constants. DIB_PAL_COLORS tells Windows that the color table in the bitmap data is relative to the currently selected palette. DIB_RGB_COLORS indicates that the color table contains RGB colors. Since you don't want to be tied to the currently selected palette, the brush-building function will specify the latter of the two constants.

CreateDIBitmap returns the handle of the brush bitmap it has created. It is necessary to remember to use the DeleteObject function to free up the memory and resources used by the brush.

CreateDIBitmap requires three type declarations: BITMAPINFOHEADER, BITMAPINFO, and RGBQUAD.

Declaring Type *BITMAPINFOHEADER*

The BITMAPINFOHEADER structure, Listing 6.6, defines the characteristics of the DIB being used to create the brush. It includes 11 parameters, five of which will be set to zero in the present application.

Listing 6.6 TRANSDEC.BAS. Declaration for type *BITMAPINFOHEADER*.

```
Type BITMAPINFOHEADER '40 bytes
    biSize As Long
    biWidth As Long
    biHeight As Long
    biPlanes As Integer
    biBitCount As Integer
    biCompression As Long
    biSizeImage As Long
    biXPelsPerMeter As Long
    biYPelsPerMeter As Long
    biClrUsed As Long
```

```
        biClrImportant As Long
        End Type
```

Table 6.4 gives the range of values and their meanings for each of the 11 parameters.

Table 6.4 Parameters for the *BITMAPINFOHEADER* Structure		
Parameter	**Value Range**	**Represents**
biSize	Always = 40	Size of BITMAPINFOHEADER structure itself
BiWidth	8 for brushes	Width of brush in pixels
BiHeight	8 for brushes	Height of brush in pixels
BiPlanes	1 for a DIB	Number of color planes
biBitCount	1 = monochrome 4 = 16 color 8 = 256 color 24 = 24-bit	Number of bits per pixel
biCompression	BI_RGB = None BI_RLE8 = 8 bit BI_RLE4 = 4 bit	Compression type
biSizeImage	0 or greater	Image size in bytes (0 if no compression used)
biXPelsPerMeter	0 for brushes	Horizontal pixels/meter
biYPelsPerMeter	0 for brushes	Vertical pixels/meter
biClrUsed	0 or greater	Number of entries in DIB color table that are actually used (0 if all will be used)
biClrImportant	0 or greater	Number of entries that are important (0 if allcolors)

Declaring Type *BITMAPINFO*

BITMAPINFO is a structure that includes the BITMAPINFOHEADER structure and a color table. This is a short declaration, for a change.

```
    Type BITMAPINFO
        bmiHeader As BITMAPINFOHEADER
        bmiColors(1) As RGBQUAD ' Monochrome bitmap
        End Type
```

II

The Graphics Interface

There are only two entries to deal with here. One (bmiHeader) is the information set up in BITMAPINFOHEADER. The other (bmiColors) is the size of the Colors array, which describes the number of colors in the color table and determines the size of the color table in bytes. Simply set this field to the same number that appears in biBitCount in the BITMAPINFOHEADER declaration. That is, make it 1, meaning that you are dealing with a monochrome bitmap. This automatically sets up the color table size as 8 bytes. As noted before, you can use a string or a long pointer to capture this color table information. Because you want to use the color table in the RGBQUAD form, all that is necessary is to declare it such.

Declaring Type *RGBQUAD*

The RGBQUAD structure, shown in Listing 6.7, is a four-byte structure that holds an RGB value for a pixel. RGBQUAD supports device-independent bitmaps and appears in the BITMAPINFO structure.

Each of the four bytes represents one parameter: Red, Green, Blue, or Reserved. The Reserved byte will always be set to 0, unless you intend to do palette animation. To set the color of an entry, enter a value between 0 and 255 for each of the Blue, Green, and Red parameters. Reserved is always 0. If you set all the values to 0, you get a black pixel. If you set all the values to 255 (except for Reserved), you get a white pixel. In other words, this works just like the RGB function in Chapter 5.

Listing 6.7   TRANSDEC.BAS Declaration for type *RGBQUAD*.

```
Type RGBQUAD
        rgbBlue      As String * 1
        rgbGreen     As String * 1
        rgbRed       As String * 1
        rgbReserved  As String * 1
        End Type
```

Making Miscellaneous Declarations Needed for Brushes

Transitions require a number of type declarations. Listing 6.8 shows the type declarations and global constants most frequently used for these effects. All are included in TRANSDEC.BAS.

> ### Listing 6.8   TRANSDEC.BAS. Type declarations and global constants for transitions.
>
> ```
> Declare Function BitBlt Lib "GDI" (ByVal hDestDC As Integer, _
>     ByVal X As Integer, ByVal Y As Integer, ByVal nWidth As _
>     Integer, ByVal nHeight As Integer, ByVal hSrcDC As Integer, _
>     ByVal XSrc As Integer, ByVal YSrc As Integer, _
> ByVal dwRop As Long) As Integer
>     Declare Function CreatePatternBrush Lib "GDI" (ByVal _
>         hBitmap As Integer) As Integer
>     Declare Function PatBlt Lib "GDI" (ByVal hDC As Integer, _
>         ByVal X As Integer, ByVal Y As Integer, ByVal nWidth As _
>         Integer, ByVal nHeight As Integer, ByVal dwRop As Long) _
>         As Integer
>     Declare Function SelectObject Lib "GDI" (ByVal hDC As _
>         Integer, ByVal hObject As Integer) As Integer
>     Declare Function DeleteObject Lib "GDI" (ByVal hObject _
>         As Integer) As Integer
>
>     Global Const lngSRCCOPY = &HCC0020 ' (DWORD) dest = source
>     Global Const lngPATCOPY = &HF00021 ' (DWORD) dest = pattern
>
>     Global Const lngCBM_INIT = &H4&    '  initialize bitmap
>     Global Const intDIB_RGB_COLORS = 0 '  color table in _
>         RGBQUAD
>     Global Const lngBI_RGB = 0&
> ```

You now have a standard module of common declarations, type statements, and constants for your multimedia projects. This module will be used soon for actually making brushes.

Writing the *MakeBrush* Function

In this part of the project, you will see how to prepare a standard module called MAKBRUSH.BAS. It contains the definition of one function, MakeBrush.

All of the code will appear in the general section of the module. You have seen the declarations of the API functions used in the module, so it should be easy to follow this.

Listing 6.9 shows how to start the function definition, and fill in the entries in the BITMAPINFOHEADER. If you are building this as you read, open MAKBRUSH.BAS and type this information into the general declarations section.

Listing 6.9   MAKBRUSH.BAS. Filling in the entries in the
BITMAPINFOHEADER.

```
Option Explicit
Function MakeBrush() As Integer
Dim intBrushBitmapInfoParameter As BITMAPINFO ' Brush bitmap _
    data used in creation
    intBrushBitmapInfoParameter.bmiHeader.biSize = 40
    intBrushBitmapInfoParameter.bmiHeader.biWidth = 8
    intBrushBitmapInfoParameter.bmiHeader.biHeight = 8
    intBrushBitmapInfoParameter.bmiHeader.biPlanes = 1
    intBrushBitmapInfoParameter.bmiHeader.biBitCount = 1
    intBrushBitmapInfoParameter.bmiHeader.biCompression = _
      lngBI_RGB
    intBrushBitmapInfoParameter.bmiHeader.biSizeImage = 0
    intBrushBitmapInfoParameter.bmiHeader.biXPelsPerMeter = 0
    intBrushBitmapInfoParameter.bmiHeader.biYPelsPerMeter = 0
    intBrushBitmapInfoParameter.bmiHeader.biClrUsed = 0
    intBrushBitmapInfoParameter.bmiHeader.biClrImportant = 0
```

Because this is a monochrome bitmap, there are going to be only two entries
in the color table—black and white. The next step is to make all the values for
the RGB components of each entry either "full on" (white) or "full off"
(black). Remember that the Reserved value is 0 because this bitmap's palette
will not be animated. Listing 6.10 shows how to do this.

**Listing 6.10   MAKBRUSH.BAS. Filling the color table with black
and white.**

```
    intBrushBitmapInfoParameter.bmiColors(0).rgbBlue = Chr$(0)
    intBrushBitmapInfoParameter.bmiColors(0).rgbGreen = Chr$(0)
    intBrushBitmapInfoParameter.bmiColors(0).rgbRed = Chr$(0)
    intBrushBitmapInfoParameter.bmiColors(0).rgbReserved = _
      Chr$(0)
    intBrushBitmapInfoParameter.bmiColors(1).rgbBlue = Chr$(255)
    intBrushBitmapInfoParameter.bmiColors(1).rgbGreen = _
      Chr$(255)
    intBrushBitmapInfoParameter.bmiColors(1).rgbRed = Chr$(255)
    intBrushBitmapInfoParameter.bmiColors(1).rgbReserved = _
      Chr$(0)
```

Initializing the Bitmap

At this point, the next step is to create a bitmap by staking out a chunk of the
computer's Random Access Memory (RAM). This is not a "clean" piece of
territory. It may have been used many times since the computer last booted
up to store information temporarily as various tasks were performed. This
previous activity may well have left various bits turned "on" or "off" in an
unpredictable pattern. Therefore, the first thing to be done is to initialize the
area of RAM reserved for storing the bitmap. This means turning "on" all the

bits the brush is going to use. You could think of this as pulling out a clean white sheet of paper before starting to write.

In setting up this clean space to work, there is another factor to consider. `CreateDIBitmap` expects that each row of the bitmap will be an exact multiple of 32 bits. Each bit represents one pixel. The bitmap is only eight pixels square, so there will be 24 unused bits on each line. That means that the program really only needs to clean up the first byte in each row of pixel entries. Listing 6.11 shows the quick, elegant way to clear off some room in which to work.

Listing 6.11 MAKBRUSH.BAS. Initializing the brush bitmap.

```
Dim intRepeat As Integer
Dim strPixelEntry As String * 32 '32 bytes reserved in RAM _
    for pixel entries (8 rows of 4 bytes each)
For intRepeat = 0 To 7 'Each "Repeat" will initialize the _
    next byte of pixel entries
        Mid$(strPixelEntry, intRepeat * 4 + 1, 1) = _
            Chr$(&HFF) 'Sets bytes 1, 5, 9 etc to white
        Next intRepeat
```

Putting the Pattern on the Bitmap

Next, the program will go back and create a patterned monochrome bitmap by turning some bits "off," or black. For this demonstration, you want to have an evenly shaded pattern. This will make it easy to see the effect of the brush when combined with the other bitmaps. Afterward, you may want to change the equations in this next part to see how many different patterns you can get. To begin with, you'll just turn off the even-numbered pixels by using the code in Listing 6.12.

Listing 6.12 MAKBRUSH.BAS. Building a 50% gray brush.

```
Dim intRow As Integer   ' A counter to keep track of the
                        ' rows in the brush bitmap.
    Dim intColumn As Integer ' A counter to keep track of
                            ' the columns in the brush bitmap.
For intRepeat = 0 To 63
        intRow = intRepeat \ 8 'Integer division: returns
                            only the whole number
        intColumn = intRepeat Mod 8 'Modulus arithmetic:
                            returns only remainder
        'The next statement turns off the even-numbered pixels.
        If (intRow Mod 2 = 0) Xor (intColumn Mod 2 = 0) Then
            Mid$(strPixelEntry, intRow * 4 + 1, 1) = _
Chr$(Asc(Mid$(strPixelEntry, intRow * 4 + 1, 1)) And _
    (Not (2 ^ intColumn)))
        End If
        Next intRepeat
```

II

The Graphics Interface

Understanding How the Code Works

The first lines after the loop starts to work through the bitmap, row by row, column by column. Each pixel entry byte is looked at eight times (once for each bit in the byte). The If statement then does the actual bit shifting with two Boolean operators.

The first part of the If statement applies the Boolean XOR operator to the results of a modulus division on the row and column numbers. In case you're rusty on your logical operations, XOR combines integers in pairs, such that if one integer is zero and the other is one, the result is one. If both integers are zero, or if both are one, the result is zero. Doing the modulus 2 operation in the preceding line of code on the row and column numbers ensures that the program will have to deal only with 0s and 1s.

The If statement regards any 0 result as a logical False, causing the program execution to go back to the top of the For intRepeat = 0 to 63 loop for the next pass. But in those cases where the row is even and the column is odd or vice versa, the program executes the Then part of the statement. This short piece of code does nearly all the work:

```
Mid$(strPixelEntry, intRow * 4 + 1, 1) = _
    Chr$(Asc(Mid$(strPixelEntry, intRow * 4 + 1, 1)) _
    And (Not (2 ^ intColumn)))
```

This expression only affects bytes 1, 5, 9, 13, 17, 21, 25, and 29 of the 32-byte pixel entry string, because of the Mid$ statement on the left side of the equation. The right side of the equation uses bit masking to turn off every other bit within the selected byte as required by its row number. This creates a "checkerboard" pattern.

Making the Actual Brush

When this process is complete, the module will have everything needed to use CreateDIBitmap. Listing 6.13 creates the brush and then destroys it.

Listing 6.13 MAKBRUSH.BAS. Creating the actual brush.

```
Dim hDeviceDependentBitmap As Integer ' Handle for DDB brush _
    created from DIB data
hDeviceDependentBitmap = CreateDIBitmap(picBrush.hDC, _
    intBrushBitmapInfoParameter.bmiHeader, lngCBM_INIT, _
    strPixelEntry, _
    intBrushBitmapInfoParameter,intDIB_RGB_COLORS)
MakeBrush = CreatePatternBrush(hDeviceDependentBitmap)
intCleanUp = DeleteObject(hDependentBitmap)
' To save system resources, it is necessary to destroy
' brushes when we are finished with them.
```

This has been a lot of work, but you now have a brush-building procedure useful in many multimedia projects.

Creating an ROP Brush Demonstration

With these standard modules, the ROPs that employ brushes can be demonstrated. All that's required is to modify the form used earlier for the ROP demo. A PictureBox makes it possible to see what the brush pattern alone looks like, applied to an area. The list of ROPs loaded at run time gets larger, and the program will call the standard modules just discussed.

The files for the ROP Brush Demostration project are on the CD-ROM as BRDEM16.VBP and BRDEM16.FRM (16-bit versions) or BRDEM32.VBP and BRDEM32.FRM (32-bit), along with MAKBRUSH.BAS, TRANSDEC.BAS and the image files STAR1.BMP and RINGS2.BMP. The code for the 16-bit and 32-bit versions is almost exactly the same, so only the 16-bit version is shown in the text. The executable versions are on the CD-ROM as BRDEM16.EXE and BRDEM32.EXE. "BRDEM" in the following discussion refers to both versions.

The setup for the form is shown in Figure 6.9. Be sure, if you are setting your own up, that ScaleMode for the PictureBoxes is set to Pixel.

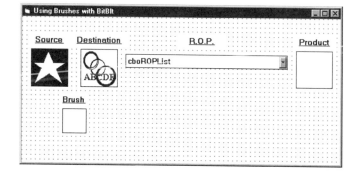

Fig. 6.9
The Brush demo uses this setup to illustrate the use of brushes with ROPs.

The events for the demonstration are a bit different from the ones used in ROPDEM.FRM. The list box in Form_Load is still set up, and the cboROPList_Click event still sets things in motion. The bitmaps get combined in picProduct_Paint, just as before, but now the new MakeBrush function is called in this event. A similar bit of code in the new picBrush_Paint event now makes the brush pattern visible to you in its own PictureBox.

Making the Event Procedures

Clicking an entry in the combo box calls the Product_Paint procedure, which is still where BitBlt and the ROPs will do their work.

```
Private Sub cboROPList_Click()
    picProduct_Paint
End Sub
```

The ROP list for the combo box loads with the form. This list now contains the four named ROPs that use brushes and 23 more that have no names but that also use brushes.

It might be hard to envision what a brush pattern actually looks like. The picBrush_Paint event uses another Blt function, PatBlt, to fill a small area with the brush pattern. The use of PatBlt is pretty straightforward and is shown in Listing 6.14. PatBlt specifies the area that is to be filled by the currently selected brush and specifies that PATCOPY will be the ROP used to do the job. Otherwise, this event looks much like the one that uses BitBlt to paint the Result PictureBox.

Listing 6.14 BRDEM.FRM. The *picBrush_Paint* event.

```
Private Sub picBrush_Paint()
'This procedure just shows you what the brush pattern looks like
'repeated over an area.
    Dim hBrush As Integer
    Dim hPreviousBrush As Integer
    Dim intShowBrush As Integer 'Placeholder used when _
        painting pattern into picBrush
    Dim intCleanUp As Integer 'Placeholder used when _
        deleting brush

    hBrush = MakeBrush()
    hPreviousBrush = SelectObject(picBrush.hDC, hBrush)
    intShowBrush = PatBlt(picBrush.hDC, 0, 0,
picBrush.ScaleWidth, picBrush.ScaleHeight, lngPATCOPY)

    intCleanUp = SelectObject(picBrush.hDC, hPreviousBrush)
    intCleanUp = DeleteObject(hBrush)

End Sub
```

The picProduct_Paint event is very similar to its earlier version in ROPDEM.FRM. However, it now calls the MakeBrush function, selects the newly created brush, and then destroys the brush after using it to paint the Product PictureBox.

Running BRDEM

Figure 6.10 shows how BRDEM looks when it's running. As before, you should notice that some of the ROPs in a series would create interesting effects and transitions, both over the entire screen and in small sections. You should experiment with changing the formulas in the MakeBrush function to see how many different patterns you can generate.

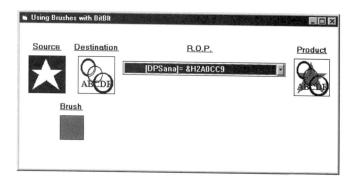

Fig. 6.10
This is the Brush demo in operation.

You probably will find that some of the patterns are useful, while many others are not. To carry out an effective fade transition, though, you can't use the mathematically generated brush patterns. You need a series of graduated, random-appearing brushes for the best results. In the next section, you'll learn how to do that and how to create those fades.

Planning the Fade Effect

The fade effect is one of the most widely used transitions in video and film, and is equally useful in multimedia. In a fade, the image gradually turns darker until it is totally black. Alternatively, an image may gradually appear out of a totally black screen. It is also possible to have a fade that goes to or from a white screen, or any other color.

In analog media (film and videotape), a fade is the result of manipulating the amount of light that falls on the light-sensitive surface being exposed in the camera. To fade to black, the camera iris is closed. To fade a picture in, the camera iris is opened. The metallic particles that capture the image appear randomly on the film or videotape. Each image or frame is actually slightly different from the ones before and after it. This causes the transition to appear "natural" to the eyes, rather than artificial or mechanical.

In digital media, a fade is the result of changing pixels on the viewing surface to black. The original bitmap image does not actually change. Because pixels are in a grid pattern on a monitor screen, rather than random, the programmer must work at making the transition appear natural.

For your fade effect, you want the capability to do three things: fade in, fade out, and fade from one image to the next. It is critical that the viewers perceive these transitions in the same way that they would perceive analogous transitions in film or video. In addition, the method chosen must allow for a range of transition speeds, from slow to fast.

Choosing Ways to Do Fades in Multimedia

There are two ways to produce a fade effect. One way is to use the palette animation method you learned in Chapter 5. To do a fade out with this method, each entry in the displayed image palette shifts in steps until all entries are pure black. However, this method has two drawbacks.

First, in actual practice, you cannot count on having access to an infinitely graduated range of colors. Windows will display the closest available color to the one specified for a palette entry, but in most cases you will not have enough shades in your series. In addition, you do not know what the user's equipment is going to be capable of displaying. Second, by shifting the entire palette or a substantial part of it, you may see some very strange effects on the colors of items in other windows.

The other way is to simply change pixels at random to black. This method does not change any palette entries, so it works around the problems encountered in the first method. However, it would be easy to end up with a transition that looks "fake," especially if the individual pixels turn on or off sequentially as the viewer looks at the image. On the whole, though, this is a better choice for most requirements, and it is the method used in this chapter.

Modifying Earlier Modules for the Fade Effect

You will find the program listings for the Fade Effect Project on the CD-ROM FADE16.VBP and FADE16.FRM, or FADE32.VBP and FADE32.FRM, along with FADEBRSH.BAS, MAKEFADE.BAS, and TRANSDEC.BAS. Most of these are modifications of modules created earlier in the chapter. However, one more file, RNDPIXEL.TXT, has been added, to hold instructions for turning on pixels in a brush bitmap at random.

While the code for the 16-bit and the 32-bit versions is largely the same, there are some differences caused by the fact that a 16-bit application cannot call functions from a 32-bit library, and vice versa. In the FADEBRSH,

MAKEFADE, and TRANSDEC modules, both the 16-bit and the 32-bit code is shown side-by-side, with the version not in use REMarked out. Only the 16-bit version is shown in the text that follows. Where necessary, REMarks in the source code explain the differences between the 16-bit and the 32-bit versions. "FADE" in the discussion refers to both versions.

The form setup for this project is shown in Figure 6.11. Just as in the Wipe demonstration, the PictureBoxes are stacked on top of each other, and the bottom one is invisible and has its AutoRedraw property set to True.

The .FRM module uses the Command_Click, Form_Load, and Timer_Timer events to call the three .BAS modules. The MAKEFADE.BAS module does the actual form painting, using a routine named FadeOne. Details of how this works are in the text. Executable versions of the code are on the CD-ROM as FADE16.EXE and as FADE32.EXE.

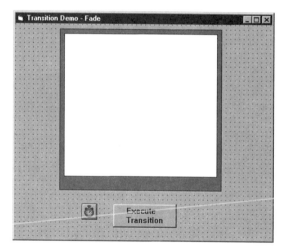

Fig. 6.11
The form for the fade is very similar to the Wipe demonstration.

This procedure builds on what you learned from the previous projects. Take, for example, the procedure used in the brush demonstration to combine bitmaps with a brush and paint the result into the picProduct box. In a fade, you need to produce a starting frame, an ending frame, and a series of frames in between. Each frame in the series will have just slightly more (or less) black pixels in it than the one before. The picProduct_Paint code will do this with a few changes, as you will see. Along the way, this code will turn into its own standard module, MAKEFADE.BAS.

MAKBRUSH.BAS did a good job of building a brush, but the pattern possibilities are limited as long as the module uses math functions to calculate the pixels to be blackened. If you experimented with the bit-masking equation, you probably were able to create some hollow squares, some stripes, a 25% gray dither, and some other nondescript (but boring) patterns. If you could tell the function directly which pixels to change to black, it would be much better. A change to MAKBRUSH.BAS will make this possible, turning the module into FADEBRSH.BAS.

The basic layout for the wipe demonstration is satisfactory for the purpose at hand, but with so much of the code now residing in standard modules, it will be necessary to rewrite the event procedures. The Form module now serves mainly to route the program flow to and between the various modules. The Timer event, however, still creates the animation effect by repeatedly causing the next fade frame to be created and displayed.

Creating the Fade Effect Demonstration

The Form_Load event does two things. So that the viewer won't see an empty PictureBox while waiting for the demo to start, the program loads an image. In addition, the event also calls a procedure that will give a random pattern to the bits in the brush used for creating the fade. You'll see more of RandomizeBrushPixels in the section "Creating Random Brushes."

```
Private Sub Form_Load()
    picProduct.Picture = LoadPicture("\vb\china1.bmp")
    RandomizeBrushPixels
End Sub
```

As in the Wipe demo, a command button will set things in motion. In this version, though, cmdFadeButton_Click has a little more work to do. Listing 6.15 shows the new version. It will track progress in the fade, determine whether it's a fade-in or a fade-out, and make sure the fade sequence begins and ends with the right image in the right condition. The main mechanism for doing this is the static variable intDirection. It is static so that it can establish a count that cues the change of pictures.

Listing 6.15 FADE.FRM. The *cmdFadeButton_Click* event.

```
Private Sub cmdFadeButton_Click()
    Static intDirection As Integer    'Fading in or out?
                                      'See MAKEFADE.BAS

    Dim intWay As Integer             'Establishes way to
                                      'start & finish fade

    intFadeFrameNumber = 0            'Tracks where we are
```

```
                                        'in this fade
        intDirection = intDirection + 1
        intWay = intDirection Mod 2
```

When the variable `intWay` is 1, the image is fading out. If 0, it is fading in. This is set by `intDirection`, which is 1 at the start of each round. This unusual `Mod 4` operation matches the switch between images to the way the command button works.

```
    If (intDirection Mod 4) < 2 Then
        picSource.Picture = LoadPicture("\vb\china1.bmp")
        Else picSource.Picture = LoadPicture("\vb\china2.bmp")
    End If
```

The button requires two clicks for each picture after the first one: once to fade in, once to fade out. Listing 6.16 shows how `intWay` determines the fade out sequence.

Listing 6.16   FADE.FRM. Causing the image to fade-out.

```
        If intWay <> 0 Then

            intFirstPic = BitBlt(picProduct.hDC, 0, 0, _
                picProduct.ScaleWidth, picProduct.ScaleHeight, _
                picSource.hDC, 0, 0, lngSRCCOPY)
            lngROP = lngMERGECOPY
            lngFinish = lngBLACKNESS
```

When fading out, the program starts by displaying the image without any brush being applied. `MERGECOPY` is the ROP of choice, and the fade out will close with a black screen. When all is ready, the fade timer is started.

When fading in, the series starts with a black screen, uses the `SPna` raster operation, and ends with a display of the unbrushed image (see Listing 6.17).

Listing 6.17   FADE.FRM. Causing the image to fade-in.

```
    Else intFirstPic = BitBlt(picProduct.hDC, 0, 0,
    picProduct.ScaleWidth, picProduct.ScaleHeight,
    picSource.hDC, 0, 0, lngBLACKNESS)
      lngROP = lngSOURCEnotPATadd
            lngFinish = lngSRCCOPY
          End If
        tmrFadeTimer.Enabled = True
```

II

The Graphics Interface

Several variables do all the tracking. Two (lngROP and lngFinish) come from the TRANSDEC.BAS module, along with the constants for the raster operations. The others appear within the Form module.

Obviously, you can improve this code snippet when you use it in your own programs. A procedure that ques up bitmap files from a slide list can replace the two lines that load either CHINA1.BMP or CHINA2.BMP. The other If...Then loop identifies MERGECOPY as the ROP of choice for fade-outs, ending in BLACKNESS. SOURCEnotPATadd (one of the "nameless" ROPs that has been given a distinctive moniker for this demonstration) creates fade-ins, with a finishing SRCCOPY.

Take a closer look at what is happening in this simple event procedure and you'll see why you want to spend some time getting to know the ROP codes. One way to handle two kinds of fade would be to use the same set of brush bitmaps in forward sequence when fading out and in reverse sequence when fading in. This would mean having a loop counter somewhere that knows how and when to count backwards. This is the kind of thing that can make you crazy when you write your program, and make you crazy again when you try to debug it.

Instead, you are using MERGECOPY for fading out, and an unnamed ROP for fading in. As it happens, the unnamed operation selected is the inverse of MERGECOPY. By using it, the same bitmaps appear in the same order, but the "negative" version does the fading in. This way the loop counter only has to count forward, the way counters should enumerate.

The Interval property for the timer control is a critical factor in the appearance of the effect. You may want to change the setting at run time, to allow some images to pass by very quickly and others to stay on the screen longer. The tmrFadeTimer_Timer event is responsible for keeping track of the current frame number in the fade-in progress and calls the function that paints the current frame into the visible PictureBox. This function is now called by a new name, FadeOne.

```
Private Sub tmrFadeTimer_Timer()
    intFadeFrameNumber = intFadeFrameNumber + 1
    FadeOne
End Sub
```

Animating the Fade: The *FadeOne()* Function

In order to animate the fade transition, you need to be able to create a frame and show it, then replace it with the next (slightly different) frame a fraction of a second later. Listing 6.18 shows how this will be done. The Paint event procedure in the brush demonstration does a good job of creating single frames. It simply has been lifted out of the `Paint` event, given the name `FadeOne()`, and made into MAKEFADE.BAS, a standard module.

Listing 6.18 MAKEFADE.BAS. Defining the function *FadeOne()*.

```
Public intFadeFrameNumber As Integer

Function FadeOne()
    Dim picProduct As Object ' Adjust the declarations
    Set picProduct = frmFadeDemo.picProduct ' of the _
        product, source
    Dim picSource As Object ' and timer objects to
    Set picSource = frmFadeDemo.picSource  ' match _
        the requirements
    Dim tmrFadeTimer As Object ' of your project.
    Set tmrFadeTimer = frmFadeDemo.tmrFadeTimer
    Dim hMakeFadeBrush As Integer
    Dim hPreviousBrush As Integer
    Dim intCombination As Integer  ' Placeholder
    Dim intCleanUp As Integer      ' Placeholder

    Static intDirection  ' Tracks fade in or out.
                         ' Same name used in .FRM module:
                         ' caution when revising.
```

The declarations at the beginning are the largest change in this transformation. In order to refer to the objects on the form, you must declare the names by which they will be called in this module. Then you set the new name equal to the object.

In its former version, the procedure had `BitBlt` call an ROP selected from a list by the user. Listing 6.19 shows how, in this version, `BitBlt` calls `lngROP`, a placeholder for the name of the ROP that will cause either a fade-in or a fade-out. You saw in the `Form` events how this ROP was determined.

Listing 6.19 MAKEFADE.BAS. Switching fade directions.

```
hMakeFadeBrush = MakeFadeBrush(intFadeFrameNumber)
    hPreviousBrush = SelectObject(picProduct.hDC, _
        hMakeFadeBrush)

    intCombination = BitBlt(picProduct.hDC, 0, 0, _
        picProduct.ScaleWidth, picProduct.ScaleHeight, _
        picSource.hDC, 0, 0, lngROP)

    intCleanUp = SelectObject(picProduct.hDC, _
        hPreviousBrush)
    intCleanUp = DeleteObject(hMakeFadeBrush)
```

Finally, FadeOne decides whether the fade has been completed. Listing 6.20 gives the details. If the fade is done, FadeOne inserts either a black slide or a copy of the image that has just been faded in. This makes a satisfying conclusion and hides any little glitches that may have crept in during the animation sequence.

Listing 6.20 MAKEFADE.BAS. *FadeOne* puts on the finishing touches.

```
    If intFadeFrameNumber = intNumberOfFrames Then
        tmrFadeTimer.Enabled = False
        intCombination = BitBlt(picProduct.hDC, 0, 0, _
            picProduct.ScaleWidth, picProduct.ScaleHeight, _
            picSource.hDC, 0, 0, lngFinish) 'to end fade
        intDirection = intDirection + 1
    End If

End Function
```

Creating Random Brushes: The *MakeFadeBrush()* and *RandomizeBrushPixels()* Functions

In the Brush demo, you saw how to use math and bit-masking to produce an evenly patterned brush bitmap. For a fade, you need a series of bitmaps (one per frame of the fade sequence), starting with only a few black pixels and ending with all black pixels. This is difficult if not impossible to do with a formula.

To create such a graduated series of bitmaps, you can either use random selection or hand-draw each and every bitmap that you are likely to need. The latter approach seems like too much work, so go with the first. However, to speed things up, this program will use a file generated by Visual Basic's RND function, containing a list made up of the numbers 1 through 64, in random order, with no repeated numbers. This list is in the file RNDPIXEL.TXT on the CD-ROM.

You can use the same technique to generate as many randomized lists as you want. Each list will produce a slightly different visual effect in a fade. Fortunately, these patterns do not seem to be so regular as to be distracting to the viewer. None of them, unfortunately, will produce a brush that when repeated over the entire display will give a totally random-appearing result. A repeating pattern of some kind will always be visible. This will be true even if you carefully work out all the dot positions for each brush by using a piece of graph paper. Each little eight-by-eight brush may be totally random, but it will populate the display with identical rubber-stamp images.

Listing 6.21 shows how the function RandomizeBrushPixels in FADEBRSH.BAS reads the number of entries required for each screen in the series and stores them in an array called intRandomPixels().

Listing 6.21 FADEBRSH.BAS. The *RandomizeBrushPixels* function.

```
Function RandomizeBrushPixels()
    Dim intRepeat As Integer
' Counter for loops
    Dim strRndPixelPosition As String * 3
' Tracks pixel entries

    Open "RNDPIXEL.TXT" For Input As #intRandomPixelFile
' Plain ASCII text
    For intRepeat = 1 To 64
        Input #intRandomPixelFile, strRndPixelPosition
        intRandomPixels(intRepeat) = Val(strRndPixelPosition)
        Next intRepeat

End Function
```

This array data is in MakeFadeBrush(), which is a very slightly modified version of the MakeBrush() function you saw in the Brush demo. Apart from a couple of name changes, the only thing new is in the routine that selects the pixels to set to 0. Formerly, this routine chose every other pixel. Now it only pulls out the ones identified in the currently selected element of intRandomPixels.

Listing 6.22 shows how the pixels to be set are changed. If there are to be eight steps in the fade (not counting the start and finish screens), the first fade bitmap will need to have eight random pixels set to black. So the first element of intRandomPixels will contain eight unique, random, non-repeating numbers between 1 and 64. The second element will contain 16 numbers (including the eight from the first element), and so on.

Listing 6.22 FADEBRSH.BAS. Stepping through the fade sequence.

```
For intRepeat = 1 To intFadeFrameNumber *
(64 / intNumberOfFrames)
        intRow = (intRandomPixels(intRepeat) - 1) \ 8 ' Integer _
            division; returns only the whole number
        intColumn = (intRandomPixels(intRepeat) - 1) Mod 8 _
            ' Modulus arithmetic: returns only remainder
```

II

The Graphics Interface

The global constant `intNumberOfFrames` is an important one, by the way. It appears in TRANSDEC.BAS. If you want to make your fade longer or shorter, change the value of `intNumberOfFrames` appropriately. You can adjust the timer interval as well to get the effect you want.

Running the Fade Demo

When you run the demonstration, the first image appears in the PictureBox immediately. Figures 6.12 and 6.13 show two frames from this sequence.

Fig. 6.12

This is how the fade effect begins...

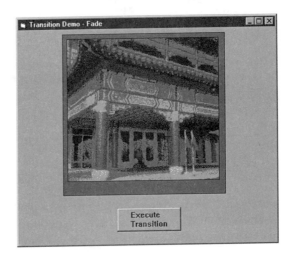

When you click the command button, this image fades out to solid black. At the next click of the button, a new image fades in. This cycle repeats as long as you like.

Fig. 6.13

This is how the fade effect progresses...

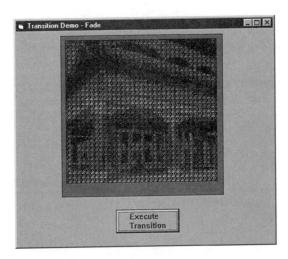

As usual, improvements are possible in this demonstration. It is certainly possible to set up the event procedures so that the images simply fade from one into the next, without requiring a button click. Likewise, you will want to modify the `Form_Load` and `cmdFadeButton_Click` events to continuously load and display a long series of images. This is another place where you can use an external text file—to hold the play list of images.

An interesting experiment you might want to try involves combining two images and a graduated brush series. You only need to add a second invisible PictureBox to the stack and make a careful choice from the list of raster operations available. How many ways can you find to simultaneously fade out one image while fading in another? The model for the `BitBlt` function needed is in the demo.

Finally, you may wish to consider loading your source bitmaps into memory. This can improve the speed of your transitions in some cases. The techniques are beyond the scope of this chapter, but are well worth investigation.

Creating Other Transition Effects

After completing the projects presented during this chapter and the one before it, you have all the tools you need to perform eight of the nine transitions in Table 6.1. The only one that requires a custom control is the Spin transition. Take a look at the list again, if you don't believe it.

The easy two, of course, are the cut and the pop on/off. If you are going to do something simple, such as putting a single full-window image up quickly, you can simply turn the `Visible` property of a PictureBox from `False` to `True`. A slide is also easy, using the `Move` method. And, of course, you have already seen how to use `PaintPicture` to produce the flip effect.

If you want to pop up or remove small images, you have the `BitBlt` and `SRCCOPY` tools at your command. These two tools are also useful for cutting from one full-window image to another. Pull down/pull up elements are nearly as easy, using the same techniques applied in the wipe effect or the slide.

You can add another PictureBox to the Fade demo, choose an appropriate raster operation, and create dissolves. You may need to make some adjustments to the palette when you do this, but the skills from Chapter 5 will show you the way.

From Here...

What you've gained here is the basic set of tools to use in creating transitions. The only limit to the effects that are possible is your imagination!

■ For more information on palette effects, check out Chapter 5, "Graphics and Palettes."

■ To learn about the use of "hot spots" in images (an idea with wide applications in multimedia), see Chapter 7, "Hypertext and Hot Spots."

■ For more information about animation techniques, see Chapter 10, "Animation."

Chapter 7

Hypertext and Hot Spots

Anyone who has used Windows for more than one hour has run into Microsoft's sophisticated Help system. This system enables the user not only to find specific topics quickly, but also to jump from topic to topic by clicking on underlined key words. The Windows Help system is an example of a *hypertext application*, which has become quite the rage in these days of multimedia. A hypertext application enables you to search through information just about any way you want, either by reading topics in order, or by jumping almost instantly from one topic to another related topic located anywhere within the hypertext document.

Although Visual Basic provides no direct support for this type of programming, you can still build a hypertext system of your own. And you can do it all within Visual Basic, without ever having to call any Windows APIs directly. As you may have guessed, building hypertext applications is the subject of this chapter. Before you're done here, you learn to:

- Design a hypertext language and document

- Display a hypertext document on-screen

- Link on-screen words to related topics

- Link graphical "hot spots" to other parts of a document

- Change the mouse pointer as it passes over different areas of a window

Understanding Hypertext Applications

As you may have gathered from this chapter's introduction, a hypertext application is a program that enables users to access information in just about any way they want. A hypertext application accomplishes this feat by providing *hyperlinks*, which are active areas in the document that lead to different topics. Hyperlinks come in two basic forms: *link words* and *hot spots*. A link word or phrase is underlined (or highlighted) text within the document. A hot spot is an active area in a picture or in text. Both types of links, when clicked with the user's mouse, lead to information related to the link.

For example, suppose you're reading a hypertext novel on your computer screen. In the first scene, Bob Nelson and Lori Anderson are on their first date, sitting in a fancy French restaurant. On your screen, you see the text for the current chapter. As you read, you see that some of the words in the text are underlined, like this:

> "This place is really something," <u>Lori</u> said, eyeing the prices on the <u>menu</u>. "I just wish I were hungrier." As she spoke, her stomach growled. She hoped that <u>Bob</u> couldn't hear it. The truth was that Lori was starving, but she knew that Bob couldn't afford the prices in this place. She would eat light this evening and then grab a real supper when she got <u>home</u>.

The underlined words are hyperlinks that lead to more in-depth information about the characters, places, and objects in the scene. If you clicked on the underlined word "Lori," for example, you might see a screen that includes a photo of Lori, as well as a short biography. Clicking the novel's Back button, would return you to the starting paragraph, where you can click on the underlined word "Bob." (In a hypertext application, a Back button returns you to the previously viewed screen.) Now, a screen that displays Bob's photo and biography might appear. Back at the main paragraph again, you could try clicking on the underlined word "menu." This time, you might see a full screen, graphic image of the menu, which lists all the dishes in French along with their prices. Ouch! No wonder Lori plans to eat light. Of course, because you read Bob's biography, you know that he just got a promotion and a raise. He really *can* afford the prices on the menu, although Lori doesn't know it yet.

Want to know a little more about the dishes on the menu? You might try clicking on a hot spot in the menu, bringing up a photo of the selected dish, along with a description. (Mmmmmm! Look at that cheesecake!) Two clicks of the Back button return you to the original paragraph, where you can continue with the story. Figure 7.1 shows the jumps you made as you read the paragraph from the novel.

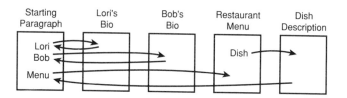

Fig. 7.1
Reading a hypertext novel often means jumping from one topic to another.

As you can see, hypertext documents provide exciting ways to present information. As you read the paragraph from the novel, you choose what information you want to know. If you want to, you can read the chapter straight through, without ever taking any of the offered "side trips." Then, you will find out about Bob's promotion at the same time Lori did. The choices you make as you read a hypertext novel can change the story significantly. Similarly, other types of hypertext documents—including software documentation, multimedia encyclopedias, help files, and more—all provide ways for users to control their viewing experience.

Using the Sample Hypertext Application

This chapter presents a program called HYPERTXT, which is an example hypertext application that can display not only topic text, but also control buttons, images with hot spots, and, of course, links to other topics in the currently loaded document. The application's instructions are included in a file called HYPERTXT.HYP, which is a hypertext document that the application can display. You can find the HYPERTXT application on this book's CD-ROM.

When you run the application, you see a window with a File menu and three buttons across the top. Choose File, Open to load the file named HYPERTXT.HYP. When you do, the first topic of the hypertext document appears. This first page is a table of contents from which you can click on a topic you want to read. You can also use the first two buttons at the top of the window to move forward or back through the topics in the document. The Back button always takes you back to the previously viewed screen.

II

The Graphics Interface

As you see, whenever the mouse pointer is over a text link or a hot spot, the mouse pointer changes from the regular arrow to an upwards-pointing arrow. This is how you know that you're pointing to a link that, when clicked, will take you to a new topic. When you're finished experimenting with the program, choose File, Exit.

In the sections that follow, you see not only how to create the HYPERTXT application, but also how to define a hypertext language and create a document using the language.

Creating a Hypertext Document

Obviously, the text that makes up a hypertext document is not the normal type of text you're used to reading. In fact, the actual text of a hypertext document is not meant for human eyes. This is because the text contains many special commands that tell the hypertext application how to display the information in the file.

For example, you know that clicking on a link word causes the hypertext application to display information related to that link word. But how does the hypertext application know where to find the information to display? How, in fact, does the application even know which are link words and which are regular words?

In this section, you'll get the answer to these questions, as you develop a simple hypertext language that you can use as the basis for your own hypertext documents.

Designing a Hypertext Document

The first step in defining a language for a hypertext document is to decide what type of information the hypertext document will contain. Most hypertext documents organize their contents into *topics*, which are short pages of text that describe a specific term or concept. Each topic is made up of several parts. Usually, a topic starts with a topic title, which briefly describes what the topic is about. For example, a topic that explains how to load a file might have the title "Loading a File."

The topic title is followed by the topic's actual text. In the case of "Loading a File," the topic text would be the paragraphs that tell the user how to accomplish that task. Often, within the topic text are link words or phrases that the user can click with the mouse to get more information about a specific subject. In the "Loading a File" topic text, for example, the word "file" might be highlighted, indicating that the user can click the word to learn more about what a file actually is.

A topic might also contain pictures that provide additional information to the user or just help make the topic page more attractive. In the "Loading a File" topic, it might be a good idea to have a picture of the application's File menu, showing the Open command selected.

The pictures in a topic might also contain hot spots, which are "live" areas that the user can click for more information. For example, in the File menu picture, there might be hot spots defined for each of the pictured commands in the menu. If the user clicks one of these hot spots, detailed information about the selected command appears on-screen.

So, to describe the hypertext language in which you'll be writing your hypertext document, you need to define the following items:

- Topic title

- Topic text

- Link words or phrases

- Image reference

- Hot spots

Of course, as you can tell from this short list, you'll be defining a very simple language for your first hypertext application. Moreover, for the sake of simplicity and clarity, you'll strictly limit how the items in the list can be used. Keep in mind that this hypertext language is only a starting point. When you finish this chapter, and are comfortable with the concepts presented here, you can modify the hypertext language in order to create more sophisticated hypertext documents.

Now that you know what types of information (items) your hypertext will contain, you need to define how that information must be organized within the document. Although most hypertext languages offer greater flexibility, the hypertext language you develop here will have a strict format. The first rules for your hypertext language, then, are as follows:

Rule #1   A hypertext document is made up of one or more topics.

Rule #2   A topic is a topic title followed by an image reference, a hot-spot list defining up to 20 hot spots, and the topic text.

In the sections that follow, you define the commands and rules that describe topic titles, image references, hot spots, and link words or phrases.

Defining the Topic Title

Because the topic title is usually displayed at the very top of a topic page, you define it first. You need some way to tell the hypertext application that the words it is currently loading from the hypertext document are a topic title, rather than just plain text. This means you must find a way to uniquely identify the topic title. In your basic hypertext language, you use the command \TITLE^ to notify the hypertext application that it's about to load a topic title. The command is followed by the text of the topic title and an ending caret, like this:

```
\TITLE^This is the Topic Title^
```

Now, as the hypertext application reads the hypertext document from a file, it can look for the \TITLE^ command, which tells the application not only that it's about to read in a topic title, but also that a new topic is about to begin. In Visual Basic, such code might look like this:

```
Open FileName For Input As #InputFileNum
While Not EOF(InputFileNum)
    Line Input #InputFileNum, Text
    If Left$(Text, 7) = "\TITLE^" Then FoundNewTopic
Wend
```

You can now write the rule that describes how to define a topic title:

Rule #3   A topic title is defined with the command \TITLE^Topic Title^, where Topic Title is the text of the topic title.

Defining an Image Reference

According to the rules you've defined so far, the item that must appear after the topic title in your hypertext document is an image reference. Because you may not want to have an image on every topic page, you need two forms of this command, one that indicates an image and one that indicates no image is to appear. The image command, then, is \IMAGE^ followed by the image's filename or the word NONE, and an ending caret. For example, the command:

```
\IMAGE^EAGLE.BMP^
```

displays the EAGLE.BMP image after the topic title, whereas the command:

```
\IMAGE^NONE^
```

displays no image after the topic title.

You must store files that contain your images in the same directory as the hypertext document. Otherwise, the application will not be able to find and display them.

Now, after the hypertext application reads a topic title from a file, it should look for the \IMAGE^ command, which tells the application which image (if any) to display after topic title. Listing 7.1 shows how the code might look in Visual Basic.

Listing 7.1   LIST7_1.BAS. Processing the *IMAGE* command.

```
Line Input #InputFileNum, Text
If Text = "\IMAGE^NONE^" Then
    Image1.Visible = False
Else
    Image = Mid$(Text, 8, Len(Text) - 8)
    Image1.Picture = LoadPicture(Image)
End If
```

You can now write the rule that describes how to define an image reference:

Rule #4   A image reference is defined with the command \IMAGE^ImageName^, where ImageName is the image's filename or the word NONE, which indicates that no image should be displayed in the topic.

Defining Hot Spots

Every image can have up to 20 hot spots defined for it. However, you may also have an image with no defined hot spots. Because an image can have a variable number of hot spots, you need a way not only to define a hot spot, but also to indicate the end of the hot-spot list. The hot-spot command is \HOTSPOT^ followed by the hot spot's definition or the word END to indicate the end of the hot-spot list. How can you define a hot spot? How about listing the coordinates of the hot spot's upper-left and lower-right corners (see Fig. 7.2) followed by the topic title to which the hot spot links? For example, the command:

```
\HOTSPOT^10 10 100 100 Topic Title^
```

indicates that the image has a hot spot whose upper-left corner is at coordinates 10,10 within the image and whose lower-right corner is at coordinates 100,100.

Fig. 7.2

Defining hot spot corners for the Open command in an image of a File menu.

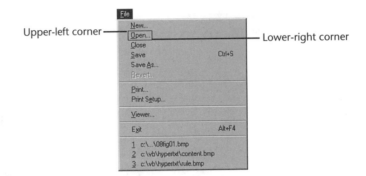

Upper-left corner

Lower-right corner

The command also indicates that if the user clicks on the hot spot, the hypertext application displays the topic titled "Topic Title." The command:

```
\HOTSPOT^END^
```

indicates the end of the hot-spot list. To define an image with hot spots, use a sequence of commands as shown in Listing 7.2.

Listing 7.2   LIST7_2.BAS. Defining images and hot spots in a hypertext document.

```
\IMAGE^CONTENT.BMP^
\HOTSPOT^10 10 1440 525 The HYPERTXT Application^
\HOTSPOT^1460 10 2925 525 Using HYPERTXT^
\HOTSPOT^2945 10 4425 525 Creating HYPERTXT Files^
\HOTSPOT^4445 10 5940 525 Glossary^
\HOTSPOT^END^
```

To define an image with no hot spots, you would use a sequence of commands like this:

```
\IMAGE^CONTENT.BMP^
\HOTSPOT^END^
```

Now, after the hypertext application reads an image reference (other than NONE) from a file, it should look for a series of \HOTSPOT^ commands. In Visual Basic, the code might look like Listing 7.3.

Listing 7.3   LIST7_3.BAS. Processing *IMAGE* commands containing *HOTSPOT* commands.

```
Line Input #InputFileNum, Text
If Text = "\IMAGE^NONE^" Then
    Image1.Visible = False
```

```
    Else
        Image = Mid$(Text, 8, Len(Text) - 8)
        Image1.Picture = LoadPicture(Image)
        Image1.Visible = True
        Line Input #InputFileNum, Text
        While Text <> "\HOTSPOT^END^"
            RecordHotSpot Text
            Line Input #InputFileNum, Text
        Wend
    End If
```

You can now write the rules that describe how to define hot spots:

Rule #5   A hot spot is defined with the command `\HOTSPOT^HotSpotDef^`, where `HotSpotDef` is the hot spot's coordinates and link, or the word `END`, which indicates the end of the hot-spot list.

Rule #6   A hot spot's coordinates and link are defined as the coordinates of the upper-left corner, the coordinates of the lower-right corner, and the topic title to which the link connects, each separated by spaces.

Defining Topic Text

The topic text always starts after the image reference (and any hot spots that might be defined for the image) and runs until the next topic title. For that reason, you really don't need a special command to indicate topic text. Just type it as normal text. However, you need a way to separate paragraphs in the topic text. To do that, just add a blank line between paragraphs. You should also keep in mind that topic text can contain link words or phrases, which you also have to define. You can now write the rule for topic text:

Rule #7   Topic text is normal ASCII text with each paragraph separated by a blank line. Topic text can contain link words or phrases.

Defining Link Words and Phrases

The most important part of a hypertext document—the part that makes a normal document hypertext—is the hyperlinks contained in the document. You've already defined hot spots, which are one type of hyperlink. The most common hyperlinks in a hypertext document, however, are link words or phrases. As you now know, these are words that are underlined or highlighted. When the user clicks on a link word, the related topic appears on-screen.

The tricky thing about link words is that they are embedded within the normal topic text. This means that the hypertext application must display the topic text word by word, always watching out for link words. As with the other hypertext items, you need a command that identifies link words. The command \LINK^, followed by the link word, a caret, the topic title to which you want to link, and an ending caret will do the trick. For example, the command

```
\LINK^Link Word^Link Topic^
```

embeds the link words Link Word within the document and links that phrase to the topic titled "Link Topic."

Now, as the hypertext application reads each word of the topic text, it watches for the \LINK^ command. When the hypertext application finds a link, it must display the link word as underlined text, as well as record the topic to which the link is associated. In Visual Basic, the code might look like Listing 7.4.

Listing 7.4   LIST7_4.BAS. Processing topic text and handling *LINK* commands.

```
Line Input #InputFileNum, Text
Do While Left$(Text, 7) <> "\TITLE^" And Not EOF(InputFileNum)
    Do Until Text = ""
        Word = GetNextWord(Text)
        If Left$(Word, 6) = "\LINK^" Then
            CreateLink Word
            Form1.FontUnderline = True
        Else
            Form1.FontUnderline = False
        End If

        Form1.Print Word; " ";
    Loop

    Line Input #InputFileNum, Text
Loop
```

You can now write the rule that describes how to define link words:

Rule #8   A link word or phrase is defined with the command \LINK^LinkWords^LinkTopic^, where LinkWords is the link text that will appear underlined in the document and LinkTopic is the topic title with which the link is associated.

Listing 7.5 is the hypertext document that you'll use as you continue on to create a simple hypertext application. In the listing, you can see first hand how to use the commands you've just defined.

Listing 7.5   HYPERTXT.HYP. A sample hypertext document.

```
\TITLE^Table of Contents^
\IMAGE^CONTENT.BMP^
\HOTSPOT^10 10 1440 525 The HYPERTXT Application^
\HOTSPOT^1460 10 2925 525 Using HYPERTXT^
\HOTSPOT^2945 10 4425 525 Creating HYPERTXT Files^
\HOTSPOT^4445 10 5940 525 Glossary^
\HOTSPOT^END^
1. \LINK^Description of the HYPERTXT application^The
HYPERTXT Application^

2. \LINK^How to use HYPERTXT^Using HYPERTXT^

3. \LINK^How to create files for HYPERTXT^Creating
HYPERTXT Files^

4. \LINK^Glossary of Terms^Glossary^

\TITLE^The HYPERTXT Application^
\IMAGE^NONE^
The HYPERTXT application is a sample
\LINK^hypertext^Hypertext^ program that shows how such
applications as the Windows Help system work.  The
application displays specially formatted text files that you
create.  These text files contain
\LINK^hyperlinks^Hyperlinks^ that enable the user to jump
to other topics in the text file.  To display other topics, the
HYPERTXT application watches for mouse clicks on topic
links.  When it senses such a mouse click, the application
finds, loads, and displays the text that's associated with the
topic link.

\TITLE^Using HYPERTXT^
\IMAGE^NONE^
When HYPERTXT starts, it displays an empty window with a
menu bar and three buttons.  To use the application, you must
first load a HYPERTXT text file.  To do this, select the File
menu's Open command.  When you do, the Open dialog box
appears from which you can select the file you want to load.
After selecting the file to load, the first topic in the file
appears on the screen.

What you actually see on the screen when the first topic loads
depends on the actual file.  Usually, the topic will contain a
number of underlined words or phrases, called
\LINK^hyperlinks^Hyperlinks^, that you can click to see
```

(continues)

The Graphics Interface

Listing 7.5 Continued

other portions of the document. You can also advance step-by-step through the document by clicking the forward browse button, which is marked by the forward arrows (>>>). To browse backwards step-by-step through the topics, click the backward browse button, which is marked by backward arrows (<<<).

HYPERTXT keeps track of the topics you've previously viewed, whether you've jumped to those topics with hyperlinks or viewed those topics using the browse buttons. To move back through these topics in the reverse order in which you viewed them, click the Back button.

To exit the HYPERTXT application, select the File menu's Exit command.

\TITLE^Creating HYPERTXT Files^
\IMAGE^NONE^
HYPERTXT files are plain ASCII text files that contain a number of special symbols that tell the HYPERTXT application how to display the file's contents. These special symbols indicate \LINK^topic^Topics^ titles, \LINK^images^Images^, and \LINK^hyperlinks^Hyperlinks^ within the document. Click a topic below:

\LINK^Creating a Topic Title^Creating a Topic Title^

\LINK^Creating a Topic Image^Creating a Topic Image^

\LINK^Creating Hot Spots^Creating Hot Spots^

\LINK^Creating Topic Text^Creating Topic Text^

\LINK^Creating Link Words or Phrases^Creating Link Words or Phrases^

\TITLE^Creating a Topic Title^
\IMAGE^NONE^
To start a new topic, use the \TITLE^ command, followed by the title text and an ending caret, as shown in the example below:

Example:\TITLE^This is a Title^

\TITLE^Creating a Topic Image^
\IMAGE^NONE^
The topic's image follows the topic title. To define the image, use the \IMAGE^ command, followed by the image's file name or the word NONE, and an ending caret, like this:

Example:\IMAGE^IMAGE.BMP^

Example:\IMAGE^NONE^

```
\TITLE^Creating Hot Spots^
\IMAGE^NONE^
```

Each topic image can have up to 20 hot spots. To create a hot spot, use the \HOTSPOT^ command, followed by the hot spot's upper left corner coordinates, lower right corner coordinates, the topic title to which the hot spot is linked, and an ending caret.

```
Example:\HOTSPOT^10 10 500 500 Topic Title^
```

To end a hot-spot list, use the \HOTSPOT^END^ command. Below, is an example that defines an image and four hot spots:

```
\IMAGE^CONTENT.BMP^

\HOTSPOT^10 10 1440 525 The HYPERTXT
Application^

\HOTSPOT^1460 10 2925 525 Using HYPERTXT^

\HOTSPOT^2945 10 4425 525 Creating
HYPERTXT Files^

\HOTSPOT^4445 10 5940 525 Glossary^

\HOTSPOT^END^

\TITLE^Creating Topic Text^
\IMAGE^NONE^
```
The body text for a topic follows the topic image, with each paragraph separated by a blank line. Topic text can contain up to 20 link words or phrases.

```
\TITLE^Creating Link Words or Phrases^
\IMAGE^NONE^
```
To create a new link word or phrase, use the "\LINK^" command, followed by the link-word text, another caret, the title of the topic to which to link, and an ending caret, as shown in the example below:

```
Example:\LINK^Link Word^Link Topic^

\TITLE^Glossary^
\IMAGE^RULE.BMP^
\HOTSPOT^END^
```
Click on a term to get its definition.

```
\LINK^Hot Spot^Hot Spots^

\LINK^Hyperlink^Hyperlinks^

\LINK^Hypertext^Hypertext^
```

(continues)

The Graphics Interface

II

Listing 7.5 Continued

```
\LINK^Image^Images^

\LINK^Topic^Topics^

\TITLE^Hot Spots^
\IMAGE^NONE^
Hot spots are hyperlinks that are part of a graphical image
displayed in a hypertext document.  For example, a hypertext
document may display an icon depicting a pair of scissors.
Clicking on the icon may cause the hypertext application to
display information about cutting text from a word-processor
document.

\TITLE^Hyperlinks^
\IMAGE^NONE^
Hyperlinks are special areas in a hypertext document that,
when clicked by the user, cause the topic associated with the
hyperlink to be displayed on the screen.  Although a
hyperlink can take many forms, it's often displayed as an
underlined word or a graphical \LINK^hot spot^Hot Spots^ in
the hypertext document.

\TITLE^Hypertext^
\IMAGE^NONE^
Hypertext is a special type of text document that contains
words or graphical images, called
\LINK^hyperlinks^Hyperlinks^, that act as links to other
information in the document. When the user clicks on a
hyperlink, a new topic related to the link appears on the
screen.

\TITLE^Images^
\IMAGE^NONE^
Images are pictures that can be included in a hypertext
document.  An image can be a static illustration or can
contain \LINK^hot spots^Hot Spots^, which act as hyperlinks
to specific topics in the hypertext document.

\TITLE^Topics^
\IMAGE^NONE^
Topics are text screens made up of one or more paragraphs.
A topic usually focuses on a specific term or concept,
explaining that term or concept in as clear and brief a manner
as possible.  Because reading text on a computer screen can
be fatiguing, topics shouldn't be longer than one screen of text
and are usually much shorter.

One of the toughest tasks in creating a useable hypertext
system is creating and organizing the topics so that they are
easy for the user to read and so that the topics follow a logical
progression.
```

Constructing the HYPERTXT Application

Now that you know how to write a simple hypertext document, you need a program that can read and display that document. In this section, you'll build that application, as well as learn how it interprets the hypertext document shown in Listing 7.1 (or you can write your own hypertext document, if you want). The HYPERTXT application is fully 16-bit and 32-bit capable; just compile the application with the appropriate version of Visual Basic. A list of all the controls used for this application and their attributes is shown in Listing 7.6.

Listing 7.6   LIST7_6.BAS. Controls used for the HYPERTXT application.

```
VERSION 4.00
Begin VB.Form Form1
   AutoRedraw      =    -1   'True
   BackColor       =    &H00FFFFFF&
   Caption         =    "Form1"
   ClientHeight    =    5940
   ClientLeft      =    1140
   ClientTop       =    1800
   ClientWidth     =    6690
   BeginProperty Font
      name             =    "MS Sans Serif"
      charset          =    1
      weight           =    400
      size             =    12
      underline        =    0   'False
      italic           =    0   'False
      strikethrough    =    0   'False
   EndProperty
   Height          =    6630
   Left            =    1080
   LinkTopic       =    "Form1"
   ScaleHeight     =    5940
   ScaleWidth      =    6690
   Top             =    1170
   Width           =    6810
   Begin VB.CommandButton btnHistoryBack
      Caption          =    "Back"
      BeginProperty Font
         name              =    "MS Sans Serif"
         charset           =    1
         weight            =    400
         size              =    8.25
         underline         =    0    'False
```

(continues)

Listing 7.6 Continued

```
            italic             =    0    'False
            strikethrough      =    0    'False
         EndProperty
         Height                =   375
         Left                  =  2280
         TabIndex              =     2
         Top                   =   120
         Width                 =   975
      End
      Begin VB.CommandButton btnForward
         Caption               =    ">>>"
         BeginProperty Font
            name               =    "MS Sans Serif"
            charset            =    1
            weight             =    400
            size               =    8.25
            underline          =    0    'False
            italic             =    0    'False
            strikethrough      =    0    'False
         EndProperty
         Height                =   375
         Left                  =  1200
         TabIndex              =     1
         Top                   =   120
         Width                 =   975
      End
      Begin VB.CommandButton btnBackward
         Caption               =    "<<<"
         BeginProperty Font
            name               =    "MS Sans Serif"
            charset            =    1
            weight             =    400
            size               =    8.25
            underline          =    0    'False
            italic             =    0    'False
            strikethrough      =    0    'False
         EndProperty
         Height                =   375
         Left                  =   120
         TabIndex              =     0
         Top                   =   120
         Width                 =   975
      End
      Begin VB.Image Image1
         Height                =  1815
         Left                  =   100
         Top                   =   840
         Width                 =  1695
      End
      Begin MSComDlg.CommonDialog CommonDialog1
         Left                  =   240
         Top                   =  5160
         _version              = 65536
```

```
            _extentx        =    847
            _extenty        =    847
            _stockprops     =    0
            cancelerror     =    -1   'True
            dialogtitle     =    "Open"
            filename        =    "*.HYP"
            filter          =    "Hypertext Files (*.HYP)"
         End
      Begin VB.Menu mnuFile
         Caption         =    "&File"
         Begin VB.Menu mnuFileOpen
            Caption         =    "&Open..."
         End
         Begin VB.Menu separator
            Caption         =    "-"
         End
         Begin VB.Menu mnuFileExit
            Caption         =    "E&xit"
         End
      End
   End
End
Attribute VB_Name = "Form1"
Attribute VB_Creatable = False
Attribute VB_Exposed = False
```

As you can see in the listing, in addition to the main form, you need several command buttons, an image control, and a common dialog box. Figure 7.3 shows the form as you should construct it with Visual Basic. Notice that you must also create a File menu containing Open and Exit commands.

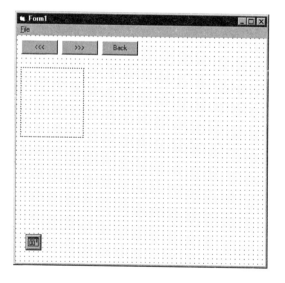

Fig. 7.3
The form for the HYPERTXT application contains a File menu, as well as several controls.

Keeping Track of Hyperlinks

Your hypertext document is going to contain a number of hyperlinks, both link words and hot spots, that the program must record and maintain. In order to know when the user has clicked on a link, the program must know the coordinates of that link. The program must also know the title of the topic to which the link leads. The easiest way to handle this data is to create a user-defined data type that holds the title topic as a string and the hot spot's coordinates as integers. This data type, called LinkType, is shown in Listing 7.7.

You can use LinkType to create arrays of this user-defined data type to hold the links. One array, Links, will be used to hold up to 20 text links, and the other array, HotSpots, will hold up to 20 hot-spot links. In order to manage these arrays, the program needs counters that store the current index into the arrays. These counters are called CurrentLink and CurrentHotSpot.

Other data items that you'll be using as you build the program are the string array History, which keeps track of which topics the user has viewed; CurrentHistory, which is used as an index into the History array; TopicCount, which holds the number of topics in the currently open hypertext document; CurrentTopicNum, which holds the number of the topic currently viewed by the user; and FileName, which contains the filename of the currently open hypertext document. As you explore the HYPERTXT application, you will see how these variables are used in the program. Listing 7.7 shows the general data declarations for HYPERTXT application.

Listing 7.7 LIST7_7.BAS. The general declarations for the HYPERTXT application.

```
Private Type LinkType
    Key As String
    LeftX As Integer
    TopY As Integer
    RightX As Integer
    BottomY As Integer
End Type

Dim Links(20) As LinkType
Dim HotSpots(20) As LinkType
Dim CurrentLink As Integer
Dim CurrentHotSpot As Integer
Dim History(100) As String
Dim CurrentHistory As Integer
Dim TopicCount As Integer
Dim CurrentTopicNum As Integer
Dim FileName As String
```

Opening a Hypertext Document

The first thing the user must do when he runs HYPERTXT is to load a
hypertext document. This is accomplished by clicking on the File menu's
Open command, and then choosing the file from the dialog box that appears
(see Fig. 7.4).

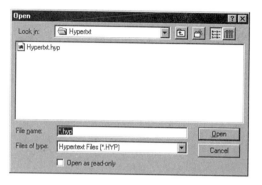

Fig. 7.4
The Open dialog
box enables you to
open a hypertext
document.

After the user selects a file, the program displays the file in the application's
window (see Fig. 7.5).

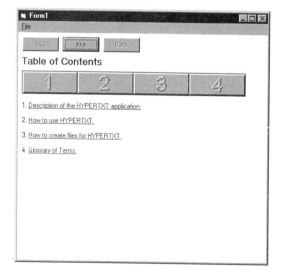

Fig. 7.5
A hypertext
document is
displayed in
HYPERTXT's
window.

The command procedure `mnuFileOpen_Click()` responds to the File menu's
Open command and handles the opening of a hypertext document. That
command procedure looks like Listing 7.8.

The Graphics Interface

Listing 7.8 LIST7_8.BAS. The *mnuFileOpen_Click( )* command procedure.

```
Private Sub mnuFileOpen_Click()
    Dim Text As String
    Dim Topic As String
    Dim InputFileNum As Integer

    On Error GoTo CancelError
    CommonDialog1.Action = 1
    CommonDialog1.Filter = "Hypertext Files (*.HYP)¦*.HYP"
    CommonDialog1.FilterIndex = 1
    FileName = CommonDialog1.FileName
    On Error GoTo FileError
    CountTopics
    InputFileNum = 1
    Open FileName For Input As #InputFileNum
    Line Input #InputFileNum, Text
    Form1.Cls
    Image1.Visible = False
    Topic = Mid$(Text, 8, Len(Text) - 8)
    PrintTopic Topic, InputFileNum
    AddToHistory Topic
    Close InputFileNum
    CurrentTopicNum = 1
    EnableButtons

CancelError:
    Exit Sub

FileError:
    MsgBox ("Cannot open selected file.")
End Sub
```

This procedure first displays the common Open dialog box, from which the user can select the hypertext file he wants to open. If the user clicks the dialog box's Cancel button, the CancelError error handler takes over, which simply ends the procedure. If the user clicks the OK button, he has selected a file. Just in case the selected file cannot be loaded properly, the FileError error handler is activated, after which the CountTopics() subroutine gets called. CountTopics(), which you see in the next section "Counting the Topics," simply counts the number of topics in the file.

Next, the mnuFileOpen_Click() procedure opens the selected file, reads in the first line of text in the file, clears the window, and makes the image control invisible. Using the Mid$() function, the program extracts the topic title from the text line and stores it in the Topic string. A call to the PrintTopic() subroutine displays the topic in the window, after which a call to the

AddToHistory() subroutine adds the first topic to the history list. (You'll read about the PrintTopic() and AddToHistory() procedures later in this chapter, in the sections "Displaying a Topic" and "Responding to the Back Button.") Finally, mnuFileOpen_Click() closes the input file, sets the current topic number to 1, and calls the EnableButtons() subroutine, which ensures that the button controls are properly enabled or disabled. (You learn about the EnableButtons() procedure later in the chapter, in the section "Enabling and Disabling Buttons.")

Counting the Topics

The CountTopics() subroutine, called by mnuFileOpen_Click(), counts the number of topics in the selected hypertext document. That subroutine, which is located in the general object, looks like Listing 7.9.

Listing 7.9   LIST7_9.BAS. The *CountTopics()* procedure.

```
Private Sub CountTopics()
    Dim InputFileNum As Integer
    Dim Text As String

    InputFileNum = 1
    Open FileName For Input As #InputFileNum
    TopicCount = 0
    While Not EOF(InputFileNum)
        Line Input #InputFileNum, Text
        If Left$(Text, 7) = "\TITLE^" Then
            TopicCount = TopicCount + 1
        End If
    Wend
    Close InputFileNum
End Sub
```

As you can see, this subroutine opens the selected file whose filename is stored in the FileName string. The While loop then reads through the file a line at a time, searching for the \TITLE^ command. Each time the subroutine finds the \TITLE^ command in the file, it increments the TopicCount variable. After reaching the end of the file, CountTopics() closes the file and ends.

Displaying a Topic

When the user opens a new hypertext document, the HYPERTXT program must display the first topic in the document. This task is handled by the PrintTopic() subroutine, which looks like Listing 7.10.

Listing 7.10 LIST7_10.BAS. The *PrintTopic( )* procedure.

```
Private Sub PrintTopic(Topic As String, InputFileNum As Integer)
    PrintTopicTitle Topic
    ShowHyperImage InputFileNum
    PrintTopicText InputFileNum
End Sub
```

This subroutine simply calls the other subroutines that display the three main parts of the hypertext document, which are the topic title, the topic image, and the topic text. The `PrintTopicTitle()` subroutine, which displays the title, looks like Listing 7.11.

Listing 7.11 LIST7_11.BAS. The *PrintTopicTitle( )* procedure.

```
Private Sub PrintTopicTitle(Topic As String)
    Form1.CurrentX = 100
    Form1.CurrentY = 600
    Form1.FontSize = 12
    Form1.FontBold = True
    Form1.FontUnderline = False
    Form1.ForeColor = &H0
    Form1.Print Topic
End Sub
```

`PrintTopicTitle()` first sets the drawing coordinates for the form. These drawing coordinates, which are given in Visual Basic's twips (the smallest unit of screen measurement in Visual Basic, equal to 1/1440 of an inch), determine where the next text will appear in the window. Next, the program sets the font attributes for a title, after which a simple call to the form's `Print()` method displays the topic title in the window.

The topic image is displayed by the `ShowHyperImage()` subroutine, which looks like Listing 7.12.

Listing 7.12 LIST7_12.BAS. The *ShowHyperImage( )* procedure.

```
Private Sub ShowHyperImage(InputFileNum As Integer)
    Dim Text As String
    Dim Image As String
    Dim Word As String
    Dim I As Integer

    Line Input #InputFileNum, Text
    If Text = "\IMAGE^NONE^" Then
        Image1.Visible = False
        Form1.Print
```

```
        Else
            Image = Mid$(Text, 8, Len(Text) - 8)
            Image1.Picture = LoadPicture(Image)
            Image1.Top = Form1.CurrentY + 100
            Form1.CurrentY = Form1.CurrentY + Image1.Height + 300
            Image1.Visible = True
            CreateHotSpots InputFileNum
        End If
    End Sub
```

This function has a lot of work to do, because it must not only display the image (if any), but also set up the image's hot spots. The following list details the subroutine:

- First, ShowHyperImage() reads a line of text from the file. If this line of text is the \IMAGE^NONE^ command, the subroutine prints a blank line in the application's window and ends. Otherwise, the document must have an image to display. A call to Mid$() extracts the image's filename from the command text, after which a call to LoadPicture() loads the image and sets the image control's Picture property.

- Next, ShowHyperImage() sets the image control's Top property, which determines the location in the window of the top of the image. In this case, the image appears just below the topic title. Because you want the topic text to appear below the image, the program must also update the form's CurrentY property, based on the current value of CurrentY and the height of the image.

- The subroutine then sets the image control's Visible property to True, which makes the image appear in the application's window.

- Finally, a call to CreateHotSpots() (a subroutine you learn about later in this chapter, in the section titled "Storing Hot Spots") sets up the hot spots associated with the image.

The PrintTopicText() subroutine, which displays the topic's text and link words, is much more complicated than ShowHyperImage(). PrintTopicText() looks like Listing 7.13.

Listing 7.13   LIST7_13.BAS. The *PrintTopicText( )* procedure.

```
Private Sub PrintTopicText(InputFileNum As Integer)
    Dim Word As String
    Dim Text As String
```

(continues)

II

The Graphics Interface

Listing 7.13   Continued

```
        CurrentLink = 0
        Form1.FontSize = 8
        Form1.FontBold = False
        Form1.CurrentX = 100

        Line Input #InputFileNum, Text
        Do While Left$(Text, 7) <> "\TITLE^" And Not EOF(InputFileNum)
            Do Until Text = ""
                Word = GetNextWord(Text)
                DoWordWrap Word
                If Left$(Word, 6) = "\LINK^" Then
                    CreateLink Word
                    Form1.ForeColor = &H8000&
                    Form1.FontUnderline = True
                Else
                    Form1.FontUnderline = False
                    Form1.ForeColor = &H0
                End If

                Form1.Print Word; " ";
            Loop

            Line Input #InputFileNum, Text

            ' Start a new paragraph for each blank line.
            If Text = "" Then
                Form1.Print
                Form1.Print
                Form1.CurrentX = 100
            End If
        Loop
    End Sub
```

PrintTopictext() sets the CurrentLink index to 0, which effectively wipes out previous links stored in the Links array. Then, it sets the form's font attributes to display normal words. A While loop reads lines of text from the file, and a nested Do Until loop extracts each word from the currently read text line.

Within the inner loop, the program calls GetNextWord(), which strips the next word from the text string and returns it from the function. A call to the DoWordWrap() subroutine updates the form's CurrentX and CurrentY coordinates if the next word to display won't fit on the current line. (You learn about these subroutines later in this chapter, in the sections "Storing Text Links" and "Handling Word Wrap.")

If the current word is the \LINK^ command, the program calls the CreateLink() subroutine (you examine this subroutine later in the "Storing Text Links" section in this chapter) to set up the new link, as well as sets the form's font attributes to display the link word in a green and underlined font. Otherwise, the program sets the font color to black and turns off underlining. A call to the form's `Print()` method displays the current word.

After extracting all words from the currently loaded line of text, the `While` loop reads in the next line and checks whether this line is blank, indicating a new paragraph. If it is, two additional calls to the form's `Print()` method, along with resetting the `CurrentX` property, begins the next paragraph.

Storing Hot Spots

As you know, a topic image can contain up to 20 hot spots, which act as graphical hyperlinks. The subroutine that extracts hot spots for a topic's image is called `CreateHotSpots()`, and it looks like Listing 7.14.

Listing 7.14   LIST7_14.BAS. The *CreateHotSpots( )* procedure.

```
Private Sub CreateHotSpots(InputFileNum As Integer)
    Dim Text As String
    Dim Word As String

    CurrentHotSpot = 0
    Line Input #InputFileNum, Text
    While Text <> "\HOTSPOT^END^"
        Text = Mid$(Text, 10)
        CurrentHotSpot = CurrentHotSpot + 1
        Word = GetNextWord(Text)
        HotSpots(CurrentHotSpot).LeftX = Val(Word)
        Word = GetNextWord(Text)
        HotSpots(CurrentHotSpot).TopY = Val(Word)
        Word = GetNextWord(Text)
        HotSpots(CurrentHotSpot).RightX = Val(Word)
        Word = GetNextWord(Text)
        HotSpots(CurrentHotSpot).BottomY = Val(Word)
        Word = Mid$(Text, 1, Len(Text) - 1)
        HotSpots(CurrentHotSpot).Key = Mid$(Text, 1, Len(Text) - 1)
        Line Input #InputFileNum, Text
    Wend
End Sub
```

Here, the `While` loop reads text lines from the hypertext file until it finds the `\HOTSPOT^END^` command. If the image has no hot spots, the `\HOTSPOT^END^` command will be the first line read in before the `While` loop begins, which means the entire loop will be skipped. Otherwise, within the loop, the program calls `Mid$()` to extract the coordinate string from the `\HOTSPOT^` command and increments `CurrentHotSpot`, which is an index that determines where the next hot spot will be stored in the `HotSpots` array.

To get the various coordinates, the program calls the GetNextWord() function, which strips the next word from the text line and returns it from the function. (You'll get a look at GetNextWord() in the next section.) In this case, the first call to GetNextWord() returns the X coordinate of the hot spot's upper-left corner. A call to the Val() function returns the value of this coordinate, which gets stored in the LeftX member of the current hot spot. The other coordinates are calculated in exactly the same way. The last call to Mid$() returns the title of the topic to which the hot spot should be linked. This title is stored as the hot spot's key.

Storing Text Links

Creating text links is a lot like creating hot spots, because you need to keep track of exactly the same information. However, before you can understand how to create text links, you need to know how the program extracts words from each text line. That task is done by the GetNextWord() function, which looks like Listing 7.15.

Listing 7.15 LIST7_15.BAS. The *GetNextWord( )* function.

```
Private Function GetNextWord(Text As String) As String
    Dim Pos As Integer

    If Left$(Text, 6) = "\LINK^" Then
        Pos = InStr(7, Text, "^", 1)
        GetNextWord = Left$(Text, Pos - 1)
        Text = Mid$(Text, Pos + 1)
    Else
        Pos = InStr(Text, " ")
        If Pos = 0 Then
            GetNextWord = Text
            Text = ""
        Else
            GetNextWord = Left$(Text, Pos - 1)
            Text = Mid$(Text, Pos + 1)
        End If
    End If
End Function
```

GetNextWord()'s single argument is the text line from which to extract the word. The function first checks whether the text line begins with \LINK^. If it does, the function must extract the entire link command, which may be comprised of several words.

Just looking for spaces won't necessarily extract the link command properly, because both the link text and the topic title portion of the command may be made up of several words each.

If the next word is a link command, the program must set up the link. This task is handled by the CreateLink() subroutine, which looks like Listing 7.16.

Listing 7.16   LIST7_16.BAS. The *CreateLink( )* procedure.

```
Private Sub CreateLink(Word As String)
    Dim Pos As Integer
    Dim LinkKey As String

    Word = Mid$(Word, 7)
    Pos = InStr(Word, "^")
    LinkKey = Mid$(Word, Pos + 1, Len(Word) - Pos - 1)
    Word = Left$(Word, Pos - 1)
    CurrentLink = CurrentLink + 1
    Links(CurrentLink).Key = LinkKey
    Links(CurrentLink).LeftX = Form1.CurrentX
    Links(CurrentLink).TopY = Form1.CurrentY
    Links(CurrentLink).RightX = Form1.CurrentX + _
        Form1.TextWidth(Word)
    Links(CurrentLink).BottomY = Form1.CurrentY + _
        Form1.TextHeight(Word)
End Sub
```

CreateLink()'s single argument is the current word extracted from the text string, which, in this case, is the entire link command. In this subroutine, the program first calls Mid$() to strip off the \LINK^ from the beginning of the link command. Calling the Pos() function then gets the position of the caret that separates the link word or phrase from the link topic title. The second call to Mid$() extracts the link word or phrase from the text and stores it in the LinkKey string. The call to Left$() leaves the string Word containing only the link text, which will be displayed as underlined on-screen.

After extracting the link topic title, the program increments the CurrentLink index, stores LinkKey in the link's Key member, and calculates and stores the link's window coordinates. These coordinates are calculated using the form's CurrentX and CurrentY properties along with the width and height of the link text.

Making the Mouse Respond to Hot Spots

Although the link words in a hypertext document are underlined and printed in green, there's no indication of where hot spots might be located in an image. How, then, can the user know when his mouse is over such a hot spot in an image? The solution to this little dilemma is to change the form of the mouse pointer whenever it's over any type of hyperlink.

 For all intents and purposes, both link words and graphic hot spots are treated as hot spots when handling the mouse pointer form.

For the text areas of the hypertext document, the form's MouseMove() event procedure handles these mousely chores. That procedure looks like Listing 7.17.

Listing 7.17 LIST7_17.BAS. The *Form_MouseMove( )* procedure.

```
Private Sub Form_MouseMove(Button As Integer, Shift As Integer, _
    X As Single, Y As Single)
    Dim I As Integer
    Dim Found As Integer

    Found = False
    For I = 1 To CurrentLink
        If X > Links(I).LeftX And X < Links(I).RightX And _
            Y > Links(I).TopY And Y < Links(I).BottomY Then
                Found = True
        End If
    Next I

    If Found Then
        Form1.MousePointer = 10
    Else
        Form1.MousePointer = 0
    End If
End Sub
```

Whenever the user moves the mouse over the form, the MouseMove() event procedure gets a call. Because this procedure's arguments include the current mouse position, it's a simple matter to compare the mouse position with the link coordinates stored in the Links array. If the program finds that the mouse pointer is over a link, it changes the mouse pointer to an up-arrow image (see Fig. 7.6), indicated by a MousePointer value of 10. Otherwise, the pointer is set to its default form.

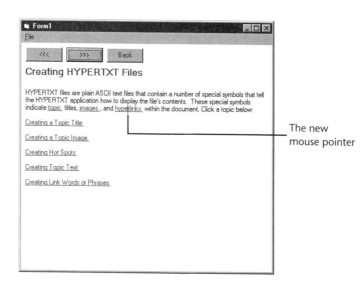

Fig. 7.6
A mouse pointer
over a hyperlink
changes to an
up-arrow image.

The new
mouse pointer

The hot spots in a topic's image are dealt with in the same way, except it's the image's MouseMove() event procedure, rather than the form's, that gets called when the mouse moves over the image. That procedure looks like Listing 7.18.

Listing 7.18   LIST7_18.BAS. The *Image1_MouseMove( )* procedure.

```
Private Sub Image1_MouseMove(Button As Integer, Shift As Integer, _
   X As Single, Y As Single)
    Dim I As Integer
    Dim Found As Integer

    Found = False
    For I = 1 To CurrentHotSpot
        If X > HotSpots(I).LeftX And X < HotSpots(I).RightX _
          And Y > HotSpots(I).TopY And Y < HotSpots(I).BottomY Then
            Found = True
        End If
    Next I

    If Found Then
        Form1.MousePointer = 10
    Else
        Form1.MousePointer = 0
    End If
End Sub
```

As you can see, this procedure works similarly to the form's `MouseMove()` procedure. The difference is that the program now searches the `HotSpots` array rather than the `Links` array.

Responding to a Link Selection

After all this work to set up hyperlinks, both in the text and in the image, and after making sure that the mouse changes when it's over a hyperlink, it would sure be a pity if the user clicked on the link and nothing happened! The `MouseDown()` event procedures are written for both the form and image objects. The form's version of `MouseDown()` looks like Listing 7.19.

Listing 7.19 LIST7_19.BAS. The *Form_MouseDown( )* procedure.

```
Private Sub Form_MouseDown(Button As Integer, Shift As Integer, _
   X As Single, Y As Single)
   Dim I As Integer
   Dim InputFileNum As Integer
   Dim Text As String
   Dim Topic As String

   If FileName <> "" Then
      For I = 1 To CurrentLink
         If X > Links(I).LeftX And X < Links(I).RightX And _
            Y > Links(I).TopY And Y < Links(I).BottomY Then
            Form1.Cls
            InputFileNum = 1
            Open FileName For Input As #InputFileNum
            CurrentTopicNum = 0
            Do Until Topic = Links(I).Key
               Line Input #InputFileNum, Text
               If Left$(Text, 7) = "\TITLE^" Then
                  CurrentTopicNum = CurrentTopicNum + 1
                  Topic = Mid$(Text, 8, Len(Text) - 8)
               End If
            Loop

            PrintTopic Topic, InputFileNum
            AddToHistory Topic
            Close InputFileNum
         End If
      Next I
      EnableButtons
   End If
End Sub
```

Whenever the user clicks the mouse button while the mouse pointer is over the form, the form's `MouseDown()` event procedure gets called. In `MouseDown()`, the HYPERTXT application first checks to see that the user has opened a hypertext file. If he has, the program next checks whether the mouse coordinates match the coordinates for a link stored in the Links array. If they don't, the procedure just returns. Otherwise, the procedure clears the window, opens the hypertext document file, and scans through the file, looking for the topic title that matches the one stored as the link's key. Each time the program finds any topic, whether it matches the key or not, the CurrentTopicNum counter gets incremented. As you see later in this chapter, in the next section "Responding to the Browse Buttons," the program uses CurrentTopicNum when the user clicks either of the browse buttons.

When the program finds the matching topic, the call to PrintTopic() displays the topic in the window, and the call to AddToHistory() adds the topic to the user's current topic history. (You see what all this history stuff is all about when you learn how the application's Back button works, in the section "Responding to the Back Button.") Finally, because displaying a new topic may change the availability of one or more buttons (for example, you can't let the user browse forward if the application is already displaying the last topic in the document), the call to EnableButtons() ensures that the buttons are properly enabled or disabled.

When the user clicks the mouse on the current topic's image, the image control's MouseDown() event procedure gets called. That procedure looks like Listing 7.20.

Listing 7.20 LIST7_20.BAS. The *Image1_MouseDown()* procedure.

```
Private Sub Image1_MouseDown(Button As Integer, Shift As Integer, _
   X As Single, Y As Single)
    Dim I As Integer
    Dim InputFileNum As Integer
    Dim Text As String
    Dim Topic As String

    For I = 1 To CurrentHotSpot
        If X > HotSpots(I).LeftX And X < HotSpots(I).RightX _
          And Y > HotSpots(I).TopY And Y < HotSpots(I).BottomY Then
            Form1.Cls
            InputFileNum = 1
            Open FileName For Input As #InputFileNum
            CurrentTopicNum = 0
            Do Until Topic = HotSpots(I).Key
                Line Input #InputFileNum, Text
                If Left$(Text, 7) = "\TITLE^" Then
                    CurrentTopicNum = CurrentTopicNum + 1
                    Topic = Mid$(Text, 8, Len(Text) - 8)
                End If
```

(continues)

The Graphics Interface

II

Listing 7.20 Continued

```
            Loop

            PrintTopic Topic, InputFileNum
            AddToHistory Topic
            Close InputFileNum
        End If
    Next I
    EnableButtons
End Sub
```

The image object's `MouseDown()` event procedure is very similar to the form's version. The main difference is that the image object's `MouseDown()` procedure searches through the `HotSpots` array rather than through the `Links` array.

Responding to the Browse Buttons

Although a hypertext document is designed to enable the user to jump around from topic to topic, most hypertext applications also enable the user to browse through topics in the order in which they appear in the document. Just like flipping through the pages of a book, this type of browsing enables the user to read the topics in a logical order. In the HYPERTXT application, clicking on the Forward Browse button (marked with >>>) causes the program to display the next topic in the document. Similarly, clicking on the Backward Browse button (marked with <<<) causes the previous topic in the document to be displayed (see Fig. 7.7).

Fig. 7.7
The browse buttons enable the user to move through a hypertext document as though flipping pages in a book.

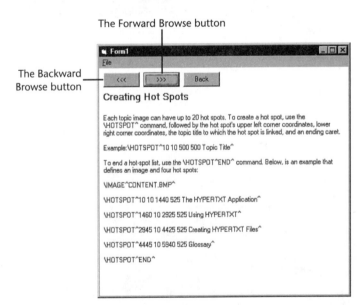

The Forward Browse button

The Backward Browse button

The browse buttons are handled by the btnForward_Click() and btnBackward_Click() command procedures, which look like Listing 7.21.

Listing 7.21   LIST7_21.BAS. The *btnForward_Click()* and *btnBackward_Click()* procedures.

```
Private Sub btnForward_Click()
    Form1.Cls
    CurrentTopicNum = CurrentTopicNum + 1
    ShowTopic
    EnableButtons
End Sub

Private Sub btnBackward_Click()
    Form1.Cls
    CurrentTopicNum = CurrentTopicNum - 1
    ShowTopic
    EnableButtons
End Sub
```

Whenever the user clicks one of the browse buttons, the program increments or decrements CurrentTopicNumber and then calls ShowTopic() to find the correct topic (see Listing 7.22).

Listing 7.22   LIST7_22.BAS. The *ShowTopic()* procedure.

```
Private Sub ShowTopic()
    Dim InputFileNum As Integer
    Dim Count As Integer
    Dim Text As String
    Dim Topic As String

    InputFileNum = 1
    Open FileName For Input As #InputFileNum
    Count = 0
    While Count <> CurrentTopicNum
        Line Input #InputFileNum, Text
        If Left$(Text, 7) = "\TITLE^" Then Count = Count + 1
    Wend
    Topic = Mid$(Text, 8, Len(Text) - 8)
    PrintTopic Topic, InputFileNum
    AddToHistory Topic
    Close InputFileNum
End Sub
```

In this subroutine, the program reads through the hypertext file counting topics until it gets to the topic whose position in the document is stored in

CurrentTopicNum. The program then calls PrintTopic() to display the topic in the window and AddToHistory() to add the topic to the user's history list. Notice that ShowTopic() does no title and key matching; it simply counts topics from the beginning of the file.

Responding to the Back Button

Often as the user is reading a topic in a hypertext document, he wants to be able to jump to a related topic and then get right back to the last topic he was reading. For this reason, the HYPERTXT application keeps a history list that stores all the topics the user has read, in the order he read them. This order is not necessarily the same order in which the topics are listed in the document. For example, if the user reads topic 1, then jumps from topic 1 to topic 5 and from topic 5 to topic 3, the history list would hold topic 1, topic 5, and topic 3 in that order.

The Back button (see Fig. 7.8) enables the user to retrace their steps. In the case presented in the previous paragraph, clicking the Back button would move the user from topic 3 to topic 5. A second click of the Back button would bring the user back from topic 5 to topic 1, where he started. At this point, the history list is empty, because the user has completely retraced his steps.

The Back button

Fig. 7.8
The Back button retraces the user's steps.

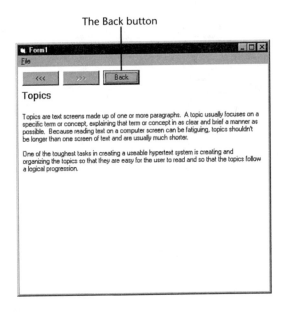

Before you can learn how the Back button works, however, you have to know how the HYPERTXT application handles its history list. Throughout the program, whenever the application displays a new topic, a call to the AddToHistory() subroutine adds the topic to the history list. That subroutine looks like Listing 7.23.

Listing 7.23   LIST7_23.BAS. The *AddToHistory( )* procedure.

```
Private Sub AddToHistory(Topic)
    CurrentHistory = CurrentHistory + 1
    History(CurrentHistory) = Topic
End Sub
```

This subroutine simply increments CurrentHistory, which is the index variable that indicates the last-used slot in the current History array, and adds the current topic title to the History array, which is just an array of strings. Every time the user views a new topic, that topic's title is added to the History array. When the user clicks the Back button, all the application must do is return to the topic whose title is listed next to last in the History array. (The last entry in the History array is always the topic currently displayed in the window.)

In the HYPERTXT application, the btnHistoryBack_Click() command procedure responds when the user clicks the Back button. That procedure looks like Listing 7.24.

Listing 7.24   LIST7_24.BAS. The *btnHistoryBack_Click( )* procedure.

```
Private Sub btnHistoryBack_Click()
    Dim Topic As String
    Dim Text As String
    Dim HistoryKey As String
    Dim InputFileNum As Integer

    Form1.Cls
    InputFileNum = 1
    Open FileName For Input As #InputFileNum
    CurrentHistory = CurrentHistory - 1
    HistoryKey = History(CurrentHistory)
    CurrentTopicNum = 0
    Do Until Topic = HistoryKey
        Line Input #InputFileNum, Text
        If Left$(Text, 7) = "\TITLE^" Then
            CurrentTopicNum = CurrentTopicNum + 1
```

(continues)

Listing 7.24 Continued

```
            Topic = Mid$(Text, 8, Len(Text) - 8)
        End If
    Loop
    PrintTopic Topic, InputFileNum
    Close InputFileNum
    EnableButtons
End Sub
```

Subroutine `btnHistoryBack_Click()` in code Listing 7.24 does the following:

- Clears the window.

- Opens the hypertext file.

- Decrements `CurrentHistory` (which effectively removes the last entry from the History array).

- Gets the target topic from the `History` array (storing it in the `HistoryKey` string.

- Initializes the `CurrentTopicNum` counter to 0.

The program then reads through the hypertext file, counting topics (so that `CurrentTopicNum` stays current) and looking for the topic whose title matches the title stored in `HistoryKey`. When the program finds the topic, a call to `PrintTopic()` displays it on-screen.

Handling Word Wrap

As you know, the HYPERTXT application displays topic text one word at a time, looking for \LINK^ commands as it goes. At some point on each line, however, the current word to be displayed will overrun the right window boundary. If this is allowed to happen, the word will be at least partially hidden from the user. To avoid this, HYPERTXT starts a new line whenever the current word won't fit completely inside the window. This task is handled by the `DoWordWrap()` subroutine, which looks like Listing 7.25.

Listing 7.25 LIST7_25.BAS. The *DoWordWrap()* procedure.

```
Private Sub DoWordWrap(Word As String)
    If Form1.TextWidth(Word) + Form1.CurrentX + _
      200 > Form1.ScaleWidth Then
        Form1.Print
        Form1.CurrentX = 100
    End If
End Sub
```

This subroutine simply sums the width of the word with the current X position in the window, adds 200 twips in order to leave an adequate right margin, and checks the sum against the width of the window. If the word won't fit, `DoWordWrap()` calls the form's `Print()` method to move to the next line and then sets `CurrentX` to the left margin.

What happens when the user resizes the window? Obviously, this action changes the window's borders; therefore, it also changes how the text should be displayed in the window. This eventuality is handled by the form's `Form_Resize()` event procedure, which looks like Listing 7.26.

Listing 7.26 LIST7_26.BAS. The *Form_Resize()* procedure.

```
Private Sub Form_Resize()
    Dim InputFileNum As Integer
    Dim Text As String
    Dim Topic As String
    Dim HistoryKey As String

    If FileName <> "" Then
        Form1.Cls
        InputFileNum = 1
        Open FileName For Input As #InputFileNum
        HistoryKey = History(CurrentHistory)
        Do Until Topic = HistoryKey
            Line Input #InputFileNum, Text
            If Left$(Text, 7) = "\TITLE^" Then
                Topic = Mid$(Text, 8, Len(Text) - 8)
            End If
        Loop
        PrintTopic Topic, InputFileNum
        Close InputFileNum
    End If
End Sub
```

First, notice that before this procedure does anything, it checks whether the `FileName` string is empty. This is important because the `Form_Resize()` procedure gets called for the first time before the user has had a chance to select a file. If `Form_Resize()` didn't check the contents of `FileName`, the program would crash almost immediately as it tried to load a file using a blank filename.

After ensuring that `FileName` is not empty, the procedure clears the window, opens the hypertext file, gets the title of the currently displayed topic (which is always the last topic in the `History` array), and then reads through the file, looking for the topic whose title matches the one stored in `HistoryKey`. When the procedure finds the topic, it calls `PrintTopic()` to display the topic in the window, using the new window dimensions.

Notice that `Form_Resize()` does not count topic titles as it reads in the file. This is because the variable `CurrentTopicNum` does not need to be updated. It already contains the right topic number because all `Form_Resize()` is doing is redisplaying the same topic. In fact, you could rewrite `Form_Resize()` to count topics rather than compare keys, like Listing 7.27.

Listing 7.27   LIST7_27.BAS. A version of the *Form_Resize( )* procedure that counts topics rather than compare keys.

```
Private Sub Form_Resize()
    Dim InputFileNum As Integer
    Dim Text As String
    Dim Topic As String
    Dim Count As Integer

    If FileName <> "" Then
        Form1.Cls
        Count = 0
        InputFileNum = 1
        Open FileName For Input As #InputFileNum
        Do Until Count = CurrentTopicNum
            Line Input #InputFileNum, Text
            If Left$(Text, 7) = "\TITLE^" Then
                Count = Count + 1
                Topic = Mid$(Text, 8, Len(Text) - 8)
            End If
        Loop
        PrintTopic Topic, InputFileNum
        Close InputFileNum
    End If
End Sub
```

Enabling and Disabling Buttons

Several variables in the HYPERTXT application determine which buttons are currently available to the user. For example, the `CurrentHistory` index variable indicates how many entries are in the `History` array. When `CurrentHistory` is 1, it's not possible for the user to move back in the history list. In this case, the Back button should be disabled.

Similarly, the `CurrentTopicNum` variable holds the position in the hypertext file of the currently displayed topic. If `CurrentTopicNum` is 1, indicating that the first topic is displayed, the Backward Browse button should be disabled. If `CurrentTopicNum` is equal to `TopicCount` (which holds the total number of topics in the file), the last topic in the file is currently displayed in the application's window. In this case, the Forward Browse button should be disabled. The subroutine that enables and disables buttons based on the aforementioned variables is `EnableButtons()`, which looks like Listing 7.28.

Listing 7.28   LIST7_28.BAS. The *EnableButtons()* procedure.

```
Private Sub EnableButtons()
    If CurrentHistory = 1 Then
        btnHistoryBack.Enabled = False
    Else
        btnHistoryBack.Enabled = True
    End If

    If CurrentTopicNum = 1 Then
        btnBackward.Enabled = False
    Else
        btnBackward.Enabled = True
    End If

    If CurrentTopicNum = TopicCount Then
        btnForward.Enabled = False
    Else
        btnForward.Enabled = True
    End If
End Sub
```

`EnableButtons()` gets called whenever a new topic is displayed on-screen. This ensures that the buttons always accurately reflect the options that are currently available to the user. At the start of the program, the buttons are all disabled by the form's `Form_Load()` procedure, which looks like Listing 7.29.

Listing 7.29   LIST7_29.BAS. The *Form_Load()* procedure.

```
Private Sub Form_Load()
    btnHistoryBack.Enabled = False
    btnBackward.Enabled = False
    btnForward.Enabled = False
    CurrentHistory = 0
    FileName = ""
End Sub
```

As you can see, the `CurrentHistory` and `FileName` variables are also initialized in `Form_Load()`.

Improving the HYPERTXT Application

The HYPERTXT application has been kept fairly simple so that it's easier to understand. There are many ways you can improve it. One way might be to manipulate the hypertext document in memory rather than always accessing the file. Such an improvement may make the application run a little faster.

You might also want to add different types of data to your hypertext documents, including sound effects and animations. By connecting hyperlinks to these new items, the user could "play" them just by clicking on them in the document.

You might also want to allow for more than one image in a topic, or even allow any number of images to be placed wherever you like within a document. To get other ideas for your hypertext, multimedia application, look at other hypertext applications, such as the Windows Help system.

From Here...

This chapter gave you an in-depth look at a simple hypertext application. If you would like to enhance this basic application as suggested in the previous section, you can find more information on related topics in the following chapters:

- For more information on the MCI, which provides easier access to all kinds of multimedia devices, see Chapter 3, "The Media Control Interface (MCI)."

- For more information on Windows' device independence, see Chapter 4, "Visual Basic Audio Capabilities."

- For coverage of animation sequences that can present information in an entertaining way, see Chapter 10, "Animation."

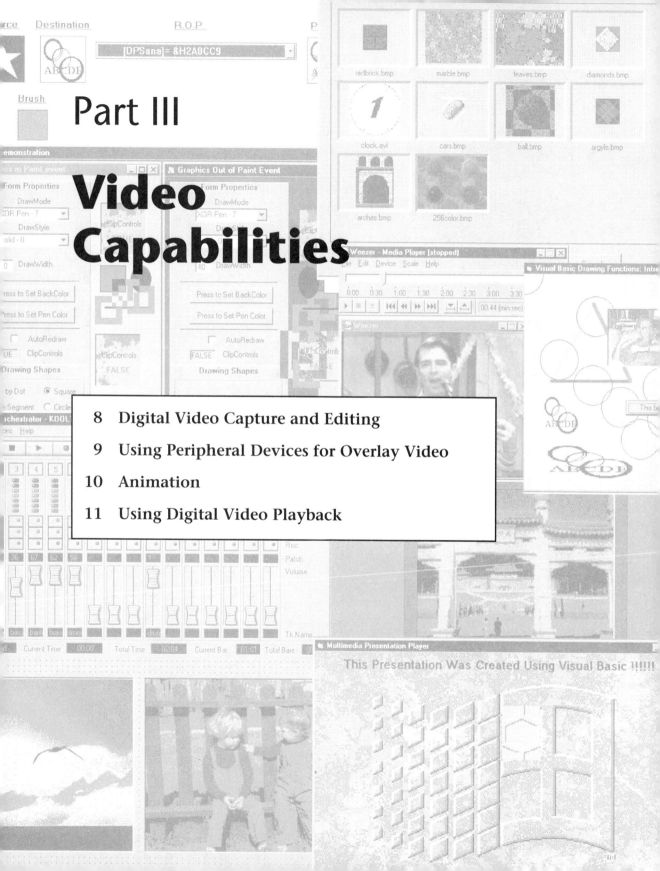

Part III

Video Capabilities

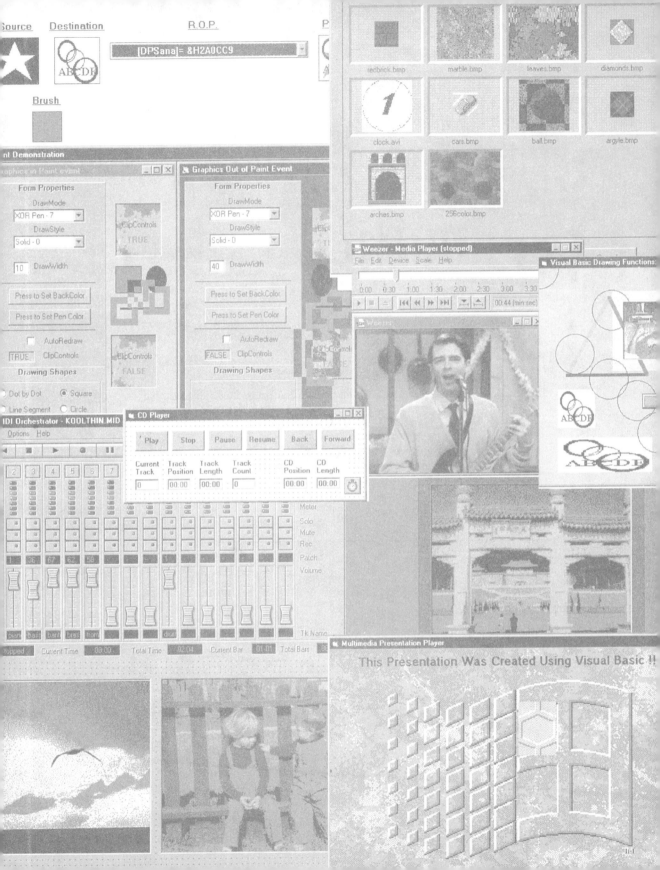

Chapter 8

Digital Video Capture and Editing

Today you can enter almost any video store and use a kiosk to preview clips from your favorite movies. It is hard to imagine that these clips are actually digital video clips played from a computer's hard disk, not a VCR or laser disc. Only a few short years ago, this was deemed impractical. Now it is commonplace. The digital revolution has begun and is one of the most highly active areas within the computer industry. Digital video is being used everywhere from computer games and CD-ROM titles to video-on-demand and interactive TV applications. In fact, CD-ROM titles such as Microsoft Encarta contain hundreds of digital video clips. Digital video is being effectively and efficiently used to create today's most innovative applications.

The dynamic nature of full-motion digital video—when combined with graphics, text, digital audio, and data—enables developers to create effective presentations, training courses, and educational material. The end result is better communication, reduced training costs, and improved decision-making capabilities.

This chapter addresses the relevant issues involved with capturing digital video on the various Windows platforms (Windows 3.x, Windows 95, and Windows NT) and from within the Visual Basic development environment.

In this chapter, the following topics are covered:

- The Video for Windows architecture
- The types of digital video

- Different techniques for capturing digital video in Visual Basic applications

- Capturing Video with Windows 95, Windows 3.x, and Windows NT

Digital Video Overview

What exactly is digital video and how is it important to programmers? Let's answer the easy part of that first. There are two types of video: *analog* and *digital*. Analog video is a constant stream of video information that is input into a display device such as a TV monitor or video overlay board for viewing. Examples of analog video are a TV tuner signal and VCR output. Digital video is an analog video stream that has been captured or digitized and stored electronically in a computer file format on storage media such as a computer hard disk or CD-ROM device.

Digital video has the advantage of being used over and over again within applications. For example, an application that controls a TV tuner cannot rewind and review the video material. If the same video from the TV tuner were digitally captured, however, the material could be viewed many times.

There is also a convenience factor associated with using digital video. There are no external devices or connections to make. Standard PC hardware—that is, a graphics display adapter—can be used. This allows more PCs, and thus more users, the ability to use your Visual Basic application. The only type of external device that may be needed is a graphics accelerator board or in the case of MPEG video, a video decoding board.

Unlike analog video, digital video files are easy to store, edit, and display. A digital file format allows the information to be accessed through a wide range of media, including CD-ROM, hard disks, and local and wide area networks.

The Various Types of Digital Video

There are several types of digital video formats that can be harnessed for use in multimedia applications. The following digital video types refer to their respective playback virtues: *software-only* digital video, *hardware-only* digital video, and a new class termed *hybrid digital video*. Each type has its own benefits and drawbacks. The type that's correct for a given application depends on the application's needs.

Software-only Digital Video

Software-only digital video refers to the ability to decompress and display digital video without the aid of any hardware other than a graphics display board. The video is compressed and decompressed in software only. This type of video, however, is very taxing on the PC's processor and results in smaller display sizes, choppy playback, and poor audio output.

Hardware-only Digital Video

With hardware-only video, captured digital video files, such as MPEG and DVI, cannot be played back without assistance from special video playback boards. An application that uses MPEG video needs a special MPEG decoder board while a DVI application requires a DVI playback board. Applications that utilize MPEG and DVI video typically are part of the mainstream commercial markets, such as the forementioned video rental kiosk. These commercial markets demand the highest quality video available.

Hybrid Digital Video

Recently there has been a surge of video playback boards that can capture and play back digital video on the same board. These video playback boards support what is known as *hybrid digital video*. Now you're probably saying that this sounds very much like hardware-only digital video and, in fact, it is. The caveat is that these boards capture video into what is termed a *native* file format, so that playback will occur with hardware assistance if the video board is present. The advantage over hardware-only digital video is that the video file can still be played back through software-only if the video board is not present.

Digital Video File Formats

Windows operating systems support various types of digital video file formats. The native format is Microsoft's Video for Windows, while other video formats include Apple Computer's QuickTime for Windows, MPEG, and DVI files. Of these video formats, Video for Windows has the most features with a variety of video capture, editing, and playback capabilities. The computer industry is spending most of its time supporting and optimizing Video for Windows technology.

The QuickTime for Windows file format was ported from the popular Macintosh QuickTime standard. Currently, this is a playback-only file format, and video capture must occur on the Mac platform. QuickTime file formats are most often used on CD-ROM titles.

The MPEG video format is quickly gaining a large following on Windows platforms. There are some capture packages available for the Windows platform but these cost in excess of $10,000. For the overwhelming majority of users, this price tag relegates MPEG to the playback-only category. MPEG playback boards can be purchased for under $300 and many of the VGA board manufacturers are placing MPEG-1 video decoders on their VGA boards. MPEG is the most widely used format for games, video on demand, and interactive video applications.

The Digital Video Interactive (.DVI) format is a proprietary Intel/IBM video format that is quietly losing what little popularity it once had. A capture board can be obtained for under $2,000 with the playback board available for under $800. This format is mostly used for specific vertical applications, such as corporate badging and security. DVI technology is also available for the OS\2 Warp platform.

Capturing Digital Video Files

Before digital video files can be played back, they must be created. Microsoft provides a standard set of digital video capture APIs and a standard file format to capture digital video. The file format is Video for Windows or *AVI (Audio-Video Interleaved)*. .AVI is the most popular video file format for the Windows operating systems.

The Microsoft .AVI file format follows the .RIFF (Resource Interchange File Format) file specification. The .AVI file format can be used with any application that can capture, edit, and play back digital video sequences. Typical .AVI files contain multiple streams of data, but most contain only one audio and one video stream. In its simplest terms, an .AVI file can be thought of as a sequence of bitmaps that are stored with corresponding chunks of audio data. The data within the .AVI file is assembled by the video capture drivers.

Before plunging into the depths of digital video capture, the following items of concern need to be discussed:

- *Storage space.* Storing digital video requires a tremendous amount of disk storage space. Knowing the factors that affect storage sizes can significantly enhance your application.

- *Playback/capture speed.* The speed or rate of video capture can affect the quality of the captured video and the storage space required.

■ *Playback/capture size.* The size or dimensions of the captured video also affects the quality of the video and the storage space required.

■ *Picture quality.* The pixel depth of the captured video also affects both the video quality and storage space requirements.

Storage Space

The space required for storing video in a digital format is incredibly high. For a typical PC, an uncompressed bitmap with a resolution of 640X480 pixels and a pixel depth of 8 bits per pixel, requires 2,457,600 bytes of storage! For full-motion video, with a playback rate of 30 frames per second, this would require 73,728,000 bytes for 1 second of uncompressed full-screen video with no audio. These types of data rates exceed all of the typical PC transfer mechanisms that currently exist.

Fortunately, the video that is stored is compressed. Video for Windows uses the *Installable Compression Manager (ICM)* to handle the compression and decompression of digital video segments. The ICM is a component of Video for Windows that allows users to select the compression codec to be used when compressing the video. The ICM also automatically determines which codec to use during playback.

When digital video files are captured, they are typically stored to a contiguous capture file in a format supported by the video capture driver. Capture drivers capture video to a known, contiguous file, which eliminates any unnecessary disk seeks or other file I/O. The capture file is allocated before capture begins and is several megabytes in size. After the video segment is completely captured, the contents of the file are compressed and read into a new file in final playback format.

Video capture boards (such as Intel's SmartRecorder) support hardware compression during capture; however, others do not. Software compression is too time-consuming to be done during capture; therefore, it is done off-line after the original video capture.

Video compression is achieved through the use of *codecs*, which stands for *co*mpression and *dec*ompression drivers. A PC can have many video codecs installed at one time; the user then chooses which codec to apply when compressing the video. During playback the correct decompressor is automatically chosen by the Video for Windows playback driver.

 NOTE Video for Windows is supplied with four codecs: RLE from Microsoft, Video 1 from Microsoft and MediaVision, SuperMac's Cinepak, and Intel's Indeo Compression. You can purchase additional codecs to install.

III

Video Capabilities

Audio compression is handled through the Audio Compression Manager. Although similar to the video codecs, audio recording is handled through a sound board, not the video capture board. The audio capture drivers are invoked by the Video for Windows record APIs, which in turn capture the incoming audio and store it in the AVI capture file. Figures 8.1 and 8.2 depict the data flow of capture video and compression.

Fig. 8.1
How data flows when capturing digital video using Video for Windows.

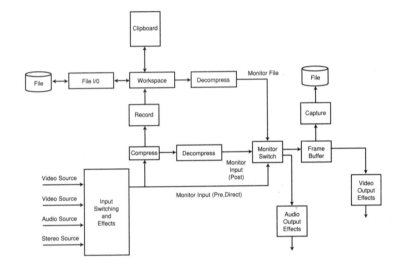

Fig. 8.2
An overview of Video for Windows compression and decompression driver architecture.

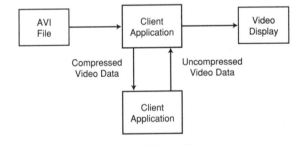

Decompression Driver Architecture

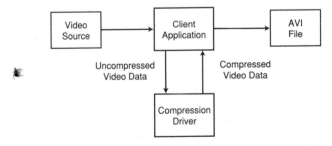

Compression Driver Architecture

Playback and Capture Speed

The playback speed of captured video can affect the storage requirements for digital video segments. For true full-motion video—defined as the rate of video playback at which the human eye cannot detect any frame breakup—the playback speed is 30 fps (frames per second). The faster your capture and playback rates, the higher the storage requirements.

Typical Video for Windows files are captured at a rate of 15 frames per second, which provides video material to the end user without incurring video or audio breakup during playback. For content that has very little movement, such as a panel of speakers, 15 fps is more than adequate; however, for content such as high-action sports clips, 15 fps is not adequate.

Playback and Capture Size

The size of video frames has the biggest effect on the storage requirements of the captured video. Until recently, the typical Video for Windows display size was 160X120 pixels, which is 1/16 of a screen for 640X480 resolution. The size of the video that can be handled during capture and playback is directly related to your PC's speed. A fast Pentium processor captures and displays video more quickly than a 386 class machine.

By shrinking the video frame size from 640X480 to 160X120, you reduce the uncompressed per frame requirements from 2,457,600 bytes to 153,600 bytes. Again, the video frame size directly affects the storage requirements of your application. For example, a CD-ROM title benefits from a larger frame size and you don't need to be as worried about storage space; however, if you are working with a security application that records video from a CCTV system to hard disk, storage space is a concern.

Picture Quality

Picture quality involves many factors that affect the storage requirements of digital video. The two variables that affect picture quality are *pixel depth* and *compression ratios.*

Pixel depth is how many bits per pixel are used to represent the color spectrum. For example, 8 bits per pixel indicates a possible range of 256 colors that can be used to represent the colors of a video frame. As the number of bits increases, so do the storage requirements. The more bits per pixel, the closer the captured video resembles the video signal being recorded. Also, because less video information is presented in an 8 bits per pixel format, the capture and playback rates are faster. Other common pixel depths are 16 bits per pixel (16,000 colors) and 24 bits per pixel (>1 million colors).

When compressing video frames, there are two types of compression techniques used: *interframe compression* and *intraframe compression*. Most codecs use both techniques.

Interframe compression eliminates interframe duplication by using the key and delta frame technique. When using interframe compression, you indicate how often to create a *key frame*. The key frame is a reference point used for marking the changes or deltas that occur in subsequent frames until the next key frame is captured. Figure 8.3 illustrates how this compression technique works.

Fig. 8.3
What interframe compression codecs actually store in a video file.

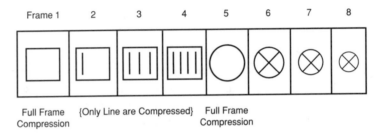

Intraframe compression is achieved on a frame-by-frame basis, where the codec compresses each individual frame independently. Most of the codecs use both techniques, where the key frame is compressed individually and only the changes between the following frames are compressed.

Both intraframe and interframe compression fall into two categories: *lossless* and *lossy*. Lossless compression allows all compressed data to be recovered after decompression. Lossless compression is appropriate for applications that cannot tolerate any lost data. The nature of lossless compression limits itself to a small compression ratio, typically 2:1. Because playing full-motion video from a CD-ROM or via a network requires compression ratios of 180:1, lossless compression is not be suitable for CD-ROM or network playback.

Lossy compression techniques yield a much higher compression ratio in addition to a resulting "loss" of data; the data is discarded during compression. Lossy techniques are based on complex algorithms that leave out information less important to the human eye. This less important information is typically where blocks of the image contain a similiar color pattern. Lossy compression enables the user to set compression ratios at arbitrary levels, which results in a compression trade-off: the higher the compression ratio, the smaller the resulting file and the more blurry the video image will be.

Compression ratios also affect the storage requirements of digital video. When setting compression ratios for digital video, you are trading lower storage requirements for less video information to represent the video frames. The ratios vary for optimal quality versus storage requirements from codec to codec.

Step Capture

If your video is being captured from a controllable video source such as a VCR or laser disc device, there is a powerful mechanism available to you for capturing digital video. This is *step capture.*

Step capture requires a computer-controllable video source (VCR or laser disc) and an MCI driver for the device. This form of capture is used for most, if not all, of the professional content that is available to end users.

When using step capture, the Video for Windows capture engine controls the video source device through the MCI driver. The device is placed in a paused mode, then is advanced frame by frame. Each frame is captured and compressed by the capture engine. After each frame is captured, the device is then rewound and the segment is played again to capture the accompanying audio track.

Step capture ensures that the intended capture/playback rate is achieved. During normal video capture, if the processor cannot keep up with the specified capture rate, padded or duplicate frames are added to achieve a constant playback rate. Step capture eliminates the redundant frame. The size of the captured video can also be increased because each frame is captured individually.

Even though high-quality video segments can be captured using step capture, the resultant video will only be as good as your video device and video signal. A frame accurate device with a stable single frame output is essential.

Video Capture Tools

There are several capture applications available in the marketplace; these can be used as stand-alone applications for video capture. The Microsoft Video for Windows SDK contains VIDCAP.EXE and VIDEDIT.EXE. These applications provide rudimentary capture and editing for digital video files. Other ISV's that have video capture products include Adobe's Premier, Lenel Systems MediaRecorder, and Splice from Splice, Inc.. Most video boards come pre-bundled with video-capturing software so be sure to check your board's documentation for included software.

III

Video Capabilities

For applications that require integrated video capture, such as a video e-mail system or a personnel database system, a stand-alone capture application will not do the job. Your application will need to provide this capability directly.

There are different methods that can be used for adding video capture to your application. The Video for Windows SDK APIs can be called directly. This moves all of the responsibility for capture directly into the calling application. This is the most flexible method for capturing video, but is also the most time-consuming and difficult. Using the Video for Windows APIs directly requires use of a language other than Visual Basic.

There are a few tools on the market available for digital video capture. Two of these tools are Microsoft's Video for Windows Capture VBX and Lenel Systems MediaRecorder Toolkit. The Microsoft Video for Windows SDK provides a video capture VBX named CAPWNDX.VBX. Lenel Systems MediaRecorder Toolkit contains a video capture OLE custom control, a VBX, OLE automation server, DLL library, and C++ class library. The OLE custom control is covered later in this chapter, "Using the MediaRecorder Toolkit OLE Custom Control."

Using the Video for Windows Capture VBX—CAPWNDX.VBX

The Video for Windows Capture VBX is relatively straightforward and easy to use. Because VBXs are limited to a 16-bit architecture, the capture VBX must be used within a 16-bit application. To create a video capture application with CAPWND.VBX, the following prerequisites are necessary:

- A Video for Windows-compatible capture board must be installed in your PC.

- The Video for Windows capture drivers shipped with the board must be installed and set up correctly. This also involves first installing Microsoft Video for Windows.

- Your video source (camera, VCR, laser disc) needs to be connected to the video input using the appropriate cables.

- Your audio source needs to be connected to the audio inputs of your soundboard (if present).

- The capture board and drivers need to be checked by using the bundled capture software that comes with the video capture board. If the capture board and drivers work correctly, then you are ready to go.

- The Video for Windows Capture VBX must be installed.

Once the hardware and drivers are installed and operating correctly, creating a capture application is relatively easy. When the capture control is placed on-screen, the control automatically initializes itself with the first video capture device present on the system.

 NOTE There can be more than one video capture device installed in your PC although this is not typically done. If more than one video capture device is installed, the user must manually select which capture device to use.

To see the video displayed in the preview window, the Connect property must be set to True. Video is displayed and you can configure the control to use the capture parameters you want. Many of the properties present on the control are run-time properties, such as the VideoSourceDlg properties. The capture program, CAPVBX.EXE, in Listing 8.1 is a sample video capture application that uses the capture VBX. The majority of work in this program is in setting up the properties correctly for capture; capturing video is the easy part.

Listing 8.1   CAPVBX.FRM. Video capture using the CAPWNDX.VBX control.

```
VERSION 4.00
Begin VB.Form CAPVBX
   BackColor       =    &H00808080&
   Caption         =    "Video Capture Using CAPWNDX.VBX"
   ClientHeight    =    5250
   ClientLeft      =    900
   ClientTop       =    1110
   ClientWidth     =    7740
   BeginProperty Font
      name             =    "MS Sans Serif"
      charset          =    1
      weight           =    400
      size             =    8.25
      underline        =    0    'False
      italic           =    0    'False
      strikethrough    =    0    'False
   EndProperty
   Height          =    5940
   Left            =    840
   LinkTopic       =    "Form1"
   ScaleHeight     =    5250
   ScaleWidth      =    7740
   Top             =    480
   Width           =    7860
   Begin VB.CommandButton CaptureAbort
      Caption          =    "Abort Capture"
```

(continues)

III

Video Capabilities

Listing 8.1 Continued

```
        Height          =    495
        Left            =    2760
        TabIndex        =    0
        Top             =    4680
        Width           =    2055
    End
    Begin VBX.CAPWND CaptureWindow
        AudioBits       =    8
        AudioChannels   =    1
        AudioRate       =    11025
        AutoSize        =    0       'False
        CaptureAudio    =    -1      'True
        CaptureDOSMem   =    0       'False
        CaptureFile     =    "C:\CAPTURE.AVI"
        CaptureHitOK    =    0       'False
        CaptureLimit    =    0
        CaptureUseLimit =    0       'False
        Connect         =    -1      'True
        DriverNum       =    0
        Height          =    3135
        Left            =    2040
        MCIDeviceEnable =    0       'False
        MCIDeviceName   =    ""
        MCIStartMS      =    0
        MCIStepCapture  =    0       'False
        MCIStopMS       =    0
        Overlay         =    0       'False
        PalNumColors    =    256
        PalNumFrames    =    20
        Preview         =    0       'False
        PreviewRate     =    15
        Top             =    360
        VideoRate       =    15
        Width           =    3990
        Yield           =    0       'False
    End
    Begin VB.Label ErrorWindow
        BackColor       =    &H00808080&
        ForeColor       =    &H00FF0000&
        Height          =    375
        Left            =    120
        TabIndex        =    2
        Top             =    4800
        Width           =    2535
    End
    Begin VB.Label StatusWindow
        BackColor       =    &H00808080&
        ForeColor       =    &H00FF0000&
        Height          =    375
        Left            =    5160
        TabIndex        =    1
        Top             =    4800
        Width           =    2535
    End
```

```
Begin MSComDlg.CommonDialog PaletteDialog
   Left            =    960
   Top             =    3960
   _version        =    65536
   _extentx        =    847
   _extenty        =    847
   _stockprops     =    0
   defaulttext     =    ".pal"
   dialogtitle     =    "Palette Open"
   filter          =    "Palette (*.pal) ¦ *.pal"
End
Begin MSComDlg.CommonDialog CaptureDialog
   Left            =    240
   Top             =    3960
   _version        =    65536
   _extentx        =    847
   _extenty        =    847
   _stockprops     =    0
   defaulttext     =    ".avi"
   dialogtitle     =    "File Open"
   filter          =    "Video (*.avi) ¦ *.avi"
End
Begin VB.Menu File
   Caption         =    "&File"
   Begin VB.Menu SaveCapturedVideoAs
      Caption         =    "&Save Captured Video As..."
   End
   Begin VB.Menu LoadPalette
      Caption         =    "&Load Palette..."
   End
   Begin VB.Menu SavePalette
      Caption         =    "Save &Palette..."
   End
   Begin VB.Menu Exit
      Caption         =    "E&xit"
   End
End
Begin VB.Menu Edit
   Caption         =    "Edit"
   Begin VB.Menu CopyFrame
      Caption         =    "&Copy Frame"
   End
End
Begin VB.Menu Options
   Caption         =    "&Options"
   Begin VB.Menu VideoSource
      Caption         =    "&Video Source..."
   End
   Begin VB.Menu VideoFormat
      Caption         =    "Video &Format..."
   End
   Begin VB.Menu VideoDisplay
      Caption         =    "Video &Display..."
   End
   Begin VB.Menu ViewAnalog
```

III

Video Capabilities

(continues)

Listing 8.1   Continued

```
            Caption         =   "View &Analog"
        End
        Begin VB.Menu CaptureAudio
            Caption         =   "&Capture Audio"
        End
    End
    Begin VB.Menu Capture
        Caption         =   "&Capture"
        Begin VB.Menu SingleFrame
            Caption         =   "&Single Frame"
        End
        Begin VB.Menu MotionVideo
            Caption         =   "&Motion Video..."
        End
        Begin VB.Menu Palette
            Caption         =   "&Palette..."
        End
    End
End
Attribute VB_Name = "CAPVBX"
Attribute VB_Creatable = False
Attribute VB_Exposed = False
```

Setting the Audio Capture Parameters

When setting up the capture control, there are a few important parameters that affect the final results of the captured video. The first set of parameters controls the type of audio that is captured with the digital video file.

Typically there are two data streams present in an .AVI file—video and audio. If there is no audio stream present, the resultant file size will be smaller; however, the video capture rate will be slightly higher because the CPU and storage systems are not being taxed by digitizing and storing audio information.

NOTE
When capturing audio with digital video, the audio capture is dependent on a separate audio board being present in the system. Audio data is not captured through the video capture board. The developer doesn't have to worry about setting up or controlling the audio board because this is automatically handled by the Video for Windows capture drivers.

As you can see in Listing 8.1, the audio parameters are set for 11 Khz `AudioRate`, 8 `AudioBits`, and 1 `AudioChannels`. This translates into an 11 Khz sample rate, 8 bits of audio data and a mono (one channel) recording. This represents the lowest possible storage requirements and also the lowest quality audio recording. By varying these parameters, the storage requirements and quality can be improved or reduced.

The typical variations for audio sample rate are 11 Khz for voice-quality recordings, 22 Khz for a good all-purpose recording rate for voice and music, and 44 Khz for CD-quality audio recordings. The quality of each sample taken can be increased by altering the amount of information captured through the `AudioBits` property. Most of the audio boards on the market are 16-bit; however, you can change this parameter to increase the audio quality, if 16-bit capture is supported by your audio board. Finally, the audio quality is affected if one audio channel is used (mono) or two channels are used (stereo).

There is also one additional factor to mention in capturing audio: the effect of the Audio Compression Manager. The Video for Windows run time comes complete with audio codecs that can reduce the storage requirements of the captured audio. If your audio board supports the real-time compression of audio files, the Audio Compression Manager loads the proper decompression codec on playback to decompress the audio file.

Initializing the Video Capture Driver

The first step that must be performed when a video capture application loads is to establish a connection with the video capture driver. This is shown in Listing 8.2. There can only be one instance of a video capture driver opened per system. This means that two capture controls cannot be placed in an application and use the video board at the same time. This also means that two separate applications cannot access the capture driver simultaneously either. If this functionality is desired, then multiple video boards and drivers must be installed.

When the CAPVBX application loads, the video capture board is loaded and initialized; this is done by setting the `DriverNum` and `Connect` properties of the CAPWND.VBX control (see Listing 8.2). In a similar fashion, the driver must be disconnected upon application exit or else the capture driver will be in use and no other application will be able to access it.

Listing 8.2 CAPVBX.FRM. How the capture application initializes the video capture control.

```
Private Sub Form_Load()
    CaptureWindow.DriverNum = 0
    CaptureWindow.Connect = True
    CenterWindow
End Sub

Public Sub CenterWindow()
    CaptureWindow.Top = _
```

(continues)

III

Video Capabilities

Listing 8.2 Continued

```
CAPVBX.Height \ 2 - CaptureWindow.Height \ 2
   CaptureWindow.Left = _
CAPVBX.Width \ 2 - CaptureWindow.Width \ 2
End Sub

Private Sub Exit_Click()
   CaptureWindow.Connect = False
   Unload CAPVBX
   End
End Sub
```

Video Capture Variations

There are five types of video captures that can be performed using Video for Windows:

- *Full-motion video capture.* This is the capture of incoming video frames at a constant frame rate. Simultaneous audio can be captured along with the video sequence.

- *Single-frame manual capture.* This type of video capture captures a single frame and appends the single frame to a capture file. No audio is captured.

- *Single-frame bitmapped capture.* This type of capture saves a single frame of video as an individual bitmapped image. No audio is captured.

- *Step capture.* Step capture is used in conjunction with MCI device drivers to control laser disc or videotape devices. The device is placed in a play/pause mode and each frame is single-stepped through in a video sequence. This allows the file capture rate to be constant. Audio is captured on the second pass through the video segment.

- *Palette capture.* Palette capture is important when the resulting .AVI or bitmapped file is being created in 256-color mode. A palette should be captured before the video is captured to prevent all images from appearing in black and white.

Listing 8.3 shows the subroutines that are called to capture full-motion video sequences.

Listing 8.3   CAPVBX.FRM. Subroutines for capturing full-motion video sequences.

```
Private Sub CaptureAudio_Click()
    If CaptureAudio.Checked Then
        CaptureWindow.CaptureAudio = False
        CaptureAudio.Checked = False
    Else
        CaptureWindow.CaptureAudio = True
        CaptureAudio.Checked = True
    End If
End Sub

Private Sub CaptureAbort_Click()
    CaptureWindow.CaptureStop = True
End Sub

Private Sub CaptureWindow_Error()
    If CaptureWindow.ErrorNum > 0 Then
        ErrorWindow = CaptureWindow.Error
    End If
End Sub

Private Sub CaptureWindow_Status()
    StatusWindow = CaptureWindow.Status
End Sub

Private Sub MotionVideo_Click()
    CaptureWindow.CaptureUseLimit = False
    CaptureWindow.Capture = True
End Sub
```

Capturing Full-Motion Video

To start full-motion video capture, simply set the Capture property to True and set the CaptureUseLimit property to False. Setting CaptureUseLimit to False allows the video capture to continue until the Esc key is pressed or until a mouse button is clicked. If the CaptureUseLimit property was set to True, the amount of video captured would be limited by the CaptureLimit property, which specifies the number of seconds of video to capture. If an error occurs during any part of the video capture process, the Error event is fired. The properties ErrorNum and Error are read-only properties that provide the error code and a string describing the error.

The Status event is fired when the status of the capture driver changes. For example, when the video capture process is started, the status of the capture driver switches from stopped to started. The current status of the capture driver can be determined by reading the Status property.

III

Video Capabilities

Video capture can be aborted at any time by setting the `CaptureStop` property to `True`. This works for full-motion video capture, step capture, and palette capture.

Capturing Single Video Frames

There are two types of single-frame captures—*single-frame manual capture* and *single-frame bitmapped capture*. Single-frame manual capture involves creating a sequence of video frames by manually selecting and saving each frame of previewed video. The frames form an .AVI file that plays back at the specified capture rate. There is no audio captured with this type of .AVI file. The subroutine `SingleFrame_Click` (see Listing 8.4) shows how this type of capture is performed. As you can see, setting the `SingleFrame` property to `True` captures a frame of video and appends the frame to the end of the capture file.

Listing 8.4 CAPVBX.FRM. Capturing and appending frames to a capture file with *SingleFrame*.

```
Private Sub CopyFrame_Click()
    CaptureWindow.EditCopy = True
End Sub

Private Sub SingleFrame_Click()
    CaptureWindow.SingleFrameOpen = True
    CaptureWindow.SingleFrame = True
    CaptureWindow.SingleFrameClose = True
End Sub
```

The single-frame bitmapped capture saves a single frame of video as a bitmapped image. For example, a frame of video can be saved as a .BMP file. For this to be performed using the CAPWNDX.VBX, the use of another control must be used. By setting the `EditCopy` property to `True`, a single frame of video is copied to the Clipboard. From there, the bitmap can be retrieved from the clipboard and pasted into a control like the Image control and saved as a bitmap file. This type of video capture is very popular and is used for many vertical market applications such as employee database applications.

Creating a Palette for Capturing Video

Creating a palette is a prerequisite for video capture if you are capturing video targeted at 256 color displays. Unless a palette is captured, the video will be captured in black and white or the video will use a previously captured palette. For the best quality video, first capture a new palette for each video sequence that is captured. Then capture the video sequence using the previously captured palette.

When Video for Windows calculates an optimal palette, it averages the palette entries for each video frame. Each incoming video frame is then mapped to the computed palette and displayed on the VGA surface. Some video boards, such as the Smart Video Recorder from Intel, calculate the palette automatically and therefore do not need to have a palette captured. If your board needs to have a palette captured, it is clearly evident because the video displayed will be black and white when the video driver is first invoked. If the video capture board supports displaying analog or overlay video and you are previewing the video on the overlay plane, the colors will appear in true-color regardless of the capture mode. This is not how the captured video will be displayed. To preview how the captured video will appear, the incoming video must be previewed on the VGA surface.

The `Palette_Click` subroutine in Listing 8.5 shows how a palette is captured using the CAPWNDX VBX. The first step is to set the number of colors to be stored in the palette by setting the `PalNumColors` property to 236 colors rather than 256. Setting the property to 236 allows room for the Windows system palette to be included in the computed palette. The next step is to indicate the number of frames to use for computing the palette by setting the `PalNumFrames` property. The palette is captured by setting the property `PalCreate` to `True`. In the following code, the subroutine `LoadPalette_Click` shows how to load a palette from disk. The subroutine `SavePalette_Click` shows how to save a palette to disk.

Listing 8.5   CAPVBX.FRM. Capturing a palette with *Palette_Click*.

```
    Private Sub LoadPalette_Click()
        PaletteDialog.DialogTitle = "File Open"
        PaletteDialog.Action = 1
        CaptureWindow.PalOpen = PaletteDialog.FileName

    End Sub

    Private Sub Palette_Click()
        CaptureWindow.PalNumColors = 236
        CaptureWindow.PalNumFrames = 30
        CaptureWindow.PalCreate = True
    End Sub

    Private Sub SavePalette_Click()
        PaletteDialog.DialogTitle = "File Save"
        PaletteDialog.Action = 1
        CaptureWindow.PalSave = PaletteDialog.FileName
    End Sub
```

III

Video Capabilities

Miscellaneous Video Capture Notes

Listing 8.6 shows how to invoke the various configuration dialog boxes to be used with Video for Windows by using the `CaptureSave` property. The `CaptureSave` property invokes the necessary dialog boxes needed for this action. One of the dialog boxes provides the capability to remove the captured AVI sequence from the capture file and stores it in an individual .AVI file. As previously mentioned, Video for Windows captures all video and audio into a previously allocated capture file. This is done to improve capture speed. Once the video is captured, it needs to be removed from the capture file and compressed using the installable codecs available on the system.

Listing 8.6 CAPVBX.FRM. Using *CaptureSave* to invoke configuration dialog boxes.

```
Private Sub SaveCapturedVideoAs_Click()
    CaptureDialog.DialogTitle = "File Save"
    CaptureDialog.Action = 1
    CaptureWindow.CaptureSave = CaptureDialog.FileName
End Sub

Private Sub VideoDisplay_Click()
    CaptureWindow.VideoDisplayDlg = True
End Sub

Private Sub VideoFormat_Click()
    CaptureWindow.VideoFormatDlg = True
    CenterWindow
End Sub

Private Sub VideoSource_Click()
    CaptureWindow.VideoSourceDlg = True
End Sub

Private Sub ViewAnalog_Click()
    If CaptureWindow.CanOverlay Then
        If ViewAnalog.Checked Then
            CaptureWindow.Overlay = False
            ViewAnalog.Checked = False
        Else
            CaptureWindow.Overlay = True
            ViewAnalog.Checked = True
        End If
    End If
End Sub
```

The Video for Windows Capture VBX Command Reference

Making video capture easy is the purpose of the Video for Windows capture control. This VBX allows the programmer control over most aspects of digital video control. Table 8.1 lists all the properties of the CAPWNDX.VBX.

Table 8.1   The Properties of CAPWNDX.VBX

Properties	Description
AudioBits	Specifies how many bits to use for capturing audio. Typically 8- or 16-bit.
AudioChannels	Specifies the number of channels to use for audio capture. 1—mono; 2—stereo.
AudioRate	Specifies the sample rate in kilohertz to use for audio capture. Typical values are 11025 (11Khz), 22050 (22Khz), and 44100 (44Khz).
AutoSize	When True, the control is sized to the size of the video image. When False, the video is stretched to fill the size of the control.
BorderStyle	Determines if a border appears around the control.
CanOverlay	Specifies whether the video driver supports overlay or live video.
Capture	Controls when video capture starts and stops. Other properties can provide control over the capture once started.
CaptureAbort	Stops the capture of audio and video.
CaptureAudio	Enables or disables the capturing of audio when capturing video.
CaptureDOSMem	When True, the memory under the 1MB boundary is used for video capture. When False, extended memory is used.
CaptureFile	Specifies the name of the file into which video is captured.
CaptureFileSize	Specifies the capture file size in kilobytes. Pre-allocating a large capture file improves capture throughput to the disk.
CaptureHitOK	Determines whether to display a dialog box when the user presses Enter to start video capture or to not display the dialog box and start video capture as soon as possible. A dialog box may be used because capture does not start instantaneously when the Capture property is set to True.
CaptureLimit	Specifies the number of seconds for which to capture video when the CaptureUseLimit property is set to True.

(continues)

Table 8.1 Continued

Properties	Description
CaptureSave	Copies the contents of the capture file to a new file.
CaptureStop	Stops audio and video capture.
CaptureUseLimit	Determines whether capture stops after a specified number of seconds or when the user presses the Esc key or clicks a mouse button.
Connect	Determines if a driver is connected to the control for video capture or connects the driver specified by the DriverNum property to the control.
DriverName	Returns the name of the capture driver specified by the DriverNum property.
DriverNum	Zero-based index that specifies the capture driver to use.
DriverVersion	Returns the version of the capture driver specified by the DriverNum property.
EditCopy	Determines whether the current frame is copied to the Clipboard.
Error	Returns a description of the last error.
ErrorNum	Returns the last error number.
Height	Specifies the height of the control on the form.
Left	Specifies the position of the left side of the control on the form.
MCIDeviceEnable	Determines whether an MCI device is to be used as the source of video for capture.
MCIDeviceName	Specifies the name of the MCI device to be used as the source for video capture. Specifies a VCR or laser disc device.
MCIStartMS	Specifies the start position on the media in the MCI device for video capture. Time is in milliseconds.
MCIStepCapture	Determines if the video driver is to record the video sequence from the MCI device in a frame-by-frame or step manner.
MCIStopMS	Specifies the end position on the media in the MCI device for video capture. Time is in milliseconds.
Name	Specifies the name of the control.

Properties	Description
Overlay	Determines if overlay mode for the capture driver is enabled. When set to True, the preview mode settings are disabled.
PalCreate	Creates a palette to be used for 8-bit palletized video capture.
PalCreateManual	Manually creates a palette for palletized video capture.
PalNumColors	Specifies the number of colors that the palette is to contain when the PalCreate method is called. The number of palette colors can range from 2 to 256.
PalNumFrames	Specifies the number of video frames to use for computing the palette.
PalOpen	Opens a palette file to be used for video capture.
PalSave	Saves the current palette to a file.
Preview	Determines if preview mode is to be used for viewing incoming video. When set to True, incoming video frames are captured at the designated PreviewRate and displayed on the screen.
PreviewRate	Specifies the rate at which incoming video frames are to be captured and displayed on the screen.
SingleFrame	Captures a single frame of video and appends it to the end of the capture file.
SingleFrameClose	Terminates single-frame capture mode.
SingleFrameOpen	Opens the capture file and prepares the capture driver for single-frame capture.
Status	Returns a description of the status of the capture process.
Top	Specifies the position of the top of the control relative to the top of the form that contains the control.
VideoCompressionDlg	Displays a dialog box listing the video compression options available on the system.
VideoDisplayDlg	Displays a dialog box containing display options that the capture driver supports.
VideoFormatDlg	Displays a dialog box for choosing video format options such as size and color depth.
VideoRate	Specifies the rate at which video is to be captured and stored to disk.

III

Video Capabilities

(continues)

Table 8.1 Continued	
Properties	**Description**
VideoSourceDlg	Displays a dialog box for choosing the input for the incoming video signal.
Visible	Determines the visibility of the control.
Width	Specifies the width of the control on the form.
Yield	Specifies if video capture occurs as a background task.

As with any VBX, there is a set of events that provides interaction with the VBX. CAPWNDX.VBX is no different. CAPWNDX contains two events that provide status and error information to the developer. Table 8.2 explains the events of CAPWNDX.VBX.

Table 8.2 Custom Event Handlers for the CAPWNDX VBX	
Event	**Description**
Error	The Error event is fired when an error occurs during video capture. The reason for the error can be determined by checking the Error property.
Status	The Status event is fired when a change in the status of the capture driver occurs. Checking the status indicates the new status of the capture driver.

Using the MediaRecorder Toolkit OLE Custom Control

One of the drawbacks to CAPWNDX.VBX is its lack of control when performing single-frame capture. Many applications can not only require motion video capture but single-frame capture. The CAPWNDX.VBX does not provide the capability to capture a single video frame and save this frame as a bitmapped graphics file. An employee database is an example of an application that would capture a single frame of video (employee photo) and save this image as a bitmapped graphic.

The CAPWNDX.VBX also lacks the capability to freeze or unfreeze the video display, which is essential for performing video capture. Using CAPWNDX.VBX results in writing a lot of setup code to properly configure the capture drivers. This is unnecessary work that can be done very easily using the MediaRecorder Toolkit.

Lenel's MediaRecorder Toolkit OCX provides the capabilities of
CAPWNDX.VBX for capturing motion video, but also provides a variety of
options for capturing still images as well. The MediaRecorder Toolkit OCX is
also available in 16-bit and 32-bit flavors, which opens your target markets up
to all of the Windows operating systems.

When creating an application with the MediaRecorder Toolkit OCX, the
same prerequisites that applied to the Video for Windows control apply:
your capture hardware and software must be installed and configured properly before starting. Then simply draw the capture control on the Visual Basic
form and you see that live video appears within the control. The control is
automatically configured to use the first available capture driver present on
the system. In addition, if menu negotiation is enabled in your form, an in-
place activation menu appears on your application when the control is activated at runtime by clicking it. The MediaRecorder menu allows all of the
setup dialogs and capture methods to be invoked without having to write any
code!

The MediaRecorder Toolkit has the capability to take advantage of video
hardware that supports hardware-assisted playback. By using the `PreviewZoom`
property, the capture and preview sizes can be altered independently of each
other. For example, this allows you to use a smaller capture size such as
160X120 and to preview the video when played back at 320X240. To see if
your video board supports this capability, invoke the following sequence of
calls:

1. Check the `CanPreviewZoom` method to determine if your capture hardware supports this capability.

2. Set the `PreviewZoom` property to `True`.

3. Set the `PreviewMode` property to `Digital`.

4. Independently alter the properties `CaptureWidth` and `CaptureHeight`
   versus `PreviewWidth` and `PreviewHeight`. This allows you to view the
   effects of hardware scaling on the captured video.

When capturing still images using the MediaRecorder Toolkit, images can
be full size or cropped using a moveable and sizable cropping rectangle. Images can be saved to a variety of formats including .JPEG, .BMP, .TGA, .TIF,
and .GIF.

The sample program STILLIMG.EXE illustrates the capabilities of still-image
capture using the MediaRecorder Toolkit. Motion video is also given as a
result of in-place activation. In Listing 8.7, you can see that all of the

III

Video Capabilities

CAPVBX program functionality plus still-image capture and the image-capture frame have been duplicated by allowing in-place activation to occur when clicking the capture control. My entire application was created by drawing a MediaRecorder control and creating a menu!

Listing 8.7 STILLIMG.FRM. Duplicating still-image capture and image-capture frame with CAPVBX.

```
VERSION 4.00
Begin VB.Form STILLIMG
   BackColor       =    &H00808080&
   Caption         =    "Video Capture Using MediaRecorder Toolkit"
   ClientHeight    =    4230
   ClientLeft      =    1095
   ClientTop       =    1740
   ClientWidth     =    6720
   BeginProperty Font
      name         =    "MS Sans Serif"
      charset      =    1
      weight       =    400
      size         =    8.25
      underline    =    0    'False
      italic       =    0    'False
      strikethrough =   0    'False
   EndProperty
   Height          =    4920
   Left            =    1035
   LinkTopic       =    "Form1"
   ScaleHeight     =    282
   ScaleMode       =    3    'Pixel
   ScaleWidth      =    448
   Top             =    1110
   Width           =    6840
   Begin L_captLib.L_capt CaptureControl
      Height       =    3615
      Left         =    960
      TabIndex     =    0
      TabStop      =    0    'False
      Top          =    360
      Width        =    4815
      _version     =    65536
      _extentx     =    8493
      _extenty     =    6376
      _stockprops  =    97
      backcolor    =    16711680
      borderstyle  =    1
      freeze       =    -1   'True
      useambientcolor =    0 'False
   End
   Begin VB.Menu File
      Caption      =    "&File"
      Begin VB.Menu Exit
         Caption   =    "E&xit"
```

```
        End
    End
End
Attribute VB_Name = "STILLIMG"
Attribute VB_Creatable = False
Attribute VB_Exposed = False

Private Sub Exit_Click()
    End
End Sub
```

Control Properties for the MediaRecorder Toolkit

Table 8.3 provides a description of the properties for the MediaRecorder Toolkit OLE control.

Table 8.3 Properties for the MediaRecorder Toolkit OCX	
Properties	**Description**
AutoPaletteCaptureMode	Determines the type of capture to perform for automatic palette capture.
BackColor	Specifies the background color of the capture window.
BorderStyle	Determines the type of border to place around the control.
BorderWidth	Determines the width of the border or frame around the capture window. 0—no frame.
BottomBorderColor	Determines the color of the bottom border around the capture window.
CaptDurationHrs	Specifies the number of hours for which to capture video.
CaptDurationMin	Specifies the number of minutes for which to capture video.
CaptDurationSec	Specifies the number of seconds for which to capture video.
CaptureAudio	Enables or disables the capturing of audio when capturing AVI video.
CaptureFile	Specifies the file to use for capturing AVI video.
CaptureFileSize	Indicates the maximum size of the capture file.

III

Video Capabilities

(continues)

Table 8.3 Continued

Properties	Description
CaptureFrameHeight	Indicates the height of the capture frame.
CaptureFrameLeft	Indicates the left position of the capture frame.
CaptureFrameTop	Indicates the top position of the capture frame.
CaptureFrameWidth	Indicates the width of the capture frame.
CaptureHeight	Indicates the height at which to capture the AVI video.
CaptureMode	Determines the duration of the video capture.
CaptureType	Determines the type of video capture—time elapsed or constant frame rate.
CaptureWidth	Indicates the width at which to capture the AVI video.
Enabled	Enables the control, if set to True; disables the control from accepting user input, if set to False.
FrameRate	Indicates the rate at which to capture AVI video.
Freeze	Freezes (if set to True) or unfreezes (if set to False) the displayed video.
Hwnd	Window handle (HWND) of the control.
LeftBorderColor	Indicates the color of the left border around the capture window.
ManualPaletteCaptureMode	Determines the type of capture to perform for manual palette capture.
PalCaptNumColors	Specifies the number of colors (1–256) to use when computing a palette.
PalCaptNumFrames	Specifies the number of frames to average when capturing a palette.
PalCaptNumMinutes	Specifies the number of minutes to average when capturing a palette.
PalCaptNumSeconds	Specifies the number of seconds to average when capturing a palette.
Picture	Returns an Ipicture pointer of the contents of the image control.
PreviewHeight	Indicates the height of the preview window within the capture object window.

Properties	Description
PreviewMode	Allows for the preview window to display in analog or digital mode.
PreviewWidth	Indicates the width of the preview window.
PreviewZoom	Allows the capture size to be a different size than the preview size. Only available in digital preview mode and if hardware supports this feature.
RightBorderColor	Indicates the color of the right border around the capture window.
TLHrsBtwFrames	Indicates the number of hours between frames; used for time lapse recording, where one video frame is captured every HH:MM:SS.
TLMinBtwFrames	Indicates the number of minutes between frames; used for time lapse recording, where one video frame is captured every HH:MM:SS.
TLSecBtwFrames	Indicates the number of seconds between frames; used for time lapse recording, where one video frame is captured every HH:MM:SS.
TopBorderColor	Indicates the color of the top border around the capture window.
UseAmbientColor	When True, the controls background is set to the background color of the control container. When False, sets the controls background to the user-specified background.
UseCaptureFrame	Invokes a sizable frame for capturing still-frame images.

Control Methods for the MediaRecorder Toolkit

Table 8.4 provides a description of the methods for the MediaRecorder Toolkit OLE control.

Table 8.4 MediaRecorder Toolkit OLE Control Methods

Method	Description
AbortAviCapture	Aborts the capture of AVI video.
AbortPaletteCapture	Aborts the capture of a palette.
AboutBox	Invokes an About dialog box for the OLE control.

(continues)

Table 8.4 Continued

Method	Description
ActualClipLengthFrames	Returns the actual length of the captured video in frames.
ActualClipLengthMS	Returns the actual length of the captured video in milliseconds.
ActualFrameRate	Returns the actual frame capture rate of the video.
AnalogDisplayDlg	Invokes the dialog box for configuring the Analog Display of the capture board. The appearance of the dialog box is board-specific.
AnalogDisplayHasDlg	Returns True if the video board has an analog display configuration dialog.
AudioFormatDlg	Invokes dialog box for configuring audio-capture formats.
AviCapture	Starts the capture of AVI video, manual or automatic.
CanDisplayAnalog	Returns True if the video capture board can display analog video.
CanPreviewZoom	Returns True if the video capture board supports hardware zooming.
CaptureFrames	Captures frames of AVI video manually through user intervention.
CapturePalette	Captures a palette for use during video capture.
CaptureVideo	Captures AVI video using the capture duration parameters or UserAbortCapture parameter.
CompressionDlg	Invokes a dialog box for choosing the AVI compressor to use for captured video.
CopyFrame	Copies the current contents of the capture window to the Clipboard.
CopyPalette	Copies the palette of the current frame in the capture window to the Clipboard.
CreateThumbnail	Returns a thumbnail of the current contents being displayed in DIB (Device Independent Bitmap) format.
FrameCompressionDlg	Invokes a dialog box to set single frame compression options.
GetBitmap	Returns a Windows DDB (Device Dependent Bitmap) from the contents of the current display.

Method	Description
GetDIB	Returns a Windows DIB (Device Independent Bitmap) from the contents of the current display.
GetPalette	Returns a palette handle from the contents of the current display.
LoadPalette	Loads a palette from a file. This palette is used for capturing AVI video.
NumFramesDropped	Returns the number of frames dropped during video capture.
PaletteCaptureDlg	Invokes a dialog box for setting up the parameters for palette capture.
PaletteRequired	Returns True if the capture format requires the capture of a palette.
PastePalette	Pastes the palette from the Clipboard to the capture window, which becomes the palette used for video capture.
Refresh	Re-paints the display window.
SaveCapturedVideoAs	Saves the most recently captured video to another file applying the compression schemes specified by the user.
SaveFrame	Saves the current frame in the capture window as a bitmap file.
SavePalette	Saves the current palette in the capture window to a file.
VideoCaptureFileDlg	Invokes a dialog box to configure capture file size and location.
VideoFormatDlg	Invokes a dialog box for choosing the video format to capture the AVI video.
VideoSourceDlg	Invokes a dialog box for configuring video source (inputs) of the capture board.
VideoSourceHasDlg	Returns True if the video capture board has a Video Source configuration dialog box.

Control Events for the MediaRecorder Toolkit

Table 8.5 provides a description of the events for the MediaRecorder Toolkit OLE control.

Table 8.5 MediaRecorder Toolkit OLE Control Events

Event	Description
CaptureCued	Fires when capture has been invoked and the capture driver is ready to begin capturing video.
CaptureDone	Fires when video capture has been completed.
PaletteCaptureCued	Fires when palette capture has been invoked and the capture driver is ready to begin capturing the palette.
PaletteCaptureDone	Fires when palette capture has been completed.

Capturing Video in the Windows 3.1 Environment

Virtually all of the video capture boards on the market have video capture drivers for the 16-bit or Windows 3.1 operating system. The components that comprise Video for Windows are additional add-on DLLs that supplement the Windows 3.1 environment to support digital video playback and capture.

Table 8.6 lists components of the Video for Windows environment.

Table 8.6 The Video for Windows Components

Component	Description
AVICAP.DLL	Contains the functions used to perform video capture. This module provides a high-level interface to the .AVI file I/O routines and the video capture and audio device drivers. The tools such as CAPWNDX.VBX and the MediaRecorder Toolkit use these functions to perform video capture.
MSVIDEO.DLL	Contains a set of fast-drawing routines used for displaying the digital video frames on the graphics display. These DrawDib functions behave similar to super-fast StretchDIBits functions. These functions also support the Installable Compression Manager (ICM) for decompressing the video frames.
MCIAVI.DRV	MCI driver for Video for Windows playback.
AVIFILE.DLL	Contains high-level .AVI file access functions. These functions manage the video frames and data streams present in an .AVI file. These data streams provide synchronized playback of multiple data channels such as video, audio, MIDI and narrations. Custom data streams can be added and supported via custom stream handlers.

Component	Description
Installable Compression Manager (ICM)	Manages the codecs that compress and decompress the video data in .AVI files.
Audio Compression Manager (ACM)	Manages the compression and decompression of audio data within .AVI files. The Audio Compression Manager can also be used independently of Video for Windows. The Audio Compression Manager is installed automatically when installing Video for Windows. The Sound Mapper application provides the capability to map audio compression drivers with waveaudio devices. The Sound Mapper application also provides audio codec configuration.

Capturing Video in the Windows 95 Environment

The Windows 95 environment is an interesting operating system for capturing digital video. Both the Video for Windows capture and playback components are included as base components of Windows 95. This relieves the developer from having to ship these components as part of their application.

Windows 95 also includes automatic detection of video capture drivers through Plug-and-Play technology. This makes the installation and setup of video capture boards a relatively simple process. Windows 95 ships with video capture drivers for Orchid Vidiola Video Capture Card.

All the 16-bit Video for Windows capture applications and tools work with Windows 95, because Windows 95 allows direct access to the capture hardware. Windows 95 also can use the 32-bit capture drivers and API that Windows NT uses. For end users, this means that configuring and using video capture applications and video boards will be an easy task. You can take the best of both worlds or choose just one (16-bit or 32-bit) world to run in.

> **Caution**
>
> The only caveat is that 16-bit DLLs or applications cannot be mixed with 32-bit DLLs or applications. This means that your 32-bit Visual Basic applications cannot call or use 16-bit DLLs on the system.

Capturing Video in the Windows NT Environment

Unlike Windows 95, the Windows NT operating system is unable to handle 16-bit video capture. All the 16-bit video capture drivers written for the Windows 3.1 environments access the capture board directly. This type of access

III

Video Capabilities

is forbidden in the protected Windows NT environment. A 32-bit protected mode device driver must be written for any hardware component to be accessed via an application. This means that the 16-bit capture applications and 16-bit capture tools will not work on Windows NT.

Microsoft has provided a Video for Windows capture API for Windows NT. The Video for Windows capture API is consistent with the Windows 95 and Windows 3.x versions of Video for Windows. With the availability of 32-bit capture drivers, it is a matter of porting the 32-bit applications and tools over to 32-bit for video capture to work under Windows NT.

With the release of Windows NT 3.1, Video for Windows capture and playback support have been included as a standard component of the operation system. This relieves the burden of providing the Video for Windows runtime diskettes and capture libraries when distributing your digital video applications. The components are located in the WINNT\SYSTEM directory of your Windows NT machine. The following are the new component names for each portion of Video for Windows:

16-bit Module Name	32-bit Module Name
AVICAPT.DLL	AVICAP32.DLL
AVIFILE.DLL	AVIFIL32.DLL
MSVIDEO.DLL	MSVIDC32.DLL
MSVFW.DLL	MSVFW32.DLL MSAVI32.DLL MSACM32.DLL
MCIAVI.DRV	MCIAVI32.DLL

From Here...

In this chapter, techniques for capturing digital video were examined and demonstrated. The Video for Windows capture architecture and how this architecture relates to the types of digital video available on the Windows platforms were explored. Video capture issues specific to the Windows 3.1, Windows 95 and Windows NT platforms were also examined.

■ For a discussion of the multimedia capabilities of the Windows 3.1, Windows 95 and Windows NT platforms, see Chapter 2, "Multimedia Development with Windows."

■ For information on techniques for playing analog video, see Chapter 9, "Using Peripheral Devices for Overlay Video." This chapter provides insight into the other types of video available for Windows applications, in order to determine the best choice for your application.

■ For more information on techniques for playing back digital video under the various Windows platforms, see Chapter 11, "Using Digital Video Playback." The integration of digital video into applications is also explored.

III

Video Capabilities

Chapter 9

Using Peripheral Devices for Overlay Video

It's the middle of the afternoon at work. The phone rings and it's a friend who is calling to tell you that a major news event is breaking on TV. He asks if you can get to a TV set to watch the broadcast. "No problem," you reply as you move to your PC and switch tasks from the spreadsheet that you were working on to your TV tuner application. You tile the application windows and now you are watching the news broadcast while continuing to work on your spreadsheet.

This scenario may seem far-fetched, but it is not. In fact, this situation may be occurring more frequently with our unending need for timely information. You are probably wondering how a TV signal can be displayed on your PC, what special hardware or software is needed, and how much it costs. Surprisingly, very little hardware, software, or money is needed for such an application.

The technology used in this situation is called *overlay video*. All that is needed to display video information on your computer screen is an additional overlay video board, which works in conjunction with your standard VGA card to combine the video and graphics signals into one cohesive display.

This chapter provides information on using overlay video in your applications. The topics include the following:

- What is overlay video

- Available video formats and standards

- Why overlay video is used in an application

III

Video Capabilities

■ How to use peripheral devices such as laser discs and videotape decks

■ A practical guide for avoiding common mistakes when using overlay video.

Understanding Overlay Video

There are two methods for viewing full-motion video on the PC: *digital video* and *analog video*. Digital video is video that has been "captured" or "digitized" from a video source and stored digitally in a file on a computer hard disk. The digital video is captured at a constant frame rate—for example, at 30 frames per second (fps). This means that 30 times per second, a frame of incoming video is stored electronically to a computer file.

Analog video, by contrast, is a constant video stream that is input to an overlay video board and displayed on a computer screen. Examples of analog video include the video signals from a TV or VCR. Unlike digital video, no storage requirements are necessary on the computer hard disk, nor is the display of analog video tax the computer's CPU. All the work of displaying analog video is placed on the overlay video board.

The term *overlay video* is derived from the technique used to display analog video on the computer screen. When you run a Windows program, all the visual components of the program (windows, menus, buttons, graphics, and so on) are displayed through the video graphics adapter (VGA adapter) within the PC. All Windows programs share the frame buffer of the VGA adapter.

Overlay video is not displayed through the VGA adapter. The overlay video board connects to the VGA adapter through a connection known as a *feature connector*. The overlay video board combines the output from the VGA adapter with the output from the overlay video board and creates a composite result that is displayed on the computer monitor. Thus, the overlay video output is overlaid on top of the graphics adapter to form a single output, which is displayed on the computer monitor. Figure 9.1 illustrates an overlay video connection.

The combination of overlay video and VGA boards is often referred to as *two-plane technology*. This is in reference to the overlay video plane and the VGA plane, respectively.

In order for the video to be displayed on your PC monitor, the video must be displayed through the VGA surface. This technique is performed through the designation of a *key-color* on the VGA surface. A key-color is one of the displayable colors of the current VGA resolution that is used by the overlay video board to pass through the analog video. The most often used key-color is magenta. When a window used to display video is created, the background of the window is filled with the key-color. The video shows through where the key-color is present on the window.

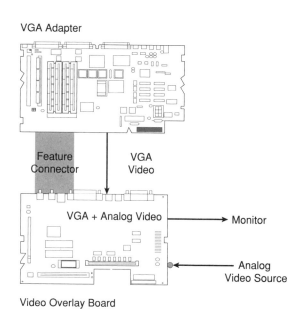

VGA Adapter

Feature Connector

VGA Video

VGA + Analog Video → Monitor

Analog Video Source

Video Overlay Board

Fig. 9.1
How overlay video boards and VGA boards are connected.

When you are developing an application that uses an overlay video board, you don't need to worry about creating a window with the appropriate key-color or how to make the video display on the screen. This is handled by the device driver for the video board. You need to interface only with the device driver.

Using Analog Video

Analog video gives you an alternative method of providing full-motion video for applications. Analog video offers a consistent delivery of *full-motion video* to the user, regardless of the size of the playback area. Full-motion video is defined as a constant frame rate for video delivery where the human eye cannot detect frame breakup. This frame rate is 30 frames per second (fps).

There are several important factors that might contribute to your decision to use analog video in an application. The most important is the type of application being developed. For instance, a training application can rely on analog video from a laser disc as well as digital video from a file. But sometimes analog video is the only choice; for example, a TV monitor application needs to use analog video because it is acting like a TV set where the incoming video signal is received from a TV tuner.

Along with the type of application being developed, there are other trade-offs to think about when choosing whether to use analog video or digital video:

- *Analog video requires less CPU usage than digital video.* Analog video is simply passed through and displayed on the overlay surface, requiring no main CPU usage by the application. Digital video is very CPU-intensive unless a digital video playback board is used (as in the case of MPEG video).

- *Analog video requires at least one nonstandard PC component, the overlay video board.* It also requires a video source such as a TV tuner or laser disc. Most digital video formats can be played back without any extra hardware assistance.

- *Analog video requires less storage than digital video.* There are no files; all video is stored on a laser disc or videotape, or it is a live signal.

- *Applications using analog video are less portable than applications using digital video.* Analog video requires an input source, which means that distributing the application requires the sending of input material such as a laser disc or videotape, or an input device. The recipient of the application must also have an overlay video board.

- *Analog video can typically provide better resolution, scalability, and playback rates than its digital counterparts.* This advantage is rapidly disappearing with the appearance of video accelerator boards and digital video playback boards.

- *Most analog video boards render VGA output to 256 colors and typically 800×600 or lower screen resolution.* The 256-color resolution is due to the limitations of the video feature connector used to connect the VGA adapter to the overlay video board. The feature connector bus width is 8-bits. Some overlay video board manufacturers are starting to take advantage of local bus and PCI bus technologies and offer true-color VGA resolutions when using their overlay board. In-Motion Corp.'s Picture Perfect Professional is an example of an overlay video board that features true-color VGA resolutions. These solutions are relatively new and more expensive than overlay video boards that use the feature connector for their VGA connection.

Analog Video Standards and Formats

There are two types of video standards that you need to consider when working with analog video. These standards are NTSC (National Television Standards Committee) and PAL (Phase Alternating Line). The video standards comprise the type of signal output from a video source. NTSC is the video standard that is used in the United States; PAL is used in Europe. When you are developing applications that use analog video, it is important to get a video board that supports both standards if your application is going to be distributed internationally. Fortunately, most overlay video boards support both NTSC and PAL video sources.

The video format refers to the type of signal that is input into the overlay video board. The types of video formats are *composite video, S-Video,* and *RGB*.

The Difficulties of Using Analog Video

Using analog video within an application is not as straightforward as using another multimedia element such as digital video or audio. Some of the difficulties include using a nonstandard MCI command set, controlling multiple devices, and addressing unique command set features. The additional hardware requirements and the need to understand peripheral devices also require more thought and planning than for other media elements.

Table 9.1 lists some of the hardware components that are used when working with analog video.

Table 9.1   Common Hardware Components Used with Applications Requiring Analog Video

Component	Purpose
Overlay video board	Displays analog video on a PC screen.
Video camera	Used as a video source.
Laser disc player	Used as a video source.
VCR	Used as a video source.

(continues)

III

Video Capabilities

Table 9.1 Continued	
Component	**Purpose**
TV tuner	Used as a video source. This is often included as a part of the overlay video board. An example of this is the WinTV overlay video board.
TV monitor	Used for applications that may require a two-monitor solution. Only video is displayed on this monitor.
Extra power strips	Used to plug in the extra peripheral devices.
Video cables	Connects the video source to the video display device.

Even with the extra hardware requirements, analog video can be used effectively for a variety of applications. Analog video is excellent for training, video-on-demand, video library, educational, and video editing applications.

Controlling Multiple Devices

When using a multimedia element such as digital video, there is only one device driver that an application must control. Unless the video input does not require application control, such as a camera, then the application must be able to control multiple devices (overlay video board and the input device, such as a laser disc or a videotape device) when using analog video.

An application must synchronize the start and stop of the overlay video board and video source. This can be difficult depending on the input source, due to mechanical latency in starting and stopping the device. Applications must take synchronization into account, or the result will be a sloppy presentation of video output to the screen. The section, "Synchronizing the Overlay Video Board," discusses this topic in greater detail.

Using a Nonstandard MCI Command Set

When using an MCI driver for an overlay video board, the command set does not follow the basic MCI commands for controlling the device. The MCI command set for overlay video relies on the `freeze`, `unfreeze` and `put` commands for basic control.

The overlay video MCI specification provides basic control over the device. Video board manufacturers added tremendous capabilities to their products, yet the command specification didn't address their needs. To provide their customers with the best possible driver for their products, the board manufacturers extended the overlay MCI specification to include nonstandard commands.

Although these extended commands provide a great capability to the developer, they also create a problem when you try to create applications that are hardware-independent. The extended commands are defined by the developer who is expanding the command set, not by a committee or standards group. Thus, commands that perform the same function—for example, adjust a TV tuner—take different commands, data structures and flags. This defeats the whole purpose of a standard and leaves the programmer stranded.

There have been some advances to address this problem. Microsoft has defined the Digital Video MCI command set. The Digital Video command set is a superset of the overlay video commands. The overlay command set will not be expanded, and all overlay video board manufacturers are asked to develop MCI drivers for their products that will use the extended set of commands offered by the digital video command set.

> Appendix A, "The MCI Command Reference," contains all of the digital video MCI commands as well as the MPEG MCI and animation MCI commands.

Understanding the Overlay Video Device

The overlay video device is a complex board with many capabilities. In order to properly use the overlay video board within an application, you must be familiar with the basic terms and concepts of overlay video.

There are four different regions that are used for presenting overlay video: *video*, *frame*, *source*, and *destination*. The video region refers to the area of incoming video being brought into the overlay video board. This region has a maximum size and extent that is equal to the dimensions of the board's video frame buffer. The frame region refers to the area of video board's frame buffer that is to receive incoming video data. The source region refers to the region of the frame buffer that is to be displayed in the destination window. The destination region refers to the area of the destination window's client area that is to display the video data from the frame buffer. Figure 9.2 illustrates the different regions of an overlay video device and how they are related.

One other note about the overlay video device: some overlay video boards can support the opening of multiple overlay video windows. Each window can have a separate device input if the overlay board supports multiple video inputs. Only one video window will be actively displaying video. The other windows are frozen until activated. This is due to the video frame buffer being able to process only one video input actively at a time.

Fig. 9.2
Understanding the different regions and relationships of the overlay video board.

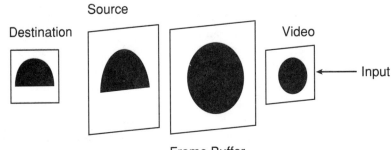

Using the Laser Disc Device

The laser disc device is one of the most popular video peripherals available when developing applications requiring analog video. The laser disc device is very useful for training, kiosk, and catalog applications. Laser disc players are popular for their virtually instant access times for searching to locations on the disc and playing video.

Laser disc devices are connected to the computer through a serial port. The serial connection allows the PC to issue control commands to the laser disc player. The video output from the laser disc player is connected to the video input of the overlay video board. The audio inputs from the laser disc player can be connected to the audio inputs of the overlay board, the line input of an audio board, or directly to a set of speakers. Figure 9.3 shows the typical laser disc connections to the PC.

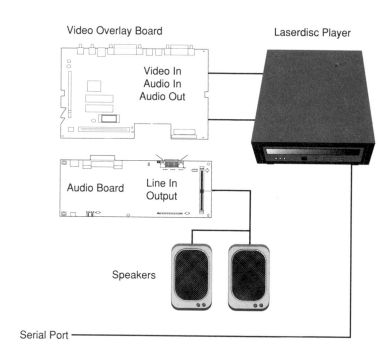

Video Overlay Board

Video In
Audio In
Audio Out

Laserdisc Player

Audio Board

Line In
Output

Speakers

Serial Port

Fig. 9.3
How a laser disc
player is connected
to a multimedia
PC.

Types of Laser Discs

There are two types of laser discs that can be used: *Constant Angular Velocity
(CAV)* and *Constant Linear Velocity (CLV)*. The type of disc that is used affects
the performance and capabilities of your laser disc player.

The CAV discs provide better performance than the CLV counterpart. CAV
discs are *frame-accurate,* which means that seeks are accurate to the exact
location specified. CAV discs allow the device to exhibit more control via the
step command.

CLV discs, by nature, are not capable of being frame-accurate, which means
that these discs should not be used for applications requiring absolute accu-
racy. When a seek is performed on a CLV disc, the location specified is not
always where the device seeks to. It seeks to the nearest location the device is
capable of providing for the disc. When a device is paused, a CLV disc may
not present as clear a picture as a CAV disc. Or, depending on the device, the
video signal may be stopped rather than held constant at the location.

III

Video Capabilities

Synchronizing the Overlay Video Board

To provide synchronization between the overlay video board and the laser disc device, both devices must be controlled at virtually the same time. Synchronization is vital to achieve a polished, professional look for your application. If you stop a device and then freeze the overlay video board, you might lose the last frame, leaving black or interference. Conversely, if the overlay video board is stopped first, then the correct last frame might not be grabbed.

Understanding how the laser disc device works is vital to achieving synchronization. The overlay video board has virtually instantaneous access to freezing and unfreezing the acquisition of incoming video data to the frame buffer. This performance is fairly constant from board to board and can be treated in this manner. This leaves the laser disc device as the unknown in the synchronization equation.

The laser disc device is an interesting blend of technologies. On one side, the laser disc device is mechanical in nature. This means that there is a built-in time lapse involved between issuing the `play` command to when the device actually starts playing. There is also a time lapse when issuing the `stop` command. The time lapse varies depending on whether the disc is spinning or not. If the disc is spinning, the start up time is less than if the disc is not spinning.

The laser disc device also behaves in a similar fashion as digital video device, such as Video for Windows, in that the seek times and response times to play video segments are very fast. The time lapse involved for playing the device is in starting the disc spinning and sending the serial command to the device. Once the command is issued, the response time is within a couple of seconds. This allows overlay video and laser discs to be a fast, responsive solution for training applications where full-screen, full-motion video is required without taxing the CPU.

The most effective method of synchronizing a laser disc with an overlay video board is to ensure the following conditions:

- Make sure that the laser disc device is spinning; this is accomplished through the `spin up` MCI command.

- Use the `pause` command to stop the laser disc device. When a laser disc player is paused, the video output signal is held constant. This means that you can grab the still image and display it in your application. When the laser disc device is stopped, there is no video output signal. Grabbing an image at this time results in a black image.

Using the Videotape Device

The videotape device is a very popular home or consumer-oriented device. Many of the newer models that are on the market have the capability to be controlled via a PC through a serial communications port. This capability allows for a very large installed base of VCR and camcorder owners to bring their video into the PC.

Some of the videotape devices have a direct serial port connection built into the device. Others, such as the devices from Sony, have what is called a Control-L jack on the device. The Control-L port can be connected to the serial port and controlled via a Control-L driver, but the most common method of controlling these devices is through a device called a VBOX. A VBOX uses a standard protocol developed by Sony called the VISCA protocol, for interfacing video peripherals to a PC. The VBOX connects the serial port on the PC to the Control-L port on the device. A VISCA driver is then used to communicate with the device. A MCI VISCA driver is available from several vendors including the Microsoft Video for Windows SDK, Sony, and Lenel Systems.

Unlike the laser disc device, the videotape device has the capability to record video. Laser disc players can also record, but the cost of read/write optical storage devices are only suitable for the most demanding applications. The capability to record video means that with a couple of controllable VCRs, a home editing system can be built utilizing the PC as the controlling interface.

Videotape devices offer a wide variety of video formats that can be used. Depending on the VCR or camcorder you are using, VHS, S-VHS, 8mm, HI-8mm, and betacam are the most popular consumer formats.

The videotape device is slightly different than a laser disc device when using it within an application. The greatest difference is the mechanical time lapse when issuing a command to the device. When a `play` command is issued, the tape must be mounted in the device, the read heads are engaged before the videotape starts to move, which takes a much longer time than laser disc.

Videotape is also a sequential access media. As compared with a laser disc, a videotape cannot instantly transport itself across the media to a specified location. The videotape device must rewind or fast-forward the media, traversing all of the tape in-between the current position and the requested position. Depending on the position, this can take several minutes.

Videotape devices are also less accurate in general than the laser disc counterparts. Some videotape devices are frame accurate and depend on an RC time code, which is placed on the tape during recording to find a location. Devices that do not support time codes are reliant upon a counter. A counter is accurate to within +/– 2 seconds for finding a location. It is also prone to human error because the counter must be reset when a new tape is inserted.

To address the needs of the videotape device, Microsoft defined a VCR or videotape command set that can be used to control the videotape device.

Synchronization between the videotape device and overlay video board is slightly different than with the laser disc device. The differences are listed below:

- There is no spin command for a videotape device. To get a device ready for playing, send the cue command. This engages the play or record heads so that the play or record commands can occur immediately.

- A videotape device has pre-roll and post-roll conditions that must be addressed. When a videotape device is playing and the stop command is sent, the tape does not stop at the current position. Instead, the tape is moved backwards a few frames. This is known as post-roll. When the play command is issued, the tape does not start outputting a stable signal immediately; instead, a few frames pass before the signal is stable. This is known as pre-roll. It is important to know these values if your application is dependent upon accurate positioning of the device.

- As with the laser disc player, pausing the videotape device results in a video signal being output from the device. Stopping the device results in no video signal being output. Unlike the laser disc player, the output signal during a pause is not as stable. You may consider freezing the image before the stop or pause command is issued.

Demonstrating a Video Center Application

To demonstrate the techniques of synchronizing overlay video with a videotape and laser disc device, I have put together a sample Video Center application. The application controls an overlay video board, a laser disc player, and a videotape device. The Video Center application can also capture single frames of video to graphic bitmap files. Figure 9.4 shows the user interface for the Video Center application. This functionality is commonly used in application such as employee databases where an employee's photo is input into a computer from a video camera then captured to a bitmapped graphics file for later display.

To run this application, you must have the following equipment:

- An overlay video board with an MCI driver. The driver alias in the MCI section of SYSTEM.INI must be called *overlay*.

- A laser disc device with an MCI driver. The driver alias must be called *laser disc*.

- If a laser disc is not available, use a videotape device with an MCI driver. The driver alias must be called *videotape*. Both a laser disc and video tape device can be used if they are available.

- The MCI driver for the overlay video board must support the save command for saving a frame of video as a bitmapped graphics file.

To demonstrate various techniques, the application uses the basic set of commands common to both the laser disc and videotape MCI command sets. This application can be enhanced by using the specific commands for each device type.

The Video Center application uses the MCI control provided with Visual Basic to control the laser disc and videotape devices. The mciSendString command is used to control the overlay device.

Fig. 9.4
Demonstrating the user interface for the Video Control Center.

III

Video Capabilities

Controls for the Application

The Video Center application is 16-bit and 32-bit capable, just compile the application with the proper version of Visual Basic. As you can see from the Video Center file listing, there are only a few controls used for this application. There is a `CommonDialog` control that is used for loading and saving video frames to files. There is a `Timer` control that is used for periodically querying the position of the laser disc and videotape devices. The current position of each device is displayed in a status box on the form. A list of all controls used for this application and their attributes are shown in Listing 9.1.

Listing 9.1 VCENTER.FRM. Controls used for the Video Center application.

```
VERSION 4.00
Begin VB.Form VCenter
    Caption         =   "Video Control Center"
    ClientHeight    =   5775
    ClientLeft      =   795
    ClientTop       =   810
    ClientWidth     =   8190
    BeginProperty Font
       name         =   "MS Sans Serif"
       charset      =   1
       weight       =   400
       size         =   8.25
       underline    =   0   'False
       italic       =   0   'False
       strikethrough =  0   'False
    EndProperty
    Height          =   6465
    Left            =   735
    LinkTopic       =   "Form2"
    ScaleHeight     =   385
    ScaleMode       =   3   'Pixel
    ScaleWidth      =   546
    Top             =   180
    Width           =   8310
    Begin VB.CommandButton LoadVideo
       Caption      =   "Load Video File..."
       Height       =   375
       Left         =   6360
       TabIndex     =   12
       Top          =   3240
       Width        =   1695
    End
    Begin VB.CommandButton SaveVideo
       Caption      =   "Save Video..."
       Height       =   375
       Left         =   6360
```

```
      TabIndex        =      11
      Top             =      2640
      Width           =      1695
   End
   Begin VB.CommandButton PlaySegment
      Caption         =      "Play Segment"
      Height          =      375
      Left            =      6360
      TabIndex        =      10
      Top             =      2040
      Width           =      1695
   End
   Begin VB.CommandButton SetEndPos
      Caption         =      "Set"
      Height          =      255
      Left            =      7440
      TabIndex        =      9
      Top             =      1320
      Width           =      615
   End
   Begin VB.CommandButton SetStartPos
      Caption         =      "Set"
      Height          =      255
      Left            =      7440
      TabIndex        =      8
      Top             =      600
      Width           =      615
   End
   Begin VB.TextBox EndPos
      Height          =      285
      Left            =      6360
      TabIndex        =      7
      Top             =      1680
      Width           =      1695
   End
   Begin VB.TextBox StartPos
      Height          =      285
      Left            =      6360
      TabIndex        =      6
      Top             =      960
      Width           =      1695
   End
   Begin VB.Timer Timer1
      Interval        =      2000
      Left            =      240
      Top             =      120
   End
   Begin MSComDlg.CommonDialog FileDlg
      Left            =      6960
      Top             =      4560
      _version        =      65536
      _extentx        =      847
      _extenty        =      847
      _stockprops     =      0
```

(continues)

III

Video Capabilities

Listing 9.1   Continued

```
            filename      =   "*.bmp"
            filter        =   "Bitmap(*.bmp)"
      End
      Begin VB.Label Label3
         Caption          =   "End Position:"
         Height           =   255
         Left             =   6360
         TabIndex         =   5
         Top              =   1320
         Width            =   975
      End
      Begin VB.Label Label2
         Caption          =   "Start Position:"
         Height           =   255
         Left             =   6360
         TabIndex         =   4
         Top              =   600
         Width            =   975
      End
      Begin VB.Label Units
         Caption          =   " "
         Height           =   255
         Left             =   4320
         TabIndex         =   3
         Top              =   5400
         Width            =   1215
      End
      Begin VB.Label CurrentPosition
         Height           =   255
         Left             =   2520
         TabIndex         =   2
         Top              =   5400
         Width            =   1695
      End
      Begin VB.Label Label1
         Caption          =   "Current Position:"
         Height           =   255
         Left             =   1200
         TabIndex         =   1
         Top              =   5400
         Width            =   1215
      End
      Begin MCI.MMControl MMDevice
         Height           =   735
         Left             =   1200
         TabIndex         =   0
         Top              =   4560
         Width            =   4995
         _version         =   65536
         _extentx         =   8811
         _extenty         =   1296
         _stockprops      =   32
         borderstyle      =   1
      End
```

```
Begin VB.Shape DisplayCenter
   Height          =   3600
   Left            =   1320
   Top             =   600
   Width           =   4800
End
Begin VB.Menu File
   Caption         =   "File"
   Begin VB.Menu Exit
      Caption      =   "Exit"
   End
End
Begin VB.Menu Device
   Caption         =   "Device"
   Begin VB.Menu Laserdisc
      Caption      =   "Laser disc"
   End
   Begin VB.Menu VCR
      Caption      =   "VCR"
   End
   Begin VB.Menu Camera
      Caption      =   "Camera"
   End
End
Begin VB.Menu Video
   Caption         =   "Video"
   Begin VB.Menu Freeze
      Caption      =   "Freeze"
   End
   Begin VB.Menu Align
      Caption      =   "Align"
   End
End
End
Attribute VB_Name = "VCenter"
Attribute VB_Creatable = False
Attribute VB_Exposed = False
```

Devices Used in the Video Center Application

Three devices are used by the Video Center application: a laser disc player, a videotape deck, and an overlay video board. The application uses two methods for interacting with these devices, the MCI control and the mciSendString. Although either method can be used with all three devices, it makes more sense to use the MCI control for interacting with the laser disc and videotape devices and the mciSendString API for controlling the overlay video board. This is because the user interface buttons on the MCI control closely represent the functionality of the laser disc and videotape devices. This coupled with the available properties and methods of the MCI control make this the easiest method for controlling these devices.

III

Video Capabilities

The overlay video device is a unique device that doesn't mimic the functionality provided by the MCI control neither in the user interface department nor by the available properties and methods. The overlay video board is really driven by the actions or modes of the videotape and laser disc devices.

Both the MCI control and the mciSendString API rely heavily on the use of command strings for controlling respective drivers. When developing an application that uses either of these methods, I like to have a set of constants that can be used for each of the commands that I might be using. VCENTER.FRM (on the CD-ROM) includes definitions for the constants that represent the modes or states that a device can be placed in. These are used when querying the mode of each device. Listing 9.2 shows these constants.

Listing 9.2 VCENTER.FRM. MCI string constants used in the Video Center application.

```
' Basic command strings for the MCI multimedia control
Const PLAY_STR = "Play"
Const STOP_STR = "Stop"
Const OPEN_STR = "Open"
Const CLOSE_STR = "Close"
Const PAUSE_STR = "Pause"
Const BACK_STR = "Back"
Const STEP_STR = "Step"
Const NEXT_STR = "Next"
Const PREV_STR = "Prev"
Const SEEK_STR = "Seek"
Const RECORD_STR = "Record"
Const EJECT_STR = "Eject"
Const SOUND_STR = "Sound"
Const SAVE_STR = "Save"
Const STATUS_STR = "Status"
Const SET_STR = "Set"
Const LOAD_STR = "Load"
'Command Strings for the overlay device type
Const FREEZE_STR = "Freeze"
Const PUT_STR = "Put"
Const WINDOW_STR = "Window"
Const WHERE_STR = "Where"
' mode constants
Const MODE_OPEN = 524
Const MODE_STOP = 525
Const MODE_PLAY = 526
Const MODE_RECORD = 527
Const MODE_SEEK = 528
Const MODE_PAUSE = 529
Const MODE_READY = 530
```

The rest of the constants found in the globals section of the Video Center form are used for two purposes, defining the logical name used for opening a device and for defining an alias for the overlay video board. Remember that all MCI drivers on a system are listed in the SYSTEM.INI file where the following syntax is used:

```
[mci]
LogicalName = mcidrvr.drv
```

`LogicalName` is the name that I have defined in the Video Center application. In order for the Video Center application to control the peripheral devices, the laser disc, videotape, and overlay MCI drivers must use the logical names defined in the globals section of the Video Center form. The constants used for each MCI device type are the typical `LogicalNames` for these drivers.

I have also defined a couple of global variables that are used for reporting the active peripheral device, the error return string and a fixed string that is used for any return string provided by the `mciSendString` command. The `mciSendString` command returns a string for the commands that provide return information. In order for this to happen, a fixed size string needs to be allocated. I have allocated one that is used for all calls to `mciSendString`. A fixed string is allocated in Visual Basic by using the following syntax:

```
Dim FixedStr As String * 50
```

This syntax indicates that 50 bytes are pre-allocated for the variable `FixedStr`.

Using Compilation Directives

For the application to be both 16-bit and 32-bit capable, compilation directives must be used. This because the 16-bit API used for `mciSendString` and `mciGetErrorString` are contained in a library named MMSYSTEM. The 32-bit APIs are contained in a library named WINMM. The compilation directives link to the appropriate library depending on the target operating system (Win32 or Win16) of the application. Listing 9.3 shows the rest of the globals section of the Video Center application.

Listing 9.3   VCENTER.FRM. Variables and API definitions used for the Video Center application.

```
' Device alias's used for the laser disc and vcr devices
Const LASERDISC_TYPE = "Laserdisc"
Const VCR_TYPE = "Videotape"
Const OVERLAY_TYPE = "Overlay"
```

(continues)

Listing 9.3 Continued

```
Const OVERLAY_ALIAS = "Board"
Const SPACE = " "
'Variables used for the Video Control Center
Dim FixedStr As String * 50
Dim ActiveDevice As String
Dim StatusReturn As String
' Declaration Statements
#If Win32 Then
Private Declare Function mciSendString Lib "WINMM"_
                    (ByVal Cmd As String, ByVal RetVal As String, _
                     ByVal Len As Integer, ByVal Notify As Integer) As Long
Private Declare Function mciGetErrorString Lib "WINMM"_
                    (ByVal Err As Long, ByVal RetVal As String, _
                     ByVal Len
                     As Integer) As Integer
#Else
Private Declare Function mciSendString Lib "MMSYSTEM"_
                    (ByVal Cmd As String, ByVal RetVal As String, _
                     ByVal Len_ As Integer, ByVal Notify As Integer) As Long
Private Declare Function mciGetErrorString Lib "MMSYSTEM"_
                    (ByVal Err As Long, ByVal RetVal As String, _
ByVal Len As Integer) As Integer
#End If
```

Because there is only one overlay video device used in this application, the overlay video device is loaded when the form loads. During the design of the application, I drew a rectangle shape in the middle of the application form. This rectangle is used as a reference to place the video provided from the overlay board. This rectangle is called DisplayCenter. When the form loads, subroutine OpenOverlayBoard is called.

The OpenOverlayBoard subroutine builds a string for opening the overlay video board. Overlay video drivers create a window that is used for displaying video. In order for this window to look like a seamless part of your application, the window must be created as a *child window*. Child windows need to have a *parent window*. As seen in Listing 9.4, the OpenOverlayBoard instructs the video board MCI driver to open a child window with the Video Center application form as the parent. Once the driver is opened, show the window with the Window MCI command because the window is initially invisible.

Once the OpenOverlayBoard routine has been completed, the overlay driver is opened, and the window is made visible. The window has not been given any

size or position yet. The `PutOverlayBoard` subroutine places the
video window within the dimensions of the rectangle shape named
`DisplayCenter`. This is done through the `Put` command where the client area
of the video window is placed at the coordinates of the `DisplayCenter` rectangle.

Listing 9.4   VCENTER.FRM. Opening and positioning the overlay video device.

```
Private Sub Form_Load()
    OpenOverlayBoard
    PutOverlayBoard
End Sub
Public Sub OpenOverlayBoard()
    Dim Cmd As String
    Dim Ret As Long
    Cmd = OPEN_STR & SPACE & OVERLAY_TYPE & SPACE & "alias " &_
                    OVERLAY_ALIAS & " parent " & VCenter.hWnd & " _
                    style child"
    Ret = mciSendString(Cmd, FixedStr, 49, 0)
    Cmd = WINDOW_STR & SPACE & OVERLAY_ALIAS & " state show"
    Ret = mciSendString(Cmd, FixedStr, 49, 0)
End Sub
Public Sub PutOverlayBoard()
    Dim Cmd As String
    Dim Ret As Long
    Cmd = PUT_STR & SPACE & OVERLAY_ALIAS & " window client at "_
      & DisplayCenter.Left & SPACE & DisplayCenter.Top & SPACE &_
      DisplayCenter.Width & SPACE & DisplayCenter.Height
    Ret = mciSendString(Cmd, FixedStr, 49, 0)
End Sub
```

Loading Peripheral Devices

To use the peripheral laser disc and videotape devices, there are menu items
located on the top of the form. When a particular device is loaded, the menu
item is checked. Let's examine the code executed when a laser disc device is
loaded.

The first action is to freeze the video display. This provides a solid, stable
image on-screen. Next, opened peripheral devices are closed, which is done
through the `ClosePeripheral` subroutine by sending the `Stop` and `Close` commands to the MCI control. After the opened peripheral devices have been
closed, the specified device needs to be opened.

The `OpenPeripheral` subroutine is called and the name of the device to open is
passed into the subroutine. As you can see from Listing 9.5, the `Notify` prop-

III

Video Capabilities

erty of the MCI control is set to False for opening the MCI device because you want to know on function return if the open succeeded. The time format is set to frames. This provides consistency between all the MCI drivers for all videotape and laser disc devices. Each MCI driver has a default time format that may vary from driver to driver. Setting the time format to frames just provides consistency for the end user.

After the time format has been set, the Notify property is set to True. This enables user interaction with the application and other applications when a command button on the MCI control has been pressed. It is important to note that if the Notify property is False, control is not returned to the user when the Play button is pressed until the command is completed. This normally doesn't occur until the end of the media. For laser disc and videotapes this could mean several hours. The Notify property should almost never be set to False for these types of peripheral devices.

Listing 9.5 VCENTER.FRM. How to open peripheral devices using the MCI control.

```
Private Sub Laserdisc_Click()
    FreezeVideo
    ClosePeripheral
    OpenPeripheral LASERDISC_TYPE
End Sub
Private Sub VCR_Click()
    FreezeVideo
    ClosePeripheral
    OpenPeripheral VCR_TYPE
End Sub
Private Sub Camera_Click()
    ClosePeripheral
    UnfreezeVideo
End Sub
Public Sub FreezeVideo()
    Dim Cmd As String
    Dim Ret As Long
    Cmd = FREEZE_STR & SPACE & OVERLAY_ALIAS
    Ret = mciSendString(Cmd, FixedStr, 49, 0)
End Sub
Public Sub UnfreezeVideo()
    Dim Cmd As String
    Dim Ret As Long
    Cmd = UNFREEZE_STR & SPACE & OVERLAY_ALIAS
    Ret = mciSendString(Cmd, FixedStr, 49, 0)
End Sub
Public Sub ClosePeripheral()
    FreezeVideo
    MMDevice.Command = STOP_STR
    MMDevice.Command = CLOSE_STR
```

```
        ActiveDevice = ""
        EndPos = ""
        StartPos = ""
    End Sub
    Public Sub OpenPeripheral(DevType As String)
        MMDevice.DeviceType = DevType
        MMDevice.Notify = False
        MMDevice.Wait = True
        MMDevice.Shareable = False
        MMDevice.Command = OPEN_STR
        ' now that the command is finished set the modes to wait
        Dim Cmd As String
        Dim Ret As Long
        Cmd = SET_STR & SPACE & DevType & " time format frames"
        Ret = mciSendString(Cmd, FixedStr, 49, 0)
        Cmd = STATUS_STR & SPACE & DevType & " time format"
        Ret = mciSendString(Cmd, FixedStr, 49, 0)
        If Ret = 0 Then
            Units = FixedStr
        End If
        ActiveDevice = DevType
        MMDevice.Wait = False
        MMDevice.Notify = True
    End Sub
```

For the Video Center application, I use all of the buttons provided by the MCI control. As you can see in Listing 9.6, every button's Click method is intercepted to provide the correct interaction with the video board driver.

Because all commands sent to the peripheral device through the MCI control interface have the Notify property set to True, the Done event needs to be intercepted and properly handled. When an MCI command issued through the MCI control is finished executing or has been superseded, the Done event is fired. What the Video Center application does is to check the mode of the peripheral device and set the mode of the overlay video board accordingly—for example, if the video peripheral stops, the video board freezes.

Notice in Listing 9.6 that I have intercepted the NextClick and the PrevClick commands and do not follow through with the default processing. This is because the default processing uses the seek command to fast-forward and rewind. The seek command moves the peripheral device to a desired location without any video output being shown. The device is scanned forwards and backwards to the desired location. This method is slower than a seek command, but the user is able to get visual feedback as to what the device is doing.

Note that when these buttons are overwritten by sending a string command to the ActiveDevice variable. This variable contains the name of the logical

III

Video Capabilities

name of the device, which was passed into the OpenPeripheral subroutine. On the PrevClick and NextClick events, default processing is avoided by setting the Cancel variable to True. If the scan command fails, then the video freezes and default processing is restored.

Listing 9.6   VCENTER.FRM. Intercepting the *Click* events for the MCI control.

```
Private Sub MMDevice_BackClick(Cancel As Integer)
    If Not MMDevice.Mode = MODE_PAUSE Then
        MMDevice.Command = PAUSE_STR
    End If
End Sub
Private Sub MMDevice_Done(NotifyCode As Integer)
    Dim DMode As Long
    DMode = MMDevice.Mode
    Select Case DMode
        Case MODE_READY, MODE_OPEN, MODE_STOP, MODE_SEEK
            FreezeVideo
        Case MODE_PLAY, MODE_RECORD, MODE_PAUSE
            UnfreezeVideo
    End Select
End Sub
Private Sub MMDevice_EjectClick(Cancel As Integer)
    FreezeVideo
    MMDevice.Wait = False
    MMDevice.Notify = False
End Sub
Private Sub MMDevice_NextClick(Cancel As Integer)
    Cancel = True
    Dim Cmd As String
    Dim Ret As Long
    UnfreezeVideo
    Cmd = PLAY_STR & SPACE & ActiveDevice & " scan"
    Ret = mciSendString(Cmd, FixedStr, 49, 0)
    If Not Ret = 0 Then
        Cancel = False
        FreezeVideo
    End If
End Sub
Private Sub MMDevice_PlayClick(Cancel As Integer)
    MMDevice.Wait = True
    MMNotify = False
    MMDevice.Command = Pause
    MMDevice.Wait = False
    MMDevice.Notify = True
    UnfreezeVideo
End Sub
Private Sub MMDevice_PrevClick(Cancel As Integer)
    Cancel = True
    Dim Cmd As String
```

```
        Dim Ret As Long
        UnfreezeVideo
        Cmd = PLAY_STR & SPACE & ActiveDevice & " scan reverse"
        Ret = mciSendString(Cmd, FixedStr, 49, 0)
        If Not Ret = 0 Then
            Cancel = False
            FreezeVideo
        End If
    End Sub
    Private Sub MMDevice_StepClick(Cancel As Integer)
        If Not MMDevice.Mode = MODE_PAUSE Then
            MMDevice.Command = PAUSE_STR
        End If
        Cancel = True
        Dim Cmd As String
        Dim Ret As Long
        UnfreezeVideo
        Cmd = STEP_STR & SPACE & ActiveDevice
        Ret = mciSendString(Cmd, FixedStr, 49, 0)
        If Not Ret = 0 Then
            Cancel = False
        End If
     End Sub
    Private Sub MMDevice_StopClick(Cancel As Integer)
        FreezeVideo
    End Sub
```

Saving Images

The Video Center application has the capability to save still images from the overlay video board and load these images from the hard disk to be displayed on the overlay video board. Most drivers support the saving of images from the overlay board to a bitmapped image file. This type of operation is essential for applications such as employee or real-estate database applications. The save is performed through the Save MCI command. Listing 9.7 shows how saving an image from the overlay video board to a bitmapped file is performed. It is important to note that the overlay drivers save the images in true-color rather than the mode that the VGA display driver is operating in.

Conversely, when loading an image onto the overlay video board, the video and any playing devices needs to be stopped. This is because the overlay frame buffer now contains the bitmapped file rather than the video stream from the video source. Notice that images are displayed in true-color even though your VGA mode may only be capable of displaying 256 colors. This is because the images are being shown on the overlay plane.

III

Video Capabilities

Listing 9.7 VCENTER.FRM. Loading and saving images from the overlay video board.

```
Private Sub Freeze_Click()
    If OverlayMode = MODE_STOP Then
        UnfreezeVideo
    Else
        FreezeVideo
    End If
End Sub
Private Sub LoadVideo_Click()
    Dim Cmd As String
    Dim Ret As Long
    FileDlg.DialogTitle = "Open File Dialog"
    FileDlg.Action = 1
    If FileDlg.CancelError = False Then
     MMDevice.Command = STOP_STR
     Cmd = LOAD_STR & SPACE & OVERLAY_ALIAS & SPACE & _
        FileDlg.FileName
     Ret = mciSendString(Cmd, FixedStr, 49, 0)
     If Ret Then
         GetErrorString Ret
         MsgBox StatusReturn
     End If
    End If
End Sub
Private Sub SaveVideo_Click()
    Dim Cmd As String
    Dim Ret As Long
    MMDevice.Command = STOP_STR
    FileDlg.DialogTitle = "Save File Dialog"
    FileDlg.Action = 1
    If FileDlg.CancelError = False Then
     Cmd = SAVE_STR & SPACE & OVERLAY_ALIAS & SPACE & _
       FileDlg.FileName
     Ret = mciSendString(Cmd, FixedStr, 49, 0)
     If Ret Then
         GetErrorString Ret
         MsgBox StatusReturn
     End If
    End If
End Sub
Public Sub GetErrorString(ErrorCode As Long)
    If mciGetErrorString(ErrorCode, FixedStr, 49) Then
        StatusReturn = FixedStr
    End If
End Sub
```

> **Caution**
>
> There is one potential problem that arises when using overlay video with an application. This problem only arises when the video window created by the MCI driver is a child window. Because the video is displayed on a separate plane from the VGA graphics, the video window must be notified when the parent moves. If the MCI driver creates a frame window, this is no problem since the frame receives WM_MOVE messages from windows. When the video window is a child window, these WM_MOVE messages aren't sent to the video window because only the parent frame window receives them. This can cause the video to be lost when the frame window is moved.
>
> The method for solving this problem is to intercept the WM_MOVE messages from the parent window and call the PutOverlayBoard subroutine shown in the Video Center application. In Visual Basic, messages cannot be intercepted without a messaging control, such as Desaware's SpyWorks VBX or by writing a callable DLL to subclass a window. The Align_Click method shown below is a manual method for correcting the video window if the application window has been moved.
>
> ```
> Private Sub Align_Click()
>     PutOverlayBoard
> End Sub
> ```

Exiting the Application

When exiting the Video Center application, the overlay video board must be closed and the peripheral devices closed. If this is not done, the application cannot run again. This is true of any application that opens MCI devices and uses the alias property. In the Video Center application, I trap the form's UNLOAD event and the Exit_Click events. This may seem redundant but it is necessary in case the application is closed through the Control menu. Listing 9.8 illustrates these events.

Listing 9.8 VCENTER.FRM. Proper clean-up of MCI devices on exiting the application.

```
Private Sub Exit_Click()
    CloseOverlayBoard
    ClosePeripheral
    End
End Sub
Private Sub Form_Unload(Cancel As Integer)
    ClosePeripheral
    CloseOverlayBoard
End Sub
```

III

Video Capabilities

(continues)

Listing 9.8   Continued

```
Public Sub CloseOverlayBoard()
    Dim Cmd As String
    Dim Ret As Long
    Cmd = CLOSE_STR & SPACE & OVERLAY_ALIAS
    Ret = mciSendString(Cmd, FixedStr, 49, 0)
End Sub
```

Playing the Peripheral Device

As you have probably noticed from looking at the Video Center application, there are text boxes that are used for defining a beginning and ending position. These two values can then be used to instruct the peripheral device to play from the beginning position to the ending position.

The subroutine PlaySegment, shown in Listing 9.9, instructs the device to play from the start position to the end position. The subroutines SetEndPos and SetStartPos get the current position of the peripheral device and place this value in the appropriate edit box. One interesting note: although this is not documented in the MCI reference, some MCI drivers actually play in reverse if the starting position is greater than the ending position. You need to experiment with your driver to see if this capability is present. The VISCA MCI driver that comes with Video for Windows has this capability.

While the peripheral device is playing, I have implemented a timer control that periodically updates a status bar with the current position of the device. This is a nice feature for an application to have for providing a visual representation as to where the device is with the current media.

Listing 9.9   VCENTER.FRM. How to play a segment and retrieve the current position using a laser disc or videotape device.

```
Private Sub PlaySegment_Click()
    Dim Cmd As String
    Dim Ret As Long
    UnfreezeVideo
    Cmd = PLAY_STR & SPACE & ActiveDevice & " from_
      " & StartPos & " to " & EndPos
    Ret = mciSendString(Cmd, FixedStr, 49, 0)
    If Not Ret = 0 Then
        FreezeVideo
    End If
End Sub
Private Sub SetEndPos_Click()
    EndPos = GetCurrentPosition()
End Sub
```

```
Private Sub SetStartPos_Click()
    StartPos = GetCurrentPosition()
End Sub
Private Sub Timer1_Timer()
    If OverlayMode = MODE_STOP Then
        Freeze.Checked = True
    Else
        Freeze.Checked = False
    End If
    CurrentPosition = GetCurrentPosition
End Sub
Public Function GetCurrentPosition() As String
    Dim Cmd As String
    Dim Ret As Long
    Dim RetVal As String
    If Not ActiveDevice = "" Then
      Cmd = STATUS_STR & SPACE & ActiveDevice & SPACE & "position"
      Ret = mciSendString(Cmd, FixedStr, 49, 0)
      If Ret = 0 Then
          RetVal = FixedStr
      End If
    End If
    GetCurrentPosition = RetVal
End Function
```

From Here...

You have learned from this chapter that analog video is an effective and alternative method for providing video without the CPU or storage bondage imposed on your applications by digital video. The MCI Command sets for overlay video, videotape, and laser disc players offer you a working toolset that embraces the common functionality for most devices. By using device-specific commands, applications can be tailored to the exact performance characteristics of the devices being used.

■ For a discussion on how to make stunning transition effects once images have been captured from an overlay video board, see Chapter 6, "Creating Transition Effects."

■ For more information on using digital video in your applications, see Chapter 8, "Digital Video Capture and Editing."

■ For more information on creating multimedia databases using all of the multimedia types including analog video, see Chapter 14, "Multimedia Databases Using the JET Engine."

III

Video Capabilities

Chapter 10

Animation

While digital video and audio receive the bulk of the attention where multimedia is concerned, animation comprises another aspect of multimedia, which is applicable to as many if not more situations than video and audio. Animation is the display of a series of graphic images that simulate motion. In many cases, there is synchronized audio included with the animation. Animation is used for multimedia titles, presentations, games, and training, as well as a host of other applications.

There are three basic types of animation that are used in multimedia applications: *frame-based, object,* and *palette animation.*

Frame-based animation is a series of screens or frames that is displayed in quick succession. The changing of the screen from frame to frame produces the animation. Frame-based animation is very similar to some digital video technologies. Each frame can be edited as a unique entity because it represents an actual picture shown for a specified time period. An example of frame-based animation is animated cartoons.

Object animation also called cast-based animation or *sprite animation* is a form of animation in which each object in the presentation is an individual element with its own pattern, size, shape, color, and speed. A script controls the placement and movement of the objects in each frame. The technique used in object animation can be applied to your application to give the illusion of motion. This can be applied to a piece of text, for example, to give the impression that the text is moving across the screen.

Palette animation is used to make changes to an application's palette and the system palette through the use of color cycling. This allows for alterations of a background bitmap without actually creating a new color palette.

Object animation is strictly time-based. There are no individual frames that can be edited separately. Each frame is a time-slice that defines the usage and position of each element in the animation. As a result, there is no picture—

only a collection of information defining the position and behavior of objects for an instant in time. Cast-based animation is created and edited through authoring packages that show all cast members relative to each other. The elements are then individually edited.

In this chapter, the following animation techniques will be covered:

- Using the *Media Control Interface* (MCI) for controlling frame-based animation

- Creating sprite animation and using it in an application

- Learning how palette animation is created and used

- Creating a *Visual Basic class* for controlling all MCI-based animation

- Converting classes to include all other MCI media types, such as digital video and audio

Playing Animation Using the MCI Command Set

One of the easiest and most effective methods for using animation to enhance your applications is to use pre-authored animation, and play it back using the Windows MCI command set. The FLI and FLC animation file formats from AutoDesk and the AWA and AWN file formats from GoldDisk are some of the most popular animation file formats. Each company provides a MCI animation driver for controlling animation using the MCI command set.

Both AutoDesk and GoldDisk file formats are created through each company's respective animation authoring package. If you do not own or wish to own either of the authoring packages, there is an abundance of each type of files available from on-line networks, such as CompuServe or the Internet. At the time this book was written, these animation drivers were only available in 16-bit versions. Each company is reported to be working on a 32-bit port for their respective drivers.

Creating an OLE Object to Handle the Playback of Animation

The animation display application depends on an *OLE* animation playback object to display animation. Visual Basic 4 provides the support for applications to create their own class modules. A class module is an OLE automation object that can be used either locally within the current Visual Basic application or remotely through external applications. Listings 10.2 and 10.3 show the implementation of the OLE animation playback object.

The primary purpose of the animation class is to provide a complete interface to *all* of the commands supported by MCI animation drivers. This is in contrast to Visual Basic's MCI control, which only supports a small subset of basic MCI commands such as `Play` and `Stop`. The secondary purpose of the animation class is to provide a high-level abstraction for common MCI commands. For example, you can use a `Rewind` command rather than the `seek to start` command. By providing these interfaces, the animation class is one of the most powerful methods of communicating with animation MCI devices available.

To create a class module, choose the <u>C</u>lass Module command located under the Visual Basic <u>I</u>nsert menu. Listing 10.1 illustrates the properties set for the animation class. The name of the class is `Animation`. The class is `MultiUse Createable`, which indicates that you can create instances of the class both inside and outside the project. Requests for an instance of the class by an OLE client outside the project will be supplied by an already running copy of the OLE server, if any. If there are no copies of the OLE server running, a copy is started to supply the class. The `Exposed` property is also `True`, which indicates that the class you create is visible both within the project and by applications outside the project.

Listing 10.1 MCI.CLS. Properties for animation class controller.

```
VERSION 1.0 CLASS
BEGIN
  MultiUse = -1  'True
END
Attribute VB_Name = "Animation"
Attribute VB_Creatable = True
Attribute VB_Exposed = True
```

The core set of functions shown in Listing 10.2 implement the foundation of the animation class. These functions implement the basic MCI interface and allow for user control of the class.

Listing 10.2 MCI.CLS. MCI animation controller class.

```
' static variables used for the animation class
Dim hParent As Integer _
  ' contains the parent window of the animation
```

(continues)

III

Video Capabilities

Listing 10.2 Continued

```
Dim zFileName As String _
    ' contains the file name loaded/ to load into mci device
Dim zAlias As String    _
    ' contains the alias of the mci device
Dim RetStr As String * 50 _
    'contains return value from mciSendString
Dim ErrorStr As String * 50 _
    ' contains any error message
Dim bOpen As Boolean _
    ' indicates if the mci device is open
Dim iAlias As Integer _
    ' integer counter
Dim zCmdStr As String _
    ' command string for issuing commands
Dim lErrorCode As Long ' error code from mciSendCommand
' Declaration Statements for 16/32 bit compiles
#If Win16 = 1 Then
Private Declare Function mciSendString Lib _
    "MMSYSTEM" (ByVal Cmd As String, ByVal RetVal As String, _
    ByVal Len As Integer, ByVal Notify As Integer) As Long
Private Declare Function mciGetErrorString Lib _
    "MMSYSTEM" (ByVal Err As Long, ByVal RetVal As String, _
    ByVal Len As Integer) As Integer
#Else
Private Declare Function mciSendString Lib _
    "WINMM" Alias "mciSendStringA" (ByVal Cmd As String, _
    ByVal RetVal As String, ByVal Len As Integer, _
    ByVal Notify As Integer) As Long
Private Declare Function mciGetErrorString Lib _
    "WINMM" Alias "mciGetErrorStringA" (ByVal Err As Long, _
    ByVal RetVal As String, ByVal Len As Integer) As Integer
#End If

Const ALIAS_STR = "alias"
Const SPACE = " "

' Basic command strings for the MCI multimedia control
Const PLAY_STR = "Play"
Const STOP_STR = "Stop"
Const OPEN_STR = "Open"
Const CLOSE_STR = "Close"
Const PAUSE_STR = "Pause"
Const BACK_STR = "Back"
Const STEP_STR = "Step"
Const SEEK_STR = "Seek"
Const STATUS_STR = "Status"
Const SET_STR = "Set"
Const FREEZE_STR = "Freeze"
Const PUT_STR = "Put"
Const WINDOW_STR = "Window"
Const WHERE_STR = "Where"
Const CAPABILITY_STR = "Capability"
Const INFORMATION_STR = "Info"
Const UPDATE_STR = "Update"
```

```
Const RESUME_STR = "Resume"
Const REALIZE_STR = "Realize"
Public Function GetErrorString(ErrorCode As Long) As Integer
    GetErrorString = mciGetErrorString(ErrorCode, ErrorStr, 49)
End Function

Public Function SendCommand(Cmd As String) As Long
    SendCommand = mciSendString(Cmd, RetStr, 49, 0)
End Function

Private Sub Class_Initialize()
    bOpen = False
    iAlias = 0
    hParent = 0
End Sub



Public Property Get ParentHwnd() As Integer
    ParentHwnd = hParent
End Property



Public Property Let ParentHwnd(vNewValue As Integer)
    If bOpen = False Then
        hParent = vNewValue
    End If
End Property

Public Property Get FileName() As String
    FileName = zFileName
End Property

Public Property Let FileName(vNewValue As String)
    If bOpen = False Then
        zFileName = vNewValue
    End If
End Property

Public Function aOpen() As Boolean
    If bOpen = True Then
        aOpen = False
    End If
    If hParent = 0 Then
        aOpen = False
    End If
    If IsNull(zFileName) Or Trim(zFileName) = "" Then
        aOpen = False
    End If
    If IsNull(zAlias) Or Trim(zAlias) = "" Then
        zAlias = iAlias
        iAlias = iAlias + 1
    End If
    zCmdStr = OPEN_STR & SPACE & zFileName & SPACE & _
      ALIAS_STR & SPACE & Alias & " style child parent " & hParent
```

(continues)

III

Video Capabilities

Listing 10.2 Continued

```
        lErrorCode = SendCommand(zCmdStr)
        If lErrorCode = 0 Then
            aOpen = True
            bOpen = True
            aPut "window at 0 0 320 240"
            Window "State visible"
        Else
            aOpen = False
            bOpen = False
        End If
End Function

Public Property Get Alias() As String
    Alias = zAlias
End Property

Public Property Let Alias(vNewValue As String)
    If bOpen = False Then
        zAlias = vNewValue
    End If
End Property

Public Property Get ErrorCode() As Long
    ErrorCode = lErrorCode
End Property


Public Property Get ReturnString() As String
    ReturnString = RetStr
End Property
```

The rest of the implementation of the animation class provides an interface
to all of the MCI commands for an animation device. Listing 10.3 shows
these implementations. For a complete reference to the animation command
set, refer to Appendix A.

**Listing 10.3 MCI.CLS. MCI implementation functions for the
animation class.**

```
Public Function Play() As Long
    zCmdStr = PLAY_STR & SPACE & zAlias
    lErrorCode = SendCommand(zCmdStr)
    Play = lErrorCode
End Function

Public Function aStop()
    zCmdStr = STOP_STR & SPACE & zAlias
    lErrorCode = SendCommand(zCmdStr)
    aStop = lErrorCode
End Function
```

```
Public Function FastForward() As Long
    zCmdStr = SEEK_STR & SPACE & zAlias & SPACE & "to end"
    lErrorCode = SendCommand(zCmdStr)
    Play = lErrorCode
End Function

Public Function Rewind() As Long
    zCmdStr = SEEK_STR & SPACE & zAlias & SPACE & "to start"
    lErrorCode = SendCommand(zCmdStr)
    Play = lErrorCode
End Function

Public Function Mode() As String
    zCmdStr = STATUS_STR & SPACE & Alias & SPACE & "mode"
    lErrorCode = SendCommand(zCmdStr)
    If 0 = lErrorCode Then
        Mode = RetStr
    Else
        Mode = "Error"
    End If
End Function

Public Function Capability(Parm As String) As String
    zCmdStr = CAPABILITY_STR & SPACE & Alias & SPACE & Parm
    lErrorCode = SendCommand(zCmdStr)
    If 0 = lErrorCode Then
        Capability = RetStr
    Else
        Capability = "Error"
    End If
End Function

Public Function aClose() As Long
    zCmdStr = CLOSE_STR & SPACE & Alias
    lErrorCode = SendCommand(zCmdStr)
    bOpen = False
    aClose = lErrorCode
End Function

Public Function Information(Parm As String) As String
    zCmdStr = INFORMATION_STR & SPACE & Alias & SPACE & Parm
    lErrorCode = SendCommand(zCmdStr)
    If 0 = lErrorCode Then
        Information = RetStr
    Else
        Information = "Error"
    End If
End Function

Public Function Status(Parm As String) As String
    zCmdStr = STATUS_STR & SPACE & Alias & SPACE & Parm
    RetStr = "                                              "
    lErrorCode = SendCommand(zCmdStr)
    If 0 = lErrorCode Then
```

III

Video Capabilities

(continues)

Listing 10.3 Continued

```
            Trim (RetStr)
            Status = RetStr
        Else
            Status = "Error"
        End If
    End Function

    Public Function Pause() As Long
        zCmdStr = PAUSE_STR & SPACE & Alias
        lErrorCode = SendCommand(zCmdStr)
        Pause = lErrorCode
    End Function

    Public Function PlayEx(Parm As String) As Long
        zCmdStr = PLAY_STR & SPACE & Alias & SPACE & Parm
        lErrorCode = SendCommand(zCmdStr)
        PlayEx = lErrorCode
    End Function

    Public Function aResume()
        zCmdStr = RESUME_STR & SPACE & Alias
        lErrorCode = SendCommand(zCmdStr)
        aResume = lErrorCode
    End Function

    Public Function aSeek(Parm As String) As Long
        zCmdStr = SEEK_STR & SPACE & Alias & SPACE & Parm
        lErrorCode = SendCommand(zCmdStr)
        aSeek = lErrorCode
    End Function

    Public Function aSet(Parm As String) As Long
        zCmdStr = SET_STR & SPACE & Alias & SPACE & Parm
        lErrorCode = SendCommand(zCmdStr)
        aSet = lErrorCode
    End Function

    Public Function aPut(Parm As String) As Long
        zCmdStr = PUT_STR & SPACE & Alias & SPACE & Parm
        lErrorCode = SendCommand(zCmdStr)
        aPut = lErrorCode
    End Function

    Public Function Realize(Parm As String) As Long
        zCmdStr = REALIZE_STR & SPACE & Alias & SPACE & Parm
        lErrorCode = SendCommand(zCmdStr)
        Realize = lErrorCode
    End Function

    Public Function Step(Parm As String) As Long
        zCmdStr = STEP_STR & SPACE & Alias & SPACE & Parm
        lErrorCode = SendCommand(zCmdStr)
        Step = lErrorCode
    End Function
```

```
Public Function Update(Parm As String) As Long
    zCmdStr = UPDATE_STR & SPACE & Alias & SPACE & Parm
    lErrorCode = SendCommand(zCmdStr)
    Update = lErrorCode
End Function

Public Function Where(Parm As String) As String
    zCmdStr = WHERE_STR & SPACE & Alias & SPACE & Parm
    lErrorCode = SendCommand(zCmdStr)
    If lErrorCode = 0 Then
        Where = RetStr
    Else
        Where = "Error"
    End If
End Function

Public Function Window(Parm As String) As Long
    zCmdStr = WINDOW_STR & SPACE & Alias & SPACE & Parm
    lErrorCode = SendCommand(zCmdStr)
    Window = lErrorCode
End Function
```

Even though the animation display class is meant to be used for MCI animation drivers, it will work for any type of MCI driver. The only additional commands that need to be added to the animation class to make it a general purpose MCI interface would be to implement the command sets for each of the MCI device types. An example is the SetVideo command for digital video devices.

Using the OLE MCI Object in an Application

Now that a standard class has been developed for controlling MCI-based animation, it is time to use this class in an application. The first application that will take advantage of this class is a simple animation viewer. The Viewer application will open and view any MCI-based animation. Figure 10.1 shows the interface for the Animation Viewer application.

The Animation Viewer application uses the animation class in conjunction with the MCI control provided with Visual Basic. The MCI control is not used to send commands to the animation MCI driver. The MCI control is used for its user interface only. When the MCI control user interface is activated through user interaction, methods for the animation class are called. The animation class then issues commands to the animation MCI driver. Figure 10.2 illustrates the command flow for the Animation Viewer application.

The Animation Viewer application uses three controls provided with Visual Basic: *MCI*, *Timer*, and *CommonDialog*.

III

Video Capabilities

■ The MCI control is only used for user-interface purposes. The only properties changed from the default settings are `AutoEnable`, `RecordVisible`, and `EjectVisible`, which are all set to `False`.

■ The Timer control is used to check the mode of the animation class every second. Upon checking the mode of the animation class, the user interface of the MCI control is updated through the enabling and disabling of the appropriate buttons.

■ The CommonDialog control is used to present an open file dialog box for opening animation files. The filters for the CommonDialog control have been changed to include AutoDesk (.FLI, .FLC) and GoldDisk (.AWA, .AWM) files.

Fig. 10.1
Constructing an easy-to-use interface for an Animation Viewer.

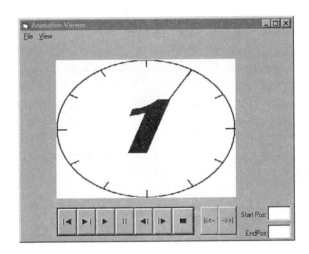

Fig. 10.2
The command flow for the Animation Viewer application.

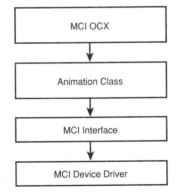

When the application first starts, the user must select a file to view by choosing Open from the File menu. When this menu item is selected, the open file dialog box is presented to the user and an animation file is opened for viewing. The code shown in Listing 10.4 illustrates the sequence of commands executed during File, Open.

Listing 10.4   ANIMMCI.FRM. Application for playing MCI-based animation files.

```
Private Sub Open_Click()
    Dim FileName As String
    Dim PutStr As String
    OpenDialog.Action = 1
    FileName = OpenDialog.FileName
    Anim.aClose
    Anim.ParentHwnd = hWnd
    Anim.FileName = FileName
    Anim.aOpen
    PutStr = " window at " & PlaybackArea.Left & " " & _
        PlaybackArea.Top & " " & PlaybackArea.Width & " " & _
        PlaybackArea.Height
    Anim.aPut PutStr
End Sub
```

After the open file dialog box is closed, the animation class is called to close any file currently open. The animation file will be opened as a child window, therefore, the `ParentHwnd` property must be set so that the form is the parent window of the animation. Then a filename is assigned to the class, and the class is opened. After the file is opened, the animation playback window is centered in `PlaybackArea` graphic through the `aPut` command.

Using the MCI Control with the Animation Class

The Animation Viewer application uses the MCI control only for its graphical user interface. This is handled by enabling the control's buttons, even though the control is not opened with a valid device. The enabling of the control is performed from the `CheckMode` subroutine, which is called every second by the Timer control. The `CheckMode` subroutine, as shown in Listing 10.5, also enables two pushbuttons, which are used for marking the beginning and ending of a segment within the animation.

III

Video Capabilities

Listing 10.5   ANIMMCI.FRM. Retrieving the status of an MCI-based animation.

```
Public Sub CheckMode()
    Dim zStatus As String
    zStatus = Anim.Status("mode")
    zStatus = Left(zStatus, 4)
    Select Case zStatus
        Case "paus"
        Case "play"
        Case "seek"
        Case "stop"
            MciCtrl.StopEnabled = True
            MciCtrl.BackEnabled = True
            MciCtrl.PrevEnabled = True
            MciCtrl.PauseEnabled = True
            MciCtrl.PlayEnabled = True
            MciCtrl.StepEnabled = True
            MciCtrl.NextEnabled = True
            StartSegment.Enabled = True
            EndSegment.Enabled = True
            Segment.Enabled = True
        Case Else
            MciCtrl.StopEnabled = False
            MciCtrl.BackEnabled = False
            MciCtrl.PrevEnabled = False
            MciCtrl.PauseEnabled = False
            MciCtrl.PlayEnabled = False
            MciCtrl.StepEnabled = False
            MciCtrl.NextEnabled = False
            StartSegment.Enabled = False
            EndSegment.Enabled = False
            Segment.Enabled = False
    End Select
End Sub
```

When any of the MCI control's buttons are pressed, the MCI control event handler for that button is called. The appropriate method of the animation class is then called. Listing 10.6 shows how all of the MCI control buttons are handled; the default processing for the MCI control buttons is circumvented by setting the parameter Cancel to True. Also shown in Listing 10.6 is the processing for setting the beginning and ending segments of an animation.

Listing 10.6   ANIMMCI.FRM. Controlling playback of MCI-based animation.

```
Private Sub MciCtrl_BackClick(Cancel As Integer)
    Anim.Step "reverse"
    Cancel = True
End Sub
```

```
Private Sub MciCtrl_NextClick(Cancel As Integer)
    Anim.aSeek "to end"
    Cancel = True
End Sub

Private Sub MciCtrl_PauseClick(Cancel As Integer)
    Anim.Pause
    Cancel = True
End Sub

Private Sub MciCtrl_PlayClick(Cancel As Integer)
    Anim.Play
    Cancel = True
End Sub

Private Sub MciCtrl_PrevClick(Cancel As Integer)
    Anim.aSeek "to start"
    Cancel = True
End Sub

Private Sub MciCtrl_StepClick(Cancel As Integer)
    Anim.Step " "
    Cancel = True
End Sub

Private Sub MciCtrl_StopClick(Cancel As Integer)
    Anim.aStop
    Cancel = True
End Sub

Private Sub StartSegment_Click()
    StartSeg = Anim.Status(" position")
End Sub

Private Sub EndSegment_Click()
    EndSeg = Anim.Status(" position")
End Sub

Private Sub Segment_Click()
    Dim zStr As String
    Anim.aStop
    zStr = " from " & StartSeg & " to " & EndSeg
    Anim.PlayEx zStr
End Sub
```

For a complete list of MCI animation commands, refer to Appendix A, "The MCI Command Reference."

III

Video Capabilities

Palette Animation

In the previous sections, you have seen how to use already created animation, which relies on an MCI animation driver to be shown. You will now discover how to create an interesting form of animation called *palette animation* or *color cycling*. This form of animation allows us to simulate effects, such as running water or lighting changes, without resorting to the resource intensive methods used for frame or cast animation.

 Palette animation will only work on graphics display adapters that support palette colors. Standard VGA adapters, as well as HiColor and TrueColor adapters may not support palette animation.

Adding Marquee Lights to the Animation Viewer

For the Animation Viewer, you will use palette animation to create the illusion of marquee lights flashing around the playback area for MCI animation. The lights will be flashing different shades of yellow.

The first order of business for creating palette animation is to create a logical palette. For this, you need to add some types and function declarations to the application. The module ANIM.BAS was added to define types for a PALETTEENTRY structure and a LOGPALETTE structure. The declarations of these types are shown in Listing 10.7.

Listing 10.7 ANIM.BAS. Declarations used for creating palette animation.

```
Type PALETTEENTRY
    peRed As String * 1
    peGreen As String * 1
    peBlue As String * 1
    peFlags As String * 1
End Type

Type LOGPALETTE
    palVersion As Integer
    palNumEntries As Integer
    palPalEntry(4) As PALETTEENTRY
End Type

'palette index used for animation
Global Const PC_RESERVED = &H1
```

The LOGPALETTE structure is used to create a logical palette using the Windows API CreatePalette. The first entry (palVersion) in the LOGPALETTE structure defines the Windows version being used. Setting this value to &H300 will ensure compatibility with Windows 3.x through Windows 95 and Windows NT. The second entry (palNumEntries) indicates how many color entries will be in the new logical palette. There can be a maximum of 236 color entries but for the Animation Viewer application, you only need 4. The array is created with 5 entries. The fifth entry, although not used for the actual palette, is used as a placeholder for the starting color for the palette entry.

> Even though a Windows palette can have 256 colors, 20 colors are normally reserved for Windows; thus, 236 user-defined color entries are left. The third entry (palPalEntry) is an array of PALETTEENTRY structures.

The PALETTEENTRY structure defines a specific color for entry in the palette. The structure entries (peRed, peGreen, and peBlue) define the RGB (red, green, blue) values for each entry in the palette. Since any data structure passed to a .DLL from a VB application needs to be of a fixed length, the data elements for the PALETTEENTRY structure are all one-byte representing a four-byte data structure. The last data element, peFlags, must be set to the defined constant PC_RESERVED. As you will see, only color entries with this setting can be altered with the AnimatePalette API. The AnimatePalette API is what is used to produce palette animation.

Drawing the Marquee Lights

To draw the marquee lights around the MCI animation playback area, another rectangle was added to the form. Figure 10.3 shows the second rectangle in design mode. The outer rectangle's Visible property is set to FALSE. This is done because you are only using this rectangle to obtain perimeter coordinates for your marquee lights.

To produce the marquee light palette animation, you will need to declare some new Windows API calls. As Listing 10.8 shows, the APIs are defined for both 16- and 32-bit usage.

Fig. 10.3

An outer rectangle was added to the Animation Viewer to serve as a guideline for the marquee lights.

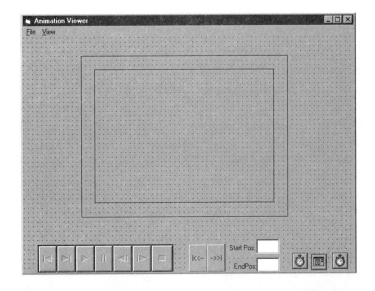

Listing 10.8 ANIMMCI2.FRM. Windows API declarations needed for performing palette animations.

```
#If Win16 = 1 Then
' new declarations to add marquee banner
Private Declare Function CreatePalette Lib _
    "GDI" (lpLogPalette As LOGPALETTE) As Integer
Private Declare Function SelectPalette Lib _
    "User" (ByVal hDC As Integer, ByVal hPalette As Integer, _
    ByVal bForceBackground As Integer) As Integer
Private Declare Function RealizePalette Lib _
    "User" (ByVal hDC As Integer) As Integer
Private Declare Function CreateSolidBrush Lib _
    "GDI" (ByVal crColor As Long) As Integer
Private Declare Function SelectObject Lib _
    "GDI" (ByVal hDC As Integer, _
    ByVal hObject As Integer) As Integer
Private Declare Function DeleteObject Lib _
    "GDI" (ByVal hObject As Integer) As Integer
Private Declare Function GetStockObject Lib _
    "GDI" (ByVal nIndex As Integer) As Integer
Private Declare Function Ellipse Lib _
    "GDI" (ByVal hDC As Integer, ByVal X1 As Integer, _
    ByVal Y1 As Integer, ByVal X2 As Integer, _
    ByVal Y2 As Integer) As Integer
Private Declare Sub AnimatePalette Lib _
    "GDI" (ByVal hPalette As Integer, _
    ByVal wStartIndex As Integer, ByVal wNumEntries As Integer, _
    lpPaletteColors As PALETTEENTRY)
#Else
Private Declare Function CreatePalette Lib _
```

```
        "GDI32" (lpLogPalette As LOGPALETTE) As Integer
    Private Declare Function SelectPalette Lib _
      "GDI32" (ByVal hDC As Integer, ByVal hPalette As Integer, _
      ByVal bForceBackground As Integer) As Integer
    Private Declare Function RealizePalette Lib _
      "GDI32" (ByVal hDC As Integer) As Integer
    Private Declare Function CreateSolidBrush Lib _
      "GDI32" (ByVal crColor As Long) As Integer
    Private Declare Function SelectObject Lib _
      "GDI32" (ByVal hDC As Integer, ByVal hObject As Integer) As
    Integer
    Private Declare Function DeleteObject Lib _
      "GDI32" (ByVal hObject As Integer) As Integer
    Private Declare Function GetStockObject Lib _
      "GDI32" (ByVal nIndex As Integer) As Integer
    Private Declare Function Ellipse Lib _
      "GDI32" (ByVal hDC As Integer, ByVal X1 As Integer, _
      ByVal Y1 As Integer, ByVal X2 As Integer, _
      ByVal Y2 As Integer) As Integer
    Private Declare Sub AnimatePalette Lib _
      "GDI32" (ByVal hPalette As Integer, _
      ByVal wStartIndex As Integer, ByVal wNumEntries As Integer, _
      lpPaletteColors As PALETTEENTRY)
    #End If
```

The first order of business is to create the logical palette that you will use to simulate the flashing marquee lights. This is done in the `Form_Load` subroutine, which is shown in Listing 10.9. The color entries for the logical palette being created are different shades of yellow. Yellow is formed by the combination of red and blue color values. The newly created logical palette contains four palette entries and is contained in the variable `hCurrentPalette`.

Listing 10.9   ANIMMCI2.FRM. Creating a logical palette for marquee lights.

```
    Private Sub Form_Load()
        Dim ColorIndex As Integer
        LogicalPalette.palVersion = &H300
        LogicalPalette.palNumEntries = 4
        For ColorIndex = 0 To 3
            LogicalPalette.palPalEntry(ColorIndex).peRed _
                = Chr$(127 + ColorIndex * 128/3)
            LogicalPalette.palPalEntry(ColorIndex).peGreen _
                = Chr$(127 + ColorIndex * 128/3)
            LogicalPalette.palPalEntry(ColorIndex).peBlue = Chr$(0)
            LogicalPalette.palPalEntry(ColorIndex).peFlags _
                = Chr$(PC_RESERVED)
        Next ColorIndex
        hCurrentPalette = CreatePalette(LogicalPalette)
    End Sub
```

III

Video Capabilities

To draw the marquee lights, the form's Paint subroutine was modified, as shown in Listing 10.10.

Listing 10.10 ANIMMCI2.FRM. Drawing the marquee lights during the form paint event.

```
Private Sub Form_Paint()
    Dim TopPos As Integer
    Dim LeftPos As Integer
    Dim BoxHeight As Integer
    Dim BoxWidth As Integer
    Dim ColorIndex As Long
    Dim TempValue As Integer
    hSystemPalette = SelectPalette(_
      ANIMVW.hDC, hCurrentPalette, False)
    TempValue = RealizePalette(ANIMVW.hDC)
    For ColorIndex = 0 To 3
        hPaintBrush(ColorIndex) = _
            CreateSolidBrush(&H1000000 Or ColorIndex)
        Next ColorIndex
    ANIMVW.Cls
    DotWidth = OuterWall.Width / 24
    ColorIndex = 0
    TopPos = OuterWall.Top + (DotWidth / 2)
    ANIMVW.CurrentX = OuterWall.Left + (DotWidth * 1.5)
    Do While CurrentX < (OuterWall.Width + OuterWall.Left) - _
        (DotWidth * 2)
        TempValue = SelectObject(ANIMVW.hDC, hPaintBrush(ColorIndex))
        TempValue = Ellipse(ANIMVW.hDC, _
            CurrentX, TopPos, CurrentX + DotWidth, TopPos + _
            DotWidth)
        CurrentX = CurrentX + DotWidth * 1.5
        ColorIndex = ColorIndex + 1
        ColorIndex = ColorIndex Mod 4
    Loop
    LeftPos = (OuterWall.Left + OuterWall.Width) - DotWidth * 1.5
    CurrentY = OuterWall.Top + (DotWidth * 1.5)
    Do While CurrentY < ((OuterWall.Top + OuterWall.Height) - _
        DotWidth * 1.5)
        TempValue = SelectObject(ANIMVW.hDC, hPaintBrush(ColorIndex))
        TempValue = Ellipse(ANIMVW.hDC, _
            LeftPos, CurrentY, LeftPos + DotWidth, CurrentY + _
            DotWidth)
        CurrentY = CurrentY + DotWidth * 1.5
        ColorIndex = ColorIndex + 1
        ColorIndex = ColorIndex Mod 4
        Loop
    TopPos = (OuterWall.Top + OuterWall.Height) - DotWidth * 1.5
    CurrentX = (OuterWall.Left + OuterWall.Width) - DotWidth * 2.5
    Do While CurrentX > OuterWall.Left + DotWidth * 1.5
        TempValue = SelectObject(ANIMVW.hDC, hPaintBrush(ColorIndex))
        TempValue = Ellipse(ANIMVW.hDC, _
            CurrentX, TopPos, CurrentX + DotWidth, TopPos + _
            DotWidth)
```

```
            CurrentX = CurrentX - DotWidth * 1.5
            ColorIndex = ColorIndex + 1
            ColorIndex = ColorIndex Mod 4
        Loop
    LeftPos = OuterWall.Left + DotWidth / 2
    CurrentY = (OuterWall.Top + OuterWall.Height) - 2 * DotWidth
    Do While CurrentY > OuterWall.Top
        TempValue = SelectObject(ANIMVW.hDC, hPaintBrush(ColorIndex))
        TempValue = Ellipse(ANIMVW.hDC, LeftPos, _
            CurrentY, LeftPos + DotWidth, CurrentY + _
            DotWidth)
        CurrentY = CurrentY - DotWidth * 1.5
        ColorIndex = ColorIndex + 1
        ColorIndex = ColorIndex Mod 4
        Loop
    TempValue = SelectObject(ANIMVW.hDC, _
        GetStockObject(GRAY_BRUSH))
    For ColorIndex = 0 To 3
        TempValue = DeleteObject(hPaintBrush(ColorIndex))
    Next ColorIndex
End Sub
```

When the Paint event is called, the logical palette, which was created during
form load, is selected and realized into the device context of the form,
ANIMVW.HDC. A solid color brush is then created for each of the colors in
the palette.

The next step is to clear the form and determine the width of each light in
the marquee. This is done by dividing the length of the outerwall by 24. To
make the lights larger in diameter, simply select a smaller number as the
divisor.

The paint routine will now draw the four walls of the rectangle and place
all of the lights on the inside of the outer rectangle. The lights are drawn
through the Ellipse API. The Ellipse API takes five parameters as inputs, the
handle to the device context to draw the ellipse into, and the top left and
bottom right bounding coordinates. The ellipse is drawn within these rectangular coordinates. Notice that before the ellipse is drawn, a new brush color is
selected into the device context. This is the new fill color for the ellipse.

Animating the Marquee Lights

Now that the marquee lights are drawn and the palette is in place, it is time
to animate the palette and produce the "flashing lights" effect. To do the
palette animation, you will need to add a new timer to the form. This timer is
called the PalTimer. When the PalTimer's interval expires, (every 1/4 second)
the palette will be animated. This is done in the PalTimer_Timer routine, as
shown in Listing 10.11.

III

Video Capabilities

Listing 10.11 ANIMMCI2.FRM. Animating the marquee lights palette during a timer event.

```
Dim ColorIndex As Integer
    For ColorIndex = 4 To 1 Step -1
        LogicalPalette.palPalEntry(ColorIndex) = _
          LogicalPalette.palPalEntry(ColorIndex - 1)
        Next ColorIndex
    LogicalPalette.palPalEntry(0) = LogicalPalette.palPalEntry(4)
    AnimatePalette hCurrentPalette, 0, 4, _
      LogicalPalette.palPalEntry(0)
```

When the timer event is invoked, the color entries in the logical palette are shifted one position to the right. The last element in the array is rotated back to the beginning. Until now, nothing has been done to effect the screen appearance. The marquee lights are set in motion with the call to AnimatePalette.

As mentioned previously, the palette animation is caused by invoking the AnimatePalette API. Let's take a closer look at this API to determine how the palette animation is created. The declaration for AnimatePalette is shown below.

```
Private Declare Sub AnimatePalette Lib "GDI" (ByVal hPalette _
    As Integer, ByVal wStartIndex As Integer, _
    ByVal wNumEntries As Integer, lpPaletteColors As PALETTEENTRY)
```

As you can see from the declaration of AnimatePalette, the following are parameters used to animate the palette:

■ The first argument to AnimatePalette is a handle to the currently realized palette (hCurrentpalette) in the application.

■ The second argument specifies the index of the first entry in the currently realized palette. For this application, the first entry is 0.

■ The third argument indicates the number of entries in the palette to change. For this application, there are only four entries and you want to effect all of them.

■ The last argument is a pointer to the first element in the palette entry array. This array contains the new color values for each entry in the logical palette. When AnimatePalette is called, the system palette is updated directly and makes the screen change instantaneously. Figure 10.4 illustrates the Animation Viewer application with the flashing marquee lights.

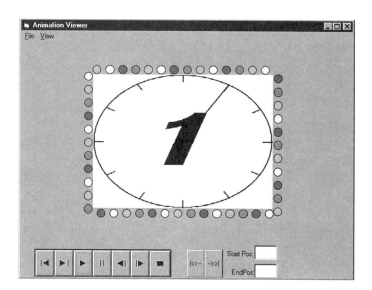

Fig. 10.4
Animation Viewer
with flashing
marquee lights.

The only thing left to do to make the application complete is to delete the logical palette that was created during form load. This is done in the form Unload routine shown in Listing 10.12.

Listing 10.12   ANIMMCI2.FRM. Deleting unused objects from memory when the form unloads.

```
Private Sub Form_Unload(Cancel As Integer)
    Dim TempValue As Integer
    PalTimer.Enabled = False
    TempValue = DeleteObject(hCurrentPalette)
End Sub
```

Adding Object-based Animation to the Animation Viewer

In object-based animation, an object such as a piece of text or a bitmap is moved across the screen over time. An example of object-based animation is the Windows marquee screensaver, where a user-defined text string is scrolled across the screen. The simplest method for creating objects in Visual Basic is to use the controls that come with Visual Basic, and move them around the screen using the top and left properties.

III

Video Capabilities

In the Animation Viewer application, I have added a text banner with the quote "Welcome To The Show!!!" to the bottom of the application. This text quote will move back and forth across the screen as time proceeds. Figure 10.5 illustrates this version of the Animation Viewer application.

Fig. 10.5

User interface for the Animation Viewer application using both Palette and object animation.

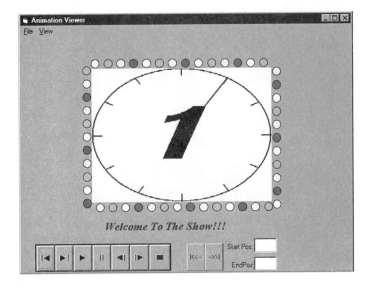

This is one of the simplest methods available for providing object animation to your Visual Basic applications. In the Animation Viewer application, all that was needed was a Timer control and a Label or Text control. The Timer control, called `TextTimer`, was added to provide regular intervals for moving the text label across the screen. The subroutine for `TextTimer`, shown in Listing 10.13, illustrates what events happen when the `TextTimer` event is called.

Listing 10.13   ANIMMCI3.FRM. Scrolling text across the screen during a Timer event.

```
Private Sub TextTimer_Timer()
    Dim NewTextLeftPos As Integer
    If (((AnimText.Left + AnimText.Width) > _
      ANIMVW.ScaleWidth) And Forward) Or _
      ((AnimText.Left < 0) And Not Forward) Then
        Forward = Not Forward
    End If
    If Forward Then
        NewTextLeftPos = AnimText.Left + 10
    Else
```

```
        NewTextLeftPos = AnimText.Left - 10
    End If
    AnimText.Move NewTextLeftPos, AnimText.Top
End Sub
```

For the TextTimer Timer event, the text label is moved back and forth across the application form. There is one variable, Forward, which is used to indicate the direction that the text is traveling. If the text label is moving from left to right, 10 pixels are added to the Left coordinate for each time interval. Otherwise, 10 is subtracted from the Left coordinate for each time interval.

This technique illustrates a simple object animation using the standard Visual Basic controls. There are no GDI calls involved. This technique will work for moving bitmaps in an image control across the screen as well. The same techniques can also be performed using the Windows GDI functions. This is more labor intensive but can also produce a smoother painting process. No matter what technique is used to implement the object, the basic premise that an object must be moved as time progresses remains the same.

From Here...

In this chapter, techniques for playing back, creating, and using animation in applications were demonstrated. A general purpose animation MCI class was developed and used for controlling all MCI animation drivers. Techniques for extending this class to encompass all MCI device types were also covered. You saw how to create and use simple palette and object animation.

The following chapters have more information related to animation:

■ For insight into the Windows MCI architecture, and an overview of all the device types and the complete MCI command set, see Chapter 3, "The Media Control Interface (MCI)."

■ To examine the graphics capabilities of Windows and how to use the Windows GDI in your applications, see Chapter 5, "Graphics and Palettes."

■ For techniques on creating and using transition effects in your applications, see Chapter 6, "Creating Transition Effects."

III

Video Capabilities

Chapter 11

Using Digital Video Playback

The ability to capture, store, transmit, and play motion video is one of the most important computing technologies available in the present and the future. The digital video revolution is bringing a new class of applications to the marketplace. Applications such as teleconferencing, on-line news and presentations, and CD-ROM titles are all using the power of digital video. Chapter 8, "Digital Video Capture and Editing," examines how to create digital video capture applications. In this chapter, you look at the architecture of digital video playback and examine how to create applications that rely on digital video playback.

Windows developers, both 16- and 32-bit, are fortunate that support for digital video is a standard part of the Windows operating systems. This means that video clips can be played back on all Windows operating systems and, if coded correctly, applications that support digital video playback can operate across the Windows platforms.

The support for digital video playback is primarily provided through the Windows MCI interface layer. Even though there are low-level APIs that will play back digital video, this method is not recommended unless a highly customized method for playing digital video is necessary. For the majority of applications, the MCI interface provides more than enough power and flexibility for both the novice and power users.

In this chapter, you learn:

- How the digital video MCI driver architecture works for playing back digital video.

- How digital video can be played using the mciSendString, MCI OLE control, and Lenel Systems MediaDeveloper Digital Video Control.

- How to use MPEG video in developing applications.

Exploring the Digital Video MCI Interface

The MCI (Media Control Interface) is the primary method for interfacing with various multimedia devices. MCI is intended to provide an abstraction layer for application programs to insulate applications from device- and driver-specific details.

NOTE The MCI interface is also cross-platform enabled, meaning that the same interface works for 16-bit Windows applications and 32-bit Windows (Win32) applications. The cross-platform compatibility of MCI holds true for digital video devices as well.

It is important to make a distinction concerning digital video on the Windows platforms. The MCI interface is the primary method used for the playback of digital video. The next section addresses the issues of digital video playback.

When a digital video file is opened for playback, the MCI driver loads the file information into memory and streams the data onto the video adapter. This is a simplistic but accurate view of the operation of a digital video MCI device driver. Figure 11.1 shows the playback data flow diagram in greater detail.

Upon loading a digital video driver and opening a file, all of the statistics of the digital video file are loaded by the device driver. The loading and opening of a digital video file are accomplished through the open MCI command.

When the play command is issued, data is loaded from the file into the device driver workspace. This is a buffer for storing a working copy of the multimedia data. The workspace audio and video data are then decompressed and passed to the *monitor switch*. The monitor switch is a router that directs audio data (if present) to the audio board and the video data to the *frame buffer*. The frame buffer is a memory buffer that contains the pixel data to be copied to the video display. Finally, the frame buffer copies the data to the video display for viewing by the end user.

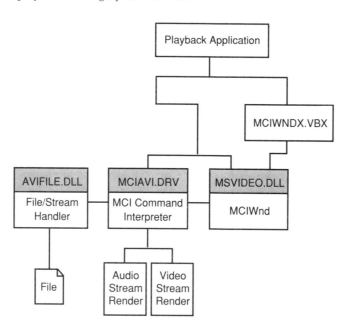

Fig. 11.1
Overview of Digital Video MCI driver playback architecture.

Methods for Digital Video Playback

The Windows operating systems, from Windows 3.x to Windows 95 and Windows NT, all support the playback of digital video. This may not seem like a great achievement, but when you consider that the same digital video files can play back under any Windows operating system with the same Windows API, the benefits are easily seen.

There are three methods that can be used to play back digital video, whether it is Video for Windows, MPEG, or DVI. These interfaces are the mciSendString function, the MCI OLE control interface provided with Visual Basic, and *Lenel System's MediaDeveloper Digital Video Control*. Each method works for 16- and 32-bit platforms.

III

Video Capabilities

It should be noted that the Video for Windows SDK provides an alternative method for playing digital video files using the MCIWNDX VBX. This isn't covered, however, because it is limited to 16-bit applications only.

Each of the applications developed in this chapter (MCISTRNG, MCICTRL, and MDEVCTRL) perform the same basic functionality: to enable the end user to open a digital video file, manipulate the basic digital video actions (play, stop, seek), stretch the display, and query various status information about the digital video file and driver. The applications in this chapter also provide code to create the digital video window as a child of the application as opposed to a free-standing window in order to tightly integrate digital video with an appplication.

Contrasting the code of each application indicates the amount of work each technique requires to integrate digital video into an application. A picture of the application is shown in Figure 11.2. As you can see from the picture of the application, the digital video player has a display area for digital video and a status to indicate the current mode (stop, play, seek) of the device. Opening and playing the digital video files are done through an application's menu items.

Fig. 11.2
Sample digital video playback application.

Using the *mciSendString* Function

When using the digital video MCI command set, the functions utilized are either `mciSendString` or `mciSendCommand`. The functions `mciSendString` and `mciSendCommand` are the Windows programming interfaces that allow developers to control digital video devices and all MCI devices. `mciSendString` is more convenient for Visual Basic developers because all of the commands are sent in the form of ASCII strings. `mciSendCommand` utilizes a set of structures that are specific to each command. Each of these structures must be defined within Visual Basic before they can be used. This is rather cumbersome, making `mciSendString` the preferred method of invoking MCI commands.

Using the `mciSendString` interface is rather easy and has the benefit of being both 16- and 32-bit portable. It does present some drawbacks, however, to the Visual Basic user. The biggest drawback is its inability to receive notifications from the MCI playback drivers.

When an MCI command is sent to the MCI driver, an optional `wait` or `notify` flag can be attached to the command. When the `wait` flag is attached, the `mciSendString` command does not return until the command has finished. For commands such as `play` this is unacceptable, because all control of the application is taken from the user until the command is finished. The `notify` flag indicates that the command returns immediately and a message, `MM_MCINOTIFY`, is sent to the window specified with the `notify` flag. The only problem, however, is that Visual Basic users cannot receive and interpret messages sent back to a Visual Basic window. There are third-party controls available, such as *Desaware's SpyWorks*, which can intercept Windows messages sent to a Visual Basic form. Other solutions, which do not require an additional control such as SpyWorks, include using the MCI OLE control or third-party multimedia controls such as Lenel System's MediaDeveloper Digital Video Control.

In the sample program MCISTRNG.EXE, you see how to play digital video via the `mciSendString` interface. As you can see from Listing 11.1, the setup of this application requires the use of a common dialog box control to load Video for Windows files and a rectangle shape that is used for displaying the video. The user interface for this application is shown in Figure 11.2.

Listing 11.1 MCISTRNG.EXE. Playing digital video through the *mciSendString* interface.

```
VERSION 4.00
Begin VB.Form MCISTRNG
   Caption        =   "Digital Video Control Using mciSendString"
   ClientHeight   =   4785
   ClientLeft     =   1140
```

(continues)

Listing 11.1 Continued

```
ClientTop        =    1395
ClientWidth      =    6930
BeginProperty Font
   name          =    "MS Sans Serif"
   charset       =    1
   weight        =    400
   size          =    8.25
   underline     =    0      'False
   italic        =    0      'False
   strikethrough =    0      'False
EndProperty
Height           =    5475
Left             =    1080
LinkTopic        =    "Form1"
ScaleHeight      =    319
ScaleMode        =    3    'Pixel
ScaleWidth       =    462
Top              =    765
Width            =    7050
Begin VB.TextBox StatusItem
   Height        =    375
   Left          =    1800
   TabIndex      =    1
   Text          =    "mode"
   Top           =    4200
   Width         =    1335
End
Begin VB.CommandButton StatusCommand
   Caption       =    "Status"
   Height        =    375
   Left          =    360
   TabIndex      =    0
   Top           =    4200
   Width         =    1215
End
Begin MSComDlg.CommonDialog OpenDialog
   Left          =    6240
   Top           =    1800
   _version      =    65536
   _extentx      =    847
   _extenty      =    847
   _stockprops   =    0
   defaulttext   =    "*.avi"
   dialogtitle   =    "File Open Dialog"
   filter        =    "Video (*.avi) ¦ *.avi"
End
Begin VB.Label StatusReturn
   Height        =    375
   Left          =    3240
   TabIndex      =    2
   Top           =    4200
   Width         =    3495
End
```

```
   Begin VB.Shape PlaybackArea
      Height          =   3600
      Left            =   840
      Top             =   240
      Width           =   4800
   End
   Begin VB.Menu File
      Caption         =   "&File"
      Begin VB.Menu Open
         Caption      =   "&Open"
      End
   End
   Begin VB.Menu Command
      Caption         =   "&Command"
      Begin VB.Menu Play
         Caption      =   "&Play"
      End
      Begin VB.Menu Stop
         Caption      =   "&Stop"
      End
      Begin VB.Menu Rewind
         Caption      =   "&Rewind"
      End
      Begin VB.Menu FastForward
         Caption      =   "&Fast Forward"
      End
      Begin VB.Menu Step
         Caption      =   "S&tep"
      End
      Begin VB.Menu ReverseStep
         Caption      =   "Reverse Ste&p"
      End
   End
   Begin VB.Menu Options
      Caption         =   "&Options"
      Begin VB.Menu Stretch
         Caption      =   "&Stretch"
      End
   End
End
Attribute VB_Name = "MCISTRNG"
Attribute VB_Creatable = False
Attribute VB_Exposed = False
```

Understanding the MCISTRNG Application

The MCISTRNG application demonstrates manipulating digital video through the mciSendString function call. When using the mciSendString interface, all of the string commands that are used in the application are defined in the general declarations section (see Listing 11.2).

Listing 11.2 MCISTRNG.FRM. Constants and declarations used in the MCISTRNG application.

```
' Constants for Program
Const ALIAS = "DvAlias"
Const ALIAS_STR = "alias"
Const SPACE = " "

' Basic command strings for the MCI multimedia control
Const PLAY_STR = "Play"
Const STOP_STR = "Stop"
Const OPEN_STR = "Open"
Const CLOSE_STR = "Close"
Const PAUSE_STR = "Pause"
Const BACK_STR = "Back"
Const STEP_STR = "Step"
Const NEXT_STR = "Next"
Const PREV_STR = "Prev"
Const SEEK_STR = "Seek"
Const RECORD_STR = "Record"
Const EJECT_STR = "Eject"
Const SOUND_STR = "Sound"
Const SAVE_STR = "Save"
Const STATUS_STR = "Status"
Const SET_STR = "Set"
Const FREEZE_STR = "Freeze"
Const PUT_STR = "Put"
Const WINDOW_STR = "Window"
Const WHERE_STR = "Where"


'Variables used for the Retrieving Status Information
Dim FixedStr As String * 50
Dim FileName As String
Dim CommandStr As String
Dim Ret As Long

' Declaration Statements - complication directive for 16 - 32 bit
#If Win32 Then
Private Declare Function mciSendString Lib "WINMM" _
    (ByVal Cmd As String, ByVal RetVal As String, ByVal _
    Len As Integer, ByVal Notify As Integer) As Long
Private Declare Function mciGetErrorString Lib "WINMM" _
    (ByVal Err As Long, ByVal RetVal As String, ByVal Len As _
    Integer) As Integer
#Else
Private Declare Function mciSendString Lib "MMSYSTEM" _
    (ByVal Cmd As String, ByVal RetVal As String, ByVal Len As _
    Integer, ByVal Notify As Integer) As Long
Private Declare Function mciGetErrorString Lib "MMSYSTEM" _
    (ByVal Err As Long, ByVal RetVal As String, ByVal Len As _
    Integer) As Integer
#End If
```

The MCISTRNG application is 16- and 32-bit ready. The compilation directive shown in Listing 11.2 illustrates this capability. As in lower-level languages such as C or C++, the directives #If, #Else, and #End If indicate to the Visual Basic compiler which set of instructions to include in the program. The variable Win32 is defined by the 32-bit version of Visual Basic and undefined by the 16-bit version.

When accessing the Windows API directly, the following is important:

- Not all of the Windows 3.1 APIs exist for Win32. Some functions have been replaced, while others were renamed.

- The libraries containing the APIs have been renamed between the Win16 and Win32 platforms.

All of the multimedia APIs in the 16-bit Windows environments are contained in a DLL library called MMSYSTEM.DLL, found in the \WINDOWS\SYSTEM directory. For 32-bit Windows applications, the multimedia APIs are contained in the DLL WINMM.DLL, found in the \WINDOWS\SYSTEM32 directory for Windows NT developers and \WINDOWS\SYSTEM directory for Windows 95 developers.

Opening and Closing Digital Video Files

There are several parameters to use when opening a digital video file through the MCI interface. Because the playback driver creates its own window for playing the digital video file, you need to change the default window style to seamlessly integrate the video within your application. The default window style as created by the driver is WS_POPUP, which needs to be changed to type WS_CHILD. When creating a child window, the parent window also needs to be specified. As shown in Listing 11.3, the open subroutine creates a string command for MCI that instructs the driver to create a child window for video playback with the parent being the form MCISTRNG. An *alias* is also specified in the command string. An alias is a logical name used when issuing subsequent commands to this instance of the MCI driver.

As with all MCI drivers, the close command must be sent whenever the application is finished using the MCI device. This is done in the form Terminate subroutine. It is also done before a new .AVI file is loaded because the AVI driver does not implement the load command, so the only method of loading an .AVI file is through the open command. Because the AVI driver is already being used, the file currently in use must be closed before another file can be loaded into memory.

Listing 11.3   MCISTRNG.FRM. Routines used for opening and closing digital video files.

```
Private Sub Open_Click()
    Dim Error As Long
    OpenDialog.Action = 1
    FileName = OpenDialog.FileName
    CommandStr = CLOSE_STR & SPACE & ALIAS
    SendCommand (CommandStr)
    CommandStr = OPEN_STR & SPACE & FileName & SPACE & ALIAS_STR &_
      SPACE & ALIAS & " style child parent " & MCISTRNG.hWnd
    Error = SendCommand(CommandStr)
    If Not Error Then
        CommandStr = PUT_STR & SPACE & ALIAS & " window at " & _
            PlaybackArea.Left & SPACE & PlaybackArea.Top & SPACE & _
            PlaybackArea.Width & SPACE & PlaybackArea.Height
        SendCommand (CommandStr)
        Stretch.Checked = True
    Else
        Stretch.Checked = False
        GetErrorString (Error)
    End If
End Sub

Private Sub Form_Terminate()
    CommandStr = CLOSE_STR & SPACE & ALIAS
    SendCommand (CommandStr)
End Sub

Public Function SendCommand(Cmd As String) As Long
    SendCommand = mciSendString(Cmd, FixedStr, 49, 0)
End Function

Public Sub GetErrorString(ErrorCode As Long)
    If mciGetErrorString(ErrorCode, FixedStr, 49) Then
        StatusReturn = FixedStr
    End If
End Sub
```

Because the video window is created as a child window, a location for playback needs to be specified. This is done through the put command. In the MCISTRNG application, a rectangular shape has been drawn on the screen. This shape represents the playback area that will be used to display digital video. Using this shape as the dimensions for playback, the rectangle representing the location of the shape is passed into the put command.

The put command modifies the position and size of the video window created by the video driver. Note that this shape may not be the original capture size of the video.

Displaying Video in Stretch Mode

The MCISTRNG application has the capability to stretch the video to fill the area defined by the rectangular shape, or the video can be played in non-stretch mode, which is done through the Stretch_Click subroutine shown in Listing 11.4.

Listing 11.4   MCISTRNG.FRM. Routine used to stretch digital video to fill a playback area.

```
Private Sub Stretch_Click()
    If Stretch.Checked = True Then
        Dim SWidth As String
        Dim SHeight As String
        Dim IHeight As Integer
        Dim IWidth As Integer
        Dim ITop As Integer
        Dim ILeft As Integer
        Dim SString As String

        CommandStr = WHERE_STR & SPACE & ALIAS & " source"
        SendCommand (CommandStr)
        SString = Left(FixedStr, 11)
        SWidth = Right(SString, 7)
        SHeight = Right(SString, 3)
        SWidth = Left(SWidth, 3)
        IWidth = CInt(SWidth)
        IHeight = CInt(SHeight)
        ILeft = PlaybackArea.Left +_
          ((PlaybackArea.Width - IWidth) /            2)
            ITop = PlaybackArea.Top + _
          ((PlaybackArea.Height - IHeight) /          2)

        CommandStr = PUT_STR & SPACE & ALIAS & " window at " _
          & ILeft & SPACE & ITop & SPACE & IWidth & SPACE & IHeight
        SendCommand (CommandStr)
        Stretch.Checked = False
    Else
        CommandStr = PUT_STR & SPACE & ALIAS & " window at " & _
         PlaybackArea.Left & SPACE & PlaybackArea.Top & SPACE & _
         PlaybackArea.Width & SPACE & PlaybackArea.Height
        SendCommand (CommandStr)
        Stretch.Checked = True
    End If
End Sub
```

III

Video Capabilities

To display the video in stretch mode, the video window is sized to the dimensions of the playback rectangle as seen in the Open_Click subroutine. For playing the video at its original captured size, you must first query the dimensions that the video was captured at. The dimensions of the video can be queried through the where command, querying the location of the source. The return value is the size that the video was captured.

The return value from the where command is centered inside of the playback rectangle again, using the put command to position the rectangle at its proper location.

The commands used for the basic control and manipulation of the .AVI files are shown in Listing 11.5. These commands include Play, FastForward, Rewind, Step, and Status.

Refer to Appendix A for the complete digital video MCI and MPEG MCI command sets and their parameters.

Listing 11.5   MCISTRNG.FRM. Routines for controlling the playback of digital video using *mciSendString*.

```
Private Sub FastForward_Click()
    CommandStr = SEEK_STR & SPACE & ALIAS & SPACE & "to end"
    SendCommand (CommandStr)

End Sub

Private Sub Play_Click()
    CommandStr = PLAY_STR & SPACE & ALIAS
    SendCommand (CommandStr)
End Sub

Private Sub ReverseStep_Click()
    Stop_Click
    CommandStr = STEP_STR & SPACE & ALIAS & " reverse"
    SendCommand (CommandStr)
End Sub

Private Sub Rewind_Click()
    CommandStr = SEEK_STR & SPACE & ALIAS & SPACE & "to start"
    SendCommand (CommandStr)
End Sub

Private Sub StatusCommand_Click()
    Dim Error As Long
    Trim (StatusItem.Text)
```

```
        If Null = Len(StatusItem.Text) Then
            StatusItem.Text = "mode"
        End If
        CommandStr = STATUS_STR & SPACE & ALIAS & SPACE & _
          StatusItem.Text
        Error = SendCommand(CommandStr)
        If 0 = Error Then
            StatusReturn = FixedStr
        Else
            GetErrorString (Error)
        End If

    End Sub

    Private Sub Step_Click()
        Stop_Click
        CommandStr = STEP_STR & SPACE & ALIAS
        SendCommand (CommandStr)
    End Sub

    Private Sub Stop_Click()
        CommandStr = STOP_STR & SPACE & ALIAS
        SendCommand (CommandStr)
    End Sub
```

Playing Digital Video from the MCI OLE Control

Visual Basic 4 includes an MCI controller OCX that is available in both 16- and 32-bit flavors. The MCI OLE control provides a high-level interface to the MCI String interface that is used in the MCISTRNG.EXE application. The MCI OLE control also provides a visual interface that consists of VCR-type controls (PLAY, STOP, FASTFORWARD, REWIND). The MCI OLE visual interface can be used for controlling the playback functions of the digital video file.

When using the MCI OLE control, the user can receive the notification messages that are sent from the MCI driver to the control when the mode of the driver changes. The control then fires an event that the application can intercept and use to perform application specific actions. The ability to receive these notification messages eliminates the problem that Visual Basic developers encountered when using the mciSendString interface.

The sample program MCICTRL.EXE, whose form attributes are shown in Listing 11.6, demonstrates playing digital video via the MCI OLE control. As you can see from comparing Listings 11.6 and 11.1, there is not much difference except for the addition of the MCI OLE control. Because the MCI OLE control doesn't provide a playback window for the drivers that it controls, you need to draw a graphical playback area using a rectangular shape and bind the playback window for digital video to it.

Listing 11.6 MCIOCX.FRM. Control setup parameters used for the MCIOCX application.

```
VERSION 4.00
Begin VB.Form MCIOCX
   Caption          =    "Digital Video Using the Mci Multimedia
                         Control"
   ClientHeight     =    5610
   ClientLeft       =    1140
   ClientTop        =    1395
   ClientWidth      =    6930
   BeginProperty Font
      name          =    "MS Sans Serif"
      charset       =    1
      weight        =    400
      size          =    8.25
      underline     =    0    'False
      italic        =    0    'False
      strikethrough =    0    'False
   EndProperty
   Height           =    6300
   Left             =    1080
   LinkTopic        =    "Form1"
   ScaleHeight      =    374
   ScaleMode        =    3    'Pixel
   ScaleWidth       =    462
   Top              =    765
   Width            =    7050
   Begin VB.TextBox StatusItem
      Height        =    375
      Left          =    1800
      TabIndex      =    1
      Text          =    "mode"
      Top           =    4920
      Width         =    1335
   End
   Begin VB.CommandButton StatusCommand
      Caption       =    "Status"
      Height        =    375
      Left          =    360
      TabIndex      =    0
      Top           =    4920
      Width         =    1215
   End
   Begin MCI.MMControl MMCtrl
      Height        =    855
      Left          =    840
      TabIndex      =    3
      Top           =    3960
      Width         =    4860
      _version      =    65536
      recordvisible =    0    'False
      ejectvisible  =    0    'False
      _extentx      =    8573
      _extenty      =    1508
```

```
      _stockprops     =    32
      borderstyle     =    1
   End
   Begin MSComDlg.CommonDialog OpenDialog
      Left            =    6240
      Top             =    1800
      _version        =    65536
      _extentx        =    847
      _extenty        =    847
      _stockprops     =    0
      defaulttext     =    "*.avi"
      dialogtitle     =    "File Open Dialog"
      filter          =    "Video (*.avi) ¦ *.avi"
   End
   Begin VB.Label StatusReturn
      Height          =    375
      Left            =    3240
      TabIndex        =    2
      Top             =    4920
      Width           =    3495
   End
   Begin VB.Shape PlaybackArea
      Height          =    3600
      Left            =    840
      Top             =    240
      Width           =    4800
   End
   Begin VB.Menu File
      Caption         =    "&File"
      Begin VB.Menu Open
         Caption         =    "&Open"
      End
   End
   Begin VB.Menu Command
      Caption           =    "&Command"
      Begin VB.Menu Play
         Caption         =    "&Play"
      End
      Begin VB.Menu Stop
         Caption         =    "&Stop"
      End
      Begin VB.Menu Rewind
         Caption         =    "&Rewind"
      End
      Begin VB.Menu FastForward
         Caption         =    "&Fast Forward"
      End
      Begin VB.Menu Step
         Caption         =    "S&tep"
      End
      Begin VB.Menu ReverseStep
         Caption         =    "Reverse Ste&p"
      End
   End
End
```

(continues)

Listing 11.6   Continued

```
    Begin VB.Menu Options
        Caption        =    "&Options"
        Begin VB.Menu Stretch
            Caption        =    "&Stretch"
        End
    End
End
Attribute VB_Name = "MCIOCX"
Attribute VB_Creatable = False
Attribute VB_Exposed = False
```

Understanding the MCICTRL Application

The MCICTRL application performs the same functions as the MCISTRNG application, only through the MCI multimedia control which is included in Visual Basic 4. While the MCI control may appear to be easy to use, it is not fully featured enough to do the job on its own.

The MCI control lacks the ability to issue commands needed for digital video control such as the put and where commands. These MCI commands need to be issued to the video driver via mciSendString to make the application function. Also, additional Windows API calls will need to be made to control the video properly. The only benefit to using the MCI OLE control is the availability of notification events to indicate when the driver's status (mode) changes. Listing 11.7 shows how the additional mciSendString commands are used with the MCI OCX.

Listing 11.7   MCIOCX.FRM. Using the MCI OCX and *mciSendString* to open a digital video file.

```
' Constants for Program
Const SPACE = " "

' Basic command strings for the MCI multimedia control
Const PLAY_STR = "Play"
Const STOP_STR = "Stop"
Const OPEN_STR = "Open"
Const CLOSE_STR = "Close"
Const PAUSE_STR = "Pause"
Const BACK_STR = "Back"
Const STEP_STR = "Step"
Const NEXT_STR = "Next"
Const PREV_STR = "Prev"
Const SEEK_STR = "Seek"
Const RECORD_STR = "Record"
Const EJECT_STR = "Eject"
```

```
Const SOUND_STR = "Sound"
Const SAVE_STR = "Save"
Const STATUS_STR = "Status"
Const SET_STR = "Set"
Const FREEZE_STR = "Freeze"
Const PUT_STR = "Put"
Const WINDOW_STR = "Window"
Const WHERE_STR = "Where"

Const GWL_STYLE = -16
Const WS_CHILD = &h40000000
Const WS_VISIBLE = &h10000000

'Variables used for the Retrieving Status Information
Dim FixedStr As String * 50
Dim FileName As String
Dim CommandStr As String
Dim Ret As Long


' Declaration Statements
#If Win32 Then
Private Declare Function mciSendString Lib "WINMM" _
  (ByVal Cmd As String, ByVal RetVal As String, ByVal Len As _
  Integer, ByVal Notify As Integer) As Long
Private Declare Function mciGetErrorString Lib "WINMM" _
  (ByVal Err As Long, ByVal RetVal As String, _
  ByVal Len As Integer) As Integer
Private Declare Function SetParent Lib "User32" _
  (ByVal Child As Integer, ByVal Parent As Integer) As Integer
Private Declare Function GetWindowLong Lib "User32" _
  (ByVal Win As Integer, ByVal Value As Integer) As Long
Private Declare Function SetWindowLong Lib "User32" _
  (ByVal Win As Integer, ByVal Offset As Integer, _
  ByVal Value As Long) As Long
#Else
Private Declare Function mciSendString Lib "MMSYSTEM" _
  (ByVal Cmd As String, ByVal RetVal As String, ByVal Len As _
  Integer, ByVal Notify As Integer) As Long
Private Declare Function mciGetErrorString Lib "MMSYSTEM" _
  (ByVal Err As Long, ByVal RetVal As String, _
  ByVal Len As Integer) As Integer
Private Declare Function SetParent Lib "User" _
  (ByVal Child As Integer, ByVal Parent As Integer) As Integer
Private Declare Function GetWindowLong Lib "User" _
  (ByVal Win As Integer, ByVal Value As Integer) As Long
Private Declare Function SetWindowLong Lib "User" _
  (ByVal Win As Integer, ByVal Offset As Integer, _
  ByVal Value As Long) As Long

#End If
```

(continues)

III

Video Capabilities

Listing 11.7   Continued

```
Private Sub Open_Click()
    Dim Error As Long
    OpenDialog.Action = 1
    FileName = OpenDialog.FileName
    MMCtrl.Command = CLOSE_STR
    MMCtrl.FileName = FileName
    MMCtrl.Command = OPEN_STR
    If Not MMCtrl.Error Then
        CommandStr = STATUS_STR & SPACE & FileName & SPACE & _
          "window handle"
        If 0 = SendCommand(CommandStr) Then
            i% = SetParent(CInt(FixedStr), MCIOCX.hWnd)
            l = SetWindowLong(CInt(FixedStr), GWL_STYLE, WS_CHILD)
        End If
        CommandStr = PUT_STR & SPACE & FileName & " window at " _
          & PlaybackArea.Left & SPACE & PlaybackArea.Top & _
          SPACE & PlaybackArea.Width & SPACE & PlaybackArea.Height
        SendCommand (CommandStr)
        Stretch.Checked = True
    Else
        Stretch.Checked = False
        GetErrorString
    End If
End Sub

Public Function SendCommand(Cmd As String) As Long
    SendCommand = mciSendString(Cmd, FixedStr, 49, 0)
End Function

Public Sub GetErrorString()
    If MMCtrl.Error Then
        StatusReturn = MMCtrl.ErrorMessage
    End If
End Sub
```

Looking at the code to open the digital video file in the Open_Click subroutine shows that the MCI control handles the opening of the video file by setting the control's FileName property, then issuing the open string via the Command property. Note that unlike the MCISTRNG application, there is no provision for setting an alias for the control. This can pose a problem when issuing subsequent MCI commands, because you need the logical name of the driver to control. Undocumented in the MCI OCX control reference is mention that in order to address the MCI driver opened by the MCI OLE control through mciSendString commands, the filename must be used for devices that use files. For devices that do not use files, such as VCRs and laser disc players, the device type specified in the DeviceType property is used.

It is important to know this because the default window style for a digital video driver is a pop-up window. For the MCIOCX application, a child window style is used. After the window is opened, the following sequence of events occurs:

1. The window handle of the digital video driver needs to be obtained. The window handle is obtained through the `status` command sent through the `mciSendString` API.

2. After the window handle is obtained, the Windows APIs are used to set the parent of the video window to the form. The function `SetParent` sets the form as the parent of the video window.

3. After the parent window is set, the style of the video window still needs to be altered. The window style of the video window is changed to `WS_CHILD`, via the API `SetWindowStyle`.

4. After the parent window and the style of the window have been changed, the `put` command is issued to place the window at its specified location.

The digital video window is not actually displayed until the `put` command is issued, so you will not see the window actually changing size and position.

The MCIOCX application is also both 16- and 32-bit ready. Listing 11.8 shows how the digital video file is positioned within the display rectangle shown on the form.

Listing 11.8 MCIOCX.FRM. Using the MCI OCX to control the playback of digital video.

```
Private Sub FastForward_Click()
    MMCtrl.Command = "Next"
End Sub

Private Sub Form_Terminate()
    MMCtrl.Command = STOP_STR
End Sub

Private Sub MMCtrl_StatusUpdate()
    Dim ll_Long As Long
    ll_Long = MMCtrl.Mode
```

(continues)

Listing 11.8 Continued

```
        Select Case ll_Long
            Case 524
                StatusReturn = "Not Opened"
            Case 525
                StatusReturn = "Stopped"
            Case 526
                StatusReturn = "Playing"
            Case 527
                StatusReturn = "Recording"
            Case 528
                StatusReturn = "Seeking"
            Case 529
                StatusReturn = "Paused"
            Case 530
                StatusReturn = "Ready"
        End Select
End Sub


Private Sub Play_Click()
    MMCtrl.Command = PLAY_STR
End Sub

Private Sub ReverseStep_Click()
    Stop_Click
    MMCtrl.Command = "Back"
End Sub

Private Sub Rewind_Click()
    MMCtrl.Command = "Prev"
End Sub

Private Sub StatusCommand_Click()
    Dim Error As Long
    Trim (StatusItem.Text)
    If Null = Len(StatusItem.Text) Then
        StatusItem.Text = "mode"
    End If
    CommandStr = STATUS_STR & SPACE & FileName & _
      SPACE & StatusItem.Text
    Error = SendCommand(CommandStr)
    If 0 = Error Then
        StatusReturn = FixedStr
    End If
End Sub

Private Sub Step_Click()
    Stop_Click
    MMCtrl.Command = "Step"
End Sub
```

```
Private Sub Stop_Click()
    MMCtrl.Command = STOP_STR
End Sub


Private Sub Stretch_Click()
    If Stretch.Checked = True Then
        Dim SWidth As String
        Dim SHeight As String
        Dim IHeight As Integer
        Dim IWidth As Integer
        Dim ITop As Integer
        Dim ILeft As Integer
        Dim SString As String

        CommandStr = WHERE_STR & SPACE & FileName & " source"
        SendCommand (CommandStr)
        SString = Left(FixedStr, 11)
        SWidth = Right(SString, 7)
        SHeight = Right(SString, 3)
        SWidth = Left(SWidth, 3)
        IWidth = CInt(SWidth)
        IHeight = CInt(SHeight)
        ILeft = PlaybackArea.Left + _
            ((PlaybackArea.Width - IWidth) /2)
        ITop = PlaybackArea.Top + _
            ((PlaybackArea.Height - IHeight) / 2)

        CommandStr = PUT_STR & SPACE & FileName & " window at " & _
            ILeft & SPACE & ITop & SPACE & IWidth & SPACE & IHeight
        SendCommand (CommandStr)
        Stretch.Checked = False
    Else
        CommandStr = PUT_STR & SPACE & FileName & " window at " & _
            PlaybackArea.Left & SPACE & PlaybackArea.Top & SPACE & _
            PlaybackArea.Width & SPACE & PlaybackArea.Height
        SendCommand (CommandStr)
        Stretch.Checked = True
    End If
End Sub
```

Obtaining Status Changes Using the MCI OCX

As mentioned earlier in the chapter, one of the advantages of using the OLE MCI control is the ability to detect the status of the MCI driver as it changes states. The driver status information is relayed to the application through the control's StatusUpdate event. When the StatusUpdate event is received, the mode of the driver can be queried through the Mode property and any actions can be taken by the developer.

III

Video Capabilities

Overall, the ability to detect the status of the MCI driver is the real advantage to using the MCI OLE control as opposed to using the mciSendString API. These two features are important if the user is not supposed to click on a specific button while the video is playing. For example, an application can disable an Exit menu item while the status of the MCI control is "playing." When the status changes from "playing" to "stopped," the Exit button can be enabled.

Playing Digital Video via the MediaDeveloper OLE Control

Lenel Systems has developed an OLE control that is specifically tailored to the playback of all digital video formats including Video for Windows, QuickTime, MPEG, and DVI Video. Using this control, applications can support all video formats without having to change any source code! The control also supports both 16- and 32-bit platforms.

The sample MDEVCTRL.EXE program shown in Listing 11.9 illustrates how the MDEVCTRL application was constructed using the MediaDeveloper Custom Control. Instead of using a shape to represent the playback area, the playback area is designated by the size of the control. The Stretch property, when set to True, fills the control with the video. When set to False, the playback area is the size of the captured video. If the video is smaller than the playback area, the video is centered within the control and can be optionally surrounded by a raised or sunken set of borders. There is also the ability to control the aspect ratio of the video through the AspectRatio property. This prevents the video from losing proportionality when being stretched. The Stretch and AspectRatio properties eliminate the need to use the put command when displaying or stretching the video.

Listing 11.9 MDEVCTRL.FRM. Control setup parameters for the MDEVCTRL application.

```
VERSION 4.00
Begin VB.Form mdevctrl
   Caption          =   "Digital Video Using MediaDeveloper Digital
                         Video Control"
   ClientHeight     =   5610
   ClientLeft       =   1080
   ClientTop        =   1005
   ClientWidth      =   6930
   BeginProperty Font
      name          =    "MS Sans Serif"
      charset       =    1
      weight        =    400
```

```
    size            =    8.25
    underline       =    0     'False
    italic          =    0     'False
    strikethrough   =    0     'False
EndProperty
Height              =    6300
Left                =    1020
LinkTopic           =    "Form1"
ScaleHeight         =    374
ScaleMode           =    3     'Pixel
ScaleWidth          =    462
Top                 =    375
Width               =    7050
Begin VB.TextBox StatusItem
    Height          =    375
    Left            =    1800
    TabIndex        =    1
    Text            =    "mode"
    Top             =    4920
    Width           =    1335
End
Begin VB.CommandButton StatusCommand
    Caption         =    "Status"
    Height          =    375
    Left            =    360
    TabIndex        =    0
    Top             =    4920
    Width           =    1215
End
Begin L_dvideoLib.L_dvideo DVCtrl
    Prop68          =    "MDEVCTRL.frx":0000
    Height          =    3600
    Left            =    960
    TabIndex        =    3
    TabStop         =    0     'False
    Top             =    360
    Width           =    4800
    _version        =    65536
    _extentx        =    8467
    _extenty        =    6350
    _stockprops     =    97
    backcolor       =    16711680
    borderstyle     =    1
    aspectratio     =    0     'False
    stretch         =    -1    'True
    timeformat      =    10
End
Begin MSComDlg.CommonDialog OpenDialog
    Left            =    6240
    Top             =    1800
    _version        =    65536
    _extentx        =    847
    _extenty        =    847
    _stockprops     =    0
```

(continues)

III

Video Capabilities

Listing 11.9 Continued

```
          defaulttext    =    "*.avi"
          dialogtitle    =    "File Open Dialog"
          filter         =    "Video (*.avi) ¦ *.avi"
      End
      Begin VB.Label StatusReturn
          Height         =    375
          Left           =    3240
          TabIndex       =    2
          Top            =    4920
          Width          =    3495
      End
      Begin VB.Menu File
          Caption        =    "&File"
          Begin VB.Menu Open
              Caption        =    "&Open"
          End
      End
      Begin VB.Menu Command
          Caption        =    "&Command"
          Begin VB.Menu Play
              Caption        =    "&Play"
          End
          Begin VB.Menu Stop
              Caption        =    "&Stop"
          End
          Begin VB.Menu Rewind
              Caption        =    "&Rewind"
          End
          Begin VB.Menu FastForward
              Caption        =    "&Fast Forward"
          End
          Begin VB.Menu Step
              Caption        =    "S&tep"
          End
          Begin VB.Menu ReverseStep
              Caption        =    "Reverse Ste&p"
          End
      End
      Begin VB.Menu Options
          Caption        =    "&Options"
          Begin VB.Menu Stretch
              Caption        =    "&Stretch"
          End
      End
   End
   Attribute VB_Name = "mdevctrl"
   Attribute VB_Creatable = False
   Attribute VB_Exposed = False
```

Understanding the MDEVCTRL Application

Using Lenel's MediaDeveloper control is probably the fastest and easiest method for developing a digital video application. The application's source code (see Listing 11.10) contains no Windows APIs or the mciSendString API. The digital video control provides all of the necessary properties and methods for fully exploiting the MCI command set.

Most of the common commands, such as play and seek, are exposed as methods. For commands such as status or any MCI command exposed or not exposed by the MediaDeveloper interface, the control provides a built-in mciSendString method. This version relieves the user from having to remember the logical name of the driver and also from building the long command strings. The mciSendString method in the MediaDeveloper control takes two parameters—the first is the actual command (such as play or status) and the second is the parameters to the command.

Listing 11.10   MDEVCTRL.FRM. Controlling digital video using Lenel's Digital Video OCX.

```
' Basic command strings for the MCI multimedia control
Const STATUS_STR = "Status"

Private Sub FastForward_Click()
    DVCtrl.FastForward
End Sub

Private Sub Form_Terminate()
    DVCtrl.Stop
End Sub

Private Sub Open_Click()
    Dim Error As Long
    OpenDialog.Action = 1
    DVCtrl.FileName = OpenDialog.FileName
    DVCtrl.Stretch = True
    Stretch.Checked = True
End Sub

Private Sub Play_Click()
    DVCtrl.Play
End Sub

Private Sub ReverseStep_Click()
    DVCtrl.Stop
    DVCtrl.Step (-1)
End Sub
```

(continues)

iii

Video Capabilities

```
Listing 11.10  Continued

Private Sub Rewind_Click()
    DVCtrl.Rewind
End Sub

Private Sub StatusCommand_Click()
    Dim Error As Long
    Trim (StatusItem.Text)
    If Null = Len(StatusItem.Text) Then
        StatusItem.Text = "mode"
    End If
    StatusReturn = DVCtrl.mciSendString(STATUS_STR, _
      StatusItem.Text)
End Sub

Private Sub Step_Click()
    Stop_Click
    DVCtrl.Step (1)
End Sub

Private Sub Stop_Click()
    DVCtrl.Stop
End Sub

Private Sub Stretch_Click()
    If Stretch.Checked = True Then
        DVCtrl.Stretch = False
        Stretch.Checked = False
    Else
        DVCtrl.Stretch = True
        Stretch.Checked = True
    End If
End Sub
```

The use of the MediaDeveloper digital video control significantly enhances the capabilities of applications while slicing the development time by a third. The MediaDeveloper control is available in both 16- and 32-bit flavors, thus making this application portable to all platforms.

MediaDeveloper Digital Video Control Reference

Table 11.1 lists all of the properties available to the digital video control object.

Table 11.1 Available Properties for Lenel's Digital Video Control	
Property	**Description**
AspectRatio	Preserves the aspect ratio of the video frame when being stretched.
AutoSize	Automatically resizes the control to the size of the video frame.
BackColor	Indicates the background color of the control.
BorderStyle	Gets/sets the border style of the control.
BorderWidth	Width of the border or frame around the video frame; 0—no frame
BottomBorderColor	Indicates the color of the bottom border around the video frame.
Driver	The digital video device driver when opening a file or device.
DropFiles	Allows the control to be a drop target for File Manager.
Enabled	Enables or disables the control.
EndPosition	Sets/gets the end position for a digital video segment.
FileName	Sets the digital video file to display in control.
Hwnd	Returns the Window handle of the control.
LeftBorderColor	Indicates the color of the left border around the video frame.
Loop	When True, digital video file will continuously play.
Mute	Enables/disables sound.
Picture	Returns a picture pointer of the contents of the video control.
RightBorderColor	Indicates the color of the right border around the video frame.
StartPosition	Sets/gets the start position for a digital video segment.
StepCount	Indicates the number of frames to move when the Step Menu Item is invoked.
Stretch	Stretches the video frame to fill the control.

(continues)

iii

Video Capabilities

Table 11.1   Continued

Property	Description
TimeFormat	The current time format of the MCI device.
TopBorderColor	Color of the top border around the control.
UseAmbientColor	When True, sets the control's background to the background color of the control container. When False, sets the control's background to the user-specified background.
UseSegmentMark	Confines the play, rewind, and fast forward methods to the begin/end segment positions.

MediaDeveloper Digital Video OLE Control Methods

Copy	Copies the current contents of the control to the clipboard.
CopyToClipboard	Copies a data handle to the Windows Clipboard.
CreateDDBThumbnail	Returns a thumbnail of the current contents being displayed in Device Dependent Bitmap (DDB) format.
CreateDIBThumbnail	Returns a thumbnail of the current contents being displayed in Device Independent Bitmap (DIB) format.
EndMedia	Returns the position of the end of the media or file.
FastForward	Positions the digital video file at the end of the file or at the end segment position.
GetBitmap	Returns a Windows Device Dependent Bitmap from the contents of the current display.
GetCurrentPosition	Returns the current position within the digital video file.
GetDIB	Returns a handle to a Windows Device Independent Bitmap.
GetMetafile	Returns a handle to a metafile from the contents of the current display.
GetMode	Returns the current mode of the digital video control.
GetObjectHeight	Returns the height of the video frame in the control.
GetObjectWidth	Returns the width of the video frame in the control.
GetPalette	Returns a palette handle from the contents of the current display.
GetSampleRate	Gets the frames per second that the digital video file is recorded at.

Property	Description
LengthMedia	Returns the length of the media.
LengthSegment	Returns the length of the segment bound by the begin and end marks.
MciSendString	Sends a string to the MCI device driver that is loaded.
Pause	Pauses/unpauses the current activity of the digital video control.
Play	Plays the digital video file.
PlaySegment	Plays the digital video file from a start position to an end position.
Refresh	Redraws or paints the control.
Resume	Resumes the paused activity of the control.
Rewind	Positions the digital video file at the beginning of the file of the start segment position.
Save	Saves the current contents of the control to a specified file format.
SaveAs	Saves what is currently showing in the control as a graphic file. User is prompted with a dialog box for the filename.
SaveFormatAs	Saves a Device Dependent Bitmap handle or a Device Independent Bitmap in a specified file format.
SeekTo	Positions the digital video file at a specified location.
SetBeginMark	Returns the current position and marks this spot as the beginning of a segment.
SetEndMark	Returns the current position and marks this as the end of a segment.
StartMedia	Returns the position of the start of the media or file.
Step	Steps the digital video forwards or backwards.
Stop	Stops the current activity within the control.

MediaDeveloper Digital Video Control Events

MciDone	Notifies application when an MCI command has been completed.

III

Video Capabilities

Working with MPEG Video

In late 1993, Microsoft worked with several hardware and software companies to create an industry standard command set for MPEG (Motion Picture Experts Group) video on the PC platform. Several commercial MPEG applications began to appear for the PC platform, but the creation of a standard playback command set was needed to ensure the widespread acceptance of MPEG video. This resulted in the creation of the MPEG video MCI command specification.

Already MPEG video is being supported and used by both commercial and professional users. MPEG is attractive because it offers state-of-the-art digital video compression, VHS-quality full-motion video, and multivendor support. MPEG video requires a decompression playback board to play MPEG files on the PC. The cost of an MPEG playback board is relatively inexpensive (less than $300) given the quality of video.

MPEG video was designed to provide 180:1 compression ratios that are required to play full-motion video at CD-ROM transfer rates. Typically MPEG video is captured and displayed at 352×240 display resolution. It can be displayed at larger resolutions through hardware scaling. The MPEG standard supports 352×250 resolution video at 30 fps synchronized with 16-bit audio. Because MPEG is an International Standards Organization (ISO) standard, compatibility is ensured among different hardware and software products and different vendors.

MPEG video drivers follow a slightly different playback model than other digital video drivers such as Video for Windows. Figure 11.3 shows the MPEG driver state transition diagram.

Fig. 11.3
Transition state diagram that shows the control paths of an MPEG video driver.

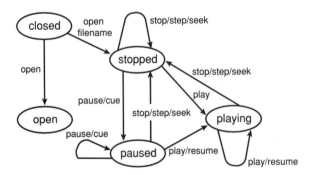

One of the quirks of working with MPEG video is the behavior of the `stop` command, which removes video display from the screen. Because the video playback is hardware-assisted, the only time video is displayed is when the driver is in the `cued` command or the `play` command has been issued. Because of this, care must be taken when the `stop` command is issued because the video will be removed from the screen.

If you have the appropiate MCI drivers and MPEG display board, the applications developed in this chapter can be modified to display MPEG files by changing the driver names and file extensions used in the common file dialog boxes.

From Here...

As demonstrated in this chapter, the use of digital video can widely enhance the appearance of your application. The programs shown in this chapter are intended to provide an introduction to the many tools and methods available for playing back digital video.

Techniques were shown for playing digital video through the use of the `mciSendString` interface, the MCI OLE control, and through Lenel System's MediaDeveloper Digital Video Control. MPEG video was discussed and how it can be used in applications in place of or along with Video for Windows.

- For more information on the MCI interface, see Chapter 3, "The Media Control Interface (MCI)," for an in-depth discussion of how the Media Control Interface works and how it is implemented on the Windows operating systems.

- For further information on how to capture digital video files on the Windows 3.x, Windows 95, and Windows NT platforms, see Chapter 8, "Digital Video Capture and Editing."

- To see how a generic MCI controller module is developed, refer to Chapter 10, "Animation." The MCI controller module uses the `mciSendString` function to control any MCI-based media type.

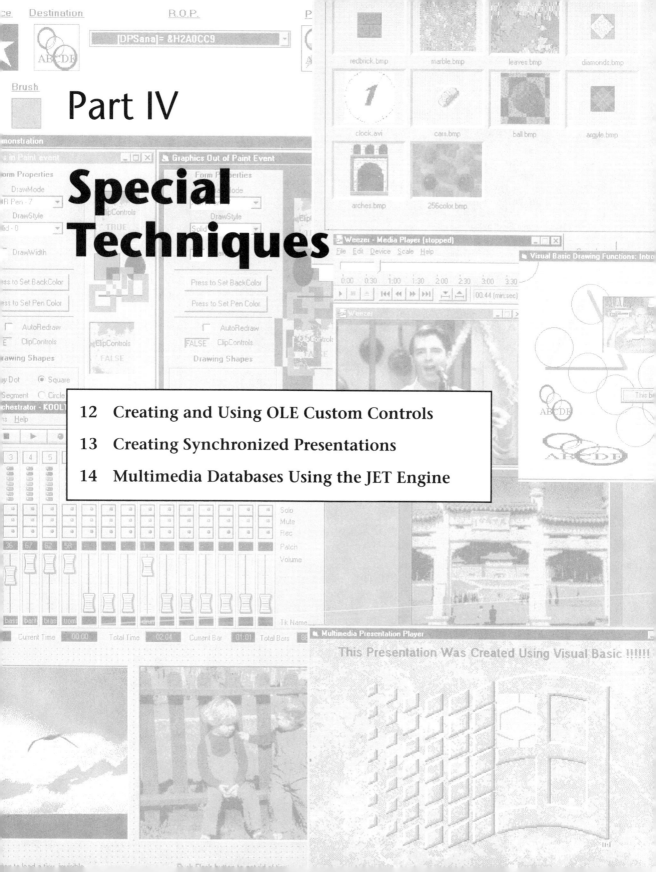

Part IV

Special Techniques

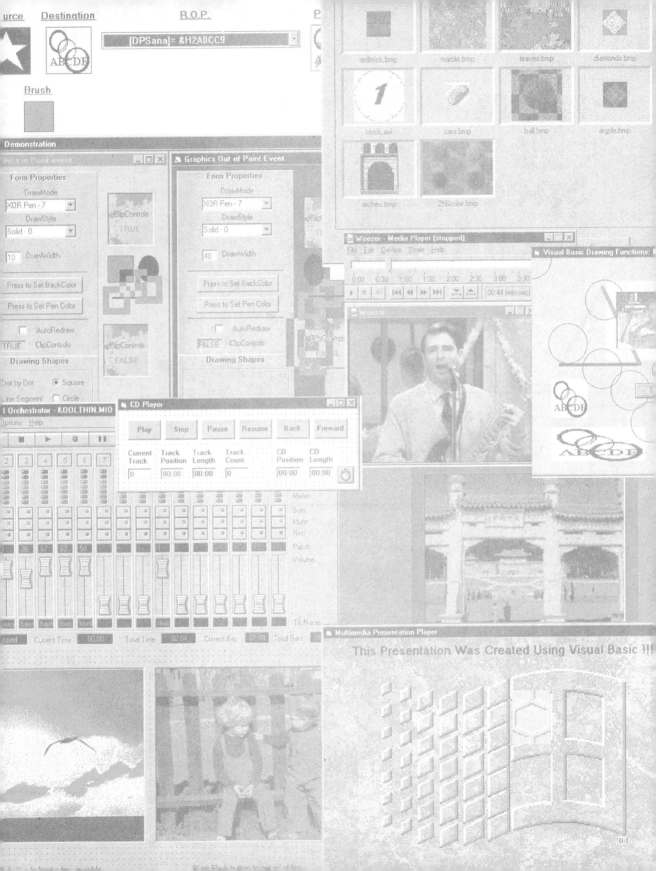

Chapter 12

Creating and Using OLE Custom Controls

OLE (Object Linking and Embedding) is the most important technology to come from the Microsoft camp this decade. It is just starting to become a mainstream feature in applications and in the new operating system releases. In fact, Windows 95 has OLE features oozing from every nook and cranny of its operating system.

In this chapter, you learn:

- Why OLE controls are important to Visual Basic developers

- How OLE custom controls work, including all of the details in building an OLE custom control

- How to create and develop a custom control. You build a shell DragDrop control that will be used in Chapter 14, "Multimedia Databases Using the JET Engine"

Why OLE and Custom Controls?

OLE technology is intended to enhance the way that a user looks at data and the applications that interact with this data. Prior to OLE, PC users had data that they needed to manipulate, and applications that manipulate the data. As an example, when a letter or memo needed to be put together, a program such as Word was used. When a spreadsheet had to be manipulated, a program such as Excel was used. Each program was isolated from the other and so was the data. If your memo needed a chart from the spreadsheet, you had to manually enter the information and make it resemble the spreadsheet.

OLE 1.0 provided basic object linking and embedding capabilities in which a Video for Windows file shown in Media Player could be inserted into a Visual Basic multimedia presentation. Chapter 13, "Creating Synchronized Presentations," demonstrates this technique. This sounds like nothing more than a Clipboard cut-and-paste operation, but with OLE, the digital video file is now an *embedded* object, which means that if the user activates the digital video picture by double-clicking on it, the native program (Media Player) is invoked and the digital video file is loaded and played by Media Player. During activation, if the digital video file is changed or updated, the new digital video can also update the presentation. The digital video file in the presentation is only updated if it is activated from within the presentation. This scenario is known as *embedding*.

The other scenario is called *linking*. Linking follows the same set of actions as embedding except that a *hot link* is maintained between Media Player and the presentation programs. A hot link means that if the digital video file is updated in any manner, the digital video is automatically updated in the presentation. This update happens no matter how the digital video file was updated. If the digital video file in Media Player is updated, the changes are automatically sent to the multimedia presentation and reflected instantaneously, if the presentation is active, or automatically the next time the presentation is viewed. This relieves the user from having to manually update any documents containing the digital video file.

While this technology in itself is useful, it is slow and not entirely friendly to both the users and developers. When Microsoft released OLE 2.0, this signaled the start of very big changes on the horizon for both end users and developers alike. The first statement to make about OLE 2.0 is that it is big: there are now many more components in OLE than just the basic linking and embedding.

OLE 2.0 is so radically different from OLE 1.0, that none of the development done for OLE 1.0 is applicable to OLE 2.0. OLE 2.0 not only encompasses the basic object linking and embedding, but also *inter-application drag and drop*, *in-place editing*, *automation*, and now *OLE controls (OCXs)*.

OLE is comprised of *interfaces*. An interface is an abstraction that represents a means of communicating with an OLE object. An interface is analogous to a C++ class without any data members. The interfaces can be inherited and derived from a C++ class. This is the reason that C++ is the preferred language for developing OLE applications and components. In Visual Basic terms, an interface is analogous to a component such as a custom control.

A custom control has properties, methods, and events that define the interface to the control.

OLE controls are an extension of the OLE 2.0 interfaces with the additional control interfaces. OLE controls heavily utilize the in-place editing and drag and drop interfaces available in OLE 2.0. OLE controls are the future of component development for the Windows operating systems.

OLE Controls: More Than an Extension to VBXs

Visual Basic 1.0 was the first product to truly establish a market for software components. These components are Visual Basic controls or *VBXs*. VBXs exploded onto the software development scene and enabled Visual Basic to be one of the premiere development environments, primarily because there are VBXs available to handle virtually any programming task from e-mail to networking and multimedia. To capitalize on the wealth of software components available in the VBX market, most major software development environments now support VBXs.

While the VBX market has rapidly expanded, it is eventually destined to wither away. The major reason for this is that the VBX architecture is inherently 16-bit in nature and cannot be expanded to a 32-bit architecture. This means that as Windows NT and Windows 95 gain more popularity, customers will demand 32-bit applications to take advantage of the performance of a 32-bit operating system. Because VBXs are 16-bit, 32-bit applications cannot use them.

VBXs are also limited by the fact that they support only user-defined properties and events. There is no support for user-defined methods. This means that every action that a VBX can perform is done through a property(s) or through a DLL function that uses the VBX. There is also no inherent support in the operating system for VBXs.

Even though VBXs may be a dead end, the software component market is not dead. In fact, it is probably poised to expand at an even faster rate than the VBX market enjoyed. This is because of OLE controls.

OLE controls are the component replacements for VBXs. OLE controls (OCXs) are expandable and can be developed and used in both 16- and 32-bit applications. The Windows operating systems (NT and 95) carry the OLE system .DLLs as a standard component of the operating system. In addition, the OLE controls support user-defined properties, events, and methods. This chapter provides a behind-the-scenes look at how OLE controls are constructed and also shows how you can easily implement your own 16- and 32-bit OLE controls through the use of the Visual C++ development environment.

An Introduction to Control Development

Building OLE controls requires C or C++ programming knowledge as well as a thorough understanding of OLE technology. Even though OLE controls can be implemented in C, this is not the smart way to build OLE controls. It is wiser to spend a week or so learning C++ than to implement OLE controls using the C interface. The OLE control you build in this chapter uses the C++ OLE control interface that is provided with Visual C++ 2.0.

To build OLE controls, you need the following items:

- *Microsoft Visual C++ 2.0 or higher*. Version 2.0 of the Visual C++ compiler is a 32-bit compiler. This can *only* be used for building 32-bit controls, DLLs, or applications. Included with Visual C++ 2.0 is the latest 16-bit compiler, Version 1.52, which can be used for building 16-bit OLE controls, DLLs, or applications.

- *The Microsoft OLE Control Development Kit (CDK)*. The Control Development Kit is included with Visual C++ 2.0. It is available in both 16-bit and 32-bit versions. Before installing either the 16-bit or 32-bit CDK, Visual C++ *must* be installed.

- *The Microsoft Foundation Classes (MFC)*. The foundation classes are included with Visual C++. While the MFC library is not specifically used, the OLE control classes in the CDK are derived from the MFC classes, therefore, understanding the MFC architecture helps to ease the control development pain. Version 3.0 of MFC is needed for the 32-bit compiler, while MFC Version 2.52 is needed for the 16-bit compiler. The MFC version can be obtained by adding 1.0 to Version 1.52 of the Visual C++ compiler.

- *Windows NT or Windows 95 for development of either 16-bit or 32-bit controls*. Windows 3.1 or higher is needed for development of 16-bit controls only. Because the 32-bit operating systems (NT or 95) can be used for both 16-bit and 32-bit development, I would recommend either of these environments.

- *Visual Basic 4.0 or a test container application to test the functionality of your OLE controls.*

- *A working understanding of OLE and C++ technologies is desireable.* If you have these two skill sets, then writing OLE controls is going to be a snap. If you do not have these two skill sets, don't worry. You are guided through how to build OLE custom controls while providing OLE and C++ overviews.

There are two major benefits provided to users of the Microsoft CDK—the assistance of the *ControlWizard* for building the control framework and the portability of the control framework to both 16-bit and 32-bit platforms. In this chapter, Visual C++ 2.0 and the 32-bit CDK is used for developing OLE controls. Later in this chapter you'll see the differences between the 16-bit and 32-bit CDK.

Generating an OLE Control with the ControlWizard

If you have purchased a product from Microsoft in the last year, you probably have noticed the inclusion of *wizards* to assist you with various tasks, depending on the product you are using. A wizard is a series of templates that guides you step-by-step through a specific process. You have to look no further than Windows 95 for an example. In Windows 95, the Add New Hardware icon in the Control Panel folder presents users with a series of dialog boxes for adding a new hardware device to your system.

To assist developers in getting started with OLE control development, the Visual C++ development environment has the ControlWizard. The ControlWizard command can be found under the Tools menu. The ControlWizard presents you with a list of all choices needed for generating an OLE control. Selecting the ControlWizard command presents you with a dialog box (see Fig. 12.1) for selecting the directory where the control is to be located and the name of the control.

Setting Control Options for a *DragDrop* Control

As an example of building an OLE control, the DragDrop control (which is used in Chapter 14, "Multimedia Databases Using the JET Engine") will be built for entering data into a multimedia database. This control intercepts the WM_DROPFILE command from the Windows Explorer and provides notification events to the application when a file(s) is dropped on the control. The application can then use the control's methods and properties to inquire about which files were dropped on the control.

Fig. 12.1
Choosing the control's Build Directory and Name using the Visual C++'s Control Development Kit.

The first step is to type **DragDrop** into the Project Name text box. This automatically adds a subdirectory of the same name to your current location on the hard disk. The current location can be changed by selecting it in the Directory list box.

After the project name and directory are established, click the Project Options button. This enables you to set up options available for the project, as shown in Figure 12.2. The project options are listed in Table 12.1.

Fig. 12.2
How to select the project options for the DragDrop control through the ControlWizard.

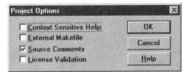

Table 12.1 Project Options for OLE Controls	
Option	**Description**
Context Sensitive Help	Generates a set of help files used by the control. The help file can be invoked at design time and is context-sensitive to the property or method the cursor is on. The Help Compiler included with Visual C++ is needed to compile these files.
External Makefile	Creates a makefile that can *only* be modified through an external text editor, not the ControlWizard or the Visual C++ environment. By default, the generated makefile is not external and can be modified by the ControlWizard, Visual C++, and/or an external editor. There is no reason to ever check this option.

Option	Description
Source Comments	Places comments into ControlWizard-generated code instructing you where the code needs to be added. This option is generally good for both inexperienced and experienced control developers. This option is checked by default.
License Validation	Generates a license (.LIC) file and inserts the licensing APIs into the control's framework. Most commercial OLE controls use this option to prevent unauthorized distribution of their controls.

For the DragDrop control, only the Source Comments option is selected by default. With the exception of External Makefile, selecting any of the other options will not affect the development of this control.

To set the Control options, click the Control Options button on the ControlWizard. The Control Options dialog box shown in Figure 12.3 enables you to set the desired options for the control. A description of the available options is provided in Table 12.2.

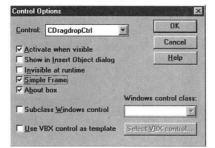

Fig. 12.3
You can specify the characteristics of the OLE control through the Control Options dialog box.

Table 12.2 Control Options for OCXs

Control Option	Description
Activate When Visible	Instructs the container to automatically "activate" the control when it is visible. Activating the control enables any user interface that the control contains, such as an in-place editing menu or toolbar. This support is not mandatory or required for in-place activation.

(continues)

Table 12.2 Continued	
Control Option	**Description**
Show in Insert Object Dialog	Places the name of the control in the Insert Object dialog box, which is invoked by applications supporting OLE. Selecting this option allows controls to be visible in the dialog box even if OLE controls are not supported by the application.
Invisible At Runtime	Select this option to have your control indicate to its container that the control should be invisible in the container's run-time mode and visible in the container's design-time mode. A container may ignore the control's preference, allowing your control to be visible at all times. Selecting this option instructs the ControlWizard to insert code that will not generate a window for the control.
Simple Frame	Select this option to have your control support the ISimpleFrameSite protocol. When the container and the control both support this protocol, the container uses simple-frame controls as parents for other controls in the container. In effect, the simple-frame control operates as an OLE compound document container, but the frame control's container does nearly all the work.
About Box	Creates a standard About dialog box for your control.
Subclass Windows Control	Subclasses common Windows controls, such as buttons, toolbars, and text boxes. This enables you to choose a Windows control from the Windows Control Class list box.
Use VBX Control as Template	Enables the Select VBX Control button, which allows you to access the Use VBX Control as Template dialog box. This dialog box is used only if you are porting a VBX to an OCX.

For the DragDrop control, the Simple Frame, Activate When Visible, and About Box options are enabled. Once the control options have been enabled, click the OK button. After the project and control options have been set, the control is ready to be built.

The last option available from the ControlWizard dialog box (refer to Fig. 12.1) is the Controls button. Clicking this button displays the OLE control's name and the classes created automatically by the ControlWizard to build this control. Figure 12.4 shows the settings used for the DragDrop control.

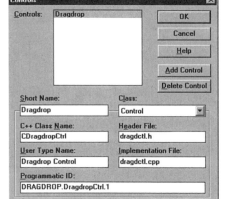

Fig. 12.4
This dialog box enables you to customize the OLE control's name(s) and source files.

The Controls box in the center of the dialog box lists all of the controls in this project. Typically, there is one control per project, but multiple controls can be added to a single project if desired.

Table 12.3 describes the options in the Controls dialog box and how they can be changed for your controls.

Table 12.3 Available options for the control's system registry names and project implementation file	
Option	**Description**
Short Name	Specifies the base name of the class. The name that appears by default is the name of the project in the Controls box.
Class	Allows you to choose a class within a project to view. By default, the Controls dialog box adds two classes to an OCX—the control itself and a property page class. Use the Class list box to select either the control class or the property page class. You can then modify various names pertaining to that class, such as the Short Name, User Type Name, and the Programmatic ID.
C++ Class Name	Specifies the name of the main class of the control or of its property page class. The class you choose in the Class list box determines whether this box displays the name of the control class or the property page class. The default name for the control class is `CPrjnameCtrl` or `CDragDropCtrl`. The default name for the property page class is `CPrjnamePropPage` or `CDragDropPropPage`.

(continues)

Table 12.3   Continued

Option	Description
Header File	Displays the name of the header file that contains the class definition.
User Type Name	Displays the name exposed to the control's user. This is name of the control that is shown to the user when inserting a control into the Visual Basic environment.
Implementation File	Displays the name of the source file that contains the class implementation.
Programmatic ID	Specifies the ID of the OLE control class. This is the name that is passed as a parameter to the Visual Basic CreateObject function if the control is created programmatically.

Once you have set all of the options for the control, click the OK button and the ControlWizard creates the project subdirectories and generates the skeleton templates for the OLE control. At this point, the control can actually be built, registered, and used within an application. Choose the Build command under the Project menu to compile the resources and code modules and to generate a working OLE control.

Registering OLE Controls

Once the control is built, it can be tested within Visual Basic, but first the control needs to be registered. This is done from the Visual C++ environment by choosing the Register Control command under the Tools menu.

An OLE control, like any OLE server, must register itself in the Registry Editor before it can be used by any applications. All controls have an exported function called DllRegisterServer, which is called to register the control. Similarly, all controls have an exported function called DllUnregisterServer to remove the control information from the Registry Editor. The ControlWizard generates this code for you so that when your control is built, the functions exist and are fully operational. To view these functions, open the PROJNAME.CPP file or in the case of the DragDrop control, DRAGDROP.CPP (see Listing 12.1).

Listing 12.1   DRAGDROP.CPP. Implementation of and DLL registration.

```cpp
#include "stdafx.h"
#include "DragDrop.h"

#ifdef _DEBUG
#undef THIS_FILE
static char BASED_CODE THIS_FILE[] = __FILE__;
#endif

CDragDropApp NEAR theApp;

const GUID CDECL BASED_CODE _tlid =
        { 0xa636d3a8, 0x37ce, 0x101c, { 0x9e, 0xee, 0x4, 0x2,_
          0x24, 0x0, 0x9c, 0x2 } };
const WORD _wVerMajor = 1;
const WORD _wVerMinor = 0;

// CDragDropApp::InitInstance - DLL initialization

BOOL CDragDropApp::InitInstance()
{
    BOOL bInit = COleControlModule::InitInstance();
    if (bInit)
    {
    // TODO: Add your own module initialization code here.
    }
    return bInit;
}

// CDragDropApp::ExitInstance - DLL termination

int CDragDropApp::ExitInstance()
{
    // TODO: Add your own module termination code here.

    return COleControlModule::ExitInstance();
}

// DllRegisterServer - Adds entries to the system registry

STDAPI DllRegisterServer(void)
{
    AFX_MANAGE_STATE(_afxModuleAddrThis);

    if (!AfxOleRegisterTypeLib(AfxGetInstanceHandle(), _tlid))
        return ResultFromScode(SELFREG_E_TYPELIB);

    if (!COleObjectFactoryEx::UpdateRegistryAll(TRUE))
        return ResultFromScode(SELFREG_E_CLASS);

    return NOERROR;
}
```

(continues)

Listing 12.1 Continued

```
// DllUnregisterServer - Removes entries from the system registry

STDAPI DllUnregisterServer(void)
{
    AFX_MANAGE_STATE(_afxModuleAddrThis);

    if (!AfxOleUnregisterTypeLib(_tlid))
        return ResultFromScode(SELFREG_E_TYPELIB);

    if (!COleObjectFactoryEx::UpdateRegistryAll(FALSE))
        return ResultFromScode(SELFREG_E_CLASS);

    return NOERROR;
}
```

Listing 12.2 contains the header or definition file for DRAGDROP.CPP, which is contained in the file DRAGDROP.H.

Listing 12.2 DRAGDROP.H. Main header file for DRAGDROP.DLL.

```
#if !defined( __AFXCTL_H__ )
    #error include 'afxctl.h' before including this file
#endif

#include "resource.h"        // main symbols

// CDragDropApp : See DragDrop.cpp for implementation.

class CDragDropApp : public COleControlModule
{
public:
    BOOL InitInstance();
    int ExitInstance();
};

extern const GUID CDECL _tlid;
extern const WORD _wVerMajor;
extern const WORD _wVerMinor;
```

The information placed in the Registry Editor is actually all of the information seen in the ControlWizard's Controls dialog box (refer to Fig. 12.4). To view the contents of the Registry Editor, the program RegEdit (Windows 3.1 and Windows 95) or RegEdt32 (Windows NT) can be used. Click Windows 95's Start button, choose Run and type in **REGEDIT** to invoke the Registry Editor (see Fig. 12.5).

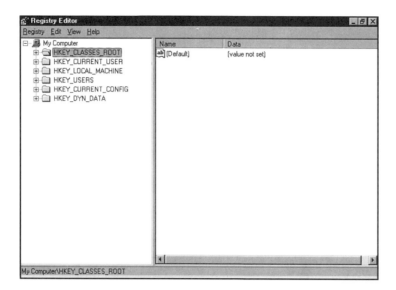

Fig. 12.5
Using the Registry
Editor for viewing
OLE control
registration
information.

To view the information about your control, expand the
HKEY_CLASSES_ROOT tree to list all of the classes registered for the system.
Scroll down the list and search for the name of your control. In the case of
the DragDrop control, the name is DRAGDROP.DragDropCtrl.1. As you may
have already noticed, this is the Programmatic ID that was in the Controls
dialog box (refer to Fig. 12.4).

Expanding the control name reveals the control's class ID or CLSID.
This is a unique identifier for your class. To find out more information
about your control, expand the CLSID folder in the main root of the
HKEY_CLASSES_ROOT tree. You notice a series of CLSIDs for all of the OLE
servers on the system. Searching for the CLSID of your control and expanding this level, as shown in Figure 12.6, reveals all of the important information about your control such as where the control is located.

Using the Template Control in Visual Basic

To this point, you have created a fully functional OCX using the Visual C++
ControlWizard, without having written one line of code. Let's now use the
control in a Visual Basic application and see what kind of control the
ControlWizard has created. To do this, use the same steps when using any
OCX in Visual Basic. If you did not create the control using Visual C++ and
would like to view the template OCX, the template control can be found in
the directory DRAGDROP\TEMPLATE on the CD-ROM that accompanies this
book.

1. Start the version of Visual Basic that corresponds to the type of OCX that was built (i.e., a 32-bit OCX can only be used with 32-bit Visual Basic).

2. Choose Tools, Custom Controls to display the Custom Controls dialog box.

3. Choose the DragDrop OCX and click OK.

4. The OCX icon is added to the Visual Basic toolbar. At this point, the generic button with the letters OCX appears.

5. Click the OCX button and draw the OCX onto a form.

6. The OCX is embedded into the form and is represented by an ellipse, which is drawn within the OCX.

Fig. 12.6

The information that is maintained about OLE controls in the Registry Editor.

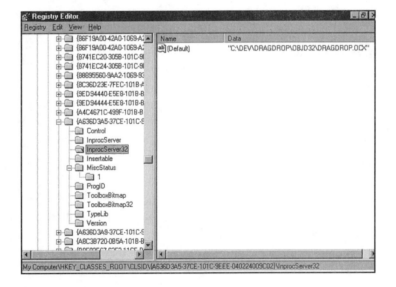

By pressing F4, the Visual Basic property sheet for the control is brought to the foreground. As you can see, there are already some properties included for the control, and you haven't written a line of code yet. These properties are known as *extended* properties. Extended properties are properties that are common to a control for an operating environment. That is, you will not see these properties anywhere within the control code or project. These properties are added by the environment, in this case Visual Basic, and can be set and manipulated like any other property. The extended properties added by Visual Basic are listed in Table 12.4.

Table 12.4	Visual Basic's Extended Properties for OCXs
Property	**Description**
DragIcon	Displayed when control is dragged.
DragMode	Indicates the drag mode for the control.
Height	Specifies the height of control in the coordinate system specified by the form.
Index	Indicates the index of control when placed in a control array.
Left	Specifies the left position of the control in the coordinate system specified by the form.
Name	Specifies the name of the control.
TabIndex	Indicates the position in the tab order.
TabStop	Specifies whether the control is in the form's tab order and can be tabbed into.
Tag	Indicates the control tag.
Top	Specifies the top of the control in the coordinate system specified by the form.
Visible	Determines visibility of the control at run time.
Width	Specifies the width of the control in the coordinate system specified by the form.

To this point, you have created a fully functioning OLE control without a single line of code. The code for the control is also both 32-bit and 16-bit ready. While the control is functional, it also performs no specific function except to draw an ellipse. It is now time to make the control work.

Defining Specifications for the *DragDrop* Control

Before developing the OLE control, you need to define the functionality of the control. This affects the properties and methods that are added to the control. In this chapter, you are developing the DragDrop control, which is used for accepting files that are dropped from the Windows File Manager and allowing a Visual Basic program to query these files and perform actions on them.

One of the inherent problems with Visual Basic is the lack of an interface for accepting Windows' messages. Windows is built entirely on a messaging interface. Every action from mouse movements to button clicks is relayed to applications through messages. The key message you are looking to intercept is the WM_DROPFILES message. Because this may be new to Visual Basic programmers, let's review the messaging interface for Windows applications.

All windows in an application have a Window procedure that processes all of the messages received for a Window class. Listing 12.3 is an interface for a Window procedure.

Listing 12.3   Window procedure function prototype.

```
LRESULT CALLBACK WindowProc(
    HWND    hwnd,        // handle of window
    UINT    uMsg,        // message identifier
    WPARAM  wParam,      // first message parameter
    LPARAM  lParam       // second message
)
```

The HWND parameter indicates which window the message is intended for. The UINT defines the type of message. WPARAM defines a 2-byte parameter for 16-bit windows and a 4-byte parameter for 32-bit windows. The LPARAM parameter defines a 4-byte parameter. The contents of WPARAM and LPARAM vary from message to message.

According to the Windows SDK, the WM_DROPFILES message is defined as follows:

```
WM_DROPFILES
hDrop = (HANDLE) wParam; //handle of internal drop structure

The WM_DROPFILES message is sent when the user releases the left
mouse button while the cursor is in the window of an application
that has registered itself as a recipient of dropped files.

Parameters - hDrop
Value of wParam. Identifies an internal structure describing the
dropped files. This handle is used by the DragFinish,
DragQueryFile, and DragQueryPoint functions to retrieve information
about the dropped files.

Return Value - An application should return zero if it processes
this message.
```

Translating the WM_DROPFILES message to a Window procedure yields the UINT parameter containing the message WM_DROPFILES and the WPARAM containing the hDrop parameter. The hDrop parameter is going to be used to query the names of the files dropped during this message.

Because there is no method of accessing messages from either Windows or other Windows applications, the DragDrop control must intercept this message and notify you through an event.

IV

When the event is fired by the control, you can query the following information from the control's properties:

- The number of files dropped during this message

- The file path and name of each file dropped

The application can then perform any operations necessary for this event.

Building Controls to Functional Specifications

Now that the purpose of the control has been defined, it is time to start building the control. An OLE control has three components that affect how you interact with the control. These components are *properties, methods,* and *events.*

- Properties are data members of the control that affect the behavior or state of the control. An example of a property is the extended property Visible, which affects the visibility of the control. The control's properties usually can be established during form design time. In a Visual Basic application, a property for an OLE control is used the same way as a property is for a VBX.

- Methods are actions that can be performed on the control. An example of a method is Copy, which copies the contents of the control to the Windows Clipboard. Methods are new to Visual Basic developers and extend the capabilities of a control.

> VBXs have methods, but these are fixed; developers cannot add additional methods to a VBX control.

- Events are actions or notifications from the control to the Visual Basic form that indicate something happened within the control. An example of an event is FilesDropped, which is used by the DragDrop control to indicate that a drag operation has occurred. Events carry the same purpose as they did in VBXs.

You start building the DragDrop control by adding an event to the control to indicate that a file drag operation has occurred. Because the number of files dropped is readily known, this number is passed back to the Visual Basic form. To add an event, press Ctrl+W to invoke the ClassWizard for class modification. The ClassWizard is used to add, modify, and delete the properties, methods, and events that a control contains. This is different from the ControlWizard, which was used to create the control's implementation files and run-time characteristics.

While class modification will occur, it does not make sense to do the class modifications manually, especially when adding properties, methods, or events. The importance of using the ClassWizard is that the control's *ODL* (Object Data Language) is also updated by the ClassWizard. The control's .ODL file is compiled into a *TLB* (Type Library) resource and compiled into the control's resources. The .TLB file contains all information about properties, methods, and events needed for external applications to use the control. If the ClassWizard is not used, the control's .ODL file must be modified manually before the control is built.

To receive the WM_DROPFILES message, the following modifications are going to be made to the control:

- An OLE event for WM_DROPFILES will be added to the control.

- A control message handler will be added to accept the WM_DROPFILES message.

- The control handler will be implemented for the WM_DROPFILES message.

The first modification you make to the control is to add an event called FilesDropped that can be fired when the control receives a WM_DROPFILES message. This is done by invoking the ClassWizard and selecting the OLE Events tab, shown in Figure 12.7.

Fig. 12.7
Use the ClassWizard to add an event to the OCX.

The `FilesDropped` event will have one parameter that will get passed to the application containing the control. The parameter will indicate the number of files that were dropped onto the control and will be a `short` or 2-bytes.

To add this event, perform the following steps:

1. Click the <u>A</u>dd Event button in the ClassWizard. This invokes the Add Event dialog box shown in Figure 12.8.

Fig. 12.8
You can name the event and its parameters to be added to the control using the ClassWizard.

2. In the <u>E</u>xternal Name combo box, type in the name **FilesDropped**.

3. In the <u>P</u>arameter List box, type in the name of the parameter for this control. Call the parameter **NumFiles**.

4. After the name is entered, tab to the next column and select the type of parameter being passed. As mentioned, this parameter is a `short`.

5. Click OK to add the event to the control.

The OLE Events tab in the ClassWizard (refer to Fig. 12.7) now shows that the event `FilesDropped` has been added to the control. In the Implementation box, the implementation of the event is called `FireFilesDropped`. The implementation name is what is called by the control to send the event to the application. This will be shown later in the chapter.

> One final note about OLE events. The combo box used for entering your custom event also contains a list of standard events for all controls. This includes `Mouse` and `Keyboard` messages. If your control needs to trigger these events, select them from the Name combo box and add them to the list of events handled by the control, as shown in the OLE Events tab.

To receive the WM_DROPFILES message, the control needs to have a message handler for this message. This is done by selecting the Message Maps tab of ClassWizard, which is shown in Figure 12.9. From the Messages list box, select the WM_DROPFILES message and click the Add Function button. Any messages that need to be interpreted by the control must be added to the control's message map. This is how MFC determines which windows are to receive each message. When the Add Function button is clicked, the OnDropFiles method appears in the Member Functions box. Double-click on the OnDropFiles method to close ClassWizard and open the source file where this method is implemented.

Fig. 12.9
Use the Message Maps tab to receive the WM_DROPFILES message.

By default, unless the filename was changed when the control was being specified in ControlWizard, the control's methods are implemented in a file called DRAGDCTL.CPP. The name of the method created by MFC in the source file is called OnDropFiles and is prototyped as void OnDropFiles(HDROP hDropInfo). The parameter that is passed into the control is a handle to a memory block containing information about the files being dropped. This handle is only valid for the duration of the method.

Because the handle has a limited life span, a member variable needs to be added to the control that can hold the HDROP information. The variable is named m_hMemory and is of type HGLOBAL.

NOTE   m_hMemory is not accessible as a property through the control. It is added as a protected member of the class as shown in Listing 12.4, DRAGCTL.H.

Now that the variable m_hMemory has been added to the control, some initialization and exit code needs to be provided to the control to ensure proper usage of the variable. During the constructor of the control, the variable is set to NULL. During the control destructor, if the variable is not NULL, the memory handle is freed and set to NULL. If the memory handle is not freed, the control will cause a memory leak whenever a Visual basic application using the control ends.

Adding Properties to Controls

Before the OnDropFiles method can be coded, there is one more matter to take care of. A variable indicating the number of files contained in the last drop operation needs to be added. This variable will be accessible as a control property, so it must be added through the ClassWizard. Adding a property through ClassWizard is similar to adding an OLE event. Properties and methods are added through the OLE Automation tab. Clicking the Add Property button displays the Add Property dialog box as shown in Figure 12.10.

To add the NumFiles property to the DragDrop control, follow these steps:

1. Click the Add Property button to display the Add Property dialog box shown in Figure 12.10.

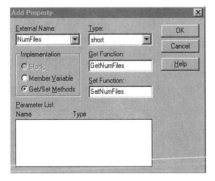

Fig. 12.10
Use the Add Property dialog box to add properties and methods to a control.

2. Type **NumFiles** into the External Name combo box.

3. Select the Get/Set Methods radio button in the Implementation box. Selecting the Get/Set Methods option allows you to write the methods for accessing and setting this property. For this property, you are only going to provide read-only access to the property value.

4. Now erase the Set Function edit control because NumFiles is a property that is only set after a drop operation; there is no reason for the application to be able to set the value in the control. This is why the Get/Set Methods was selected and the Set Function was erased.

If the Member Variable implementation was used, then the Get Function and Set Function of the property would have directly affected the variable placed inside of the control. Now it goes through the Get method, which must be implemented.

5. You need to select the type of property NumFiles will represent. For the DragDrop control, select short (2-bytes) from the Type list box.

6. Click OK to add the NumFiles property to the control.

There are two types of properties a control can have: *custom* and *stock*. A custom property is unique to your control only. A stock property is a standard property that is implemented by the OLE control's base class, COleControl. The property NumFiles is a custom property. ClassWizard also allows for the addition of stock properties. A stock property, such as BackColor, can be added by selecting from the External Name combo box instead of typing in a custom property.

Implementing OLE Controls

By browsing the DRAGDCTL.CPP file, you see that ClassWizard has added the method GetNumFiles to the module. Now you have to complete the implementation of this method. When the Get/Set Methods implementation is selected from ClassWizard, there is no member variable added for the property. This must be done manually. Add the property m_NumFiles as a short to the DRAGDCTL.H file. This variable must be set to 0 (zero) in the control's constructor. In the method GetNumFiles, return the variable m_NumFiles, as shown in Listing 12.4.

Now the implementation of OnDropFiles can be completed. Listing 12.4 shows the completed implementation. The following steps occur when the WM_DROPFILES message is received:

1. When this method is called, any existing memory contained in the variable m_hMemory is freed. This is done by calling the Windows API GlobalFree. The variable m_NumFiles must be set to 0.

2. The next step is to query the size of the parameter hDropInfo. This is done to allocate memory to m_hMemory so a copy of the information is made.

3. After the memory is copied into m_hMemory, the Windows API
DragQueryFile is called to determine the number of files contained in
the drop.

4. Next, the OLE event that was created is fired through the call
FireFilesDropped. This makes a call to the containing application noti-
fying it that a drag files' operation was completed.

5. At this point, program control is relinquished to the application.

**Listing 12.4   DRAGDCTL.CPP. Implementing the CDragDropCtrl
OCX class.**

```cpp
#include "stdafx.h"
#include "DragDrop.h"
#include "dragdctl.h"
#include "dragdppg.h"

#ifdef _DEBUG
#undef THIS_FILE
static char BASED_CODE THIS_FILE[] = __FILE__;
#endif

IMPLEMENT_DYNCREATE(CDragDropCtrl, COleControl)

// Message map

BEGIN_MESSAGE_MAP(CDragDropCtrl, COleControl)
    //{{AFX_MSG_MAP(CDragDropCtrl)
    ON_WM_DROPFILES()
    //}}AFX_MSG_MAP
    ON_OLEVERB(AFX_IDS_VERB_EDIT, OnEdit)
    ON_OLEVERB(AFX_IDS_VERB_PROPERTIES, OnProperties)
END_MESSAGE_MAP()

// Dispatch map

BEGIN_DISPATCH_MAP(CDragDropCtrl, COleControl)
    //{{AFX_DISPATCH_MAP(CDragDropCtrl)
    DISP_PROPERTY_EX(CDragDropCtrl, "AcceptDropFiles", _
        GetAcceptDropFiles, SetAcceptDropFiles, VT_BOOL)
    DISP_PROPERTY_EX(CDragDropCtrl, "NumFiles", _
        GetNumFiles, SetNotSupported, VT_I2)
    DISP_FUNCTION(CDragDropCtrl, "GetFileName", _
        GetFileName, VT_BSTR, VTS_I2)
    //}}AFX_DISPATCH_MAP
    DISP_FUNCTION_ID(CDragDropCtrl, "AboutBox", _
        DISPID_ABOUTBOX, AboutBox, VT_EMPTY, VTS_NONE)
END_DISPATCH_MAP()
```

(continues)

Listing 12.4 Continued

```
// Event map

BEGIN_EVENT_MAP(CDragDropCtrl, COleControl)
    //{{AFX_EVENT_MAP(CDragDropCtrl)
    EVENT_CUSTOM("FilesDropped", FireFilesDropped, VTS_I2)
    //}}AFX_EVENT_MAP
END_EVENT_MAP()

// Property pages

// TODO: Add more property pages as needed.
// Remember to increase the count!
BEGIN_PROPPAGEIDS(CDragDropCtrl, 1)
    PROPPAGEID(CDragDropPropPage::guid)
END_PROPPAGEIDS(CDragDropCtrl)

// Initialize class factory and guid

IMPLEMENT_OLECREATE_EX(CDragDropCtrl, _
    "DRAGDROP.DragDropCtrl.1",
    0xa636d3a5, 0x37ce, 0x101c, 0x9e, _
        0xee, 0x4, 0x2, 0x24, 0x0, 0x9c, 0x2)

// Type library ID and version

IMPLEMENT_OLETYPELIB(CDragDropCtrl,_
    tlid, _wVerMajor, _wVerMinor)

// Interface IDs

const IID BASED_CODE IID_DDragDrop =
        { 0xa636d3a6, 0x37ce, 0x101c, { 0x9e, _
            0xee, 0x4, 0x2, 0x24, 0x0, 0x9c, 0x2 } };
const IID BASED_CODE IID_DDragDropEvents =
        { 0xa636d3a7, 0x37ce, 0x101c, { 0x9e, _
            0xee, 0x4, 0x2, 0x24, 0x0, 0x9c, 0x2 } };

// Control type information

static const DWORD BASED_CODE _dwDragDropOleMisc =
    OLEMISC_SIMPLEFRAME |
    OLEMISC_ACTIVATEWHENVISIBLE |
    OLEMISC_SETCLIENTSITEFIRST |
    OLEMISC_INSIDEOUT |
    OLEMISC_CANTLINKINSIDE |
    OLEMISC_RECOMPOSEONRESIZE;

IMPLEMENT_OLECTLTYPE(CDragDropCtrl, _IDS_DRAGDROP, _
    _dwDragDropOleMisc)

// CDragDropCtrl::CDragDropCtrlFactory::UpdateRegistry -
// Adds or removes system registry entries for CDragDropCtrl
```

```
BOOL CDragDropCtrl::_CDragDropCtrlFactory::UpdateRegistry(BOOL
bRegister)
{
    if (bRegister)
        return AfxOleRegisterControlClass(
            AfxGetInstanceHandle(),
            m_clsid,
            m_lpszProgID,
            IDS_DRAGDROP,
            IDB_DRAGDROP,
            TRUE,                           //  Insertable
            _dwDragDropOleMisc,
            _tlid,
            _wVerMajor,
            _wVerMinor);
    else
        return AfxOleUnregisterClass(m_clsid, m_lpszProgID);
}

// CDragDropCtrl::CDragDropCtrl - Constructor

CDragDropCtrl::CDragDropCtrl()
{
    InitializeIIDs(&IID_DDragDrop, &IID_DDragDropEvents);

    EnableSimpleFrame();

    m_NumFiles = 0;
    m_FileName.Empty();
    m_hMemory = NULL;
}

// CDragDropCtrl::~CDragDropCtrl - Destructor

CDragDropCtrl::~CDragDropCtrl()
{
    m_FileName.Empty();
    if ( m_hMemory )
    {
        GlobalFree(m_hMemory);
        m_hMemory = NULL;
    }
}

// CDragDropCtrl::OnDraw - Drawing function

void CDragDropCtrl::OnDraw(
            CDC* pdc, const CRect& rcBounds, const CRect&
rcInvalid)
{
    // TODO: Replace the following code with your own drawing
    // code.
    pdc->FillRect(rcBounds, CBrush::FromHandle(_
        (HBRUSH)GetStockObject(WHITE_BRUSH)));
```

(continues)

Listing 12.4 Continued

```
        pdc->Ellipse(rcBounds);
        pdc->DrawText( "Drop Files Target" , -1 , _
            rcBounds, DT_CENTER ¦ DT_VCENTER ¦ DT_SINGLELINE);
}

// CDragDropCtrl::DoPropExchange - Persistence support

void CDragDropCtrl::DoPropExchange(CPropExchange* pPX)
{
        ExchangeVersion(pPX, MAKELONG(_wVerMinor, _wVerMajor));
        COleControl::DoPropExchange(pPX);

        PX_Bool ( pPX , "AcceptDropFiles" , _
            m_AcceptDropFiles , TRUE );
}

// CDragDropCtrl::OnResetState - Reset control to default state

void CDragDropCtrl::OnResetState()
{
        COleControl::OnResetState();
// Resets defaults found in DoPropExchange

        // TODO: Reset any other control state here.
}

// CDragDropCtrl::AboutBox - Display an "About" box to the user

void CDragDropCtrl::AboutBox()
{
        CDialog dlgAbout(IDD_ABOUTBOX_DRAGDROP);
        dlgAbout.DoModal();
}

// CDragDropCtrl message handlers

void CDragDropCtrl::OnDropFiles(HDROP hDropInfo)
{
        // free any existing memory
        if ( m_hMemory )
        {
            GlobalFree(m_hMemory);
            m_NumFiles = 0;
        }

        long ll_Size = GlobalSize(hDropInfo);
        m_hMemory = GlobalAlloc( GHND , ll_Size );
        BYTE *prv_Data = (BYTE *)GlobalLock(hDropInfo);
        BYTE *plv_NewData = (BYTE *)GlobalLock(m_hMemory);
        memcpy( plv_NewData , prv_Data , ll_Size );
        GlobalUnlock(m_hMemory);
        GlobalUnlock(hDropInfo);
```

```
      // find out how many there are
      m_NumFiles = (short)::DragQueryFile ( hDropInfo , -1 , _
        NULL , 0);
      ::DragFinish ( hDropInfo );
      COleControl::OnDropFiles(hDropInfo);
      FireFilesDropped( m_NumFiles );
}

BOOL CDragDropCtrl::GetAcceptDropFiles()
{
      return m_AcceptDropFiles;
}

void CDragDropCtrl::SetAcceptDropFiles(BOOL bNewValue)
{
      m_AcceptDropFiles = bNewValue;
      ::DragAcceptFiles( this->GetSafeHwnd(),
m_AcceptDropFiles);
}

short CDragDropCtrl::GetNumFiles()
{
      return m_NumFiles;
}

BSTR CDragDropCtrl::GetFileName(short FileNumber)
{
      char ls_Buffer[_MAX_PATH];
      m_FileName.Empty();
      if ( FileNumber < m_NumFiles )
      {
           ::DragQueryFile ( (HDROP)m_hMemory , _
             FileNumber , ls_Buffer , _MAX_PATH);
           m_FileName = ls_Buffer;
      }
      return SysAllocString(m_FileName);
}

void CDragDropCtrl::OnEventAdvise(BOOL bAdvise)
{
      COleControl::OnEventAdvise(bAdvise);
      if (bAdvise)
          SetAcceptDropFiles(m_AcceptDropFiles);
}
```

To complete the code for the control, there are two items that need to be added:

- A property for turning the acceptance of drag/drop operations on or off.

- A method that applications can call to retrieve the filenames of each file dropped on the control.

Adding Properties for Drop-File Operations

First, the property for accepting or denying drop-file operations must be added. This property will be called AcceptDropFiles. This property can be added to the control repeating the same steps that were used for adding the NumFiles property, with the following exceptions:

- Do not remove the implementation method SetAcceptDropFiles. You will need to implement this method in the control.

- The type of property is a BOOL or Boolean because the property has only two values, to accept or to not accept drop files.

- Manually add the member variable m_AcceptDropFiles as a BOOL to the DRAGDCTL.CPP and DRAGDCTL.H files (refer to Listings 12.3 and 12.4).

- In the implementation for the method GetAcceptDropFiles, simply return the variable m_AcceptDropFiles.

- For the implementation of the method SetAcceptDropFiles, assign the new value of the property, which was passed into the SetAcceptDropFiles method, to m_AcceptDropFiles. To actually turn on or off the capability to accept or refuse drop-file operations, the Windows API DragAcceptFiles must be called with the HWND of the control and the BOOL flag.

- As you have noticed, the value of m_AcceptDropFiles is not set or initialized in the constructor of the control as is done for other properties. That is because this property needs to maintain *persistence*. Persistence is the ability to save the value of the property when the program is saved and load the saved value into the control when the program is loaded from disk. Control persistence is done in the control's method DoPropExchange. This method controls both the saving of the properties state to disk and loading the control with the value of the properties from disk (or defaults if no values were saved). The following line of code must be added to this method:

```
PX_Bool(pPX, "AcceptDropFiles" ,m_AcceptDropFiles , TRUE);
```

The PX_Bool macro is used for Boolean properties. The first parameter pPX determines the direction of control (control loading or saving) and the second parameter is the external name of the property. The third parameter is the member variable to set or get information from. And the last parameter is the initial value of the property.

The `AcceptDropFiles` property is the only property that needs persistence because all of the other properties are dependent on the drag operation, not design-time values.

■ One final action that must be implemented for the control to function properly is to override the method `OnEventAdvise`.

The method `OnEventAdvise` is called when the control is being loaded and unloaded because OLE controls do not always perform the same steps when a developer is going repeatedly from design time to run time. This means that there must be one spot where the function to enable file drag/drop operations can occur. This spot must also occur *after* the control's window is created, because the Windows API (`DragAcceptFiles`) must be called with a valid window handle representing the window to accept the drop-file message. In this case, it is the control window.

The parameter passed into `OnEventAdvise` is TRUE if the control is being loaded and FALSE if the control is unloading. When the control is being loaded, the API `DragAcceptFiles` must be called with the value of the member variable `m_AcceptDropFiles`. Listings 12.4 and 12.5 show how to override the `OnEventAdvise` method.

Listing 12.5 DRAGCTL.H. *DragDrop* **control declaration file.**

```
// dragdctl.h : Declaration of the CDragDropCtrl OLE control class.

// CDragDropCtrl : See dragdctl.cpp for implementation.

class CDragDropCtrl : public COleControl
{
    DECLARE_DYNCREATE(CDragDropCtrl)

    BOOL m_AcceptDropFiles;
    short m_NumFiles;
    CString m_FileName;
    HGLOBAL m_hMemory;

// Constructor
public:
    CDragDropCtrl();

// Overrides

    // Drawing function
    virtual void OnDraw(
                CDC* pdc, const CRect& rcBounds, _
                  const CRect& rcInvalid);
```

(continues)

Listing 12.5 Continued

```
        // Persistence
        virtual void DoPropExchange(CPropExchange* pPX);

        // Reset control state
        virtual void OnResetState();
        virtual void OnEventAdvise(BOOL bAdvise);

// Implementation
protected:
    ~CDragDropCtrl();

    DECLARE_OLECREATE_EX(CDragDropCtrl)
// Class factory and guid
    DECLARE_OLETYPELIB(CDragDropCtrl)
// GetTypeInfo
    DECLARE_PROPPAGEIDS(CDragDropCtrl)
// Property page IDs
    DECLARE_OLECTLTYPE(CDragDropCtrl)
// Type name and misc status

// Message maps
    //{{AFX_MSG(CDragDropCtrl)
    afx_msg void OnDropFiles(HDROP hDropInfo);
    //}}AFX_MSG
    DECLARE_MESSAGE_MAP()

// Dispatch maps
    //{{AFX_DISPATCH(CDragDropCtrl)
    afx_msg BOOL GetAcceptDropFiles();
    afx_msg void SetAcceptDropFiles(BOOL bNewValue);
    afx_msg short GetNumFiles();
    afx_msg BSTR GetFileName(short FileNumber);
    //}}AFX_DISPATCH
    DECLARE_DISPATCH_MAP()

    afx_msg void AboutBox();

// Event maps
    //{{AFX_EVENT(CDragDropCtrl)
    void FireFilesDropped(short NumFiles)
        {FireEvent(eventidFilesDropped,_
            EVENT_PARAM(VTS_I2), NumFiles);}
    //}}AFX_EVENT
    DECLARE_EVENT_MAP()

// Dispatch and event IDs
public:
    enum {
    //{{AFX_DISP_ID(CDragDropCtrl)
    dispidAcceptDropFiles = 1L,
    dispidNumFiles = 2L,
    dispidGetFileName = 3L,
    eventidFilesDropped = 1L,
    //}}AFX_DISP_ID
    };
};
```

Retrieving Filenames

To complete the control, a method for retrieving each filename dropped on the control must be added. This method is added in a similar manner as when adding a property, except that the <u>A</u>dd Method button is clicked and the Add Method dialog box shown in Figure 12.11 is displayed.

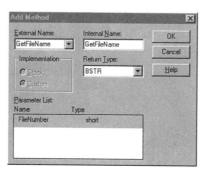

Fig. 12.11
Using the Control-
Wizard to add a
method to an
OCX.

In the <u>E</u>xternal Name combo box, enter **GetFileName**. This will also be added to the Internal <u>N</u>ame text box. This is the name of the method as called from Visual Basic. Because this method returns a string, the BSTR type must be selected in the Return <u>T</u>ype text box. This method will take one parameter that is a short, indicating which filename to retrieve from the file dropped on the control (refer to Listing 12.3).

Finally, the drawing routine for the control must be customized to reflect the visual representation of the control during application execution. The OnDraw method performs all drawing of an OLE control. For the DragDrop control, this is modified to add the text "Drop Files Target" to the center of the control. For other controls, such as an image control, this is where the code would be placed to paint the image on-screen.

Customizing an OLE Control's Property Page

OLE controls support the capability to contain their own private *property pages*. A property page is a tab within a sheet that represents properties of the control that can be set to specific values during application or form design time.

All properties of a control can be seen through Visual Basic by selecting the control and pressing the F4 key. This invokes the standard Visual Basic property viewer.

The private property pages available in OLE custom controls are used for environments that do not support property viewers like the one in Visual Basic, or to set custom control properties through a property viewer when the user may not know the proper values for the property. An example of the former is the test container in the OLE CDK. An example of the latter is the FileName property in Lenel's Digital Video control.

The Lenel Digital Video is used for the playback and control of digital video files including Video for Windows and MPEG files. Chapter 11, "Using Digital Video Playback," discusses how to use this control in applications.

When the FileName property is selected in the Visual Basic property viewer, the value selection button changes to "...", which when selected, invokes a private property page in the Digital Video control. The user can change any of the available properties and when the property page is closed, the updated values are shown in Visual Basic's property viewer.

Creating Property Pages

When a control is created through ControlWizard, a class and resource for the property page are created automatically. All that is left is for the user to design the property page dialog box and connect the controls on the property page to the persistent storage component of the control. Actually, these steps are very easy.

To design the control's property page, follow these steps:

1. Select the PROJNAME.RC file from the project's make window. For the DragDrop control, this is the DRAGDROP.RC file.

2. Next, expand the dialog tree from the DRAGDROP.RC window. The property page resource is called IDD_PROPPAGE_PROJNAME or for the DragDrop control, IDD_PROPPAGE_DRAGDROP. The property page is initially blank.

3. Draw the appropiate controls on the property page needed to reflect the properties of the control. For the DragDrop control, draw a check box and label it **Accept Drop Files from File Manager**.

4. Assign a resource ID of IDC_ACCEPTDRAGDROP to the control.

Connecting Property Pages to Controls

At this point, the property page is completed and the resources drawn on the property page can be connected to the control's persistent storage mechanism. To connect the property page to the control's persistent storage mechanism:

1. Invoke the ClassWizard by pressing Ctrl+W. Select the Member Variables tab (see Fig. 12.12). The IDs for the resources on the property page appear in the dialog box.

2. Select the ID and click the <u>A</u>dd Variable button. Enter the variable name.

3. From the Optional OLE Property Name combo box, enter the property name to link the variable with. For the DragDrop control, this is the property **AcceptDropFiles**.

Fig. 12.12
How to connect property page controls to persistent storage.

Now, the resources drawn on the property page are connected to the control's property storage. When the property is updated in the property page, the result is immediately reflected in the control. Listings 12.6 and 12.7 represent the code generated by ClassWizard and ControlWizard for the control's property page. As with the properties on a control, when the property page is changed, the control's .ODL file is affected as well.

Listing 12.6 DRAGDPPG.CPP. Implementation of the
***CDragDropPropPage* property page class.**

```cpp
#include "stdafx.h"
#include "DragDrop.h"
#include "dragdppg.h"

#ifdef _DEBUG
#undef THIS_FILE
static char BASED_CODE THIS_FILE[] = __FILE__;
#endif


IMPLEMENT_DYNCREATE(CDragDropPropPage, COlePropertyPage)

// Message map

BEGIN_MESSAGE_MAP(CDragDropPropPage, COlePropertyPage)
    //{{AFX_MSG_MAP(CDragDropPropPage)
    // NOTE - ClassWizard will add and remove message map entries
    // DO NOT EDIT what you see in these blocks of generated
    // code !
    //}}AFX_MSG_MAP
END_MESSAGE_MAP()


// Initialize class factory and guid

IMPLEMENT_OLECREATE_EX(CDragDropPropPage, _
  "DRAGDROP.DragDropPropPage.1",
  0xa636d3a9, 0x37ce, 0x101c, 0x9e, 0xee, 0x4, 0x2, 0x24, 0x0,
0x9c, 0x2)


// CDragDropPropPage::CDragDropPropPageFactory::UpdateRegistry -
// Adds or removes system registry entries for CDragDropPropPage

BOOL CDragDropPropPage::CDragDropPropPageFactory_
   ::UpdateRegistry(BOOL bRegister)
{
    if (bRegister)
        return
AfxOleRegisterPropertyPageClass(AfxGetInstanceHandle(),
            m_clsid, IDS_DRAGDROP_PPG);
    else
        return AfxOleUnregisterClass(m_clsid, NULL);
}

// CDragDropPropPage::CDragDropPropPage - Constructor

CDragDropPropPage::CDragDropPropPage() :
    COlePropertyPage(IDD, IDS_DRAGDROP_PPG_CAPTION)
{
    //{{AFX_DATA_INIT(CDragDropPropPage)
    m_AcceptDragDrop = FALSE;
```

```
        //}}AFX_DATA_INIT
}



// CDragDropPropPage::DoDataExchange
// Moves data between page and properties

void CDragDropPropPage::DoDataExchange(CDataExchange* pDX)
{
        //{{AFX_DATA_MAP(CDragDropPropPage)
        DDP_Check(pDX, IDC_ACCEPTDRAGDROP, _
           m_AcceptDragDrop, _T("AcceptDropFiles") );
        DDX_Check(pDX, IDC_ACCEPTDRAGDROP, m_AcceptDragDrop);
           //}}AFX_DATA_MAP
        DDP_PostProcessing(pDX);
}



// CDragDropPropPage message handlers
```

The header file, DRAGDPPG.H is the declaration file for the
CDragDropPropPage class.

Listing 12.7   DRAGDPPG.H. Declaration of the
***CDragDropPropPage* property page class.**

```
// CDragDropPropPage : See dragdppg.cpp for implementation.

class CDragDropPropPage : public COlePropertyPage
{
        DECLARE_DYNCREATE(CDragDropPropPage)
        DECLARE_OLECREATE_EX(CDragDropPropPage)

// Constructor
public:
        CDragDropPropPage();

// Dialog Data
        //{{AFX_DATA(CDragDropPropPage)
        enum { IDD = IDD_PROPPAGE_DRAGDROP };
        BOOL      m_AcceptDragDrop;
        //}}AFX_DATA

// Implementation
protected:
        virtual void DoDataExchange(CDataExchange* pDX);
        // DDX/DDV support
```

(continues)

Listing 12.7 Continued

```
// Message maps
protected:
    //{{AFX_MSG(CDragDropPropPage)
        // NOTE - ClassWizard will add and remove member
        // functions here.
        // DO NOT EDIT what you see in these blocks of
        // generated code !
    //}}AFX_MSG
    DECLARE_MESSAGE_MAP()

};
```

Using Definition Files

In Windows, all .DLLs and .EXEs contain a *module definition file* that represents what subroutines are exported and imported into a module and how the code and data segments of a module behave. In the 32-bit environments, the code and data segments are somewhat irrelevant because of the flat memory space of the module, but the definition file (.DEF) still exists. Even Visual Basic uses these files, although the .DEF file is not seen by the user when an .EXE file is created.

A definition file is used when building OLE controls because, after all, an OLE control is a .DLL with an .OCX extension. The definition file in Listing 12.8 is automatically generated by ControlWizard, and it shows the four functions necessary for an OLE control to be loaded and used. Table 12.5 lists each function automatically provided by MFC.

Table 12.5 Definition of functions exported from an OCX

Function	Description
DllRegisterServer	Enables external programs to load the control and have the control add its class information to the Registry Editor.
DllUnregisterServer	Enables external programs to load the control and have the control remove its class information from the Registry Editor.
DllGetClassObject	This is the entry point for OLE. When an instance of the control is dropped on a Visual Basic form during design time, or when the control is loaded at run time, this function is called to retrieve an Idispatch or OLE interface object to the control. The OLE interface object contains all of the property, method, and event information for a control.

Function	Description
DllCanUnloadNow	This function is called on program termination. When the function returns TRUE, the application is safe to terminate. When FALSE is returned, it indicates that OLE is busy and the application cannot exit yet.

Listing 12.8   DRAGDR32.DEF. Module definition file for the *DragDrop* control.

```
; dragdr32.def : Declares the module parameters.

LIBRARY        DRAGDROP.OCX

EXPORTS
        DllCanUnloadNow      @1
        DllGetClassObject    @2
        DllRegisterServer    @3
        DllUnregisterServer  @4
```

Identifying Available Properties, Methods, and Events

When an OLE control is drawn on a Visual Basic form, the Visual Basic property viewer lists all of the control's properties. The Visual Basic Object Browser indicates all of the methods for a control. The Visual Basic Object Browser is a utility provided for examining the property, method, and event interface for an OLE object. By double-clicking on the DragDrop control in the Object Browser, all of the control's events are listed. How does Visual Basic or any other OLE control container know this information? The answer lies in the control's .ODL and .TLB files.

When a control is generated with ControlWizard, one of the files that is generated is a PROJNAME.ODL file. For the DragDrop control, it is named DRAGDROP.ODL.

The .ODL extension stands for Object Description Language and contains a description of the control's properties, methods, and events. The .ODL file orginates from OLE automation, which is the primary interface to OLE controls.

As the control is being developed through the use of ClassWizard, the control's .ODL file is modified to reflect the changes. The .ODL file for the DragDrop control is shown in Listing 12.9. This is why the ClassWizard should be used for modifying the control's properties, methods, and events.

Caution

If properties, methods, or events are added manually, the .ODL file must be correctly modified to reflect the changes or the control will not function.

When the control is built, the first step is to compile the control's .ODL file into a .TLB file, which is the control's table file. A .TLB file is analagous to compiling a resource (.RC) into a .RES file. The .TLB file is linked into the resource of the control when the control is built.

When Visual Basic needs to access the properties, methods, or events of the control, the .TLB file is accessed through OLE APIs, and the appropiate information is returned. This is how Visual Basic performs its magic. If the .TLB file was removed from the control, Visual Basic would not know of any properties, methods, or events that the control contains.

NOTE

It is important to note that in the 32-bit Visual C++ environment, the .ODL file is automatically compiled into the project when it is changed. In the 16-bit environment, this is not automatically done. The developer must first run the tool Make TypeLib from the Tools menu of Visual C++. If this is not done, the control's changes will not be reflected when the control is run.

Listing 12.9 The .ODL file for the *DragDrop* control that is used for modifying the control's properties, methods and events.

```
// DragDrop.odl : type library source for OLE Custom Control
// project.

// This file will be processed by the
// Make Type Library (mktyplib) tool to
// produce the type library (DragDrop.tlb)
// that will become a resource in
// DragDrop.ocx.

#include <olectl.h>

[ uuid(A636D3A8-37CE-101C-9EEE-040224009C02), version(1.0),
  helpstring("DragDrop OLE Custom Control module"), control ]
library DragDropLib
{
```

```
    importlib(STDOLE_TLB);
    importlib(STDTYPE_TLB);

    //  Primary dispatch interface for CDragDropCtrl

    [ uuid(A636D3A6-37CE-101C-9EEE-040224009C02),
      helpstring("Dispatch interface for DragDrop Control"),
hidden ]
    dispinterface _DDragDrop
    {
        properties:
// NOTE - ClassWizard will maintain property information here.
            //    Use extreme caution when editing this section.
            //{{AFX_ODL_PROP(CDragDropCtrl)
            [id(1)] boolean AcceptDropFiles;
            [id(2)] short NumFiles;
            //}}AFX_ODL_PROP

        methods:
// NOTE - ClassWizard will maintain method information here.
            //    Use extreme caution when editing this section.
            //{{AFX_ODL_METHOD(CDragDropCtrl)
            [id(3)] BSTR GetFileName( short FileNumber );
            //}}AFX_ODL_METHOD

            [id(DISPID_ABOUTBOX)] void AboutBox();
    };

    //  Event dispatch interface for CDragDropCtrl

    [ uuid(A636D3A7-37CE-101C-9EEE-040224009C02),
      helpstring("Event interface for DragDrop Control") ]
    dispinterface _DDragDropEvents
    {
        properties:
            //  Event interface has no properties

        methods:
// NOTE - ClassWizard will maintain event information here.
            //    Use extreme caution when editing this section.
            //{{AFX_ODL_EVENT(CDragDropCtrl)
            [id(1)] void FilesDropped( short NumFiles);
            //}}AFX_ODL_EVENT
    };

    //  Class information for CDragDropCtrl

    [ uuid(A636D3A5-37CE-101C-9EEE-040224009C02),
      helpstring("DragDrop Control"), control ]
    coclass DragDrop
    {
        [default] dispinterface _DDragDrop;
        [default, source] dispinterface _DDragDropEvents;
    };

    //{{AFX_APPEND_ODL}}
};
```

Viewing Resource Scripts

The last set of files generated are shown in Listings 12.10 and 12.11. These are the control's resource files. These files reflect the control's icon and bitmap, the property page resource, and also control version information. These files, when compiled, compose the control's resource files (.RES).

Listing 12.10 DRAGDROP.RC. Resource definition file for the *DragDrop* control.

```
//Microsoft App Studio generated resource script.
//
#include "resource.h"

#define APSTUDIO_READONLY_SYMBOLS
//
// Generated from the TEXTINCLUDE 2 resource.
//
#include "afxres.h"

#undef APSTUDIO_READONLY_SYMBOLS

#ifdef APSTUDIO_INVOKED
//
// TEXTINCLUDE
//

1 TEXTINCLUDE DISCARDABLE
BEGIN
    "resource.h\0"
END

2 TEXTINCLUDE DISCARDABLE
BEGIN
    "#include ""afxres.h""\r\n"
    "\0"
END

3 TEXTINCLUDE DISCARDABLE
BEGIN
    "#include ""DragDrop.rc2"""
// non-App Studio edited resources\r\n"
    "#if 0\r\n"
    "#include "".\\tlb16\\DragDrop.tlb"""
// 16-bit: force dependency on .TLB file\r\n"
    "#endif\r\n"
    "\0"
END
```

IV

Special Techniques

```
#endif    // APSTUDIO_INVOKED

//
// Icon
//

IDI_ABOUTDLL            ICON    DISCARDABLE    "DRAGDROP.ICO"

//
// Bitmap
//

IDB_DRAGDROP        _
   BITMAP  DISCARDABLE    "DRAGDCTL.BMP"

//
// Dialog
//

IDD_ABOUTBOX_DRAGDROP DIALOG DISCARDABLE  34, 22, 260, 55
STYLE DS_MODALFRAME ¦ WS_POPUP ¦ WS_CAPTION ¦ WS_SYSMENU
CAPTION "About DragDrop Control"
FONT 8, "MS Sans Serif"
BEGIN
    ICON            IDI_ABOUTDLL,IDC_STATIC,10,10,20,20
    LTEXT           "DragDrop Control, Version
1.0",IDC_STATIC,40,10,170,8
    LTEXT           "Copyright \251 1995,
Nielsen",IDC_STATIC,40,25,170,8
    DEFPUSHBUTTON   "OK",IDOK,220,10,32,14,WS_GROUP
END

IDD_PROPPAGE_DRAGDROP DIALOG DISCARDABLE  0, 0, 250, 62
STYLE WS_CHILD
FONT 8, "MS Sans Serif"
BEGIN
    CONTROL _
      "Accept Drop Files From File Manager",IDC_ACCEPTDRAGDROP, _
        "Button",BS_AUTOCHECKBOX ¦ WS_TABSTOP,5,5,132,16
END


//
// String Table
//

STRINGTABLE DISCARDABLE
BEGIN
    IDS_DRAGDROP            "DragDrop Control"
    IDS_DRAGDROP_PPG        "DragDrop Property Page"
END
```

(continues)

Listing 12.10   Continued

```
STRINGTABLE DISCARDABLE
BEGIN
    IDS_DRAGDROP_PPG_CAPTION "General"
END


#ifndef APSTUDIO_INVOKED
//
// Generated from the TEXTINCLUDE 3 resource.
//
#include "DragDrop.rc2"   // non-App Studio edited resources
#if 0
#include ".\tlb16\DragDrop.tlb"
// 16-bit: force dependency on .TLB file
#endif

#endif     // not APSTUDIO_INVOKED
```

Listing 12.11 shows the code that AppStudio does not directly edit.

Listing 12.11   DRAGDROP.RC2. Resources *AppStudio* does not edit directly.

```
#ifdef APSTUDIO_INVOKED
    #error this file is not editable by App Studio
#endif //APSTUDIO_INVOKED

// Version stamp for this DLL

#ifdef _WIN32
#include "winver.h"
#else
#include "ver.h"
#endif

VS_VERSION_INFO     VERSIONINFO
  FILEVERSION       1,0,0,1
  PRODUCTVERSION    1,0,0,1
  FILEFLAGSMASK     VS_FFI_FILEFLAGSMASK
#ifdef _DEBUG
  FILEFLAGS         VS_FF_DEBUG¦VS_FF_PRIVATEBUILD¦VS_FF_PRERELEASE
#else
  FILEFLAGS         0 // final version
#endif
#ifdef _WIN32
  FILEOS            VOS__WINDOWS32
#else
  FILEOS            VOS__WINDOWS16
#endif
  FILETYPE          VFT_DLL
```

```
      FILESUBTYPE       0   // not used
BEGIN
     BLOCK "StringFileInfo"
     BEGIN
#ifdef _WIN32
        BLOCK "040904B0" // Lang=US English, CharSet=Unicode
#else
        BLOCK "040904E4"
// Lang=US English, CharSet=Windows Multilingual
#endif
        BEGIN
            VALUE "CompanyName",      "\0"
            VALUE "FileDescription", _
               "DRAGDROP OLE Control DLL\0"
            VALUE "FileVersion",     "1.0.001\0"
            VALUE "InternalName",    "DRAGDROP\0"
            VALUE "LegalCopyright",  "Copyright \251 1995, \0"
            VALUE "LegalTrademarks", "\0"
            VALUE "OriginalFilename","DRAGDROP.DLL\0"
            VALUE "ProductName",     "DRAGDROP\0"
            VALUE "ProductVersion",  "1.0.001\0"
            VALUE "OLESelfRegister", "\0"
        END
    END
    BLOCK "VarFileInfo"
    BEGIN
#ifdef _WIN32
        VALUE "Translation", 0x409, 1200
// English language (0x409) and the Unicode codepage (1200)
#else
        VALUE "Translation", 0x409, 1252
// English language (0x409) and the Windows ANSI codepage (1252)
#endif
    END
END

// Type library for controls in this DLL

1 TYPELIB DragDrop.tlb
```

From Here...

OLE controls represent an important part in the future of Windows programming. To the Visual Basic programmer, they represent a roadway into the 32-bit programming environments of Windows 95 and Windows NT as well as a replacement for VBXs. OLE controls are also an open-architecture component that can be used and incorporated into any development environment that supports OLE.

■ For more information on using Lenel's Digital Video control to develop applications that use digital video, see Chapter 11, "Using Digital Video Playback." This includes Video for Windows and MPEG video.

■ For a great reference on how to use many different types of OCXs to display multimedia elements in presentations, see Chapter 13, "Creating Synchronized Presentations."

■ For an illustration of the usage of the DragDrop control developed in this chapter, see Chapter 14, "Multimedia Databases Using the JET Engine." The usage of a memory control and Gallery control are also covered in this chapter.

Chapter 13

Creating Synchronized Presentations

A *synchronized presentation* is a formatted display of text—audio and video information—shown in a finite period of time where all of the presentation's elements are displayed. An example of a synchronized presentation can be a Microsoft PowerPoint presentation, where the presentation is shown in self-running mode without user intervention.

This chapter shows the concepts behind developing synchronized presentations while developing your own Presentation Player application. In this chapter, you learn

- How to determine and establish a baseline for a self-running, synchronized presentation

- How to develop a file format for storing a presentation script

- How to combine all of the multimedia elements (audio, video, animation and graphics) into a synchronized presentation

- Different storage and distribution techniques for multimedia presentations

- What the components of a presentation are and how they relate to each other

Using Synchronized Presentations

Besides CD-ROM titles, presentation software is one of the leading, off-the-shelf consumer applications that utilizes multimedia technologies. Examples of popular presentation applications include Microsoft Powerpoint, Lotus Freelance, and Software Publishing's Harvard Graphics. Because Windows 95 has built-in multimedia capabilities, it is very easy to add audio, video and graphics to a presentation.

For application developers, there are many situations where the concepts of a synchronized presentation are useful. For example, let's take an application that is used for training assembly-line workers to construct a widget. Your application can invoke a short presentation on how to assemble the widget and then a test can be given when the presentation is done. In short, the concepts used for synchronized presentations can be used in a wide variety of applications, not just presentation software.

Defining the Presentation Layout

Before building a presentation, the capabilities of the presentation software must be defined. Your presentation package will consist of three major components:

- *A background image.* The background image fills the form, which displays the presentation.

- *Text information.* Bullet items are shown on-screen; they can appear at any location on-screen.

- *Multimedia elements.* Multimedia elements consist of digital video, audio, and images to be used in the presentation.

Figure 13.1 illustrates the various components of the presentation.

Using Visual Basic Components to Display the Presentation

The Presentation Player application includes the ability to play many types of multimedia elements. Fortunately, Visual Basic has the ability to use these elements directly. For the background image of the presentation, an image control is used to load and display this image. You actually use two controls for background images. Because background images have the ability to change during the presentation, the second image control is used to pre-load secondary backgrounds. When the background needs to be changed, the next background becomes visible and the current background becomes invisible.

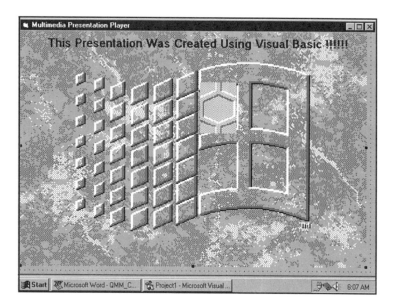

Fig. 13.1
Using Visual Basic components to construct a presentation application.

Static text controls are used for displaying text against the presentation background. The presentation package has a pre-allocated number of text controls for this purpose. For audio playback, Lenel Systems MediaDeveloper Audio Control is utilized.

Lenel Systems MediaDeveloper Digital Video control is used for the playback of Video for Windows files. This digital video control was also used in Chapter 11, "Using Digital Video Playback."

Defining the Capabilities of the Presentation Software

The presentation software will have the ability to use images, digital video, audio and text within a presentation. There will be an input or script file, which the Presentation Player application will read and use to perform various actions during the presentation.

All of the controls used in the presentation will be pre-allocated during software design. This will make the presentation play back much smoother than if the controls were not pre-loaded. The side effect of pre-allocating controls is that the number of items of each multimedia type to be shown on-screen at one time is limited to the number of pre-loaded controls.

The assumption is also made that the presentation will be self-running. This indicates that once the presentation is started, it will continue until the end of the presentation script or an error is encountered.

Constructing a Presentation File Format

All presentations follow a script, which indicates the elements that need to be played in the presentation and the element's playback characteristics, which include

■ *The location of the multimedia file.* The location of the multimedia file is a path (drive:\directory\file.ext) that indicates where to load the file from. For your presentation package, all of the multimedia files will be located external to the script file. This will present a slight problem in packaging up all of the files for presentation distribution.

The best method for distributing the files needed for the presentation is to install them all into one common directory from which the presentation is to be played. This ensures that all of the elements can be found.

In some presentation packages, such as Microsoft Powerpoint, all of the elements of the presentation including the presentation script are located in one presentation file. This makes distributing presentations very easy. A drawback is that the elements cannot be extracted for use within other applications because the presentation elements are contained within one file.

■ *The type of multimedia element to be played.* The type of multimedia element indicates to the presentation interpreter which pre-allocated control to use for the element. The valid multimedia types are digital video, audio, images and text.

■ *When the multimedia element should be played and for how long.* When the element should be played involves deciding the exact time from the beginning of the presentation to when the current command needs to be executed. This works in conjunction with the duration of the element. After the element's duration is unloaded, the multimedia element is released from memory and the control used to display the element is hidden.

■ *The playback size and position of the multimedia element.* The last components of the playback characteristics are the position of the multimedia element and its size. The size represents the display size of the element and the position indicates the element's location on-screen in pixels.

> **Caution**
>
> Care must be taken when adjusting the multimedia element's size and location. If the elements are adjusted incorrectly, the presentation could suffer greatly from the overlapping of multimedia controls. This can lead to such problems as palette flicker when running in 256 color mode.

Adding Scripting Commands to the Presentation File Format

To make your presentation flexible, the notion of script commands is used. A script command is similar to a keyword in the Visual Basic language. A script command instructs the presentation software how to interpret the line of text that is being read.

The format of the presentation file has the following syntax:

```
<Beginning of File>
SCRIPT_COMMAND = PARAMETER,PARAMETER,...,PARAMETER
SCRIPT_COMMAND = PARAMETER,PARAMETER,...,PARAMETER
SCRIPT_COMMAND = PARAMETER,PARAMETER,...,PARAMETER
...
SCRIPT_COMMAND = PARAMETER,PARAMETER,...,PARAMETER
<End of File>
```

The presentation software developed in this chapter will have a limited set of script commands. The set of script commands can be expanded to add even more flexibility to the presentation software. The following are the set of script commands that your application will use:

Script Command	Description
BACKGROUND	Instructs the presentation software to load in a new background image for the presentation.
DIGITALVIDEO	Instructs the presentation software to load and play a digital video file such as Video for Windows or MPEG.

(continues)

IV

Special Techniques

Script Command	Description
AUDIO	Indicates that an audio file should be loaded and played.
IMAGE	Indicates that an image file should be loaded into the presentation and shown for a duration of time.
TEXT	Indicates to the presentation software that the following line of text is to be added to the presentation background.

Adding Parameters to the Script Commands

Now that the script commands needed for the presentation package are defined, the parameters now need to be defined for each command.

BACKGROUND

The BACKGROUND command is used for loading a new background image into the presentation. The syntax for the BACKGROUND command is:

```
BACKGROUND = FILE.BMP;STARTTIME
```

The only two parameters needed for the BACKGROUND command are:

Parameter	Description
FILE.BMP	Indicates the name of the image to be loaded into the background.
STARTTIME	Indicates how many seconds from the start of the presentation before the new background is loaded.

There are no additional parameters to the BACKGROUND command because a background remains in effect until a new background is loaded.

DIGITALVIDEO

The DIGITALVIDEO command is used to load and play a new multimedia file in the presentation. The syntax for the DIGITALVIDEO command is:

```
DIGITALVIDEO = FILE.EXT;STARTTIME;DURATION;XPOSITION; _
    YPOSITION;WIDTH;HEIGHT
```

The following are parameters needed for the DIGITALVIDEO command:

Parameter	Description
FILE.EXT	Indicates the name of the multimedia file to load and play in the presentation.
STARTTIME	Indicates how many seconds from the start of the presentation before the new multimedia file is loaded.
DURATION	Indicates how many seconds the multimedia file should play for. A value of 0 (zero) indicates that the multimedia element should play until it's finished.
XPOSITION	Defines the location of the x-coordinate of the upper-left corner for the multimedia element.
YPOSITION	Indicates the location of the y-coordinate of the upper-left corner of the multimedia element.
WIDTH	Indicates the playback width of the element. A 0 (zero) indicates to use the width at which the digital video was recorded.
HEIGHT	Indicates the playback height of the element. A 0 (zero) indicates to use the height at which the digital video was recorded.

AUDIO

The AUDIO command is used to load and play a new audio file in the presentation. The syntax for the AUDIO command is:

```
AUDIO = FILE.EXT;STARTTIME;DURATION
```

There are a few parameters needed for the AUDIO command.

Parameter	Description
FILE.EXT	Indicates the name of the audio file to load and play in the presentation.
STARTTIME	Indicates how many seconds from the start of the presentation before the new multimedia file is loaded.
DURATION	Indicates how many seconds the multimedia file should play for. A value of 0 (zero) indicates that the multimedia element should play until it finishes playing. For time-based media such as audio, a 0 means play until the element finishes.

IMAGE

The IMAGE command is used to load and play a new image or bitmapped file in the presentation. The syntax for the IMAGE command is:

```
IMAGE = FILE.EXT;STARTTIME;DURATION;XPOSITION;YPOSITION; _
    WIDTH;HEIGHT
```

There are a few of parameters needed for the IMAGE command.

Parameter	Description
FILE.EXT	Indicates the name of the multimedia file to load and play in the presentation.
STARTTIME	Indicates how many seconds from the start of the presentation before the new multimedia file is loaded.
DURATION	Indicates how many seconds the multimedia file should play for. A value of 0 (zero) indicates that the multimedia element should play until the end of the presentation.
XPOSITION	Defines the location of the x-coordinate of the upper-left corner for the multimedia element.
YPOSITION	Indicates the location of the y-coordinate of the upper-left corner of the multimedia element.
WIDTH	Indicates the playback width of the element. A 0 (zero) indicates to use the width at which the image was captured.
HEIGHT	Indicates the playback height of the element. A 0 (zero) indicates to use the height at which the image was captured.

TEXT

The TEXT command is used to display a line of text in the presentation. The syntax for the TEXT command is:

```
TEXT =
TEXT;STARTTIME;DURATION;XPOSITION;YPOSITION;WIDTH;HEIGHT
```

The following are the TEXT command parameters:

Parameter	Description
TEXT	Represents a literal text string. The entire line of text up to the first semi-colon is displayed in the presentation.
STARTTIME	Indicates how many seconds from the start of the presentation before the text is displayed.
DURATION	Indicates how many seconds the text will be displayed. A value of 0 (zero) indicates that the multimedia element should play until it's finished.
XPOSITION	Defines the location of the x-coordinate of the upper-left corner for the multimedia element.
YPOSITION	Indicates the location of the y-coordinate of the upper-left corner of the multimedia element.
WIDTH	Indicates the playback width of the element. A 0 (zero) indicates to use the width at which the image was captured.
HEIGHT	Indicates the playback height of the element. A 0 (zero) indicates to use the height at which the image was captured.

Storing the Command Script into a User-Defined Data Type

Because each line of the presentation script contains a command that the Presentation Player application must interpret, a method of storing each command needs to be created. For the Presentation Player application, the storage mechanism that is used is a user-defined data type called PresentationCommand. The PresentationCommand data type is stored in the file PLAYER.BAS, as shown in Listing 13.1.

Listing 13.1 PLAYER.BAS. User data type for storing presentation command scripts.

```
Type PresentationCommand
    Cmd As String      _
    ' String variable stores the command for input line
    InputData As String _
    ' String for storing the input file name or text
    StartTime As Integer   _
    ' Integer variable stores start time of element
    Duration As Integer _
```

(continues)

Listing 13.1 Continued

```
        ' Stores the duration that the element is to be displayed
        XPos As Integer        ' Stores the upper coordinate
        YPos As Integer        ' Stores the left coordinate
        Width As Integer       ' Stores the display width
        Height As Integer      ' Stores the display height
        EndTime As Integer     ' start time + duration
        DataCtrlNum As Integer ' indicates which control contains
                               ' element
    End Type
```

Each data member of the `PresentationCommand` data type, with the exceptions
of `EndTime` and `DataCtrlNum`, contains information read from the command
script. The `EndTime` data member is used for storing the ending time of the
multimedia element. The `DataCtrlNum` data member is used at presentation
run time for storing the number of the control used to display this multimedia element.

Reading a Presentation Script

Before a presentation can be played, the script governing the presentation
must be read and interpreted by the Presentation Player application. This is
done through the Open command located under the File menu of the Presentation Player application. Listing 13.2 shows what happens when the Open
command is executed.

**Listing 13.2 PLAYER.FRM. Routines used for reading a
presentation command script.**

```
    Private Sub Open_Click()
    Dim OpenFileName As String
    Dim FileNumber As Integer
    PlayerDlg.Flags = cdlOFNFileMustExist
    PlayerDlg.Action = 1
    If Not (PlayerDlg.Flags And cdlOFNExtensionDifferent) = 0 Then
        OpenFileName = PlayerDlg.FileName
        FileNumber = FreeFile
        NumElements = GetNumElements(OpenFileName)
        AllocatePresentationArray (NumElements)
        Open OpenFileName For Input As FileNumber
        ReadInputFile (FileNumber)
        Close FileNumber
    End If
    End Sub
    Public Function ReadInputFile(FileNum As Integer) As Integer
    Dim InputLine As String
    Dim InputNumber As Integer
    InputNumber = 0
```

```
Do While Not EOF(FileNum)
    Input #FileNum, InputLine
    ParseFileInput InputLine, InputNumber
    InputNumber = InputNumber + 1
Loop
End Function
Public Function GetNumElements(FileName As String) As Integer
    Dim FileNumber As Integer
    Dim InputLine As String
    Dim NumElements As Integer
    NumElements = 0
    FileNumber = FreeFile
    Open FileName For Input As FileNumber
    Do While Not EOF(FileNumber)
        Input #FileNumber, InputLine
        NumElements = NumElements + 1
    Loop
    Close FileNumber
    GetNumElements = NumElements
End Function
Public Sub AllocatePresentationArray(NumElements As Integer)
ReDim PlayerElements(NumElements)
End Sub
Public Function ParseFileInput(InputData As String, InputNumber _
  As Integer) As Integer
' first remove leading/trailing blanks
InputData = Trim(InputData)
If (1 = InStr(InputData, BACKGROUND_CMD)) Then
    ParseFileInput = ParseBackgroundCmd(InputData, InputNumber)
End If
If (1 = InStr(InputData, DIGITALVIDEO_CMD)) Then
    ParseFileInput = ParseCmd(DIGITALVIDEO_CMD, InputData, _
      InputNumber)
End If
If (1 = InStr(InputData, IMAGE_CMD)) Then
    ParseFileInput = ParseCmd(IMAGE_CMD, InputData, InputNumber)
End If
If (1 = InStr(InputData, TEXT_CMD)) Then
    ParseFileInput = ParseCmd(TEXT_CMD, InputData, InputNumber)
End If
If (1 = InStr(InputData, AUDIO_CMD)) Then
    ParseFileInput = ParseCmd(AUDIO_CMD, InputData, InputNumber)
End If
ParseFileInput = 0
End Function
Public Function ParseBackgroundCmd(InputData As String, _
  InputNumber As Integer) As Integer
Dim StartPos As Integer
Dim EndPos As Integer
PlayerElements(InputNumber).Cmd = BACKGROUND_CMD
StartPos = InStr(InputData, CMDSTART)
EndPos = InStr(StartPos + 1, InputData, DELIMITER)
PlayerElements(InputNumber).InputData = Mid(InputData, _
  StartPos + 1, EndPos - (StartPos + 1))
```

(continues)

Listing 13.2 Continued

```
        StartPos = EndPos
        EndPos = InStr(StartPos + 1, InputData, DELIMITER)
        PlayerElements(InputNumber).StartTime = CInt(Mid(InputData, _
          StartPos + 1))
        Debug.Print PlayerElements(InputNumber).Cmd
        Debug.Print PlayerElements(InputNumber).InputData
        Debug.Print PlayerElements(InputNumber).StartTime
        ParseBackgroundCmd = 1
        End Function
        Public Function ParseCmd(CmdType As String, InputData As String, _
          InputNumber As Integer) As Integer
        Dim StartPos As Integer
        Dim EndPos As Integer
        PlayerElements(InputNumber).Cmd = CmdType
        StartPos = InStr(InputData, CMDSTART)
        EndPos = InStr(StartPos + 1, InputData, DELIMITER)
        PlayerElements(InputNumber).InputData = Mid(InputData, _
          StartPos + 1, EndPos - (StartPos + 1))
        StartPos = EndPos
        EndPos = InStr(StartPos + 1, InputData, DELIMITER)
        PlayerElements(InputNumber).StartTime = CInt(Mid(InputData, _
          StartPos + 1, EndPos - (StartPos + 1)))
        StartPos = EndPos
        EndPos = InStr(StartPos + 1, InputData, DELIMITER)
        PlayerElements(InputNumber).Duration = CInt(Mid(InputData, _
          StartPos + 1, EndPos - (StartPos + 1)))
        StartPos = EndPos
        EndPos = InStr(StartPos + 1, InputData, DELIMITER)
        PlayerElements(InputNumber).XPos = CInt(Mid(InputData, _
          StartPos + 1, EndPos - (StartPos + 1)))
        StartPos = EndPos
        EndPos = InStr(StartPos + 1, InputData, DELIMITER)
        PlayerElements(InputNumber).YPos = CInt(Mid(InputData, _
          StartPos + 1, EndPos - (StartPos + 1)))
        StartPos = EndPos
        EndPos = InStr(StartPos + 1, InputData, DELIMITER)
        PlayerElements(InputNumber).Width = CInt(Mid(InputData, _
          StartPos + 1, EndPos - (StartPos + 1)))
        StartPos = EndPos
        EndPos = InStr(StartPos + 1, InputData, DELIMITER)
        PlayerElements(InputNumber).Height = CInt(Mid(InputData, _
          StartPos + 1))
        End Function
```

When the Open file menu item is invoked, the following sequence of events occurs:

1. The common dialog box used for choosing a file to open is displayed. This allows the user to choose a presentation file to open.

2. A file handle is retrieved from the Visual Basic function FreeFile.

3. The input filename is passed into the routine `GetNumElements`, which reads the input file and returns the number of elements contained in the input file.

4. An array of `PresentationCommand` data types, called `PlayerElements`, is then allocated to hold each command that the input file contains. The array is allocated in the function `AllocatePresentationArray`.

5. Once the `PlayerElements` array is allocated, the command script is then opened and read by the function `ReadInputFile`.

6. `ReadInputFile` reads the command script one line at a time. Because each line contains a presentation command, each line is passed to the function `ParseFileInput`.

7. `ParseFileInput` first removes any leading and trailing whitespace characters from the input line. Next the input line is scanned in search of a command. If a valid command is found within the input line, the appropriate command parser is called. For the Presentation Player application, this is either `Parsebackground` for background commands, or `ParseCmd` for each additional command. If additional presentation commands are to be added to the command language, this is where they would be distinguished and sent to an appropriate parser.

8. Once the appropriate parser (`ParseBackgroundCmd` or `ParseCmd`) is called, the contents of the command are retrieved and placed in a `PresentationCommand` data type. You will notice that each line read from the input file has a unique number. This number corresponds to the data structure for the input line within the `PlayerElements` array.

At this point, the input file has been read and all of the commands are contained in memory with the `PlayerElements` array. The presentation is now ready to be played.

Establishing a Baseline for the Presentation

Before a presentation can be shown, a baseline needs to be created. A *baseline* determines what all the elements in the presentation are going to be synchronized to. The baseline also determines when a particular element is to be displayed and for how long.

As an example, let's examine a sample presentation script that the Presentation Player application can play.

The sample presentation follows the following script:

1. When the presentation is first started, a background image is shown on-screen.

2. After five seconds, the background is replaced and a line of text is added.

3. After three seconds, the second line of text appears on the slide.

4. After three more seconds, a third line of text appears on the slide.

5. And finally, five seconds after the third line is shown, all of the text is removed and a new background is displayed.

While this example is relatively simple it illustrates the following points:

■ There are two types of changes that take place with respect to time. The first is changing an entire background. The second is changing elements within a slide and maintaining the same background.

■ Even in this simple example, there is a baseline that determines when elements and slides in the presentation will change. In this example, the baseline is simply the time from when the presentation was loaded.

Using the *Playback* Timer

To establish a baseline for the presentation, a timer needs to be added to the main form of the application. The timer called, Playback, will establish the baseline for your presentation.

The Playback timer will be set to have an interval of 1000 milliseconds or one second. This indicates that every second a timer event will occur and the presentation application will have to load and play the next element while cleaning any residual elements that have already been played. The Timer event is what will keep the presentation moving and flowing.

Whenever a timer event occurs, the following three items occur:

■ Any new elements in the PlayerElements array scheduled to play at the occurring time interval are loaded into memory.

■ Any elements that have finished playing are removed from memory.

■ The elements that were just loaded into memory are now played.

Playing the Presentation

To play the presentation, the following tools will be needed to play back the various multimedia elements:

- *Visual Basic image controls.* The image controls display the presentation backgrounds and any other presentation images.

- *Visual Basic static text controls.* The static text controls display text for the presentation.

- *MCI class objects.* The MCI class object was developed in Chapter 10, "Animation." A generic MCI class was developed to play back MCI-based animation files. The same class module can be used to play back audio and digital video files in your presentation.

For the presentation, all of the presentation tools have been pre-allocated at presentation design time. The Presentation Player application uses the following number of tools:

- *Image controls.* Two controls for background images and two controls for images to be used during the presentation.

- *Static text controls.* An array of five static text controls are available for use during the presentation.

- *Lenel MediaDeveloper audio and digital video controls.* Two digital video objects and two audio objects have been allocated.

To start playing the presentation, select the Play command on the Presentation Player application. All of the variables used for the presentation are cleared and the presentation starts playing. Listing 13.3 shows the player portion of the presentation.

Listing 13.3   PLAYER.FRM. Playing the presentation.

```
Private Sub Play_Click()
StartTime = 0
NextText = 0
NextDigitalVideo = 0
NextAudio = 0
NextImage = 0
NextBackground = 0
FinishedPlayingList = False
```

(continues)

Listing 13.3   Continued

```
PlayPresetation (StartTime)
End Sub

Public Sub PlayPresentation(PlayTime As Integer)
    ' first load any elements into memory
    LoadElementsIntoMemory (PlayTime)
    RemoveElementsFromMemory (PlayTime)
    PlayElements (PlayTime)
End Sub
```

Loading Elements into Memory

At each timer interval, the elements of the presentation are loaded into memory. When an element is loaded into memory, it is loaded into an off-screen or invisible control. This is done to reduce any on-screen painting or delays to the user. Only after the presentation elements are loaded into memory are the controls made visible to the user.

Listing 13.4 illustrates how the presentation elements are loaded into the Presentation Player application's memory. The function LoadElementsIntoMemory is called. This routine searches each element in the presentation for an entry that is supposed to start at the current time.

Listing 13.4   PLAYER.FRM. Loading elements into memory.

```
Public Sub _
    LoadElementsIntoMemory(PlayTime As Integer)
    Dim I As Integer
    For I = 0 To NumElements - 1 Step 1
        If PlayerElements(I).StartTime = PlayTime Then
            Select Case PlayerElements(I).Cmd
                Case BACKGROUND_CMD
                    LoadBackground I
                Case IMAGE_CMD
                    LoadImage I
                Case TEXT_CMD
                    LoadText I
                Case DIGITALVIDEO_CMD
                    LoadDigitalVideo I
                Case AUDIO_CMD
                    LoadAudio I
            End Select
        End If
    Next I
End Sub
```

When an entry to be loaded is found, the appropriate loading method is called and the element is loaded, as in Listings 13.5 and 13.6.

Listing 13.5   PLAYER.FRM. Loading the image.

```
Public Sub LoadImage(Element As Integer)
    PlayerElements(Element).DataCtrlNum = NextImage
    If NextImage = 0 Then
        Image1.picture = _
            LoadPicture(PlayerElements(Element).InputData)
        Image1.Left = PlayerElements(Element).XPos
        Image1.TOP = PlayerElements(Element).YPos
        Image1.Width = PlayerElements(Element).Width
        Image1.Height = PlayerElements(Element).Height
        NextImage = 1
    Else
        Image2.picture = _
            LoadPicture(PlayerElement(Element).InputData)
        Image2.Left = PlayerElements(Element).XPos
        Image2.TOP = PlayerElements(Element).YPos
        Image2.Width = PlayerElements(Element).Width
        Image2.Height = PlayerElements(Element).Height
        NextImage = 0
    End If
End Sub
```

Listing 13.6   PLAYER.FRM. Loading text.

```
Public Sub LoadText()
    PlayerElements(Element).DataCtrlNum = NextText
    Text1(NextText).Caption = _
        LoadPicture(PlayerElements(Element).InputData)
    Text1(NextText).Left = PlayerElements(Element).XPos
    Text1(NextText).TOP = PlayerElements(Element).YPos
    Text1(NextText).Width = PlayerElements(Element).Width
    Text1(NextText).Height = PlayerElements(Element).Height
    NextText = NextText + 1
    If NextText > 4 Then
        NextText = 0
    End If
End Sub
```

Variables such as Nextbackground (see Listing 13.7) are used to depict the next available control to load a background into.

Listing 13.7   PLAYER.FRM. Loading the background.

```
Public Sub LoadBackground(Element As Integer)
    PlayerElements(Element).DataCtrlNum = NextBackground
    If NextBackground = 0 Then
        Background1.picture = _
            LoadPicture(PlayerElements(Element).InputData)
        Background1.Left = 0
        Background1.TOP = 0
        Background1.Width = Player.Width
        Background1.Height = Player.Height
        NextBackground = 1
    Else
        Background2.picture = _
            LoadPicture(PlayerElements(Element).InputData)
        Background2.Left = 0
        Background2.TOP = 0
        Background2.Width = Player.Width
        Background2.Height = Player.Height
        NextBackground = 0
    End If
End Sub
```

Removing Elements from Memory

After the elements are loaded into memory, any elements on the presentation display that have finished playing must be removed. This is done through the function RemoveElementsFromMemory.

All elements on the PlayerElements array are searched for entries that have an EndTime equal to the current time. When a match is found, the appropriate removal function is called. Listing 13.8 illustrates the removal of elements from the presentation.

Listing 13.8   PLAYER.FRM. Removing elements from memory.

```
Public Sub _
    RemoveElementsFromMemory(Element As Integer)
    Dim I As Integer
    For I = 0 To NumElements - 1 Step 1
        If PlayerElements(I).EndTime = PlayTime Then
            Select Case PlayerElements(I).Cmd
                Case BACKGROUND_CMD
                    RemoveBackground I
                Case IMAGE_CMD
                    RemoveImage I
                Case TEXT_CMD
                    RemoveText I
                Case DIGITALVIDEO_CMD
                    RemoveDigitalVideo I
```

```
                    Case AUDIO_CMD
                        RemoveAudio I
                End Select
            End If
        Next I
End Sub

Public Sub RemoveBackground(Element As Integer)
    If PlayerElements(Element).DataCtrlNum = 0 Then
        Background1.Visible = False
    Else
        Background2.Visible = False
    End If
End Sub
Public Sub RemoveImage(Element As Integer)
    If PlayerElements(Element).DataCtrlNum = 0 Then
        Image1.Visible = False
    Else
        Image2.Visible = False
    End If
End Sub
Public Sub RemoveText(Element As Integer)
    Text1(PlayerElements(Element)._
        DataCtrlNum).Vlsible = False
End Sub
```

Playing the Multimedia Elements

The final piece to the Presentation Player application is to play the multimedia elements. This is shown in Listing 13.9. As you can see, the concept is similar to removal and loading of elements. The PlayerElements array searches for entries that need to be played at the current time. When one is found, a player function for that element type is called.

Listing 13.9   PLAYER.FRM. Playing the presentation elements.

```
Public Sub PlayElements(PlayTime As Integer)
    Dim I As Integer
    For I = 0 To NumElements - 1 Step 1
        If PlayerElements(I).StartTime = PlayTime Then
            Select Case PlayerElements(I).Cmd
                Case BACKGROUND_CMD
                    PlayBackground I
                Case IMAGE_CMD
                    PlayImage I
                Case TEXT_CMD
                    PlayText I
                Case DIGITALVIDEO_CMD
                    PlayDigitalVideo I
                Case AUDIO_CMD
                    PlayAudio I
```

(continues)

Listing 13.9 Continued

```
                End Select
                If I = NumElements - 1 Then
                    FinishedPlayingList = True
                End If
            End If
        Next I
    End Sub

    Public Sub PlayImage(Element As Integer)
        If PlayerElements(Element).DataCtrlNum = 0 Then
            Image1.Visible = True
        Else
            Image2.Visible = True
        End If
    End Sub

    Public Sub PlayBackground(Element As Integer)
        If PlayerElements(Element).DataCtrlNum = 0 Then
            Background1.Visible = True
        Else
            Background2.Visible = True
        End If
    End Sub

    Public Sub PlayText(Element As Integer)
        Text1(PlayerElements(Element).DataCtrlNum).Visible = True
    End Sub
```

From Here...

In this chapter, you learned how to create a self-running, synchronized presentation. A file format was developed to store the presentation and a command parser was built to interpret the presentation script. You have also seen how to use various multimedia elements within a presentation.

For a discussion of other multimedia techniques, see the following chapters:

■ For information on creating your own transition effects, see Chapter 6, "Creating Transition Effects." These effects can be used to enhance your presentations.

■ To find out how the MCI object used in the Presentation Player application is developed, see Chapter 10, "Animation."

■ To examine various techniques for playing digital video clips, see Chapter 11, "Using Digital Video Playback." These techniques can be adapted for use in the Presentation Player application.

Chapter 14

Multimedia Databases Using the JET Engine

Only a few short years ago, text was the primary interface for most PC users. With the popularity of the graphical Windows interface, other information media such as graphics, images, animation, audio, and even video are now appearing in mainstream applications on the computer desktop. Many applications have benefited from multimedia technology, but one area in particular has been empowered by the arrival of multimedia—database applications.

Think about the typical employee database at most corporations. This is traditionally a text-oriented application with alphanumeric information that describes a company's employees. While this is important, it doesn't provide other descriptive information that distinguishes a person like a photograph, voice sample, video segment, or signature does.

Because of the built-in support for both multimedia and database technologies, Visual Basic is an ideal environment for the integration of these diverse technologies. Integrating multimedia technology in applications through the use of the Visual Basic Data Access Objects is the subject of this chapter. The techniques learned are readily applicable to the other methods of database access.

In this chapter, you learn

- How to use the Visual Basic Data Manager for database creation

- How to use the Data Access Objects and data control for accessing and manipulating multimedia information

- How to effectively use BLOB fields for storing and retrieving multimedia information

- Creating multimedia front ends to database information by using a multimedia thumbnail Gallery control

- Effective methods for designing multimedia databases

Visual Basic Database Access Features

Visual Basic 4.0 uses the *JET (Joint Engine Technology)* database engine as its native database format. This is the same database used in Microsoft Access. Visual Basic also has the capability to access and use other database formats such as FoxPro, dBASE, Paradox, Btrieve, ODBC (Open Database Connectivity), and compliant databases that include client-server databases such as SQL Server, Informix, Oracle, and Sybase.

Starting with Version 3.0, Visual Basic has included database access as a standard component. With the release of Visual Basic 4.0, support for the following features has been added:

- An object-oriented Data Definition Language (DDL) for creating and editing database, table, query, field, security, and referential-integrity objects.

- New data-bound controls including a grid, list box, and combo box.

- Support for user-defined properties on most data access objects.

- New Recordset objects for more consistent database manipulation and enhanced performance.

- Improved security features including new Group, User, and Workspace objects.

- Support for defining and enforcing referential integrity with Relation objects.

- Multiple Workspace objects to support advanced security and multiple transaction spaces.

- Improved support for ODBC databases, full cursor support, updatable query result sets, enhanced error reporting, and multiple sets.

- Improved query performance using Rushmore optimization.

Visual Basic provides many routes with which to access database information. Two of these techniques, data controls and the Data Access Objects (DAO), utilize the JET Engine. Database information can also be accessed via the Open Database Connectivity (ODBC) libraries or the Visual Basic SQL libraries. Database information can also be accessed through a variety of third-party controls and libraries; an example is Intersolv's Q+E Data Access controls.

The Data Access Objects are the primary method for accessing data within Visual Basic. The Data Access Objects are a set of object-oriented classes, implemented as OLE automation servers, with which databases can be designed, created, and manipulated. Figure 14.1 shows the class hierarchy for the Data Access Objects.

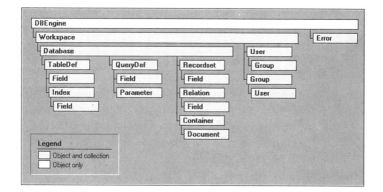

Fig. 14.1
The class hierarchy for the Visual Basic Data Access Objects.

Data Access Objects Reference Guide

The class hierarchy (refer to Fig. 14.1) outlines the classes that comprise the Data Access Objects for the Visual Basic JET Engine interface. The definitions that follow provide an overview of each class.

DBEngine Object
The DBEngine object is the top-level database object that corresponds to the JET Engine. The DBEngine object is used to set systemwide parameters for the database engine and also to set up the default workspace.

Workspace Object
The Workspace object is used to support simultaneous transactions. It also acts as a container for open databases, and identifies a security context for operations on the database. A default Workspace, Workspaces(0) is automatically

created when data access objects are first referenced in the language at run time. The default Workspace, unlike other Workspace objects, is always available and can never be closed or removed from a collection.

Database **Object**

The Database object represents a physical database, either a JET native or external database. A Database object can also represent a physical client-server database via a direct ODBC connection. The Database object is used to define the database's tables, relations, and stored queries. It also is used to open Recordset objects.

TableDef **Object**

The TableDef object represents a stored table definition. Each TableDef object in a TableDefs collection represents the definition of a table in the current database or an attached table in an external database. The table definition defines the fields and indexes of the table.

QueryDef **Object**

A QueryDef object is a stored query definition. A stored query represents a compiled SQL statement. Even though the stored query is predefined, it is possible to read and modify the SQL statement in a QueryDef, change the query parameters and then execute the query.

Recordset **Object**

The Recordset object corresponds to the results of a database query, or a *cursored view* into a database table. A cursored view is one that stores rows of data in a buffer and points to one row of data at a time, called the *current record*. The current record can be changed at any time via the Move, Seek, or Find methods. The Recordset object enables you to browse, update, and delete data in the underlying tables.

NOTE It is important to note that the Recordset object is a temporary object. When a Recordset object is closed, it is removed from the Recordsets collection and all associated resources are freed from memory.

For developers familiar with Visual Basic 3.0, the Recordset object is replaced by Dynaset, Table and Snapshot objects in Version 4.0. When creating a Recordset object, one of three types can be created.

Table-type Recordset
The table-type `Recordset` is analogous to the `Table` object in Version 3.0. It represents a table in a native or external database. This type of `Recordset` can only be opened for ISAM databases, not ODBC databases or attached tables. When opened, you have direct access to the underlying database table. This type of `Recordset` is created using the `DB_OPEN_TABLE` flag when creating the object.

Dynaset-type Recordset
The `Dynaset-type Recordset` corresponds to a dynamic table that is the result of a query on one or more database tables. It can be updated and changed because this type of `Recordset` directly reflects and is directly reflected by the underlying tables. This type of `Recordset` is created using the `DB_OPEN_DYNASET` flag when creating the object.

Snapshot-type Recordset
The `Snapshot-type Recordset` is similar to a `Dynaset-type Recordset` except that it represents a set of static information as a result of a query. Unlike a `Dynaset`, it is not updatable and updates to the table are not reflected in the `Snapshot-type Recordset`. Because the overhead of managing updates is removed, this type of `Recordset` is faster than a `Dynaset-type Recordset`. This type of `Recordset` is created using the `DB_OPEN_SHAPSHOT` flag when creating the object.

Field Object

The `Field` object represents a column of data with a common data type and set of properties. There is a collection of `Field` objects within the `TableDef`, `QueryDef`, `Recordset` and `Index` objects. The collection of `Field` objects associated with a `Recordset` object cursor position represents a single row of data. Actual data values for the `Recordset` are read and updated through the `Field` object's `Value` property. `Field` objects are automatically updated with new values as the cursor position moves within a `Recordset` object.

Index **Object**

The `Index` object is a stored index associated with a `Table`-type `Recordset` object or a `TableDef` object. When used with a `Table`-type `Recordset`, the current index may be specified by setting its `Index` property to the name of one of the indexes in the `Index` collection. Setting the `Index` allows for quick reordering of the records in a table.

Parameter **Object**

The `Parameter` object is a stored query parameter associated with a parameterized query. Developers can get and set query parameters through the Parameters collection in the `QueryDef` and `Recordset` objects.

User **Object**

The `User` object defines and enforces database security. A collection of system users is located in the `DBEngine`. Users' accounts are created or dropped from the system by adding or deleting members from the User collection. Each `User` object is created with a name and password. Access permissions to system objects such as `TableDefs` and `QueryDef` objects can be individually assigned.

Group Object

A `Group` object represents a collection of users with similar access rights. The `DBEngine` objects support a collection of system groups. Each user in a group inherits the permissions to access all objects that the group can access. For example, access rights can be assigned to an object such as a `TableDef`; this enables all users in the group to access the object.

Relation **Object**

The `Relation` object represents information about any relationships that exist between fields of two `TableDef` objects. Each `Database` object has a single collection of `Relation` objects. The JET Engine can enforce certain update and delete conditions (triggers) on the data associated with the fields of the `Relation` objects. These update and delete conditions maintain the referential integrity of the database.

Property **Object**

The `Property` object represents a stored property associated with an object. Both default or "built-in" properties and user-defined properties are stored in the object's Properties collection. User-defined properties for any object are created by appending to the object's Properties collection. User-defined properties allow developers to associate new properties with the Data Access Objects they create, and save these properties in the database. User-defined properties are supported by the following data access objects:

- `Database`

- `TableDef`

- `QueryDef`

- `TableDef.Index`

- `TableDef.Field`

- `QueryDef.Field`

Container object

`Container` objects are used in conjunction with `Document` objects to enumerate all objects stored in the database. This includes objects that are defined by client applications. Each `Database` object has a single `Container` collection. The main use of the `Container` and `Document` objects is to enumerate all objects stored in the database, and set user permissions and ownership.

Document Object

`Document` objects are objects of a common type that share a container. User permissions can be set of `Document` objects to grant or revoke security privileges.

The objects that comprise the Data Access Objects fall into the following two categories of database functionality:

- *Data Definition Language (DDL)*. These objects are used for creating and defining the database layout.

- *Data Manipulation Language (DML)*. These objects are used for the manipulation of the database contents once the database structure has been created.

The Data Definition Language

The objects comprising the Data Definition Language are used to define and create the database itself, including its tables, fields, relations, queries, and so on. The objects that comprise the Data Definition Language are often referred to as the *database schema*.

The database definition is typically a one-time operation, because the JET Engine stores the data access objects that define the database schema in the database itself. Once the database has been defined and created, there is no need to specify its structure in order to access it. Simply opening the database brings all of its objects, including those that define its structure, under the control of the DAO interface.

The Data Manipulation Language

The Data Manipulation Language consists of the objects used to write applications that access and manipulate existing databases. This includes facilities for querying the database, navigating through its tables, performing updates, and adding or deleting records.

This is where the majority of work is done not only with multimedia database applications, but with all database applications in general. Database structures are generally created through an external database application, such as Visual Basic's Data Manager application. In the section "Using the Data Manager Application," a database structure will be defined for the Multimedia Content Browser application.

Methods for Storing Multimedia Data in Databases

There are a few basic methods for storing multimedia data in databases. One method involves the traditional file system approach, while the other uses binary field types in the Database Engine. Each method has benefits and drawbacks. You can choose the appropriate method, depending on the needs of the application.

Examining File-based Multimedia Databases

File-based multimedia databases do not store the actual multimedia information in the database. Instead, the location and name of the file containing the multimedia information are stored in the database. This eliminates incompatibility problems if the application needs to work with a variety of databases because the only type of field type that the database needs to support is the Text or Alphanumeric field type.

The alternative to file-based multimedia databases is *BLOB (Binary Large Object)* databases. In the BLOB database, the multimedia content or information is stored in a database field. When a record is retrieved that contains the

BLOB field, the information is extracted and displayed like other nonmultimedia information.

File-based multimedia databases are typically easier to create than a BLOB-based database. The code to create and use this type of database is simpler to use because the developer is only dealing with text information. The biggest benefit to file-based multimedia databases is that because the multimedia information is stored in external files, the files can be accessed and used by external applications. This benefit can also cause administrative nightmares because the files can be deleted, moved or renamed outside of the database application. The following lists the benefits and drawbacks of file-based multimedia databases:

Benefits of file-based multimedia databases

> Ensures compatibility with all database engines.

> Networked applications can be created.

> Multimedia information can be used in external applications.

> Easy to develop.

> The data-binding feature can be used to link the multimedia files to a Visual Basic control.

Drawbacks of file-based multimedia databases

> Only file-based multimedia information can be stored.

> Special administrative care needs to be provided for networked applications. Any path information stored in the database must use UNC notation for resolving paths. Any information stored must be accessible from all networked stations.

> Additional care must be provided for distributing applications. All of the multimedia files must be collected and distributed. Any path information in the database tables must be updated.

> Multimedia information can be used by external applications.

In this chapter, you develop both a file-based multimedia database and a BLOB multimedia database. You first create a file-based application, then port this to a BLOB-based application, which is a Multimedia Content Browser that can be used for cataloging multimedia information residing on your computer.

Creating a Multimedia Content Browser

With the various types of multimedia data present and the large number of files needed for multimedia content, one of the logical applications for integrating multimedia and database technology is *content cataloging applications*. A content cataloging application is a multimedia database used for locating and retrieving multimedia data.

NOTE There are several commercial multimedia cataloging applications available. Lenel Systems has MpcOrganizer, Eastman Kodak has ShoeBox, U-Lead technologies has ImagePals.

When designing any database, it is essential that the format of the database be known *before* coding the application. The database design affects the layout of the application screens and functionality of the application.

In this chapter, you develop a multimedia content browser application. This application can store and retrieve information about any multimedia data present on your system. One of the side effects of multimedia is the amount of information each element represents. This information is primarily stored in files. Being able to quickly search and retrieve this information can greatly improve your project delivery schedule as well as effectively manage your disk space.

For the Content Browser application, the primary goal is to locate and identify multimedia content that resides on a computer system. For this purpose, you create a database using the fields found in Table 14.1.

Table 14.1 Fields Used to Create a Database

Field Name	Type	Length	Description
Title	Text	50 bytes	Title of the multimedia object (for example, Windsurfing Video).
Type	Numeric	1 byte	Type of multimedia object indicated by numeric constants (for example, 0—Audio Wave File).
Description	Memo	Variable	Text description of the multimedia object.
Location	Text	255 bytes	File specifications of the multimedia object (for example, c:\windows\cars.bmp).

To create this database, two techniques are used. The first technique is through the Data Manager application, included with Visual Basic. The second technique is using the Data Access Objects. Each technique is used at different points in time. Data Manager is used for creating the initial database for the application. The Data Access Objects are used for re-creating the database once the application has been deployed.

Creating Databases in Visual Basic

Databases can be created either through the Data Manager application or programmatically via the Data Access Objects. Developers know the type of data used and the database layout before the application ships. Databases for these types of applications are designed by the developer before application run time and use the Data Manager for the database design and creation. Alternatively, applications that allow users to design and create their own applications, use the Data Access Objects because the application must programmatically create the database layout based on the user input.

Using the Data Manager Application

The Data Manager is a stand-alone application that is integrated into the Visual Basic development environment. The Data Manager is used to design, view and modify new and/or existing databases. This alleviates the need to create your database design through the DAO interface.

To create the database for your Multimedia Content Browser application, first start the Data Manager by choosing Add-in, Data Manager from the Visual Basic main menu, then perform the following steps:

1. Choose the New command from the Data Manager's File menu to invoke the New Database dialog box. You notice that Data Manager can only create native (JET) databases. To create other database formats, such as Paradox, a creation tool native to that database can be used. (Figure 14.2 demonstrates this step.) Type in the name of the database to create. For the Content Browser application, type **mmdb1.mdb** in the File Name text box, then click OK.

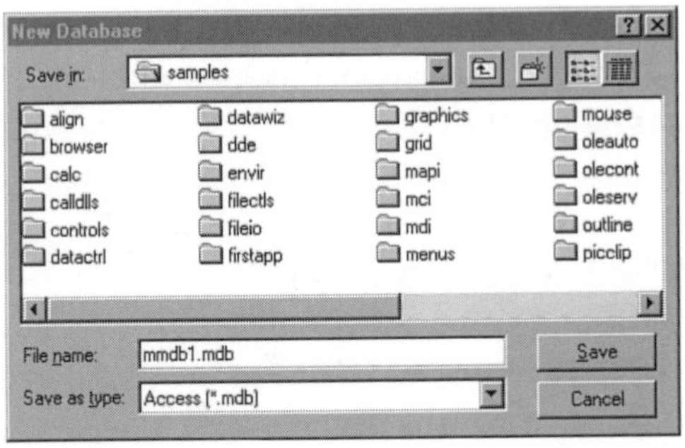

Fig. 14.2
The New Database dialog box creates a new database via Data Manager.

2. A MDI window for the database file has been created (see Fig. 14.3). Most of the buttons have been disabled. Click the New button to display the Add Table dialog box (see Fig. 14.4) to add database tables to the database definition.

Fig. 14.3
The Data Manager MDI window is used for editing and designing database tables.

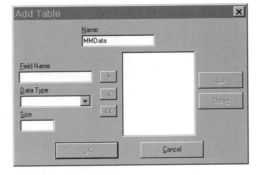

3. Enter the table name **MMData** in the Name text box in the Add Table dialog box.

Fig. 14.4
Using the Data Manager application to create a new database table.

4. Now the field names for the MMData database table need to be added. Follow Table 14.1 in the previous section for a list of the fields needed. Fill out the dialog box for each field then click OK.

5. To add the indexes or keys used for searching, select the MMData table name from the list box in the MCI window (refer to Fig. 14.3), then click the <u>D</u>esign button. The Table Editor dialog box shown in Figure 14.5 is displayed. Any additional fields or field modifications can be performed at this time.

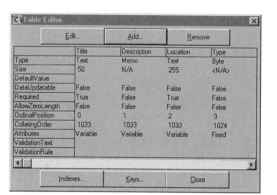

Fig. 14.5
You can add fields, keys and indexes through the Table Editor.

6. To add keys for the MMData table, click the <u>K</u>eys button from the Table Editor. The Keys dialog box (see Fig. 14.6) enables you to choose a primary key from the list of fields added to the table. For the Content Browser application, a Title field is the primary key. To set the Title as a primary key, choose the Title field from the <u>P</u>rimary combo box, then click OK. The Title field is now a primary key for the MMData table.

Fig. 14.6
Using Data Manager to add a primary key to a database table.

7. Any additional indexes can now be added to the database table. Click the <u>I</u>ndexes button in the Table Editor (refer to Fig. 14.5) and the Add Index dialog box is shown as in Figure 14.7. The Primary Index option is already checked, which indicates the Primary index already exists. The Primary index is the same as the Primary key that was added in the preceding step. Additional indexes can be added by clicking the Add button in the Add Index dialog box. Ckick OK when finished.

Fig. 14.7
Creating addi-
tional indexes for
a database table is
easy using Data
Manager.

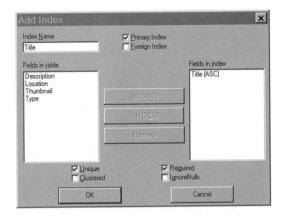

8. At this point, the database table has been created and the appropriate fields and indexes used by the Multimedia Content Browser have been added. Exit the Data Manager application.

The preceding steps indicate how to create the database used by the Multimedia Content Browser application. Shown in Table 14.2 is a list of the field types supported by the JET Engine. These types of fields can be added through Data Manager for further expansion of the Content Browser application or for your own applications.

Table 14.2	**Field Types Used by Data Manager**	
Field Type	**Description**	**Length**
Byte	Numeric value that is one byte in length.	1 byte
Integer	Number value that is two bytes in length.	2 bytes
Long	Numeric value that is 4 bytes in length.	4 bytes
Single	Floating-point value that is 4 bytes in length.	4 bytes
Double	Floating-point value that is 8 bytes in length.	8 bytes
Text	Alphanumeric value that has a maximum length of 255 characters.	Variable length— maximum length of 255 bytes.

Field Type	Description	Length
Boolean	A Yes/No field.	1 byte
Currency	A numeric value used to represent money.	8 bytes
Date/Time	A numeric value used to represent date/time values.	8 bytes
Memo	Alphanumeric value that can be longer than 255 characters.	Variable length field with no maximum value.
Long Binary	BLOB field.	A variable length binary field with no maximum length.

Using the Data Access Objects

Creating databases using the Data Manager application is not the only method for creating a database. The Data Access Objects can be used also. To create the database for the Multimedia Content Browser, the following Data Access Objects are used:

Object	Description
DBEngine	The DBEngine is used as the top-level interface for accessing all subsequent Data Access Objects.
Workspace	You only use the default workspace provided with DBEngine. This is used to provide access to the real objects that are going to be used—the Database, TableDef, Field, and Index objects. The Workspace object is used to create the database file, in this case MMDB1.MDB.
Database	This is the object used for adding the database TableDefs, Indexes, and Fields necessary for your database definition. The Database object is used to create the table definition or TableDef object.

(continues)

Object	Description
TableDef	The table definition contains collections of the fields and indexes created for the table. This object is also used for creating Index and Field objects.
Field	The Field object defines the characteristics of a field in the database table.
Index	The Index object defines the characteristics of a key or index for the database table.

Before creating a database with Data Access Objects, you must close any database files that the application has opened. Because the database files will be deleted and re-created, the files must not be opened. To create a database using the Data Access Objects, perform the following steps:

1. If the application has opened the database files that are going to be created, these files must be closed. In the Content Browser application, this is performed by closing the open Recordsets and databases. Even though the default workspace is opened, you do not have to explicitly close it because it will be closed automatically when the database is closed. After the database is closed, the database file is deleted by performing the Kill function.

 NOTE Operations, which define the database, are not typically performed within an application that manipulates the data. Data-definition operations are usually reserved for system administration applications.

2. To construct a database definition using the Data Access Objects, create the database file. The Workspace object creates the database via the CreateDatabase method, which creates the JET database file for your application. In the Content Browser application, this database file is MMDB1.MDB.

3. After the database file is created, the table definitions need to be created. The Data Access Objects create a database table through the TableDef object, which is created by calling the CreateTableDef method of the Database object. The Content Browser application uses the MMData table for storing its information.

IV

4. Once the `TableDef` object is created, the fields that define the table need to be added. This is a two-step process. The first step is to call the `CreateField` method of the `TableDef` object. This method takes three parameters. The first is the name of the field; the second parameter is the type of field to create; the third parameter is the length of the field.

The third parameter is optional and is only needed for field types, such as `text` that require a specific length.

After the field is created, the properties for that field must be set. For the Content Browser application, this requires only setting the `Required` property to `True`. After the field is created and the specific properties are set, the field is appended to the `TableDef` object by calling the `Append` method and passing in the variable holding the field object as the only parameter. The following code sample copied from Listing 14.1 illustrates this concept:

```
Set TempFld1 = TempTable.CreateField("Title", dbText, 50)
TempFld1.Required = True
TempTable.Fields.Append TempFld1
```

5. Once the fields have been added to the `TableDef` object, an index(s) must be created. An index or key dictates how the database engine will store information to allow for fast, efficient searching and retrieval of the data. The JET Engine requires that at least one key be created for each table. One of the keys must be a *primary key*. A primary key is the index that is most likely to be used when querying information.

6. An index is created by calling the `CreateIndex` method of the `TableDef` object. After an `Index` object is created, the specific properties of the index must be set. For the Content Browser application, the properties `Required`, `Unique`, and `Primary` are set to `True`. Setting the `Required` property indicates that the fields, which compose this index, cannot be empty. The `Unique` property indicates that the fields composing the index cannot be duplicates; for example, the Content Browser application uses the Title field for its primary key. The value of Title must be unique for all records. The `Primary` property sets this index to be the primary index for the table.

There can only be one primary index per table and the primary index must have the `Required` and `Unique` properties set to `True`.

7. After the index object's properties have been set, a field object for each field in the index must be created and appended to the Index object. This is similar to the operations performed for adding fields to the TableDef object. All fields created for an index must already exist in the TableDef object. The following code fragment from Listing 14.1 demonstrates these techniques:

```
Set TempIndex = TempTable.CreateIndex("Title")
    TempIndex.Required = True
    TempIndex.Primary = True
    TempIndex.Unique = True
    Set TempFld1 = TempTable.CreateField("Title")
```

8. The last step required for creating the database is to append the TableDef and Index objects to the Database object. Once this is done, the database definition is complete and stored within the database file. You can now close the database and reinitialize the programs database variables with the newly created database structure.

Listing 14.1 is from the Content Browser application. This code is invoked when the CreateDatabase menu item is selected in the database.

Listing 14.1   DACCESS1.FRM. Creating a database using the Data Access Objects.

```
Private Sub CreateDatabase_Click()
    Dim LastDB As String
    Dim TempDB As Database
    Dim TempTable As TableDef
    Dim TempFld1 As Field
    Dim TempFld2 As Field
    Dim TempFld3 As Field
    Dim TempFld4 As Field

    Dim TempIndex As Index
    ' first close the open databases
    Rs.Close
    Db.Close
    LastDB = "MMDB1.MDB"
    Kill LastDB
    ' second create a database file

    Set TempDB = _
      DBEngine.Workspaces(0).CreateDatabase(LastDB, _
        dbLangGeneral, dbVersion20)
    Set TempTable = TempDB.CreateTableDef("MMData")
    Set TempFld1 = TempTable.CreateField("Title", dbText, 50)
    TempFld1.Required = True
    TempTable.Fields.Append TempFld1
```

```
Set TempFld2 = TempTable.CreateField("Description", dbMemo)
TempTable.Fields.Append TempFld2
Set TempFld3 = TempTable.CreateField("Location", dbText, 255)
TempFld3.Required = True
TempTable.Fields.Append TempFld3
Set TempFld4 = TempTable.CreateField("Type", dbByte)
TempFld4.Required = True
TempTable.Fields.Append TempFld4

Set TempIndex = TempTable.CreateIndex("Title")
TempIndex.Required = True
TempIndex.Primary = True
TempIndex.Unique = True
Set TempFld1 = TempTable.CreateField("Title")

TempIndex.Fields.Append TempFld1
TempTable.Indexes.Append TempIndex
TempDB.TableDefs.Append TempTable

' close the temporary database objects
TempDB.Close
'OpenOriginalDatabase variables

Set Db = Workspaces(0).OpenDatabase("MMDB1.MDB")
Set Rs = Db.OpenRecordset("MMData", dbOpenDynaset)
If Rs.BOF = False Then
    Rs.MoveLast
    Total = Rs.RecordCount
End If
If Total = -1 Then
    RecPos = 0
    RecCount = 0
Else
    RecCount = Total
End If

End Sub
```

Building a File-based Multimedia Content Browser

File-based multimedia database applications are fairly straightforward to develop as long as you are prepared to handle the limitations of this type of database application. What makes these applications easy to develop is that they have only requirement: the database engine must support the Text (Alphanumeric) field type. Because all database engines support the text data type, this is not a concern.

The Content Browser database field, Location, is a text field that is used to store the location and name of the file. When adding a record to the database, simply fill in the appropriate field with the file specification of the multimedia data and add the record to the database. Retrieval works in the reverse order: query the record from the database and place the information in the text field.

Figure 14.8 shows a picture of the Multimedia Content Browser. As you can see, there are text fields used for storing information about the multimedia file. There is also a viewing area used for displaying the multimedia information.

Fig. 14.8

Screen shot showing the user interface of the Multimedia Content Browser.

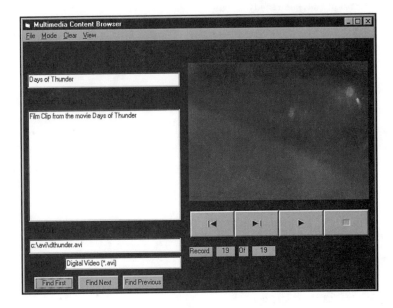

For displaying multimedia information, standard Visual Basic controls are used. While these controls allow you to construct your application with no third-party controls, they also limit the available functionality and types of information that can be displayed for the same reasons.

Table 14.3 shows the types of multimedia data supported by the Content Browser application and the type of control used for displaying the information.

Table 14.3 Multimedia Data Types Supported by the Multimedia Content Browser Application

Data Type	File Extension	Control Used for Display
Digital video	.AVI	MCI control
Wave audio	.WAV	MCI control
MIDI audio	.RMI, .MID	MCI control

Data Type	File Extension	Control Used for Display
Bitmapped graphics	BMP, .ICO, .CUR,	Image control
Vector graphics	.DIB, .WMF	Image control
Animation	.FLI, .FLC	MCI control

The controls and layout of the Multimedia Content Browser application are shown in Listing 14.2.

Listing 14.2   DACCESS1.FRM. Form Layout for Multimedia Browser application.

```
VERSION 4.00
Begin VB.Form DAccess1
   BackColor       =    &H00FF0000&
   Caption         =    "Multimedia Database -
     File Specification Technique"
   ClientHeight    =    6615
   ClientLeft      =    765
   ClientTop       =    585
   ClientWidth     =    9405
   BeginProperty Font
      name         =    "MS Sans Serif"
      charset      =    1
      weight       =    400
      size         =    8.25
      underline    =    0    'False
      italic       =    0    'False
      strikethrough =   0    'False
   EndProperty
   Height          =    7305
   Left            =    705
   LinkTopic       =    "Form1"
   ScaleHeight     =    441
   ScaleMode       =    3    'Pixel
   ScaleWidth      =    627
   Top             =    -45
   Width           =    9525
   Begin VB.CommandButton FindPrevious
      Caption      =    "Find Previous"
      Height       =    375
      Left         =    2640
      TabIndex     =    17
      Top          =    6120
      Width        =    1095
   End
   Begin VB.CommandButton FindNext
      Caption      =    "Find Next"
```

(continues)

Listing 14.2   Continued

```
         Height          =    375
         Left            =    1440
         TabIndex        =    16
         Top             =    6120
         Width           =    1095
      End
      Begin VB.CommandButton FindFirst
         Caption         =    "Find First"
         Height          =    375
         Left            =    240
         TabIndex        =    15
         Top             =    6120
         Width           =    1095
      End
      Begin VB.CommandButton Cancel
         Caption         =    "Cancel"
         Height          =    375
         Left            =    6480
         TabIndex        =    10
         Top             =    6120
         Visible         =    0     'False
         Width           =    1095
      End
      Begin VB.CommandButton OK
         Caption         =    "OK"
         Height          =    375
         Left            =    4920
         TabIndex        =    9
         Top             =    6120
         Visible         =    0     'False
         Width           =    1095
      End
      Begin VB.ComboBox MMType
         Height          =    300
         ItemData        =    "DACCESS1.frx":0000
         Left            =    1080
         List            =    "DACCESS1.frx":001C
         Style           =    1     'Simple Combo
         TabIndex        =    7
         Top             =    5640
         Width           =    3135
      End
      Begin VB.TextBox Location
         Height          =    375
         Left            =    120
         TabIndex        =    5
         Top             =    5160
         Width           =    4095
      End
      Begin VB.TextBox Description
         Height          =    2895
         Left            =    120
         MultiLine       =    -1    'True
         TabIndex        =    1
         Top             =    1800
```

```
      Width         =    4095
   End
   Begin VB.TextBox Title
      Height        =    375
      Left          =    120
      TabIndex      =    0
      Top           =    840
      Width         =    4095
   End
   Begin DragdropLib.Dragdrop DropFiles
      Height        =    615
      Left          =    2040
      TabIndex      =    19
      TabStop       =    0        'False
      Top           =    120
      Visible       =    0        'False
      Width         =    2175
      _version      =    65536
      _extentx      =    3836
      _extenty      =    1085
      _stockprops   =    0
   End
   Begin VB.Label AudioDesc
      Caption       =    "Label4"
      Height        =    255
      Left          =    7560
      TabIndex      =    18
      Top           =    5640
      Visible       =    0        'False
      Width         =    495
   End
   Begin VB.Label RecCount
      Alignment     =    2        'Center
      Caption       =    "0"
      Height        =    255
      Left          =    6120
      TabIndex      =    14
      Top           =    5400
      Width         =    615
   End
   Begin VB.Label RecPos
      Alignment     =    2        'Center
      Caption       =    "0"
      Height        =    255
      Left          =    5160
      TabIndex      =    13
      Top           =    5400
      Width         =    495
   End
   Begin VB.Label Label3
      Caption       =    "Of"
      Height        =    255
      Left          =    5760
      TabIndex      =    12
      Top           =    5400
```

(continues)

```
Listing 14.2   Continued
        Width            =   255
     End
     Begin VB.Label Label2
        Caption          =   "Record"
        Height           =   255
        Left             =   4440
        TabIndex         =   11
        Top              =   5400
        Width            =   615
     End
     Begin VB.Image Graphics
        Height           =   495
        Left             =   8640
        Stretch          =   -1   'True
        Top              =   6000
        Width            =   495
     End
     Begin MCI.MMControl MMCtrl
        Height           =   735
        Left             =   4440
        TabIndex         =   8
        Top              =   4440
        Width            =   4815
        _version         =   65536
        pausevisible     =   0    'False
        backvisible      =   0    'False
        stepvisible      =   0    'False
        recordvisible    =   0    'False
        ejectvisible     =   0    'False
        _extentx         =   8493
        _extenty         =   1296
        _stockprops      =   32
        borderstyle      =   1
     End
     Begin VB.Shape Display
        Height           =   3600
        Left             =   4440
        Top              =   600
        Width            =   4800
     End
     Begin VB.Label Label1
        BackColor        =   &H00FF0000&
        Caption          =   "Type:"
        BeginProperty Font
           name          =   "Courier New"
           charset       =   1
           weight        =   700
           size          =   12
           underline     =   0    'False
           italic        =   0    'False
           strikethrough =   0    'False
        EndProperty
        Height           =   255
```

```
      Index            =    3
      Left             =    120
      TabIndex         =    6
      Top              =    5640
      Width            =    855
   End
   Begin VB.Label Label1
      BackColor        =    &H00FF0000&
      Caption          =    "Location:"
      BeginProperty Font
         name          =    "Courier New"
         charset       =    1
         weight        =    700
         size          =    12
         underline     =    0    'False
         italic        =    0    'False
         strikethrough =    0    'False
      EndProperty
      Height           =    255
      Index            =    2
      Left             =    120
      TabIndex         =    4
      Top              =    4800
      Width            =    1335
   End
   Begin VB.Label Label1
      BackColor        =    &H00FF0000&
      Caption          =    "Description:"
      BeginProperty Font
         name          =    "Courier New"
         charset       =    1
         weight        =    700
         size          =    12
         underline     =    0    'False
         italic        =    0    'False
         strikethrough =    0    'False
      EndProperty
      Height           =    255
      Index            =    1
      Left             =    120
      TabIndex         =    3
      Top              =    1440
      Width            =    1695
   End
   Begin VB.Label Label1
      BackColor        =    &H00FF0000&
      Caption          =    "Title:"
      BeginProperty Font
         name          =    "Courier New"
         charset       =    1
         weight        =    700
         size          =    12
         underline     =    0    'False
         italic        =    0    'False
         strikethrough =    0    'False
```

(continues)

Listing 14.2 Continued

```
        EndProperty
        Height          =   255
        Index           =   0
        Left            =   120
        TabIndex        =   2
        Top             =   480
        Width           =   975
    End
    Begin VB.Menu File
        Caption         =   "&File"
        Begin VB.Menu CreateDatabase
            Caption         =   "&Create Database"
        End
        Begin VB.Menu Exit
            Caption         =   "E&xit"
        End
    End
    Begin VB.Menu Mode
        Caption         =   "&Mode"
        Begin VB.Menu Search
            Caption         =   "&Search"
            Checked         =   -1  'True
        End
        Begin VB.Menu Add
            Caption         =   "&Add"
        End
        Begin VB.Menu Modify
            Caption         =   "&Modify"
        End
        Begin VB.Menu Delete
            Caption         =   "&Delete"
        End
    End
    Begin VB.Menu Clear
        Caption         =   "&Clear"
    End
End
Attribute VB_Name = "DAccess1"
Attribute VB_Creatable = False
Attribute VB_Exposed = False
```

Adding Multimedia Information to the Content Browser

As with any database application, before the application is useful, the database must be populated with information. In order for the Content Browser application to add multimedia data, the application must be placed in Add mode. The application is placed in Add mode by choosing the Add command from the Mode menu. Choosing the Add command disables the search buttons used for navigating through the database. Listing 14.3 illustrates placing the Content Browser into Add mode.

Listing 14.3 DACCESS1.FRM. Switching the application into Add mode.

```
Private Sub Add_Click()
    DisableChecks
    Add.Checked = True
    OK.Visible = True
    Cancel.Visible = True
    ShowSearchButtons False
    DropFiles.Visible = True
    DropFiles.AcceptDropFiles = True
    ClearFields
End Sub

Public Sub DisableChecks()
    Search.Checked = False
    Add.Checked = False
    Modify.Checked = False
    Delete.Checked = False
    DropFiles.Visible = False
End Sub

Public Sub ClearFields()
    Title.Text = ""
    Description.Text = ""
    Location.Text = ""
    MMType.ListIndex = -1
    HideControls
End Sub

Public Sub HideControls()
' hide all of the controls then turn on the appropriate control
    MMCtrl.Command = CLOSE_STR
    Graphics.Visible = False
    AudioDesc.Visible = False
End Sub
```

Adding a Single Record

Since populating the database is the most tedious and time-consuming effort for the user, the application offers two modes of adding multimedia information. The first mode is a normal single record add, where the user enters the information about a multimedia file and clicks the OK button to add the record to the database.

The second method is a bulk add, which is done by selecting files from the Windows Explorer (or File Manager) and dropping these files onto the visible drop target on the Add form.

Listing 14.4 illustrates how the Content Browser adds a single record to the multimedia database. When adding a record to a database using the Data

Access Objects, a Recordset object is used. For the Content Browser application, the Recordset object used is global to the application and called Rs. The first step is to place the Recordset object into Add mode by calling the method AddNew.

Once the AddNew method is called, the fields for a new record can be filled. Remember that a Recordset object contains a collection of fields for the table that the Recordset represents. The fields for a new record are filled in by assigning data to them. The subroutine FillRecordFromForm assigns each field of the Recordset with data contained in the form fields. Once the fields are populated, the database is updated by calling the Update method on the Recordset object.

 Inspecting the OK_Click method shows that the routines used for deleting and modifying records are similar in nature to that of adding records.

Listing 14.4 DACCESS1.FRM. Adding a single record to the Multimedia Content Browser database.

```
' general constants
Const Error = -1

'global constants for Content Browser Application
Dim Db As Database
Dim Rs As Recordset
Dim Total As Long
Dim SearchCriteria As String

Private Sub OK_Click()
    If Delete.Checked = True Then
        Rs.Delete
        Rs.MoveNext
    End If
    If Modify.Checked = True Then
        Rs.Edit
        FillRecordFromForm Rs
        Rs.Update
    End If
    If Add.Checked = True Then
        Rs.AddNew
        FillRecordFromForm Rs
        Rs.Update
    End If
    DisableChecks
    Search.Checked = True
    OK.Visible = False
    Cancel.Visible = False
    ShowSearchButtons True
```

```
        UpdateCounts
    End Sub

    Public Sub UpdateCounts()
        RecPos = Rs.AbsolutePosition
        Rs.MoveLast
        RecCount = Rs.RecordCount
    End Sub

    Public Sub FillRecordFromForm(RecSet As Recordset)
        RecSet.Fields("Title").Value = Title
        RecSet.Fields("Description").Value = Description
        RecSet.Fields("Location").Value = Location
        RecSet.Fields("Type").Value = MMType.ListIndex
    End Sub

    Public Sub ShowSearchButtons(vb_Show As Boolean)
        FindFirst.Visible = vb_Show
        FindNext.Visible = vb_Show
        FindPrevious.Visible = vb_Show
    End Sub

    Private Sub Cancel_Click()
        DisableChecks
        Search.Checked = True
        OK.Visible = False
        Cancel.Visible = False
        UpdateCounts
    End Sub
```

Adding Multiple Records

While adding records one at a time is useful, it is not practical when you have to catalog a CD full of multimedia data. For this type of situation, bulk adding of information is essential. The Content Browser achieves bulk adding of records through the use of the DragDrop custom control. The DragDrop custom control enables a form to accept WM_DROPFILE messages that are issued from the Windows Explorer (or File Manager). This allows users to catalog multimedia data by simply selecting files in Explorer and dragging them onto the Content Browser application.

Listing 14.5 demonstrates the adding of files to the Content Browser database using File Manager drag and drop. When a file(s) are dropped from File Manager onto the DragDrop control, the control fires the event FilesDropped. The number of files dropped onto the application is passed into the event. When this event is called, the Content Browser application loops through each file and tries to add it to the database (if the file is a valid multimedia file). This is done by checking for a supported multimedia extension at the end of the filename. If the file is supported, it is added to the database in the same manner that a single record is added.

Listing 14.5 PROJ2\BULKADD.FRM. Bulk adding of records to the Multimedia Content Browser.

```
' list of multimedia extensions that we recognize
Const BMP_EXT = "BMP"
Const AVI_EXT = "AVI"
Const WAV_EXT = "WAV"
Const MID_EXT = "MID"
Const WMF_EXT = "WMF"
Const RMI_EXT = "RMI"
Const FLI_EXT = "FLI"
Const FLC_EXT = "FLC"
Const CUR_EXT = "CUR"
Const ICO_EXT = "ICO"
Const DIB_EXT = "DIB"

'indexes for combobox
Const WAVE_IDX = 0
Const MIDI_IDX = 1
Const BITMAP_IDX = 2
Const CURSOR_IDX = 3
Const ICON_IDX = 4
Const DV_IDX = 5
Const ANIM_IDX = 6
Const METAFILE_IDX = 7

Private Sub DropFiles_FilesDropped(ByVal NumFiles As Integer)
    Dim Cntr As Integer
    Dim FileNm As String
    For Cntr = 0 To NumFiles Step 1
        FileNm = DropFiles.GetFileName(Cntr)
        AddFileToDatabase (FileNm)
    Next Cntr
End Sub

Public Function AddFileToDatabase(FileName As String) As Integer
    If Not Error = FindValidExtension(FileName) Then
        Rs.AddNew
        '// strip the path and just store the file itself
        Rs.Fields("Title").Value = FileName
        Rs.Fields("Description").Value = FileName
        Rs.Fields("Location").Value = FileName
        Rs.Fields("Type").Value = FindValidExtension(FileName)
        Rs.Update
    End If
End Function

Public Function FindValidExtension(File As String) As Integer_
' strip the last 3 characters off of the
' file spec and convert to uppercase
' Then map the extension value to the combobox index

    Dim liststr As String
```

```
        liststr = Right(File, 3)
        liststr = UCase(liststr)
        Select Case liststr
            Case BMP_EXT, DIB_EXT
                FindValidExtension = BITMAP_IDX
            Case WAV_EXT
                FindValidExtension = WAVE_IDX
            Case RMI_EXT, MID_EXT
                FindValidExtension = MIDI_IDX
            Case AVI_EXT
                FindValidExtension = DV_IDX
            Case WMF_EXT
                FindValidExtension = METAFILE_IDX
            Case FLI_EXT, FLC_EXT
                FindValidExtension = ANIM_IDX
            Case CUR_EXT
                FindValidExtension = CURSOR_IDX
            Case ICO_EXT
                FindValidExtension = ICON_IDX
            Case Else
                FindValidExtension = Error
        End Select
    End Function
```

Searching and Locating Multimedia Data

Once the database is populated, you can utilize the application to help locate
your multimedia files. Listing 14.6 demonstrates the search capabilities of the
Content Browser application. When the application form loads, the application database (MMDB1.MDB) is opened using the default workspace object.
Once the database is opened, a Recordset needs to be created. Use a dynaset-
type Recordset so that changes to the database are immediately accessible to
your application. Once the database and Recordset objects are created, the
Recordset is moved to the last record. This operation enables you to determine the number of records the database table contains. The subroutine
Form_Load shows these operations.

To search for information, a search key must be built. Once the search key is
built, a call to the Recordset object's FindFirst method is made with the
search key as the parameter. As you notice, only the Title field is used for
searching. This can be expanded to include any or all of the fields of the
database table. After calling the FindFirst method, the property NoMatch can
be checked to determine if a record was found. The FindNext and FindPrev
methods perform similiar actions to the FindFirst method. FindPrev and
FindNext are used for traversing backwards and forwards through the
database.

If a record is found, the subroutine FillForm is called to display the multimedia data. The filename and path of the file are passed into the subroutine. If the file is a valid multimedia file, the appropriate controls are loaded onto the form and the data file is loaded.

Listing 14.6 PROJ2\BULKADD.FRM. Searching for multimedia data.

```
Private Sub Form_Load()
    Set Db = Workspaces(0).OpenDatabase("MMDB1.MDB")
    Set Rs = Db.OpenRecordset("MMData", dbOpenDynaset)
    If Rs.BOF = False Then
        Rs.MoveLast
        Total = Rs.RecordCount
    End If
    If Total = -1 Then
        RecPos = 0
        RecCount = 0
    Else
        RecCount = Total
    End If
End Sub

Private Sub FindFirst_Click()
    Dim Value As String

    Value = Trim(Title.Text)
    If Len(Value) = 0 Then
        SearchCriteria = "Title > ' '"
        Rs.FindFirst SearchCriteria
    Else
        SearchCriteria = "Title >= '" & Value & "'"
        Rs.FindFirst SearchCriteria
    End If
    If Not Rs.NoMatch Then
        FillForm Rs
    End If

End Sub

Private Sub FindNext_Click()
    Rs.FindNext SearchCriteria
    If Not Rs.NoMatch Then
        FillForm Rs
    End If

End Sub

Private Sub FindPrevious_Click()
    Rs.FindPrevious SearchCriteria
    If Not Rs.NoMatch Then
        FillForm Rs
    End If
```

```
End Sub

Public Sub FillForm(CurrentRecord As Recordset)
    Title = CurrentRecord.Fields("Title").Value
    If Len(CurrentRecord.Fields("Description").Value) Then
        Description = CurrentRecord.Fields("Description").Value
    Else
        Description = ""
    End If
    Location = CurrentRecord.Fields("Location").Value
    DisplayMultimediaObject
End Sub

Private Sub DisplayMultimediaObject()
' this event occurs when the data control
' has been repositioned
    ' first see if the location field is valid
    RecPos = Rs.AbsolutePosition + 1
    Dim File As String
    Dim CBIndex As Integer
    Dim Err As Long
    File = Location.Text
    ' remove the any leading or trailing spaces
    Trim (File)
    If Len(File) = Null Then
        Exit Sub
    End If
    ' check that the file spec is valid
    CBIndex = FindValidExtension(File)
    If CBIndex = Error Then
        Exit Sub
    End If
    ' hide all other multimedia controls
    HideControls
    ' load the object
    Err = LoadMMObject(CBIndex, File)
End Sub

Public Function LoadMMObject(_
    Index As Integer, File As String) As Long
' first set the index of the combobox
    MMType.ListIndex = Index
    Select Case Index
        Case DV_IDX, ANIM_IDX
            LoadMMObject = MciOpen(File, hWnd, MMCtrl, Display)
        Case BITMAP_IDX, CURSOR_IDX, ICON_IDX, METAFILE_IDX
            LoadMMObject = GraphicsOpen(File, Display)
        Case WAVE_IDX, MIDI_IDX
            LoadMMObject = AudioOpen(File,_
                MMCtrl, Display, AudioDesc)
    End Select
End Function

Public Function GraphicsOpen(_
    FileName As String, ViewArea As Object)
```

(continues)

Listing 14.6 Continued

```
        Graphics.Picture = LoadPicture(FileName)
        Graphics.Top = ViewArea.Top
        Graphics.Left = ViewArea.Left
        Graphics.Width = ViewArea.Width
        Graphics.Height = ViewArea.Height
        Graphics.Visible = True
        GraphicsOpen = 0
End Function

'located in mcidefs.bas
Const SPACE = " "

' Basic command strings for the MCI multimedia control
Public Const PLAY_STR = "Play"
Public Const STOP_STR = "Stop"
Public Const OPEN_STR = "Open"
Public Const CLOSE_STR = "Close"
Public Const PAUSE_STR = "Pause"
Public Const BACK_STR = "Back"
Public Const STEP_STR = "Step"
Public Const NEXT_STR = "Next"
Public Const PREV_STR = "Prev"
Public Const SEEK_STR = "Seek"
Public Const RECORD_STR = "Record"
Public Const EJECT_STR = "Eject"
Public Const SOUND_STR = "Sound"
Public Const SAVE_STR = "Save"
Public Const STATUS_STR = "Status"
Public Const SET_STR = "Set"
Public Const FREEZE_STR = "Freeze"
Public Const PUT_STR = "Put"
Public Const WINDOW_STR = "Window"
Public Const WHERE_STR = "Where"

Const GWL_STYLE = -16
Const WS_CHILD = &h40000000
Const WS_VISIBLE = &h10000000

'Variables used for the Retrieving Status Information
Dim FixedStr As String * 50
Dim FileName As String
Dim CommandStr As String
Dim Ret As Long


' Declaration Statements
#If Win32 Then
Private Declare Function mciSendString Lib "WINMM" (_
   ByVal Cmd As String, ByVal RetVal As String, ByVal Len As
Integer, _
        ByVal Notify As Integer) As Long
Private Declare Function mciGetErrorString Lib "WINMM" (_
```

```
    ByVal Err As Long, ByVal RetVal As String, _
        ByVal Len As Integer) As Integer
Private Declare Function SetParent Lib "User32" ( _
    ByVal Child As Integer, ByVal Parent As Integer) As Integer
Private Declare Function GetWindowLong Lib "User32" ( _
    ByVal Win As Integer, ByVal Value As Integer) As Long
Private Declare Function SetWindowLong Lib "User32" ( _
    ByVal Win As Integer, ByVal Offset As Integer, _
    ByVal Value As Long) As Long
#Else
Private Declare Function mciSendString Lib "MMSYSTEM" ( _
    ByVal Cmd As String, ByVal RetVal As String, ByVal Len As _
    Integer, ByVal Notify As Integer) As Long
Private Declare Function mciGetErrorString Lib "MMSYSTEM" ( _
    ByVal Err As Long, ByVal RetVal As String, ByVal Len As Integer)
As Integer
Private Declare Function SetParent Lib "User" ( _
    ByVal Child As Integer, ByVal Parent As Integer) As Integer
Private Declare Function GetWindowLong Lib "User" ( _
    ByVal Win As Integer, ByVal Value As Integer) As Long
Private Declare Function SetWindowLong Lib "User" ( _
    ByVal Win As Integer, ByVal Offset As Integer, ByVal Value _
    As Long) As Long

#End If

  Public Function MciOpen(FileName As String, FrmHwnd As Integer, _
    MMCtrl As Object, PlaybackArea As Object) As Long
    MMCtrl.Command = CLOSE_STR
    MMCtrl.FileName = FileName
    MMCtrl.Command = OPEN_STR
    If Not MMCtrl.Error Then
        CommandStr = STATUS_STR & SPACE & FileName & _
          SPACE & "window handle"
        If 0 = SendCommand(CommandStr) Then
            i% = SetParent(CInt(FixedStr), FrmHwnd)
            l = SetWindowLong(CInt(FixedStr), GWL_STYLE, WS_CHILD)
        End If
        CommandStr = PUT_STR & SPACE & FileName & " window at " & _
          PlaybackArea.Left & SPACE & PlaybackArea.Top & SPACE & _
          PlaybackArea.Width & SPACE & PlaybackArea.Height
        MciOpen = SendCommand(CommandStr)
    Else
        MciOpen = MMCtrl.Error
    End If
End Function

Public Function SendCommand(Cmd As String) As Long
    SendCommand = mciSendString(Cmd, FixedStr, 49, 0)
End Function

Public Sub MciClose(MMCtrl As Object)
    MMCtrl.Command = CLOSE_STR
End Sub
```

(continues)

Listing 14.6 Continued

```
Public Function AudioOpen(FileName As String, _
  MMCtrl As Object, ViewArea As Object, AudLabel As Object) As Long
    AudLabel.Top = ViewArea.Top
    AudLabel.Left = ViewArea.Left
    AudLabel.Width = ViewArea.Width
    AudLabel.Height = ViewArea.Height
    AudLabel.Caption = "Playing Audio File " & FileName
    AudLabel.Visible = True

    MMCtrl.Command = CLOSE_STR
    MMCtrl.FileName = FileName
    MMCtrl.Command = OPEN_STR
    AudioOpen = MMCtrl.Error
End Function
```

BLOB-based Multimedia Databases

BLOB or Binary Large Objects is a technique where the multimedia information is stored in a database field rather than in a file. This technique provides information security and a common repository for storing the multimedia information. It is also more demanding for the database engine and the developer. An example of an application that utilizes BLOB information stored in a database is an insurance damage claims application. Here the insurance agent stores pictures of the damaged property in a database along with damage report information.

The JET Engine utilized by Visual Basic, supports the use of BLOB fields. Actually, JET supports two types of BLOB fields—the Memo field and the OLE field. The Memo field is used primarily for large text objects and can contain up to 1.2 GB of information per record. An OLE field is used for large binary data such as images or audio and contains up to 1.2 GB of information per record.

Not all databases support BLOB fields. There is also a lack of consistency between database implementations, such as the largest size of information that can be stored in an individual record. If you are developing applications that are to be database-independent, then you must examine the specific BLOB limitations on a per database basis.

As with file-based multimedia databases, there are benefits and drawbacks to BLOB databases.

Benefits of BLOB-based multimedia databases

Multimedia information is secured from external applications.

Networked applications can be created and are easily administered.

Fast performance for retrieving information into global memory handles.

Easy to distribute applications.

Drawbacks of BLOB-based multimedia databases

Multimedia information cannot be shared between applications.

External DLLs or tools must be used for storing global memory handles such as bitmaps and palettes in a BLOB field.

BLOB fields are not supported by all database engines.

Slow performance if BLOB information must be retrieved into a file before it can be used by a display tool.

Extending the Content Browser to BLOB Fields

In the preceding sections, you saw how a file-based multimedia Content Browser application was created. In this section, the file-based Content Browser is extended into a BLOB Content Browser. This is done by storing thumbnail images of each multimedia data item into a BLOB field associated with each record. When a search is performed, the thumbnail images will be retrieved and displayed in a `Gallery` control.

For this application, two specialty controls are utilized:

- Lenel Systems `Gallery` control displays thumbnail images of any type of multimedia file. A thumbnail is a scaled down version of the original multimedia file. An example is a 60×90 bitmap of the first frame of a Video for Windows file. This thumbnail image graphically represents the Video for Windows file. The `Gallery` control allows for a graphical content viewer for your application.

- A memory controller control, developed in Chapter 12, "Creating and Using OLE Custom Controls," is used for storing and retrieving global memory handles of thumbnail images to the database.

To extend the Content Browser application to accept BLOB information, a field of type `BLOB` must be added to the database record layout. This is accomplished by adding a field of type `LongBinary` to the database table through the Data Manager. Extend the MMData table definition to include a field named `Thumbnail` of type `LongBinary` (refer to "Using the Data Manager Application," in this chapter for information on the MMData table). The following is the resulting table layout for the Content Browser application:

Field Name	Type	Length	Description
Title	Text	50 bytes	Title of the multimedia object (for example, Windsurfing Video).
Type	Numeric	1 byte	Type of multimedia object indicated by numeric constants (for example, 0—Audio Wave File).
Description	Memo	Variable	Text description of the multimedia object.
Location	Text	255 bytes	File specification of the multimedia object (for example, c:\windows\cars.bmp).
Thumbnail	LongBinary	Variable	Contains thumbnail bitmap of multimedia object.

To add the thumbnail field to the database using the Data Access Objects, the function CreateDatabase_Click is expanded as shown in Listing 14.7.

Listing 14.7   PROJ2\BULKADD.FRM. Creating a database containing BLOB fields.

```
Private Sub CreateDatabase_Click()
    Dim LastDB As String
    Dim TempDB As Database
    Dim TempTable As TableDef
    Dim TempFld1 As Field
    Dim TempFld2 As Field
    Dim TempFld3 As Field
    Dim TempFld4 As Field
    Dim TempFld5 As Field

    Dim TempIndex As Index
    ' first close the open databases
    Rs.Close
    Db.Close
    LastDB = "MMDB1.MDB"
    Kill LastDB
    ' second create a datbase file

    Set TempDB = DBEngine.Workspaces(0).CreateDatabase( _
      LastDB, dbLangGeneral, dbVersion20)
    Set TempTable = TempDB.CreateTableDef("MMData")
    Set TempFld1 = TempTable.CreateField("Title", dbText, 50)
    TempFld1.Required = True
    TempTable.Fields.Append TempFld1
    Set TempFld2 = TempTable.CreateField("Description", dbMemo)
    TempTable.Fields.Append TempFld2
    Set TempFld3 = TempTable.CreateField("Location", dbText, 255)
```

```
                TempFld3.Required = True
                TempTable.Fields.Append TempFld3
                Set TempFld4 = TempTable.CreateField("Type", dbByte)
                TempFld4.Required = False
                TempTable.Fields.Append TempFld4
                Set TempFld5 = TempTable.CreateField( _
                    "Thumbnail", dbLongBinary)
                TempFld5.Required = False
                TempTable.Fields.Append TempFld5

                Set TempIndex = TempTable.CreateIndex("Title")
                TempIndex.Required = True
                TempIndex.Primary = True
                TempIndex.Unique = True
                Set TempFld1 = TempTable.CreateField("Title")

                TempIndex.Fields.Append TempFld1
                TempTable.Indexes.Append TempIndex
                TempDB.TableDefs.Append TempTable

                ' close the temporary database objects
                TempDB.Close
                Set Db = Workspaces(0).OpenDatabase("MMDB1.MDB")
                Set Rs = Db.OpenRecordset("MMData", dbOpenDynaset)
                If Rs.BOF = False Then
                    Rs.MoveLast
                    Total = Rs.RecordCount
                End If
                If Total = -1 Then
                    RecPos = 0
                    RecCount = 0
                Else
                    RecCount = Total
                End If
            End Sub
```

Adding Multimedia Data to BLOB Fields

Once the database layout is completed, two new forms are added to the
project. One form adds multimedia data to the database, while the other
provides a visual display or thumbnail image based on the form search
criteria.

The form BulkFrm is used for adding multimedia records and thumbnails to
the database. As mentioned previously, this form uses two special controls,
the Gallery control from Lenel Systems, which is used for displaying thumbnail images of any data type. The second is a memory manager control,
which is developed in Chapter 12, "Creating and Using OLE Custom Controls." This control accepts any Windows global memory handle and returns
the data represented by these handles to the user. It also constructs a memory
handle if data buffers are passed into it. Listing 14.8 shows the form setup
parameters for the bulk add form.

Listing 14.8   PROJ2\BULKADD.FRM. Control settings for the BulkFRM form.

```
VERSION 4.00
Begin VB.Form BulkFrm
   BorderStyle     =   1  'Fixed Single
   Caption         =   "Bulk Add of Multimedia Files"
   ClientHeight    =   6630
   ClientLeft      =   390
   ClientTop       =   480
   ClientWidth     =   9375
   Height          =   7035
   Left            =   330
   LinkTopic       =   "Form1"
   ScaleHeight     =   6630
   ScaleWidth      =   9375
   Top             =   135
   Width           =   9495
   Begin VB.CommandButton Cancel
      Caption      =   "Cancel"
      Height       =   495
      Left         =   5640
      TabIndex     =   1
      Top          =   6000
      Width        =   1575
   End
   Begin VB.CommandButton OK
      Caption      =   "OK"
      Height       =   495
      Left         =   1200
      TabIndex     =   0
      Top          =   6000
      Width        =   1695
   End
   Begin TnglryLibCtl.TNGallery AddGallery
      Height       =   5535
      Left         =   240
      TabIndex     =   2
      TabStop      =   0     'False
      Top          =   240
      Width        =   8655
      _version     =   65536
      _extentx     =   15266
      _extenty     =   9763
      _stockprops  =   100
      borderstyle  =   1
      BeginProperty altfont _
         {FB8F0823-0164-101B-84ED-08002B2EC713}
         name         =   "Arial"
         charset      =   1
         weight       =   400
         size         =   9.75
         underline    =   0     'False
         italic       =   0     'False
         strikethrough =  -1    'True
      EndProperty
```

```
      End
      Begin MemctrlLib.Memctrl MemMngr
         Left          =   3840
         Top           =   5880
         _version      =   65536
         _extentx      =   1720
         _extenty      =   1085
         _stockprops   =   0
      End
   End
   Attribute VB_Name = "BulkFrm"
   Attribute VB_Creatable = False
   Attribute VB_Exposed = False
```

As shown in Listing 14.8, the DragDrop property of the Gallery control is set to True. This property enables the Gallery control to accept WM_DROPFILES messages from the Windows Explorer. Any file that is dropped will appear in the control as a thumbnail image. If the file is a multimedia file, the contents of the file will be represented in the thumbnail image. If the file data cannot be displayed, such as for audio data, a default thumbnail is provided. Figure 14.9 illustrates the form use for adding records to the database through the Gallery control.

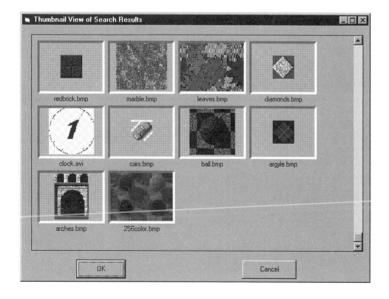

Fig. 14.9
You can add multimedia data through the Gallery control.

Once the multimedia records are placed in the Gallery control, the records are ready to be added to the database. This is done by clicking the form's OK button. Listing 14.9 demonstrates how thumbnail images are retrieved from the Gallery control and added as new records to the database.

Listing 14.9   PROJ2\BULKADD.FRM. Adding multimedia data to database BLOB fields.

```
Public Function AddFile(ByRef FileName As String, _
  Thumbnail As Integer) As Integer
    Dim Ext As String
    Ext = RightB(FileName, 3)
    If Not Error = IsValidExtension(Ext) Then
        Rs.AddNew
        '// strip the path and just store the file itself
        Rs.Fields("Title").Value = FileName
        Rs.Fields("Description").Value = FileName
        Rs.Fields("Location").Value = FileName
        Rs.Fields("Type").Value = IsValidExtension(Ext)
        AddThumbnailToDB Thumbnail
        Rs.Update
    End If
End Function

Private Sub OK_Click()
    Dim Cnt As Integer
    Dim FileSpec As String
    Dim Thumbnail As Integer
    For Cnt = 0 To (AddGallery.NumThumbNails - 1) Step 1
        Thumbnail = AddGallery.GetHDIBThumbNail(Cnt, True)
        FileSpec = AddGallery.GetFileSpec(Cnt)
        AddFile FileSpec, Thumbnail
    Next Cnt
    Cancel_Click
End Sub

Public Sub AddThumbnailToDB(Thumbnail As Integer)
    Const ChunkSize = 16384 ' Set size of chunk.
    Dim NumChunks As Integer, TotalSize As Long, X As Integer
    Rs!Thumbnail = ""   ' Initialize Notes field.
    MemMngr.MemoryHandle = Thumbnail
    NumChunks = MemMngr.GetNumBuffers(ChunkSize)
    Dim Buffer As String * ChunkSize
    Dim LastBuffer As String
    For X = 0 To (NumChunks - 1) Step 1
        TotalSize = MemMngr.GetBuffer(Buffer, ChunkSize, X)
        If Not TotalSize = ChunkSize Then
            LastBuffer = LeftB(Buffer, TotalSize)
            Rs![Thumbnail].AppendChunk LastBuffer
        Else
            Rs![Thumbnail].AppendChunk Buffer
        End If
    Next X
End Sub
```

When the OK button is clicked, a query of the Gallery control is performed to get the total number of thumbnails present in the control. For each image in the Gallery control, the file information and handle to the thumbnail are retrieved. The file information is checked against the file formats in your Content Browser application. If the file format is valid, then the AddNew method on the Recordset object is called. This prepares the Recordset data buffers to accept a new record. All of the field's values, except for the thumbnail, are assigned at this time in the same manner that a single record is added to the database as shown on the application's main form in the previous section, "Adding Multimedia Information to the Content Browser."

To add the thumbnail, the handle representing a DIB for each image in the Gallery control is used. It is best to use DIB (device-independent) memory handles rather than HBITMAP or device-dependent memory handles. This enables your application to be portable regardless of the display resolutions. The handle to the DIB is owned by the Gallery, so the AutoDelete property on your memory manager control is set to False. This property indicates that the control is not to delete the handle from memory when the MemoryHandle property is changed or the control is deleted.

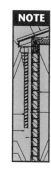

NOTE

For those of you who do not know about Windows memory handles, I will provide a short background on them for you now. Most Windows GDI and User resources such as bitmaps, menus, brushes, HDCs, hWnds, and so on are represented by memory handles. In 16-bit Windows these are 16-bit integer values while in 32-bit Windows, they are 32-bit integer values. These handles represent a block of memory that contains data. The data cannot be directly obtained through the memory handle. In order for the memory to be accessed or changed, the memory handle must be de-referenced through the Windows API GlobalLock. This returns a pointer to the block of memory. Once the pointer to the memory is obtained, the standard memory manipulation routines can be performed.

Because Visual Basic is not designed to manipulate pointers, a memory manager control (developed in Chapter 12) handles this task for you. All you have to do is supply the control with a memory handle and provide a fixed string to the control and it fills the string with the data. Once the data is retrieved from the control, the method AppendChunk is called on the Recordset's BLOB field. The AppendChunk method calculates the length of the string passed into it and appends the data contained in the string to the end of the field. As can be seen from the subroutine AddThumbnailToDB, the memory manager control is queried to see how many buffers of a fixed size are needed to retrieve the thumbnail information. A loop is executed to retrieve each buffer and append it to the end of the Recordset's Thumbnail field. As you can see, for the last buffer, the memory is transferred from the fixed buffer to a variable-length buffer. If this is not done, the BLOB field contains all of the information contained in the fixed buffer rather than the amount returned by the memory manager method GetBuffer.

Now that the thumbnail images are added into the database, they need to be retrieved. A search form was created to fill a Gallery control with thumbnail images from the database, based on the Recordset's search criteria. As you can see from Listing 14.10, the form layout looks very similar to the bulk add form except that the Gallery control's DragDrop property is set to False. You do not want any additional thumbnail images added to the gallery in the search results form.

Listing 14.10 PROJ2\SEARCHVI.FRM. Viewing controls used for viewing thumbnails in the Lenel Gallery.

```
VERSION 4.00
Begin VB.Form SearchView
   Caption         =   "Thumbnail View of Search Results"
   ClientHeight    =   6645
   ClientLeft      =   375
   ClientTop       =   390
   ClientWidth     =   9270
   Height          =   7050
   Left            =   315
   LinkTopic       =   "Form1"
   ScaleHeight     =   6645
   ScaleWidth      =   9270
   Top             =   45
   Width           =   9390
   Begin VB.CommandButton Cancel
      Caption      =   "Cancel"
      Height       =   495
      Left         =   5880
      TabIndex     =   1
      Top          =   6120
      Width        =   1455
   End
   Begin VB.CommandButton OK
      Caption      =   "OK"
      Height       =   495
      Left         =   1440
      TabIndex     =   0
      Top          =   6120
      Width        =   1335
   End
   Begin TnglryLibCtl.TNGallery SearchGallery
      Height       =   5655
      Left         =   240
      TabIndex     =   2
      TabStop      =   0    'False
      Top          =   240
      Width        =   8895
      _version     =   65536
      _extentx     =   15690
```

```
            _extenty        =    9975
            _stockprops     =    100
            borderstyle     =    1
            BeginProperty altfont _
                {FB8F0823-0164-101B-84ED-08002B2EC713}
                name            =    "Arial"
                charset         =    1
                weight          =    400
                size            =    9.75
                underline       =    0     'False
                italic          =    0     'False
                strikethrough   =    -1    'True
            EndProperty
        End
        Begin MemctrlLib.Memctrl SrchMem
            Left            =    3360
            Top             =    6120
            _version        =    65536
            _extentx        =    1508
            _extenty        =    873
            _stockprops     =    0
        End
    End
End
Attribute VB_Name = "SearchView"
Attribute VB_Creatable = False
Attribute VB_Exposed = False
```

Listing 14.11 shows how the search form manipulates the application's `Recordset` upon form load. The `Recordset` is traversed for each record that matches the search criteria. For each record, an entry is made to the `Gallery` control.

To retrieve the thumbnail from the database, the converse of the operations performed in the bulk add form is done. The field size of the current record's `Thumbnail` field is obtained. Using this value, the number of fixed size buffers needed to represent the image is calculated. The memory manager control is asked to create a new global memory handle of the size of the image through the method `CreateMemoryHandle`. Once this memory handle is created, the memory block is filled with data buffers obtained from calls to `GetChunk` on the `Thumbnail` field. This data buffer is transferred to the memory manager control and once filled, the memory handle is retrieved and passed to the `Gallery` control. The `Gallery` control only makes a copy of the handle, so you are responsible for deleting the memory handle. This is done by setting the `AutoDelete` property of the memory control to `True`. Figure 14.10 shows the visual results of a database query.

Fig. 14.10
Using the Lenel
gallery of visual
images to
represent a
database query.

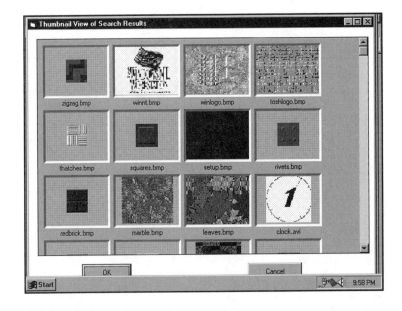

Listing 14.11 PROJ2\SEARCHVI.FRM. How the search form manipulates the application's *Recordset* upon form load.

```
Private Sub Form_Load()
    Rs.FindFirst SearchCriteria
    While Not Rs.NoMatch
        AddToGallery
        Rs.FindNext SearchCriteria
    Wend

End Sub


Public Sub AddToGallery()
    Dim Path As String
    Dim Thumbnail As Integer
    Dim Ret As Boolean
    Path = Rs.Fields("Location").Value
    Thumbnail = GetThumbnailFromDB
    If Thumbnail Then
        Ret = SearchGallery.AddThumbNailFirst(Path, Thumbnail)
    End If
End Sub

Public Function GetThumbnailFromDB() As Integer
    Const ChunkSize = 16384 ' Set size of chunk.
    Dim NumChunks As Integer, TotalSize As Long, _
      X As Integer, Ret As Long
    Dim Buffer As String * ChunkSize
```

```
            TotalSize = Rs![Thumbnail].FieldSize()
            If TotalSize = 0 Then
                GetThumbnailFromDB = 0
            Else
                ' How many chunks?
                NumChunks = TotalSize \ ChunkSize - _
                  (TotalSize Mod ChunkSize <> 0)
                SrchMem.CreateMemoryHandle (TotalSize)

                For X = 0 To (NumChunks - 1) Step 1
                    If X = (NumChunks - 1) Then
                        Buffer = Rs![Thumbnail].GetChunk(X * _
                          ChunkSize, TotalSize Mod ChunkSize)
                        Ret = SrchMem.SetBuffer(Buffer, ChunkSize, X)
                    Else
                        Buffer = Rs![Thumbnail].GetChunk(X * ChunkSize, _
                          ChunkSize)
                        Ret = SrchMem.SetBuffer(Buffer, ChunkSize, X)
                    End If
                Next X
                GetThumbnailFromDB = SrchMem.MemoryHandle
            End If
        End Function
```

This extension of the Content Browser shows how to use and manipulate
BLOB fields to store multimedia data. This data is obtained from memory
handles. The same procedure can be used to retrieve data from files in order
to store the file's contents in a BLOB field. All that is needed is to replace the
memory manager calls with the Visual Basic calls for opening and accessing
files.

From Here...

This chapter has demonstrated the benefits and usefulness from integrating
multimedia and database technologies. Two types of database techniques
were discussed—the file-based multimedia database and the BLOB multimedia database.

You learned how to create databases using the Visual Basic Data Manager and
through the Data Access Objects. Search and retrieval techniques and methods for effectively using BLOB fields with the JET Engine were shown.

■ For a discussion on the use of the audio capabilities of Visual Basic and
the Windows operating systems, see Chapter 4, "Visual Basic Audio
Capabilities."

■ For coverage on the use of graphics, see Chapter 5, "Graphics and Palettes."

■ For more information on the use of digital video within applications, see Chapter 8, "Digital Video Capture and Editing." The use of Lenel Systems Digital Video Data bound control, which can be bound to database applications, is covered.

■ For more information on OLE controls and to view the source code used for developing the controls in the Content Browser application, see Chapter 12, "Creating and Using OLE Custom Controls."

Appendix A

The MCI Command Reference

The MPEG MCI command set is a subset of the digital video MCI command set. This appendix contains all of the MPEG MCI commands, digital video MCI commands, and animation MCI commands.

MPEG MCI Commands

capability

The capability command returns a string containing additional information about the capabilities of MCIAVI.

> capability devicename *parameters*

The following parameters can modify capability:

Parameter	Description
can eject	Returns False.
can freeze	Returns True if the device can freeze data in the frame buffer.
can lock	Returns True if the device can lock portions of the image with the freeze and unfreeze commands.
can play	Returns True.
can record	Returns True if the device can record video.

(continues)

Parameter	Description
can reverse	Returns True if the device can play in reverse.
can save	Returns True if the device can store digitized images, audio and/or video to disk.
can stretch	Returns True if the device can resize an image or motion video in the process of writing it from the frame buffer to the display.
can stretch input	Returns True if the device can resize an image or motion video in the process of digitizing it into the frame buffer.
can test	Returns True if the device recognizes the test keyword.
compound device	Returns True.
device type	Returns MPEG video.
has audio	Returns True if the device supports audio playback.
has still	Returns True if the device works better with single images than motion video files.
maximum play rate	Returns the maximum play rate supported in frames per second.
minimum play rate	Returns the minimum play rate supported in frames per second.
has video	Returns True if the device supports video playback.
uses files	Returns True.
uses palettes	Returns True if video and images use a palette for display.
windows	Returns the number of simultaneous display windows the device can support.

capture

The capture command starts the capture of MPEG video.

> capture devicename *parameters*

The following parameter modifies the capture command:

Parameter	Description
as file	Captures the video to the specified filename.

createvideodc

Creates a `VideoDC` on which the application can draw the sprite to be displayed. The application uses the HBRUSH returned from the status `video brush` command to paint areas where the video will be displayed.

> createvideodc devicename *parameters*

The following parameter modifies the `createvideodc` command:

Parameter	Description
at rect	Specifies the size of the `VideoDC` to be created. If not specified, then the `VideoDC` has the same dimensions as the video window. The coordinates of rect are relative to the video window.

close

The `close` command closes this instance of the MPEG driver and releases all resources associated with it.

> close devicename

configure

The `configure` command invokes an MPEG driver specific dialog box used to configure the MPEG driver.

> configure devicename

copy

The `copy` command copies the current video frame to the Clipboard.

> copy devicename

cue

The `cue` command prepares MPEG driver for playback and leaves it in a paused state.

> cue devicename *parameters*

The following optional parameters modify `cue`:

Parameter	Description
output	Prepares the MPEG driver for playing.
to position	Positions the workspace to the specified position.

freeze

The `freeze` command freezes the video output.

> `freeze` devicename

info

The `info` command returns a string containing information about MPEG driver.

> `info` devicename *parameters*

The following optional parameters modify `info`:

Parameter	Description
file	Returns the name of the file currently loaded.
product	Returns product ID for MPEG manufacturer.
version	Returns the release level of the MPEG driver.
window text	Returns the text string in the title bar of the window associated with the MPEG driver.
video streams	Returns number of video streams in the System stream. Returns 0, if the System stream contains no video stream.
video bitrate	Indicates bitrate of the video stream that is the current stream.
video maxbitrate	Indicates maximum bitrate accepted by the device.
audio streams	Returns number of audio streams in the system stream. Returns 0, if the System stream contains no audio stream.
audio bitrate	Indicates bitrate of the audio stream that is the current stream.
audio samplerate	Sample rate for the audio stream being played back. (For example, 44 or 22 or 11 standing for 44Khz, 22Khz, and 11Khz, respectively.)

open

The open command opens an instance of the MPEG driver.

> open devicename *parameters*

The following parameters modify open:

Parameter	Description
alias alias	Specifies an alias used to reference this instance of the MPEG driver.
elementname	Specifies the name of the device element (file) loaded when the MPEG driver opens.
parent hwnd	Specifies the parent of the default window.
style stylevalue	Specifies the style used for the default window. The following constants are defined for stylevalue: overlapped, popup, and child.
type MPEGVideo	Specifies the device type of the device element.

pause

The pause command pauses playing of motion video or audio.

> pause devicename

play

The play command starts playing the video sequence.

> play devicename *parameters*

The following optional parameters modify play:

Parameters	Description
from position	Specifies the position to seek to before beginning the play.
to position	Specifies the position at which to stop playing.
repeat	Specifies that the video is to be played again, automatically when the end of the video segment is reached.

put

The put command specifies a rectangular region that describes a cropping or scaling option. The rectangular region is defined by the upper-left corner, the width, and the height of the rectangle.

put devicename *parameters*

One of the following parameters must be present to indicate the specific type of rectangle:

Parameter	Description
destination	Restores the initial destination window associated with this instance of the MPEG driver.
destination at rectangle	Specifies which portion of the destination window associated with this instance of MPEG driver is used.
source	Restores the initial source rectangle. The image from this rectangle is scaled to fit in the destination rectangle.
source at rectangle	Specifies which portion of the source is scaled to fit in the destination rectangle. The units for the source rectangle are based on the units for the MPEG file.
window	Restores the initial window size on the display. This command also displays the window.
window at rectangle	Changes the size and location of the display window. The rectangle specified with the at flag is relative to the parent window of the display window (usually the desktop) if the style child flag has been used for the open command. To change the location of the window without changing its height or width, specify zero for the height and width.
window client	Restores the client area of the window.
window client at rectangle	Changes the size and location of the client area of the window. The rectangle specified with the at flag is relative to the parent window of the client window. To change the location of the window without changing its height or width, specify zero for the height and width.

releasevideodc

Releases the VideoDC obtained by the application using the createvideodc command.

releasevideodc devicename *parameter*

Parameter	Description
HDC	VideoDC to release.

resume

The resume command specifies that operation should continue from where it was interrupted by a pause command.

resume devicename

seek

The seek command positions and cues the workspace to the specified position showing the specified frame.

seek devicename *parameters*

One of the following parameters can modify seek:

Parameter	Description
offset bytes	Specifies an absolute byte offset from the beginning of the file at which to begin decoding. It is the application's responsibility to ensure that the offset in the MPEG bitstream is a location that the device can start decoding. This is device-specific.
to position	Specifies the desired new position, measured in units of the current-time format.
to end	Moves the position after the last frame of the workspace.
to start	Moves the position to the first frame of the workspace.

set

The set command sets the state of control items.

set devicename *parameters*

The following parameter can modify set:

Parameter	Description
time format format	Sets the time format to format. The default time format is frames. Milliseconds can be abbreviated as ms. MPEG supports frames and milliseconds.

setaudio

The setaudio command sets various values associated with audio playback and capture.

> setaudio devicename *parameters*

Only one of the following parameters can be present in a setaudio command unless otherwise noted:

Parameter	Description
off	Disables audio.
on	Enables audio.
stream to number	Changes the current audio stream to a new audio stream indicated by number.

setvideo

The setvideo command sets various values associated with video playback.

> setvideo devicename *parameters*

The following optional parameters modify setvideo:

Parameter	Description
off	Disables video display in the window.
on	Enables video display in the window.
stream to number	Changes the current video stream to a new video stream indicated by number.

signal

The signal command identifies a specified position in the workspace.

> signal devicename *parameters*

The following parameters modify signal:

Parameter	Description
at position	Specifies the frame to invoke a signal.
cancel	Indicates the active signal should be removed from the workspace.
every interval	Specifies the period (in the current-time format) to send signals.
return position	An optional parameter that indicates the MPEG driver should send the position value instead of the uservalue value in the window message.
uservalue id	Specifies a value associated with this signal request that is reported back with the window message.

status

The status command returns status information about this instance of the MPEG driver.

> status devicename *parameters*

One of the following parameters modifies status:

Parameter	Description
audio	Returns on if either or both speakers are enabled, and off otherwise.
audio stream	Returns the number of the current audio stream.
length	Returns the length of the longest stream in the .AVI file in the current-time format.
mode	Returns one of the following: not ready, paused, playing, seeking, or stopped.
nominal frame rate	Returns the nominal frame rate associated with the file in units of frames per second times 1000.

(continues)

Parameter	Description
position	Returns the current position in the workspace in the current-time format.
ready	Returns True if this instance of the MPEG driver is ready to accept another command.
speed	Returns the current playback speed.
start position	Returns the start of the media.
time format	Returns the current-time format (frames or milliseconds).
video	Returns on or off, depending on the most recent setvideo.
video brush	Returns the ASCII decimal value for the handle to a brush (HBRUSH) to be used by the application to indicate areas where video should be displayed. Any areas without the HBRUSH color will contain the graphics data that was painted into them.
video stream	Returns the number of the current video stream.
window handle	Returns the ASCII decimal value for the window handle associated with this instance of the MPEG driver.
window visible	Returns True if the window is not hidden.
window minimized	Returns True if the window is minimized.
window maximized	Returns True if the window is maximized.

step

The step command advances the sequence to the specified image.

step devicename *parameters*

The following optional parameters modify step:

Parameter	Description
by frames	Specifies the number of frames to advance before showing another image. You can specify negative values for frames.

Parameter	Description
key	The key modifier indicates that steps occur in increments of *key frames* or as referred to with MPEG, *I frames*.

stop

The stop command stops playing.

> stop devicename

update

The update command repaints the current frame into the specified display context.

> update devicename *parameters*

The following optional parameters modify update:

Parameter	Description
hdc hdc at rect	Specifies the clipping rectangle relative to the client rectangle.
hdc hdc	Specifies the handle of the display context to paint.
paint hdc hdc	An application uses the paint flag with update when it receives a WM_PAINT message intended for a display context.

updatevideodc

The updatevideodc command causes the contents of the VideoDC to be updated onto the screen into the video window with any sprite/text that was rendered into the DC by the application. Areas of the DC containing the HBRUSH color display video. The rest display the information rendered into the DC.

> updatevideodc devicename *parameter*

The following parameter modifies `updatevideodc`:

Parameter	Description
hdc hdc	The hdc parameter is a handle to a device context used by the MPEG driver to display video and graphics information.

unfreeze

The `unfreeze` command enables the frame buffer to acquire and display video data.

> unfreeze devicename

where

The `where` command returns the rectangular region that has been previously specified, or defaulted, using the `put` command. The rectangular region coordinates are defined by the upper-left corner, the width, and the height of the rectangle.

> where devicename *parameters*

The following parameters modify `where`:

Parameter	Description
destination	Returns a description of the rectangular region used to display video and images in the client area of the current window.
destination max	Returns the current size of the client rectangle.
video	Returns a description of the rectangular region cropped from the frame buffer, which is stretched to fit the destination rectangle on the display.
video max	Returns the maximum size of the frame buffer.
video min	Returns the minimum resolution that the video can be played back in.
window	Returns the current size and position of the display-window frame.
window max	Returns the size of the entire display.

window

The `window` command provides an instance of the MPEG driver with a window handle used to display images or motion video.

> `window` devicename *parameters*

The following parameters modify `window`:

Parameter	Description
handle hwnd	Specifies a window to be used with this instance.
handle default	Restores playback to the default window created during the open operation.
state showvalue	Issues a ShowWindow call for the current window. The following constants are defined for showvalue: hide minimize restore show show maximized show minimized show min noactive show na show noactivate show normal
text caption	Specifies the text placed in the title bar of the window.

Digital Video MCI Command Reference

The digital video MCI command set contains more commands than the command set of any other MCI device type. Before using any of the MCI digital video MCI commands, check the MCI device driver that you are using to ensure that the command is supported. An example of an MCI command that is not widely supported is the `setaudio` command.

capability

The capability command returns a string containing additional information about the capabilities of MCIAVI.

capability devicename *parameters*

One of the following parameters can modify capability:

Parameter	Description
can eject	Returns False.
can freeze	Returns False.
can lock	Returns False.
can play	Returns True.
can record	Returns False.
can reverse	Returns False.
can save	Returns False.
can stretch	Returns True.
can stretch input	Returns False.
can test	Returns True.
compound device	Returns True.
device type	Returns digital video.
has audio	Returns True.
has still	Returns False.
has video	Returns True.
uses files	Returns True.
uses palettes	Returns True.
windows	Returns the number of simultaneous display windows the device can support.

close

The `close` command closes this instance of the MCIAVI and releases all resources associated with it.

> `close` devicename

configure

The `configure` command displays a dialog box used to configure MCIAVI.

> `configure` devicename

The Configure dialog box contains the following options:

Option	Description
Window	Displays the video in a window.
Full Screen	Displays the video using the full screen with 320×240 resolution. This allows a 256-color display on 16-color devices.
Zoom By 2	Stretches the video to twice its normal size.
Skip Video Frames If Behind	Specifies dropping frames if the video falls behind. If this isn't selected, all the video frames will be shown and the audio will break up as necessary.
Don't Buffer Offscreen	Specifies that a copy of the display window should not be maintained.
Information list box	Contains information about the open file. Additional information might be listed after the file is played.

cue

The `cue` command prepares MCIAVI for playback and leaves it in a paused state.

> `cue` devicename *parameters*

The following optional parameters modify `cue`:

Parameter	Description
output	Prepares MCIAVI for playing.
to position	Positions the workspace to the specified position.

info

The info command returns a string containing information about MCIAVI.

info devicename *parameters*

The following optional parameters modify info:

Parameter	Description
file	Returns the name of the file currently loaded.
product	Returns Video for Windows.
version	Returns the release level of MCIAVI.
window text	Returns the text string in the title bar of the window associated with MCIAVI.

open

The open command initializes MCIAVI.

open devicename *parameters*

The following parameters modify open:

Parameter	Description
alias alias	Specifies an alias used to reference this instance of MCIAVI.
elementname	Specifies the name of the device element (file) loaded when MCIAVI opens.
parent hwnd	Specifies the parent of the default window.
style stylevalue	Specifies the style used for the default window. The following constants are defined for stylevalue: overlapped, popup, and child.
type AVIVideo	Specifies the device type of the device element.

pause

The pause command pauses playing of motion video or audio.

pause devicename

play

The `play` command starts playing the video sequence.

> `play` devicename *parameters*

The following optional parameters modify `play`:

Parameter	Description
`from position`	Specifies the position to seek to before beginning the play.
`to position`	Specifies the position at which to stop playing.
`fullscreen`	Specifies that playing should use a full-screen display. Use this flag only when playing compressed files; uncompressed files won't play full-screen.
`window`	Specifies that playing should use the window associated with a device instance (the default).

put

The `put` command specifies a rectangular region that describes a cropping or scaling option. The rectangular region is defined by the upper-left corner, the width, and the height of the rectangle.

> `put` devicename *parameters*

One of the following parameters must be present to indicate the specific type of rectangle:

Parameter	Description
`destination`	Restores the initial destination window associated with this instance of MCIAVI.
`destination at rectangle`	Specifies which portion of the destination window associated with this instance of MCIAVI is used.
`source`	Restores the initial source rectangle. The image from this rectangle is scaled to fit in the destination rectangle.
`source at rectangle`	Specifies which portion of the source is scaled to fit in the destination rectangle. The units for the source rectangle are based on the units for the .AVI file.

(continues)

Parameter	Description
`window`	Restores the initial window size on the display and also displays the window.
`window at rectangle`	Changes the size and location of the display window. The rectangle specified with the `at` flag is relative to the parent window of the display window (usually the desktop) if the style `child` flag has been used for the open command. To change the location of the window without changing its height or width, specify 0 for the height and width.
`window client`	Restores the client area of the window.
`window client at rectangle`	Changes the size and location of the client area of the window. The rectangle specified with the `at` flag is relative to the parent window of the client window. To change the location of the window without changing its height or width, specify 0 for the height and width.

realize

The `realize` command tells MCIAVI to select and realize its palette into a display context of the displayed window. Use this command only if your application uses a window handle and receives a WM_QUERYNEWPAL or WM_PALETTECHANGED message.

> `realize` devicename *parameters*

One of the following parameters can modify `realize`:

Parameter	Description
`background`	Realizes the palette as a background palette.
`normal`	Realizes the palette used for a top-level window (the default).

resume

The `resume` command specifies that operation should continue from where it was interrupted by a `pause` command.

> `resume` devicename

seek

The seek command positions and cues the workspace to the specified position showing the specified frame.

> seek devicename *parameters*

One of the following parameters can modify seek:

Parameter	Description
to position	Specifies the desired new position, measured in units of the current-time format.
to end	Moves the position after the last frame of the workspace.
to start	Moves the position to the first frame of the workspace.

set

The set command sets the state of control items.

> set devicename *parameters*

One of the following parameters can modify set:

Parameter	Description
seek exactly on seek exactly off	Selects one of two seek modes. With seek exactly on, seek always moves to the frame specified. With seek exactly off, seek moves to the closest key frame prior to the frame specified.
speed factor	Sets the relative speed of video and audio playback from the workspace. Factor is the ratio between the nominal frame rate and the desired frame rate, where the nominal frame rate is designated as 1000. Setting the speed to 0 plays the video as fast as possible without dropping frames and without audio.
time format format	Sets the time format to format. The default time format is frames. Milliseconds can be abbreviated as ms.; MCIAVI supports frames and milliseconds.

(continues)

Parameter	Description
`audio all off`	Disables audio.
`audio all on`	Enables audio.
`video off`	Disables video.
`video on`	Enables video.

setaudio

The `setaudio` command sets various values associated with audio playback and capture.

> `setaudio` devicename *parameters*

Only one of the following parameters can be present in a `setaudio` command unless otherwise noted:

Parameter	Description
`off`	Disables audio.
`on`	Enables audio.
`volume to factor`	Sets the average audio volume for both audio channels.

setvideo

The `setvideo` command sets various values associated with video playback.

> `setvideo` devicename *parameters*

The following optional parameters modify `setvideo`:

Parameter	Description
`off`	Disables video display in the window.
`on`	Enables video display in the window.
`palette handle to handle`	Specifies the handle to a palette.

signal

The `signal` command identifies a specified position in the workspace. MCIAVI supports only one active `signal` at a time.

> `signal` devicename *parameters*

The following parameters modify `signal`:

Parameter	Description
`at position`	Specifies the frame to invoke a signal.
`cancel`	Indicates the active signal should be removed from the workspace.
`every interval`	Specifies the period (in the current-time format) to send signals.
`return position`	An optional parameter that indicates the MCIAVI should send the position value instead of the `uservalue` value in the window message.
`uservalue id`	Specifies a value associated with this signal request that is reported back with the window message.

status

The `status` command returns status information about this instance of MCIAVI.

> `status` devicename *parameters*

One of the following parameters modifies `status`:

Parameter	Description
`audio`	Returns on if either or both speakers are enabled, and off otherwise.
`forward`	Returns True if playing forward.
`length`	Returns the length of the longest stream in the AVI file in the current-time format.
`media present`	Returns True.
`mode`	Returns one of the following: not ready, paused, playing, seeking, or stopped.

(continues)

Parameter	Description
monitor	Returns file.
nominal frame rate	Returns the nominal frame rate associated with the file in units of frames per second×1000.
number of tracks	Returns the number of tracks in a video sequence (usually 1).
palette handle	Returns the palette handle.
position	Returns the current position in the workspace in the current-time format.
ready	Returns True if this instance of MCIAVI is ready to accept another command.
reference frame	Returns the nearest key-frame number that precedes frame.
seek exactly	Returns on or off, indicating whether or not seek exactly is set.
speed	Returns the current playback speed.
start position	Returns the start of the media.
time format	Returns the current-time format (frames or milliseconds).
unsaved	Returns False.
video	Returns on or off, depending on the most recent setvideo.
volume	Returns the average volume to the left and right speaker. This returns an error if the device has not been played or volume has not been set.
window handle	Returns the ASCII decimal value for the window handle associated with this instance of MCIAVI.
window visible	Returns True if the window is not hidden.
window minimized	Returns True if the window is minimized.
window maximized	Return True if the window is maximized.

step

The step command advances the sequence to the specified image.

>   step devicename *parameters*

The following optional parameters modify step:

Parameter	Description
by frames	Specifies the number of frames to advance before showing another image. You can specify negative values for frames.
reverse	Requests that the step be taken in the reverse direction.

stop

The stop command stops playing.

>   stop devicename

update

The update command repaints the current frame into the specified display context.

>   update devicename *parameters*

The following optional parameters modify update:

Parameter	Description
hdc hdc at rect	Specifies the clipping rectangle relative to the client rectangle.
hdc hdc	Specifies the handle of the display context to paint.
paint hdc hdc	Specifies that an application uses the paint flag with update when it receives a WM_PAINT message intended for a display context.

where

The where command returns the rectangular region that has been previously specified, or defaulted, using the put command. The rectangular region coordinates are defined by the upper-left corner, the width, and the height of the rectangle.

> where devicename *parameters*

The following parameters modify where:

Parameter	Description
destination	Returns a description of the rectangular region used to display video and images in the client area of the current window.
destination max	Returns the current size of the client rectangle.
source	Returns a description of the rectangular region cropped from the frame buffer, which is stretched to fit the destination rectangle on the display.
source max	Returns the maximum size of the frame buffer.
window	Returns the current size and position of the display-window frame.
window max	Returns the size of the entire display.

window

The window command provides an instance of MCIAVI with a window handle used to display images or motion video.

> window devicename *parameters*

The following parameters modify window:

Parameter	Description
handle hwnd	Specifies a window to be used with this instance.
handle default	Restores playback to the default window created during the open operation.
state showvalue	This command issues a ShowWindow call for the current window. The following constants are defined for showvalue: hide minimize restore

Parameter	Description

	`show`
	`show maximized`
	`show minimized`
	`show min noactive`
	`show na`
	`show noactivate`
	`show normal`

`text caption`	Specifies the text placed in the title bar of the window.

The Animation MCI Command Reference

The animation MCI device drivers use a subset of the total MCI command specification.

capability

The `capability` command returns a string containing additional information about the capabilities of the animation driver.

> `capability` devicename *parameters*

One of the following parameters can modify `capability`:

Parameter	Description
`can eject`	Returns True if the device can eject the media.
`can play`	Returns True if the device can play.
`can record`	Returns False. Animation devices cannot record.
`can reverse`	Returns True if the animation device can play in reverse.
`can save`	Returns False. Animation devices cannot save data.
`can stretch`	Returns True if the device can stretch frames to fill a given display rectangle.
`compound device`	Returns True if the device supports an element name.

(continues)

Parameter	Description
device type	Animation devices return animation.
fast play rate	Returns fast play rate in frames per second.
has audio	Returns True if the device supports audio playback.
has video	Returns True.
normal play rate	Returns normal play rate in frames per second.
slow play rate	Returns the slow play rate in frames per second.
uses files	Returns True if the element of a compound device is a file pathname.
uses palettes	Returns True if the device uses palettes.
windows	Returns the number of windows the device can support.

close

The close command closes this instance of the animation driver and releases all resources associated with it.

    close devicename

info

The info command returns a string containing information about the animation driver.

    info devicename *parameters*

The following optional parameters modify info:

Parameter	Description
file	Returns the name of the file used by the animation device.
product	Returns the product name and model of the current device.
window text	Returns the caption of the window used by the device.

open

The open command initializes the animation driver.

open devicename *parameters*

The following parameters modify open:

Parameter	Description
alias device_alias	Specifies an alternate name for the animation element. If specified, it must be used as the device_id in subsequent commands.
nostatic	Indicates that the device should reduce the number of static (system) colors in the palette. Reducing the number of static colors increases the number of colors controlled by the animation.
parent hwnd	Specifies the window handle of the parent window.
shareable	Initializes a device element as shareable. Subsequent attempts to open it fail unless you specify shareable in both the original and subsequent open commands. MCI returns an error if the device is already open and not shareable.
style style_type	Indicates a window style.
style child	Opens a window with a child window style.
style overlapped	Opens a window with an overlapped window style.
style popup	Opens a window with a popup window style.
type device_type	Specifies the device type of the device element. As an alternative to type, MCI can use the [mci extension] entries in the SYSTEM.INI file to select the controlling device based on the extension used by the device element.

pause

The pause command pauses playback of the animation. If the animation is stopped, pause displays the animation window if it is not already visible and in the foreground.

pause devicename

play

The play command starts playing the animation sequence.

> play devicename *parameters*

The following optional parameters modify play:

Parameter	Description
fast	Plays the animation sequence at a fast rate.
from position	Specifies the starting position for the playback. If the from parameter is not specified, playback begins at the current frame.
to position	Specifies the ending position for the playback. If the to parameter is not specified, play stops at the end of the media. You cannot specify the reverse keyword with an ending position.
reverse	Specifies that the play direction is backwards. You cannot specify an ending playback position with the reverse keyword.
scan	Plays the animation sequence as fast as possible without disabling video.
slow	Plays the animation sequence at a slow rate.
speed fps	Plays the animation sequence at the specified speed. Speed is specified in frames per second (fps).

put

The put command specifies a rectangular region that describes a cropping or scaling option. The rectangular region is defined by the upper-left corner, the width, and the height of the rectangle.

> put devicename *parameters*

One of the following parameters must be present to indicate the specific type of rectangle:

Parameter	Description
destination	Sets the whole window as the destination window.

Parameter	Description
destination at rectangle	Specifies a rectangle for the area of the window used to display the image. The rectangle coordinates are relative to the window origin and are specified as X1 Y1 X2 Y2. The coordinates X1 Y1 specify the top, left corner, and the coordinates X2 Y2 specify the width and height of the rectangle. When an area of the display window is specified and the device supports stretching, the source image is stretched to the destination offset and extent.
source	Selects the whole image for display in the destination window.
source at rectangle	Specifies a rectangle for the image area used for display. The rectangle coordinates are relative to the image origin and are specified as X1 Y1 X2 Y2. The coordinates X1 Y1 specify the top, left corner, and the coordinates X2 Y2 specify the width and height of the rectangle. When an area of the source image is specified and the device supports stretching, the source image is stretched to the destination offset and extent.

realize

The realize command tells the animation driver to select and realize its palette into a display context of the displayed window. Use this command only if your application uses a window handle and receives a WM_QUERYNEWPAL or WM_PALETTECHANGED message.

    realize devicename *parameters*

One of the following parameters can modify realize:

Parameter	Description
background	Realizes the palette as a background palette.
normal	Realizes the palette used for a top-level window (the default).

resume

The resume command specifies that operation should continue from where it was interrupted by a pause command.

    resume devicename

seek

The seek command positions and cues the workspace to the specified position showing the specified frame.

> seek devicename *parameters*

One of the following parameters can modify seek:

Parameter	Description
to position	Specifies the desired new position, measured in units of the current-time format.
to end	Moves the position after the last frame of the workspace.
to start	Moves the position to the first frame of the workspace.

set

The set command sets the state of control items.

> set devicename *parameters*

One of the following parameters can modify set:

Parameter	Description
audio all off	Disables audio output.
audio all on	Enables audio output.
audio left off	Disables output to the left audio channel.
audio left on	Enables output to the left audio channel.
audio right off	Disables output to the right audio channel.
audio right on	Enables output to the right audio channel.
time format frames	Sets the time format to frames. All commands that use position values will assume frames. When the device is opened, frames is the default mode.
time format milliseconds	Sets the time format to milliseconds. All commands that use position values will assume milliseconds. (You can abbreviate milliseconds as ms.)

Parameter	Description
video off	Disables video output.
video on	Enables video output.

status

The status command returns status information about this instance of the animation driver.

> status devicename *parameters*

One of the following parameters modifies status:

Parameter	Description
current track	Returns the current track.
forward	Returns True if the play direction is forward or if the device is not playing.
length	Returns the total number of frames.
length track track_number	Returns the total number of frames in the track specified by track_number.
media present	Returns True if the media is inserted in the device; otherwise, it returns False.
mode	Returns Not Ready, Paused, Playing, Seeking, or Stopped for the current mode.
number of tracks	Returns the number of tracks on the media.
palette handle	Returns the handle of the palette used for the animation.
position	Returns the current position.
position track number	Returns the position of the start of the track specified by number.
ready	Returns True if the device is ready.
speed	Returns the current speed of the device in frames per second.
start position	Returns the starting position of the media.

(continues)

Parameter	Description
stretch	Returns True if stretching is enabled.
time format	Returns the current time format.
window handle	Returns the handle of the window used for the animation.

step

The step command advances the sequence to the specified image.

> step devicename *parameters*

The following optional parameters modify step:

Parameter	Description
by frames	Specifies the number of frames to advance before showing another image. You can specify negative values for frames.
reverse	Requests that the step be taken in the reverse direction.

stop

The stop command stops playing.

> stop devicename

update

The update command repaints the current frame into the specified display context.

> update devicename *parameters*

The following optional parameters modify update:

The HDC parameter must be included when issuing the update command. The clipping rectangle is an optional argument.

Parameter	Description
hdc hDC	Specifies the handle to the device context to update.
at rectangle	Specifies the clipping rectangle.

where

The where command returns the rectangular region that has been previously specified or defaulted using the put command. The rectangular region coordinates are defined by the upper-left corner, the width, and the height of the rectangle.

> where devicename *parameters*

The following parameters modify where:

Parameter	Description
destination	Requests the destination offset and extent.
source	Requests the source offset and extent.

window

The window command controls the animation display window. You can change the display characteristics of the window or provide a display window for the driver to use in place of the default display window.

Generally, animation devices create a window when opened but don't display the window until they receive a play command. If your application provides a window to the driver, your application is responsible for managing the messages sent to the window.

The window command provides several flags that let you manipulate the window. Because you can use the status command to get the handle to the driver display window, you can also use the standard window manager functions (such as ShowWindow) to manipulate the window.

> window devicename *parameters*

The following parameters modify `window`:

Parameter	Description
`fixed`	Disables stretching of the image.
`handle window_handle`	Specifies the handle of the destination window to use instead of the default window.
`handle default`	Specifies that the animation device should set the display window back to the driver's default window.
`state hide`	Hides the display window.
`state iconic`	Displays the window as iconic.
`state maximized`	Maximizes the display window.
`state minimize`	Minimizes the display window and activates the top-level window in the window-manager's list.
`state minimized`	Minimizes the display window.
`state no action`	Displays the window in its current state. The window that is currently active remains active.
`state no activate`	Displays the window in its most recent size and state. The window that is currently active remains active.
`state normal`	Activates and displays the display window in its original size and position.
`state show`	Shows the display window.
`stretch`	Enables stretching of the image.
`text caption`	Specifies the caption for the display window.

Index

C

M

capability, 518
cue, 519
info, 520
open, 520
play, 521
put, 521-522
realize, 522
seek, 523
set, 523-524
setaudio, 524
setvideo, 524
signal, 525
status, 525-526
step, 527
update, 527
where, 527-528
window, 528-529
hDrop, 408
inserting in script
  commands, 442-445
MPEG commands (MCI)
  capability, 505-506
  capture, 506
  createvideodc, 507
  cue, 507-508
  info, 508
  open, 509
  play, 509
  put, 510
  releasevideodc, 511
  seek, 511
  set, 511-512
  setaudio, 512
  setvideo, 512
  signal, 513
  status, 513-514
  step, 514-515
  update, 515
  updatevideodc, 515-516
  where, 516
  window, 517
script commands
  (presentations)
  AUDIO, 443-444
  BACKGROUND, 442
  DIGITALVIDEO, 442-443
  IMAGE, 444
  TEXT, 444-445
sndPlaySound( ), 86-87
parent windows, 367
ParentHwnd property, 345

PASTEL.DIB bitmap, 160
PastePalette method (OCX),
  299
PatBlt( ) function, 187
patterns, inserting in brush
  bitmaps, 211
pause command (MCI), 509,
  520, 531
Pause method
  (MediaDeveloper), 387
pausing CDs, 106-107
PC_RESERVED constant, 169
PCM Converter (Pulse Code
  Modulation), 43
pen color functions
  (DrawMode property),
  143-144
performance
  digital video, 275
  images, 126
persistence (OLE controls),
  420
Phase Alternating Line (PAL)
  standard, 309
picColorBox_Paint event, 153
picPalAnim_Paint event, 171
picProduct_Paint event, 184,
  194
picSpinner_Paint event, 183
picture boxes (DrawMode/
  BackColor/ForeColor
  properties), 125
Picture Clip control, 25
Picture property
  MediaDeveloper, 385
  OCX, 296
PictureBox control, 25,
  125-126
Pioneer LaserDisk MCI driver,
  47
pixel depth, 275
pixels (palette animation),
  162-164
play command (MCI), 509,
  521, 532
Play method
  (MediaDeveloper), 387
playback
  animation, 336-343
  digital video, 361-362
  frame size, 275

MCI interface, 360-361
MCI OLE control,
  371-380
mciSendString( ), 362-365
MediaDeveloper OLE
  control, 380-389
performance, 275
**Playback timer
  (presentations), 450**
PLAYER.BAS (13.1), 445
PLAYER.FRM (13.2), 446
PLAYER.FRM (13.3), 451
PLAYER.FRM (13.4), 452
PLAYER.FRM (13.5), 453
PLAYER.FRM (13.6), 453
PLAYER.FRM (13.7), 454
PLAYER.FRM (13.8), 454
PLAYER.FRM (13.9), 455
PlayerElements array, 449
playing
  CDs, 105-106
  devices
    MCI command-message
      interface, 95-96
    peripheral devices (Video
      Center application),
      332-333
  MIDI files, 115-117
  presentations, 451-452
    loading elements,
      452-454
    multimedia elements,
      playing, 455-456
    removing elements,
      454-455
  waveform files
    command-message
      interface (MCI), 89-100
    command-string interface
      (MCI), 100-115
    high-level functions,
      83-88
**PlaySegment method
  (MediaDeveloper), 387**
PlaySound( ) function, 87-88
**PlaySound( )'s declaration
  (4.3), 88**
Plug-and-Play BIOS, 37
  event manager, 38-39
  resource manager, 38-39
  run-time manager, 38

X–Y–Z

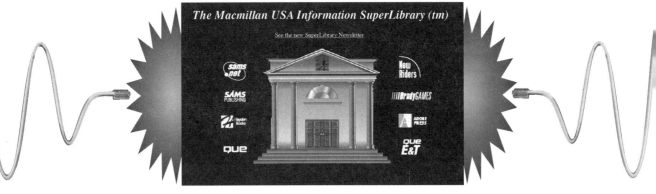

MediaDeveloper

Provides tools to build powerful imaging and multimedia applications. With virtually any Windows-compatible development environment, and MediaDeveloper, you can write interactive multimedia programs that play video, animation, graphics and audio. Cut your multimedia development time from weeks to hours. Over 100 APIs included to create interactive multimedia. Thumbnails and hot spots, unique Media Segmenting, Database Interface, universal media format support-over 20 in all. Available in three versions: (1) *OLE Controls*, (2) *VBX*, or (3) *DLL, OLE Automation, C and C++ Libraries.*

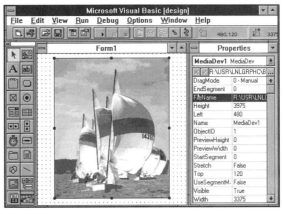

MediaRecorder Toolkit

Enables your application to capture full-motion videos from camcorders, VCRs, laser disc players, or cable TV. Features palette capture, still-frame capture, compression options, dialog boxes, resizable windows, and support for all Windows-compatible video capture boards. Available in two versions: (1) as an *OLE Control* or (2) as a *OLE 2.0 Automation Server, C++ Libraries and DLL package.*

Lenel MCI Drivers Kit

Provides enhanced support for industry leading boards and allows you to control a wide range of consumer and prosumer camcorders, VCRs, and laser disc players right from your computer!

Lenel Systems International Inc.

LENEL SYSTEMS ▼ INTERNATIONAL INC.

290 Woodcliff Office Park
Fairport, New York, USA 14450-4212
Phone: 716-248-9720
Fax 716-248-9185
CompuServe: 71333.622

Lenel Gallery™

Integrates Thumbnail Images of multimedia data into your applications. Customizable user interface, set background colors, gallery size, thumbnail size, thumbnail border width, highlighting color, and text color. Supports more than 30 digital video, analog video, graphics and audio formats. Features include: Database Interface, Databinding, User Defined Interface and events, Hot Spots and more. Provides a visual representation of your media in an entirely new way. Available in three versions: (1) as an *OLE* Control (2) as a VBX or (3) as an *OLE 2.0 Automation Server, C++ Libraries and DLL package.*

Development Environments Supported by Lenel's Development Tools

- Microsoft® Visual Basic®
- Borland® Delphi
- Microsoft Access
- Visual FoxPro
- Visual C++
- Paradox
- PowerBuilder
- INFORMIX—NewEra
- Oracle Workgroup/2000
- CA-Visual Objects
- CA-Realizer
- dBase
- Pascal
- SmallTalk
- Microsoft Word and Excel
- Any environment that supports OLE Controls, OLE 2.0 Automation, C++ libraries or DLLs.

Development Environments Supported by Lenel's Development Tools

- Visual Basic
- Delphi
- Access
- Visual FoxPro
- Visual C++
- Paradox
- PowerBuilder
- Informix New-Era
- Oracle Developer/2000
- CA-Visual Objects
- CA-Realizer
- dBase
- Pascal
- SmallTalk
- Word and Excel
- Any environment that supports OLE Controls, OLE 2.0 Automation, C++ libraries or DLLs.

Development Environments Supported by Lenel's Development Tools

- Visual Basic
- Delphi
- Access
- Visual FoxPro
- Visual C++
- Paradox
- PowerBuilder
- Informix New-Era
- Oracle Developer/2000
- CA-Visual Objects
- CA-Realizer
- dBase
- Pascal
- SmallTalk
- Word and Excel
- Any environment that supports OLE Controls, OLE 2.0 Automation, C++ libraries or DLLs.

Complete and Return this Card
for a *FREE* Computer Book Catalog

Thank you for purchasing this book! You have purchased a superior computer book written expressly for your needs. To continue to provide the kind of up-to-date, pertinent coverage you've come to expect from us, we need to hear from you. Please take a minute to complete and return this self-addressed, postage-paid form. In return, we'll send you a free catalog of all our computer books on topics ranging from word processing to programming and the internet.

Mr. ☐ Mrs. ☐ Ms. ☐ Dr. ☐

Name (first) ☐☐☐☐☐☐☐☐☐☐☐☐ (M.I.) ☐ (last) ☐☐☐☐☐☐☐☐☐☐☐☐☐☐☐☐☐

Address ☐☐☐☐☐☐☐☐☐☐☐☐☐☐☐☐☐☐☐☐☐☐☐☐☐☐☐☐☐☐☐☐

☐☐☐☐☐☐☐☐☐☐☐☐☐☐☐☐☐☐☐☐☐☐☐☐☐☐☐☐☐☐☐☐

City ☐☐☐☐☐☐☐☐☐☐☐☐☐☐☐ State ☐☐ Zip ☐☐☐☐☐ ☐☐☐☐

Phone ☐☐☐ ☐☐☐☐ Fax ☐☐☐ ☐☐☐ ☐☐☐☐

Company Name ☐☐☐☐☐☐☐☐☐☐☐☐☐☐☐☐☐☐☐☐☐☐☐☐☐☐☐☐

E-mail address ☐☐☐☐☐☐☐☐☐☐☐☐☐☐☐☐☐☐☐☐☐☐☐☐☐☐☐☐

1. Please check at least (3) influencing factors for purchasing this book.

Front or back cover information on book ☐
Special approach to the content ☐
Completeness of content ☐
Author's reputation ☐
Publisher's reputation ☐
Book cover design or layout ☐
Index or table of contents of book ☐
Price of book ☐
Special effects, graphics, illustrations ☐
Other (Please specify): _____ ☐

2. How did you first learn about this book?

Saw in Macmillan Computer Publishing catalog ☐
Recommended by store personnel ☐
Saw the book on bookshelf at store ☐
Recommended by a friend ☐
Received advertisement in the mail ☐
Saw an advertisement in: _____ ☐
Read book review in: _____ ☐
Other (Please specify): _____ ☐

3. How many computer books have you purchased in the last six months?

This book only ☐   3 to 5 books ☐
2 books ☐   More than 5 ☐

4. Where did you purchase this book?

Bookstore ☐
Computer Store ☐
Consumer Electronics Store ☐
Department Store ☐
Office Club ☐
Warehouse Club ☐
Mail Order ☐
Direct from Publisher ☐
Internet site ☐
Other (Please specify): _____ ☐

5. How long have you been using a computer?

☐ Less than 6 months   ☐ 6 months to a year
☐ 1 to 3 years   ☐ More than 3 years

6. What is your level of experience with personal computers and with the subject of this book?

	With PCs	With subject of book
New	☐	☐
Casual	☐	☐
Accomplished	☐	☐
Expert	☐	☐

Source Code ISBN: 07897-0139-1

7. Which of the following best describes your job title?

- Administrative Assistant ☐
- Coordinator ☐
- Manager/Supervisor ☐
- Director ☐
- Vice President ☐
- President/CEO/COO ☐
- Lawyer/Doctor/Medical Professional ☐
- Teacher/Educator/Trainer ☐
- Engineer/Technician ☐
- Consultant ☐
- Not employed/Student/Retired ☐
- Other (Please specify): _____ ☐

8. Which of the following best describes the area of the company your job title falls under?

- Accounting ☐
- Engineering ☐
- Manufacturing ☐
- Operations ☐
- Marketing ☐
- Sales ☐
- Other (Please specify): _____ ☐

9. What is your age?

- Under 20 ☐
- 21-29 ☐
- 30-39 ☐
- 40-49 ☐
- 50-59 ☐
- 60-over ☐

10. Are you:

- Male ☐
- Female ☐

11. Which computer publications do you read regularly? (Please list)

_____
_____
_____
_____
_____
_____
_____
_____
_____

Comments: _____
_____

Fold here and scotch-tape to mail

Licensing Agreement